The
Book
of
Rules

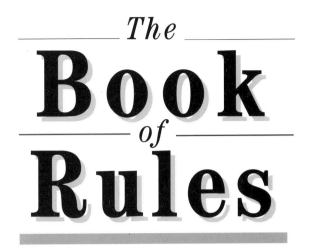

The Book of Rules

of

The

A visual guide to the laws
of every commonly played
sport and game

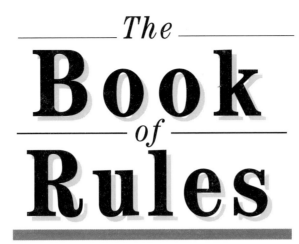

☑®
Checkmark Books™
An imprint of Facts On File, Inc.

OUACHITA TECHNICAL COLLEGE

The Book of Rules

Copyright © 1998 by Duncan Petersen Publishing Ltd

Checkmark Books
An imprint of Facts On File, Inc.
11 Penn Plaza
New York NY 10001

Library of Congress Cataloging-in-Publication Data

The book of rules: a visual guide to the laws of every commonly
played sport and game.
p. cm.
First published in 1997 by Ebury Press, London.
Includes index.
ISBN 0-8160-3919-4
1. Sports—Rules. 2. Games—Rules.
GV731.B56 1998
796—dc21   98-24910

Checkmark Books are available at special discounts when purchased in bulk quantities for businesses, associations, institutions or sales promotions. Please call our Special Sales Department in New York at (212) 967-8800 or (800) 322-8755.

You can find Facts On File on the World Wide Web at http://www.factsonfile.com

Conceived, edited and designed by
Duncan Petersen Publishing Ltd,
31, Ceylon Road, London W14 OPY

Printed by DELO tiskarna, d.d., Slovenia

Typeset by Duncan Petersen Publishing Ltd

10 9 8 7 6 5 4 3 2
This book is printed on acid-free paper.

Introduction

*T*he *Book of Rules* presents an illustrated, easy-to-use, functional guide to the rules of more than 30 of the world's most popular sports and games (the count reaches many more than 30 if all the various track-and-field events are considered separately). Our goal was to create something much more friendly and stimulating than the dense text of official rules books, quicker to use and easily understood by readers of any age or level of expertise. By assembling within two covers a full set of rules for most of the world's commonly played or watched sports—a major feat of compilation—we hoped to create a uniquely valuable reference work for any individual or organization with an interest in understanding and participating in the rich sporting traditions that pervade the world we live in.

The truth is that few people are likely to possess detailed knowledge about all of the sports found in this book. Readers will approach this book with a variety of needs. Some will have knowledge about a specific sport but may desire exposure to some little-understood rules or regulations. Others may approach a sport as a beginner, hoping to acquire the basics necessary to play or appreciate the game. Still others may want to gain familiarity with unfamiliar games in an effort to develop a sports program. *The Book of Rules* serves these and many other needs. This book can be used both as a guide to major commercial games that pervade American culture—occupying huge chunks of television time, entire newspaper sections, and drawing huge crowds—as well as a blueprint for stranger, less familiar games, a few of which are rarely played in North America but enjoy substantial appeal in other places. This book mixes the needs of the spectator with the needs of the player, organizer, or coach, providing a cross section of the full range of great games found around the globe.

To serve diverse audiences, we present most sports in two parts: an Essentials section, which lays clear all the basic requirements and principles of a sport, backed by the official rules book for that sport. We devised the color pages of the book (those headed Essentials) with accessibility and simplicity in mind. Featuring full-color action shots of both amateur and many of the world's greatest players showcasing their skills, the illustrations and diagrams are an ideal way to come to grips with basic techniques and principles, and they help solve commonplace queries about how the games should be played. In addition, because official rule books spend much of their time talking about what can happen (as opposed to what does happen), these Essentials pages give us an opportunity to provide the reader with an overview of what they are likely to encounter in playing or watching a typical game.

These Essential pages could, of course, be superficial on their own, as it is impossible for them to cover everything that can happen in sporting contests—many of which are quite chaotic by their nature. We, therefore, generally back up the Essentials section with the text of the official rule books, point-by-point, on double-page spreads with clear cross-referencing. These two different types of information—summary and detailed backup—thread their way through the whole book, making an understanding of the games at any level possible.

Organized sports and games can represent the best of human potential and achievement. At any level, they present the opportunity for substantial challenge and fun. We hope that *The Book of Rules* will increase your enjoyment and understanding of this important part of our world.

General Editor: Mark Paluch
• **Australian rules football** Andrew Watt • **Baseball** Steve Meyerhoff and Wendy Macadam • **Basketball** Alan Richardson and Albert Schencking • **Boxing** Karl-Heinz Wehr • **Cricket** John Jamieson • **Croquet** Paul Campion • **Field Hockey** Jane Nuckolds, George Croft and Mary Coyle • **Football** David Rossell • **Lawn Bowling** David Johnson • **Men's lacrosse** Rodney Burns and Mark Coups • **Netball** Maria Harding • **Rounders** Brian Mackinney • **Rugby League** Neil Tunnicliffe • **Soccer** David Barber • **Softball** Merle Butler • **Squash** Ted Wallbutton • **Table tennis** Colin Clemett • **Tennis** Nicola Bickord • **Track and Field** David Littlewood and Pat Liddiard • **Volleyball** Bernard Kilkenny

Main contents list

The sports and games as they appear in the book

Alphabetical contents list

How to use this book

What's in, what's out

The Book of Rules presents a generous cross section of the world's major sports and games. You will find games played by both teams and individuals, and sports that are either American or international in origin. All of America's major professional games are represented (baseball, football, basketball, and ice hockey), as are most of the games played recreationally (tennis, volleyball, softball, etc.). A few of the games (e.g., Australian rules football) are rarely played in North America, but the advent of cable television sports channels means that Americans have increased access to them. Still others are international games gaining in popularity in this country (e.g., soccer and rugby). Finally, there is a smattering of games that are not widely known, but simple to understand, organize, and play (e.g., rounders, netball, korfball). Whatever your needs or interests, you should find a sport in *The Book of Rules* to excite your curiosity.

Topics covered

For easy reference a consistent sequence of headings explains each sport:

Playing surface, equipment, players, and officials

The information in the captions, the illustrations, and any annotations on the diagrams and artwork are derived from the official rule book.

How to play/ How to win

This section briefly summarizes how play starts, how it proceeds, and how it ends.

Measurements

An effort is made to present measurements that are true to a game and meaningful to most Americans. Generally, if a game measures distances and units in metric terms, that unit is given first, with the English equivalent following in parentheses. For a few sports, only metric measurements are provided.

5.18 m (17 ft)

76 cm (2 ft 6 in)

1.98 m (6 ft 6 in)

3.96 m (13 ft)

1.55 m (5 ft 1 in)

76 cm (2 ft 6 in)

13.40 m (44 ft)

6.10 m (20 ft)

The following conversion chart may help some readers:

	multiply by
inches to centimeters	2.54
centimeters to inches	0.39
feet to meters	0.30
meters to feet	3.28
yards to meters	0.91
meters to yards	1.09
ounces to grams	28.35
grams to ounces	0.035

Key rules

This important feature simplifies points that are essential, controversial, or difficult to understand.

Skills and tactics

Whole books have been written on these; here we provide a brief summary of the important points.

Gray areas

These boxed sections focus on controversial, evolving, or little understood aspects of a game.

The rules point by point

Generally we provide the most "senior" official version available—typically the international rules. Otherwise we give the most widely used version. Note that for boxing we provide the amateur, rather than the professional, rules.

For each sport, some of the most important rules, such as those governing playing surface and equipment, are covered by a cross-reference to an "Essentials" page, where they are explained in simple terms, and illustrated.

The rules are produced as completely as possible for every sport, but constraints of space have meant that in some instances the rules have been abridged. Where abridgements or summaries occur, they are made clear by italics or notes in the text.

Thus the rules as given are a true working version, which can provide rulings on most issues experienced by most people.

Please note that some sports update their rule books regularly.

Soccer
Essentials

The world's most popular game to play as well as its most popular spectator sport, soccer is an obsession across much of the globe, but only in the last 20 years has soccer made major inroads in the United States. It is now firmly established as an organized sport for young people, and a professional league has taken root. In 1994, the U.S. hosted the World Cup, an international event held once every four years.

Manchester United, Britain's most popular team

The field

Rectangular, traditionally with a grass surface, divided into two equal halves. Its length is between 110 and 120 yds and its breadth between 70 and 80 yds.

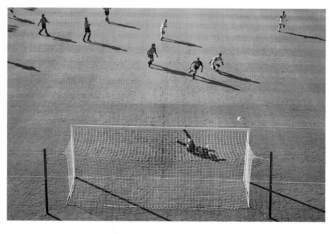

Corner flag

Corner flag

Sideline

20 yds

44 yds

18 yds

Optional halfway flagpole

Halfway

Center circle

20 yds

Line

70–80 yds

110–120 yds

Sideline

1 yd

Corner flag

6 yds

Penalty area

Goal line

10 yds

12 yds

Penalty mark

Goal area

Goal line

Corner flag

The teams

Two teams of 11 players each, including one goalkeeper, or goalie. A maximum of three substitutes is permitted. Any of the other players may change places with the goalie.

The goals

Placed on the center of the goal lines at each end of the field and must consist of two upright posts, 8 yards apart and joined by a horizontal crossbar. Both posts and crossbar should be of equal width, not exceeding 5 in. A net attached to posts, bars and the ground behind them is optional. The whole structure must stand 8 feet above the ground (inside measurement).

Soccer fans

Perhaps the biggest soccer crowd ever was the 199,854 who crammed into the Maracaña Municipal Stadium in Rio de Janeiro in Brazil to watch the World Cup final on the 16th of July 1950. Pictured right is Wembley Stadium, outside of London.

The ball

Spherical with an outer casing of leather or approved substitute material. Its circumference must be 27–28 in and it must weigh between 14 and 16 oz. Its pressure should be equal to 0.6–1.1 atmospheres.

HOW TO PLAY

Each team attempts to score goals by kicking or heading the ball into the goal defended by the opposing side. The ball must not be touched by the hands of any player other than the goalkeeper.

Starting

The team who wins a coin toss chooses to defend one end of the field or to the kickoff. At least two players from the team kicking off position themselves behind the halfway line and inside the center circle. (At this point every player must be within his team's half of the field. The defending team's players must also remain outside the center circle.) The ball is placed on the center spot and the game starts on the referee's whistle. The first kick must enter the opponent's half.

How to win

The team scoring the highest number of goals by kicking or heading the ball into the opposition's goal wins the game. The goal zone is defined in *Law 10, Method of Scoring (page 12).*

Officials

A referee and two assistant referees (linesmen).

Dressing for goal
A goalie wears colors that distinguish him from the other players—so that he is instantly identifiable. Some goalies may wear gloves to help grip the ball and occasionally a cap to shade the eyes.

Dress

A jersey or shirt with shorts and socks. These are the same color for a whole team, although the goalie must wear colors that distinguish him from the other players. Suitable footwear and protective shin guards (covered entirely by the socks) are also worn. A player must not wear anything that is dangerous to other players.

Superstars
In much of Europe (as well as Central and South America and parts of Africa and Asia), star soccer players inspire a devotion equal to that of rock stars. Frenchman Eric Cantona (left) is an idol not only at home, but also in England, where he played for the popular Manchester United team for a number of years.

KEY RULES

A game lasts 90 minutes, divided into two halves. Teams change ends at halftime. Although the clock runs continually, a referee tracks the time lost to injuries and penalties and adds it back at the end of either half. Because only he knows how much "extra time" there is, no one knows precisely when a half will end until his whistle blows. In addition, some important games are extended by 30 minutes of overtime in the event of a tie. If the tie remains, a series of penalty kicks may decide the issue.

• A player can be penalized for being offside, i.e., being in front of the ball, in the opposite side's half and without at least two opponents between him and the goal. *See Law 11, Offside (page 12).*

• If a player commits a major foul such as kicking, striking, or pushing an opponent, a direct free kick is awarded to the opposing team. This also applies if the ball is deliberately handled by any player other than the goalie. Other offenses such as delay of game or dangerous play are penalized with an indirect free kick for the other team.

For any free kick, the kicker's opponents must keep a distance of 10 yards between themselves and the ball.

• A player who argues with the referee or persistently breaks the rules is shown the yellow card (an official caution), while more serious conduct such as violent behavior or foul language results in the player being sent out of the game (shown the red card). See pages 12–13 and 16 for *Law 12, Fouls and Misconduct.*

• Some fouls, if they take place within the penalty area, incur a penalty kick against the offending team. *See Law 14, Penalty Kick (page 16).*

SOCCER
THE RULES

Law 1

The Field of Play
See The field (page 10).

Law 2

The Ball
See The ball (page 10).

Law 3

Number of Players
See The teams (page 10).

Law 4

Players' Equipment
See The Ball (page10).

Laws 5 & 6

Referees

Law 7

Duration of the Game
The duration of the game shall be two equal periods of 45 minutes, unless otherwise mutually agreed upon, subject to the following:
a) Allowance shall be made in either period for all time lost through substitution, the transport from the field of injured players, time-wasting or other cause, the amount of which shall be a matter for the discretion of the Referee.
b) Time shall be extended to permit a penalty kick being taken at or after the expiration of the normal period in either half.
The halftime interval shall not exceed 15 minutes.
Competition rules shall clearly stipulate the duration of the halftime interval.
The duration of the halftime interval may be altered only with the consent of the Referee.

Law 8

The Start of Play
a) At the beginning of the game, choice of ends and the kickoff shall be decided by the toss of a coin. The team winning the toss shall have the option of choice of ends or the kickoff. The Referee having given a signal, the game shall be started by a player taking a placekick (i.e., a kick at the ball while it is stationary on the ground in the center of the field of play) into his opponents' half of the field of play. Every player shall be in his own half of the field and every player of the team opposing that of the kicker shall remain not less than 10 yards from the ball until it is kicked off; it shall not be deemed in play until it has

traveled the distance of its own circumference. The kicker shall not play the ball a second time until it has been touched or played by another player.
b) After a goal has been scored, the game shall be restarted in like manner by a player of the team losing the goal.
c) After halftime: when restarting after halftime, ends shall be changed and the kickoff shall be taken by a player of the opposite team to that of the player who started the game.

Punishment
For any infringement of this Law, the kickoff shall be retaken, except in the case of the kicker playing the ball again before it has been touched or played by another player; for this offense, an indirect free kick shall be taken by a player of the opposing team from the place where the infringement occurred, subject to the overriding conditions imposed in Law 13. A goal shall not be scored direct from a kickoff.
d) After any other temporary suspension: when restarting the game after a temporary suspension of play from any cause not mentioned elsewhere in these Laws, provided that immediately prior to the suspension the ball has not passed over the sideline or goal lines, the Referee shall drop the ball at the place where it was when play was suspended, unless it was within the goal area at that time, in which case it shall be dropped on that part of the goal area line which runs parallel to the goal line, at the point nearest to where the ball was when play was stopped. It shall be deemed in play when it has touched the ground; if, however, it goes over the sideline or goal lines after it has been dropped by the Referee, but before it is touched by a player, the Referee shall again drop it. A player shall not play the ball until it has touched the ground. If this section of the Law is not complied with the Referee shall again drop the ball.

Law 9

Ball In and Out of Play
The ball is out of play:
a) When it has wholly crossed the goal line or sideline, whether on the ground or in the air.
b) When the game has been stopped by the Referee.
The ball is in play at all other

times from the start of the match to the finish including:
a) If it rebounds from a goalpost, crossbar or corner flag post into the field of play.
b) If it rebounds off either the Referee or Assistant Referees when they are in the field of play.
c) In the event of a supposed infringement of the Laws, until a decision is given.

Law 10

Method of Scoring
Except as otherwise provided by these Laws, a goal is scored when the whole of the ball has passed over the goal line, between the goalposts and under the crossbar, provided it has not been thrown, carried or intentionally propelled by hand or arm, by a player of the attacking side, except in the case of a goalkeeper, who is within his own penalty area. The team scoring the greater number of goals during a game shall be the winner; if no goals, or an equal number of goals are scored, the game shall be termed a "draw."

Law 11

Offside
1. A player is in an offside position if he is nearer to his opponents' goal line than the ball, unless:
a) he is in his own half of the field of play, or
b) he is not nearer to his

opponents' goal line than at least two of his opponents.

2. It is not an offense in itself to be in an offside position. A player shall only be penalized for being in an offside position if, at the moment the ball touches, or is played by one of his team, he is, in the opinion of the Referee, involved in active play by:
a) interfering with play, or
b) interfering with an opponent, or
c) gaining an advantage by being in that position.

3. A player shall not be declared offside by the Referee
a) merely because of his being in an offside position, or
b) if he receives the ball, direct from a goal kick, a corner kick, or a throw-in.

4. If a player is declared offside, the Referee shall award an indirect free kick, which shall be taken by a player of the opposing team from the place where the infringement occurred, unless the offense is committed by a player in his opponents' goal area, in which case the free kick shall be taken from any point within the goal area.

Law 12

Fouls and Misconduct
A player who commits any of the following six offenses in a

Keep it clean
Soccer is not a contact sport and any kind of interference with an opponent is a foul penalized by a direct free kick by the opposition.

manner considered by the Referee to be careless, reckless or involving disproportionate force:

a) kicks or attempts to kick an opponent; or
b) trips an opponent; or
c) jumps at an opponent; or
d) charges an opponent; or
e) strikes or attempts to strike an opponent; or
f) pushes an opponent;

or who commits any of the following four offenses:
g) when tackling an opponent makes contact with the opponent before contact is made with the ball; or
h) holds an opponent; or spits at an opponent; or
i) handles the ball deliberately, i.e., carries, strikes, or propels the ball with his hand or arm (this does not apply to the goalkeeper within his own penalty area);

shall be penalized by the award of a **direct free kick** to be taken by the opposing team from the place where the offense occurred, unless the offense is committed by a player in his opponents' goal area, in which case the free kick shall be taken from any point within the goal area. Should a player of the defending team commit one of the above 10 offenses within the penalty area, he shall be penalized by a **penalty kick.** A penalty kick can be awarded irrespective of the position of the ball, if in play, at the time an offense within the penalty area is committed.

A player committing any of the following five offenses:
1. playing in a manner considered by the referee to be dangerous;
2. charging fairly, i.e., with the shoulder, when the ball is not within playing distance of the players concerned and they are definitely not trying to play it;
3. when not playing the ball, impeding the progress of an opponent, i.e., running between the opponent and the ball, or interposing the body so as to form an obstacle to an opponent;
4. charging the goalkeeper except when he:
a) is holding the ball;
b) is obstructing an opponent;
c) has passed outside his goal area;
5. when playing as a goalkeeper and within his own penalty area:
a) from the moment he takes

Fair tackle?
Defenders often resort to desperate measures to take the ball away from an opponent. But the rules are very clear about what constitutes a legal tackle. See Rule 12, part g.

control of the ball with his hands, he takes more than four steps in any direction while holding, bouncing, or throwing the ball in the air and catching it again, without releasing it into play, or
b) having released the ball into play before, during or after the four steps, he touches it again with his hands, before it has

been touched or played by a player of the opposing team either inside or outside of the penalty area, or by a player of the same team outside the penalty area, subject to the overriding conditions of 5c), or
c) touches the ball with his hands after it has been deliberately kicked to him by a teammate, or

Playing dirty
If the referee sees something like this, the guilty party is likely to be shown the yellow card, but often players will hide their rough play from the referee.

d) indulges in tactics which, in the opinion of the Referee, are designed merely to hold up the game and thus waste time and so give an unfair advantage to his own team, shall be penalized by the award of an **indirect free kick** to be taken by the opposing side from the place where the infringement occurred, subject to the overriding conditions imposed in Law 13.

A player shall be **cautioned** and shown the **yellow card** if:
j) he enters or re-enters the field of play to join or rejoin his team after the game has commenced, or leaves the field of play during the progress of the game (except through accident) without, in either case, first having received a signal from the Referee showing him that he may do so. If the Referee stops the game to administer the caution, the game shall be restarted by an indirect free kick taken by a player of the opposing team from the place where the ball was when the Referee stopped the game, subject to the overriding conditions imposed in Law 13.

If, however, the offending player has committed a more serious offense, he shall be penalized according to that section of the law he infringed;
k) he persistently infringes the Laws of the Game;
l) he shows, by word or action, dissent from any decision given by the Referee;
m) he is guilty of ungentlemanly conduct.

For any of these last three offenses, in addition to the caution an **indirect free kick** shall be awarded to the opposing side from the place where the offense occurred, subject to the overriding conditions imposed in Law 13, unless a more serious infringement of the Laws of the Game was committed.

A player shall be sent off the field of play and shown the **red card** if, in the opinion of the Referee, he:
n) is guilty of violent conduct;
o) is guilty of serious foul play;
p) uses foul or abusive language;
q) is guilty of a second cautionable offense after having received a caution.

If play is stopped by reason of a player being ordered from the

➡ *page 16*

SKILLS
• • • • •

Although all players require stamina, speed, and the ability to control a ball, particular qualities are desirable for each for the four positions on a team. *Defenders* must be skilled at tackling and heading. *Midfield Players* need the stamina to keep up with play at all times and the flexibility to play defense or offense as required. *Forwards* need to be especially skillful with the ball and good at heading. They also need to be able to respond quickly and accurately to goal opportunities. *Goalies* must have the agility and reflexes to block balls coming in from all kinds of angles. They also need a high level of concentration and good judgment.

Passing

There are a number of different passes that can be used by a player, depending on the direction and distance that the ball needs to travel. The direction the ball takes will depend on which part of it is kicked and with which part of the foot (e.g. the heel, toe, instep etc.), while the distance will depend on the length of the backswing (the backwards lift of the foot prior to kicking). For example, a *lofted pass* combines a long backswing with an instep kick to the lower part of the ball to produce a high, long flight through the air, whereas a swerving pass, made by kicking the ball to left or right of center with the inside or outside of the foot, may be used to curve the ball past an opponent.

Ball control

Controlling the ball with the feet is the most important of all soccer skills. The most skilled players can dribble the ball rapidly down the field changing direction at will to trick an opponent.

Playing on
The ball is much easier to control when it is traveling away from you. Players try to pass the ball in front of a teammate so he can catch up to it.

Foul play
This is an illegal tackle. The defender is in danger of kicking the attacker's legs and has missed the ball completely.

Attacker   Defender

Kicking

The direction and distance a ball travels when kicked depend not only on the length and power of the leg swing but what part of the foot makes contact with the ball—and where on the ball it makes contact.

Tackling

The *block tackle* is used by a player to take posession of the ball from an opponent by approaching head-on or from the side, snatching the ball and continuing on with it in another direction. The *sliding tackle* simply clears the ball from the opponent's control without actually taking posession of it. Successful tackling requires balance, tenacity, and a good sense of timing.

Attacker

Defender

Fair play
This is a legal tackle. The defender has gone for the ball and strikes it cleanly.

Too late
A late tackle—that is, an attempt to tackle an attacker after the ball has gone past—will almost certainly lead to a penalty kick if it occurs within the goal area.

Ball control and dribbling

The ball can be received and brought under control with any part of the body other than the arms and hands. A player can then travel down the field with it by dribbling, i.e., keeping it rolling slightly in front of him with quick controlled taps. A skilled player can incorporate sudden changes in direction and pace to outmaneuver opponents.

Body control
A player may bring down and control a high ball with his chest but he must not let the ball touch his arms or hands.

Dribbling
A good forward can fake and swerve through a whole bank of defenders, leaving them lunging in his wake.

Scoring attempt

Ideally shots should be kept low, since the course of a high shot is clearly visible and more predictable—and therefore easier to block or intercept. But when a direct ground shot is not possible different techniques are employed. A *volley shot* directs the ball into the goal while it is still in the air. A *chip shot* is a steep, short shot that takes advantage of a goalie who has moved off the goal line by sending the ball over his head. Heading is another way of deflecting the ball neatly into the net.

Heading

Heading can be used for scoring, passing, or defense. By meeting the ball with the forehead and using the body to provide force, the ball can be directed forward, backward, or to one side.

No "climbing"
Players are allowed to strike the ball with their forehead as well as their feet but they are not allowed to climb an opponent to reach the ball for a header.

Goalkeeping

The goalie is the only player permitted to use his hands. Taking advantage of this to catch the ball is generally the safest way of saving a goal. A goalie has to be constantly on the alert, ready to leap into the air, plunge to the ground, or stand securely in the net to receive shots. When it is not possible to catch the ball, a goalkeeper can "palm," or punch it, diverting its course away from the goal.

Shooting
The best forwards swoop in on balls in the goal area getting a shot away before defenders can intercept

continued from page 13

field for an offense without a separate breach of the Law having been committed, the game shall be resumed by an **indirect free kick** awarded to the opposing side from the place where the infringement occurred, subject to the overriding conditions imposed in Law 13.

Law 13
Free Kick

Free kicks shall be classified under two headings: "Direct," from which a goal can be scored direct against the **offending side**, and "Indirect," from which a goal cannot be scored unless the ball has been played or touched by a player other than the kicker before passing through the goal.

When a player is taking a direct or an indirect free kick inside his own penalty area, all of the opposing players shall be at least 10 yards from the ball and shall remain outside the penalty area until the ball has been kicked out of the area. The ball shall be in play as soon as it has traveled the distance of its own circumference and is beyond the penalty area. The goalkeeper shall not receive the ball into his hands, in order that he may thereafter kick it into play. If the ball is not kicked direct into play, beyond the penalty area, the kick shall be retaken.

When a player is taking a direct or an indirect free kick outside his own penalty area, all of the opposing players shall be at least 10 yds from the ball, until it is in play, unless they are standing on their own goal line, between the goal posts. The ball shall be in play when it has traveled the distance of its own circumference.

If a player of the opposing side encroaches into the penalty area, or within 10 yards of the ball, as the case may be, before a free kick is taken, the Referee shall delay the taking of the kick, until the Law is complied with.

The ball must be stationary when a free kick is taken, and the kicker shall not play the ball a second time, until it has been touched or played by another player.

Notwithstanding any other reference in these Laws to the point from which a free kick is to be taken:
1. any free kick awarded to the

The yellow card
Any player who persistently breaks the rules or argues with the referee is given an official warning with a yellow card held high in the air. A player guilty of violent behavior or foul language is shown a red card and expelled from the game.

defending team, within its own goal area, may be taken from any point within the goal area,
2. any indirect free kick awarded to the attacking team within its opponent's goal area shall be taken from the part of the goal-area line that runs parallel to the goal line, at the point nearest to where the offense was committed.

Punishment

If the kicker, after taking the free kick, plays the ball a second time before it has been touched or played by another player an indirect free kick shall be taken by a player of the opposing team from the spot where the infringement occurred, unless the offense is committed by a player in his opponents' goal area, in which case the free kick shall be taken from any point within the goal area.

Law 14
Penalty Kick

A penalty kick shall be taken from the penalty mark and, when it is being taken, all players with the exception of the player taking the kick, properly identified, and the opposing goalkeeper, shall be within the field of play but outside the penalty area, at least 10 yds from

the penalty mark and must stand behind the penalty mark.

The opposing goalkeeper must stand (without moving his feet) on his own goal line, between the goalposts, until the ball is kicked. The player taking the kick must kick the ball forward; he shall not play the ball a second time until it has been touched or played by another player. The ball shall be deemed in play directly it is kicked, i.e., when it has traveled the distance of its circumference. A goal may be scored directly from a penalty kick. When a penalty kick is being taken during the normal course of play, or when time has been extended at halftime or full time to allow a penalty kick to be taken or retaken, a goal shall not be nullified if, before passing between the posts and under the crossbar, the ball touches either or both of the goalposts, or the crossbar, or the goalkeeper, or any combination of these agencies, providing that no other infringement has occurred.

Punishment

For any infringement of this Law:
a) by the defending team, the kick shall be retaken if a goal has not resulted;
b) by the attacking team, other

than by the player taking the kick, if a goal is scored it shall be disallowed and the kick retaken;
c) by the player taking the committed after the ball is in play, a player of the opposing team shall take an indirect free kick from the spot where the infringement occurred, subject to the overriding conditions imposed in Law 13.

Law 15
Throw-In

When the whole of the ball passes over the sideline, either on the ground or in the air, it shall be thrown in from the point where it crossed the line, in any direction, by a player of the team opposite to that of the player who last touched it. The thrower at the moment of delivering the ball must face the field of play and part of each foot shall be either on the sideline or on the ground outside the sideline. The thrower shall use both hands and shall deliver the ball from behind and over his head. The ball shall be in play immediately it enters the field of play, but the thrower shall not again play the ball until it has been touched or played by another player. A goal shall not be scored direct from a throw-in.

Punishment

a) If the ball is improperly thrown in, the throw-in shall be taken by a player of the opposing team.
b) If the thrower plays the ball a second time before it has been touched or played by another player, an indirect free kick shall be taken by a player of the opposing team from the place where the infringement occurred, subject to the overriding conditions imposed in Law 13.

Law 16
Goal Kick

When the whole of the ball passes over the goal line excluding that portion between the goalposts, either in the air or on the ground, having last been played by one of the attacking team, it shall be kicked direct into play beyond the penalty area from any point within the goal area, by a player of the defending team. A goalkeeper shall not receive the ball into his hands from a goal kick in order that he may thereafter kick it into play. If the ball is not kicked beyond the penalty area, i.e., direct into play, the kick shall be retaken. The kicker shall not play the ball a second time until it has been touched or been played by another player. A goal shall not be scored direct from such a kick. Players of the team opposing that of the player taking the goal kick shall remain outside the penalty area until the ball has been kicked out of the penalty area.

Punishment

If a player taking a goal kick plays the ball a second time after it has passed beyond the penalty area, but before it has touched or been played by another player, an indirect free kick shall be awarded to the opposing team, to be taken from the place where the infringement occurred, subject to the overriding conditions imposed in Law 13.

Law 17

Corner Kick

When the whole of the ball passes over the goal line, excluding that portion between the goalposts, either in the air or on the ground, having last been played by one of the defending team, a member of the attacking team shall take a corner kick, i.e., the whole of the ball shall be placed within the quarter circle at the nearest corner flagpost, which must not be moved, and it shall be kicked from that position.

A goal may be scored direct from such a kick. Players of the team opposing that of the player taking the corner kick shall not approach within 10 yds of the ball until it is in play, i.e., it has traveled the distance of its own

circumference, nor shall the kicker play the ball a second time until it has been touched or played by another player.

Punishment

a) If the player who takes the kick plays the ball a second time before it has been touched or played by another player, the referee shall award an indirect free kick to the opposing team, to be taken from the place where the infringement occurred, subject to the conditions imposed in Law 13.
b) For any other infringement the kick shall be retaken.

International Board Decisions

Above are listed all the basic rules of soccer. However, these rules are continually qualified year-by-year by additional rulings called International Board Decisions. For the latest Decisions, contact your national Soccer governing body.

Reprinted by permission of The Football Association (England). Local rules, which may be slightly different, should be obtained by the relevant governing body in your area.

TACTICS

Most teams choose one of three main formations to make effective use of their players. Defensemen-midfielders-forwards are arranged as 4-2-4 (four defenders, two midfielders, and four strikers), 4-3-3, or 4-4-2. This last formation is the most defensive. The arrangement chosen will depend on a number of factors such as the strengths of the individual players and those of the opposing team, the conditions, and the venue.

The decision may be made to change the formation during play if, for example, a team desperately needs to score. In this instance more forwards will be allocated to strengthen the attack.

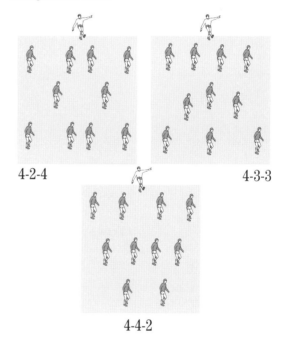

4-2-4   4-3-3

4-4-2

GRAY AREA

Q. Player A passes the ball up the field to Player B who is currently standing in an offside position. In running back to receive the pass, Player B passes two opponents, thus placing them between himself and the goal. Would he be penalized for being offside?

A. Yes. Player B cannot return to an onside position by running back down the field once the ball has been played to him. *See Law 11, Offside (page 12).*

Dropkick
A goalkeeper can send the ball upfield either by kicking it or throwing it with a single arm. A goalkeeper who holds the ball too long may be penalized for delaying the game.

Australian rules football
Essentials

Australia's national winter sport, Australian rules football, is a fast-moving, physical game in which points are generally scored by kicking the ball through any of three sets of posts set up side-by-side. Although the game is infrequently played in North America, professional contests from Australia are now occasionally broadcast on cable television sports channels.

The field

Oval, grass, 135–185 m (148–202 yds) in length and 110–155 m (120–170 yds) in width. Two goalposts, 6.4 m (21 ft) apart and at least 6 m (20 ft) in height) are placed at each end of the ground. Two "behind posts," 3 m (10 ft) minimum height are placed in line with the goalposts, at a distance of 6.4 m (21 ft) from each. The line between the goalposts is the goal line and the lines between the goalposts and the behind posts are the behind lines. A goal square is marked out using the goal line as one of its sides, as well as two 9-m (30-ft) lines drawn at right angles to the goalposts (kickoff lines) and a line connecting the outer end of these kickoff lines. The center circle is 3 m (10 ft) in diameter, divided into two semicircles and enclosed in a square with 45-m (49-yds) sides.

Grand Final day
The Super Bowl of Australian rules football is Grand Final day, played at the Melbourne Cricket Ground, and seen below.

The players

Two teams of 18 players on the field at a time, plus up to four substitutes.

Officials

A field umpire, two boundary umpires, and two goal umpires.

The ball

Oval, 720–730 mm (29 in) by 545–555 mm (approx 21 in) and weighing 450–500 g (approx 17 oz).

Dress

Sleeveless shirts (referred to as "guernseys" in Australia), shorts, socks, and boots. Players must not wear anything that may cause injury during a match, such as jewelry, guards, or dangerous footwear.

Playing area
The field is one of the biggest for any sport—up to 185m (202 yds) long.

50 m
110–155 m
9 m
3 m
45 m
135–185 m
50 m
6.4 m
6.4 m
6.4 m

Basic dress
Surprisingly for such a tough, physical game, Australian rules players wear no protective clothing.

Player positions

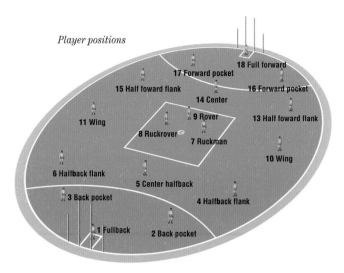

18 Full forward
17 Forward pocket
15 Half foward flank
16 Forward pocket
14 Center
11 Wing
9 Rover
13 Half foward flank
8 Ruckrover
7 Ruckman
10 Wing
6 Halfback flank
5 Center halfback
3 Back pocket
4 Halfback flank
1 Fullback
2 Back pocket

Playing positions

In Australian Rules the forwards' main function is to score goals, the midfield players pass the ball up the field, and the backs attempt to prevent the opponents from scoring.

Rovers

Autralian rules is not only for big men. Rovers are often small, combining speed and agility to grab a loose ball and dart away with it, carrying the ball to the forwards.

HOW TO PLAY

Players attempt to score goals by kicking the ball in between their opponents' goalposts. They may run with the ball, kick it or hit it, but they are not allowed to throw it.

Starting

A toss decides the choice of ends. The umpire then starts the first quarter with a center bounce. This takes place inside the center circle, with a maximum of four players from each team allowed inside the center square at the time. The umpire holds up the ball, blows the whistle, and then bounces the ball in the circle. Only one player from each team may then try to take possession of the ball. In muddy conditions the umpire may need to throw the ball up into the air rather than bounce it— a "ball-up."

How to win

A ball kicked between the goalposts (the central posts) without being touched by a player other than the kicker scores a goal (6 pts). A *behind* (1 pt) is scored if the ball is kicked through either of the other two sets of posts, if it is kicked over the central crossbar, if it is kicked through the goalposts but has touched a post or another player, or if a defender causes the ball to cross the goal or behind lines. The team with the most points wins.

KEY RULES

• A match consists of four quarters of 20 to 25 minutes each. Teams change ends after every quarter.

Ball-up

Australian rules games begin with the umpire bouncing the ball in a circle surrounded by up to four players from each team.

• Play is fast-moving and restricted by just a few basic rules. The ball may be kicked or handballed (held in one hand and then punched with the fist of the other hand) in any direction. Throwing is not allowed as a means of moving the ball. *See Law 9, Ball Disposal (page 21).*

• Players may also run with the ball, unless tackled, provided they bounce it on the ground at every 15 m (16 yds). *See Law 10, Ball Possession (pages 21–22).*

• If a player catches a ball from a teammate's kick, that is called a "mark." The kick must travel at least 10 m, and no one else may have touched it. Following a mark, the player has the choice of putting the ball into play or taking a free kick.

• Breaches of the laws are penalized by a free kick to the opposition. Violations include throwing the ball, illegal tackling *(see Law 11, How a Player May Be Checked or Tackled, page 22),* charging an opponent and kicking the ball out of bounds. *See Law 12, Free Kicks (page 23).*

AUSTRALIAN RULES FOOTBALL

THE LAWS

1 Playing Field, Oval, Goal, and Behind Posts
See The field (page 18).
2 The Ball
See The ball (page 18).
3 Teams
See The players (page 18).
4 Players' Boots, Jewelry and Protective Equipment
See Dress (page 18).
5 Starting the Match
See How to play (page 19).

6 Goals and Behinds
6.1 A goal shall register six points and a behind one point. The team scoring the greater number of points shall win the match. If the points are equal, the match shall be drawn.
6.2 When a ball crosses a goal or behind line or hits a goalpost, the field umpire shall give the goal umpire an "All clear" signal if there have not been any incidents in play which the field umpire intends to penalize.
6.3 A score cannot be registered unless the field umpire calls or indicates "All clear," or "Touched, all clear" to the goal umpire.
6.4 Subject to the "All clear" signal, a goal shall be scored when the ball is kicked over the

goal line by a player of the attacking team without touching a player or a goalpost. A behind shall be scored in any other case when the ball passes over the goal line, or touches or passes over a goalpost or passes over a behind line without touching or passing over a behind post.
6.4.1 If a defending player kicks or takes the ball over the goal or behind line, a behind shall be scored.
6.4.2 If the ball touches or passes over a behind post, it shall be out of bounds.
6.4.3 The fact that the ball has struck or touched an umpire (or any other authorized official or replaced player) shall not prevent the scoring of a goal or a behind.
6.4.4. While the ball is on the ground and a player has his hands on it, and if another player kicks the ball, it shall be deemed to have been touched in transit. If the ball goes over the goal or behind lines, the field umpire shall call "Touched, all clear" and a behind shall be registered.
6.4.5 In the event that the ball crosses a goal or behind line, or hits a goalpost, and the goal umpire does not receive an all clear from the field umpire and play continues, the goal umpire shall run after the field umpire and notify him at once.

On receipt of such advice, the field umpire shall stop play and give the all clear.
The goal umpire shall signal and record the score and play shall recommence in accordance with these laws.
In the event that a free kick has been awarded after the ball crosses the line and before the all-clear has been given, the field umpire shall give the all-clear and the goal umpires shall signal and record the score. The free kick shall then be taken where the infringement occurred or where the ball is at the time, whichever is the greater penalty against the offending team.
6.4.6 In the event that, after the all-clear has been given for a goal, an infringement occurs to a player of the defending team prior to the ball being bounced in the center circle, the resultant free kick shall be taken at the spot where the infringement occurred, or at the center circle, whichever is the greater penalty against the offending team.
6.4.7 In the event that, after the all-clear has been given for a behind, an infringement occurs to a player of the defending team prior to the ball being kicked off after the behind, the resultant free kick shall be taken at the spot where the infringement occurred, or at the back line of

the center square, whichever is the greater penalty against the offending team.
6.5 The goal umpires shall be the sole judges of goals and behinds and their decisions are final, except when the ball has become dead by a decision of the field umpire.
6.5.1 Upon receiving "All clear," the goal umpire shall initially indicate a goal by raising both index fingers, and a behind by raising one index finger.
6.5.2 The goal umpire shall then signal a goal by waving two flags, and a behind by waving one flag. A score cannot be annulled unless the goal umpire immediately rectifies a mistake by notifying the field umpire before the ball is bounced in the center if he has wrongly signaled a goal or before the ball is kicked off in the case of a behind except when the ball has been signaled out of bounds and the signal has not been seen by the field umpire.
6.5.3 When a score has been annulled, the goal umpire shall immediately stand on the center of the goal line and hold both flags above his head in crossed position.
6.6 At the first sound of the siren, the ball shall be dead, but a player who has, prior to the first sound of the siren, taken a mark or been awarded a free kick shall be allowed to kick or handball the ball. A goal or behind obtained therefrom or from a ball that is in transit prior to the first sound of the siren shall be counted.
In the event that the siren sounds while the ball is in transit, or while the player taking a kick after the siren is preparing to kick the ball, or after he has kicked the ball, an infringement occurs to a player of the attacking team before the all-clear has been given, the field umpire shall blow his whistle and consult with the goal umpire as to whether a goal or behind has been kicked.
If a goal has been kicked the field umpire shall give the all-clear and the goal shall be registered. In the event that a behind has been kicked, the player offended against shall be

Loose ball
On the run, players have to be dextrous to cleanly pick up the ball while surrounded by opponents—they can be tackled the moment they touch it.

given the option of taking the free kick at the spot the infringement occurred, or allowing the behind to be registered.

Should the siren sound while the ball is in transit, or while the player taking a kick after the siren is preparing to kick the ball, or after he has kicked the ball, an infringement occurs to a player of the defending team before the all-clear has been given, the field umpire shall award a free kick to the player offended against at the spot where the infringement occurred.

6.6.1 In the event that two or more field umpires are officiating, the ball shall be deemed dead when one of the field umpires hears the first sound of the siren. That field umpire shall be the sole judge of whether the ball has been kicked or handled or whether a free kick has been awarded prior to the first sound of the siren.

6.6.2 If the ball is touched in transit the field umpire must be satisfied that the score was not assisted by another player, but if the ball touches any player below the knee it shall become dead and no score recorded.

6.7 Controlling bodies shall authorize such officials as they deem appropriate to record scores, separate from the goal umpires. In the event of the goal umpires disagreeing on the final scores, the controlling body may take the separately recorded scores into consideration in determining the result of the match.

7 Kicking Off from Behind
7.1 When a behind has been scored, unless a subsequent free kick has been given, any player of the defending team shall kick the ball into the field of play from within the kickoff lines, the ball contact being made before the ball completely crosses the line. When the ball is being kicked off, no player shall be allowed within 5 m (approx. 16 ft) of the kickoff lines.

7.2 The player kicking off may regain possession provided the ball has been kicked into the field of play beyond the kickoff lines.

7.3 If the ball is not brought into play correctly, the field umpire shall bounce the ball on the center of the kickoff line.

7.4 The ball shall not be kicked off until the goal umpire has finished waving the flag.

7.5 If an opposing player attempts to delay play by moving to, or standing within, 5 m (approx. 16 ft) of the kickoff line or prevents the player from kicking off, the field umpire shall penalize the offending team by advancing the mark from the kickoff line to the back line of the center square—the kick to be taken at the center of the line by the nearest player of the team offended against.

In the event of a further offense against this law, the mark to be advanced to the forward line of the center square—the kick to be taken at the center of the line by the nearest player of the team offended against.

7.6 If after the goal umpire has finished waving the flag a player will not kickoff (time being added) when directed to do so by the field umpire, or kicks the ball over the goal or behind line, the field umpire shall bounce the ball on the center of the kickoff line.

8 Marking the Ball
8.1 A mark is catching the ball directly from the kick of another player, not less than 10 m (33 ft) distant, the ball being held a reasonable time and not having been touched in transit from kick to catch.

8.1.1 A mark shall be awarded to a player who crosses the boundary line from the playing ground but controls the ball before it has passed completely over the boundary line. If the field umpire is in doubt he should consult the boundary umpire.

8.1.2 A mark shall be allowed when the ball is caught and controlled on the goal, behind or boundary lines.

8.1.3 A mark will be awarded where a ball in flight strikes an umpire, or any other authorized official or replaced player.

8.2 When a player takes a mark or is given a free kick, an opponent is permitted to stand on the mark or spot where this occurrence took place.

8.2.1 Only one opponent may stand on a player's mark.

8.2.2 No other player is allowed within a corridor which extends from 5 m (approx. 16 ft) either side of the mark to 5 m either side of, and a 5 m radius behind, the player with the ball. This corridor is to be known as the 10 m protected area.

8.2.3 In the event of an opponent encroaching over the mark when a player is kicking for

goal and a goal is kicked, the field umpire shall give the "All clear" and the goal shall be registered. If a goal has not been kicked, the player shall be given the option of another kick, and the mark shall be advanced 50 m (approx. 55 yds).

9 Ball Disposal
The ball may be kicked or handballed.

9.1 A player shall handball the ball by holding the ball in one hand and hitting it with the clenched fist of the other hand. If the ball is not handballed correctly, a free kick shall be given to the nearest opponent.

9.2 A player may kick the ball by

Handballing See 9.1.

making contact with the ball below the knee.

9.2.1 A player who takes a mark or is awarded a free kick shall play the ball from directly behind the spot where the mark or free kick was awarded. The 10 m protected area shall apply. If the player attempts to play the ball other than in a direct line over the mark, the field umpire shall call "Play on" and the ball shall immediately be in play.

9.2.2 When it is necessary for a defending player, from a free kick or mark, to play the ball from beyond the goal or behind line, the player on the mark shall not be permitted to come within 5 m (16 ft) of the goal or behind lines. In such cases, the ball must be played directly over the mark.

If there is no player on the mark, the ball may be played in any direction provided it is brought into play over the goal, behind or boundary line originally

crossed.

9.2.3 When a player is kicking for goal from a mark or a free kick, the kick shall be taken along a direct line through the mark to the center of the goal line.

9.2.4 The ball shall be deemed to be brought into play when any portion of it is on or above the boundary line.

9.2.5 If a player taking his kick from outside the boundary line after having been awarded a mark or a free kick, fails to take the ball into play, or attempts to play on outside the boundary line, the ball shall be deemed to be out of bounds. The ball will then be thrown into play by the boundary umpire from the spot where the original mark or free kick took place.

9.2.6 If a player on the defending team, from a free kick or mark, kicks from behind the goal or behind lines and the ball hits either a goalpost or behind post, the field umpire shall direct the timekeepers to add time on and give the player another kick to put the ball into play.

10 Ball Possession
10.1 A player may hold the ball for any length of time provided he is not held by an opponent.

10.2 If he runs with the ball he must bounce it or touch it on the ground at least once within every 15 m (approx. 16 yds) from the commencement of his run, whether running in a straight line or turning and dodging.

10.3 If a player with the ball bounces it, he is deemed to be in possession of the ball.

➡ *page 22*

Below, see 10.2.

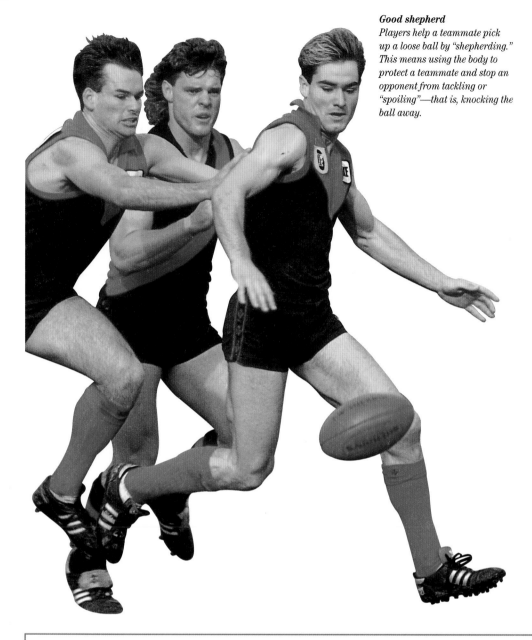

Good shepherd
Players help a teammate pick up a loose ball by "shepherding." This means using the body to protect a teammate and stop an opponent from tackling or "spoiling"—that is, knocking the ball away.

SKILLS AND TACTICS

Both teams try to maintain possession of the ball, moving it quickly into the forward area to score points.

Marking is an acquired skill. The high mark is one of the game's main characteristics: leaping into the air to catch the ball directly from a kick. The ball is difficult to catch because of its shape and frequent foul weather conditions. Players need the strength to mark the ball against the pressure of leaping opponents trying to do the same. Being able to *kick* with the left or right foot, for distance and accuracy, is also important, particularly when kicking for goal. *Handballing* (i.e. punching the ball with one hand while held in the other hand) is left- or right-handed. The emphasis is on accuracy. *Running with the ball* requires agility and strength as players must bounce the ball as they run, dodging opponents. *Tapping* the ball in *ruck duels* to fellow players is frequently used to clear blocked play. As with the center bounce, the umpire blows his whistle to restart play and bounces the ball between two rucks who then attempt to gain possession.

Shepherding is using the body to stop an opponent from tackling or spoiling (knocking the ball away from) a teammate. Players must be able to *tackle* effectively, bringing an opponent to a halt and preventing him from disposing of the ball cleanly in order to gain a chance at possession.

continued from page 21

10.4 If he runs with the ball and handballs it over an opponent's head and catches it, he must, within 15 m (approx 16 yds) of commencing his run or striking the ball on the ground, bounce it or touch the ground with it or dispose of the ball.
10.5 A player who lies on or over the ball is deemed to be in possession of the ball.

11 How a Player May Be Checked or Tackled
11.1 A player may be fairly met or checked by an opponent by the use of the hip, shoulder, chest, arms or open hand provided the ball is not more than 5 m (16 ft) away.
11.2 A player may be pushed in the chest or side or shepherded by an opponent provided the ball

is not more than 5 m (16 ft) away.
11.3 A player in possession of the ball may fend off a prospective tackler by pushing him with an open hand in the chest, shoulder or side.
11.4 A player in possession of the ball may be tackled and grasped in the area below the top of the shoulders and on or above the knees. The tackle may be from front, side or behind provided that the tackle from behind does not thrust forward the player with the ball.
11.5 Procedures for administering this law are as follows:
   11.5.1 A player in possession of the ball, when held by an opponent firmly enough to retard his progress, should be given a reasonable chance of disposing of it by kicking or handball, otherwise a free kick shall be

awarded to his opponent for holding the ball.
   11.5.2 The field umpire shall bounce the ball when the player with the ball has the ball held to his body by an opponent, unless the player has had a reasonable time to dispose of the ball prior to being tackled, in which case a free kick shall be awarded for holding the ball.
   11.5.3 A player not in possession of the ball when held by an opponent, shall be awarded a free kick.
   11.5.4 When a player claims a mark, the ball having been touched in transit, and retains possession when held by an opponent, the field umpire shall not award a free kick but bounce the ball if he is satisfied that the player did not hear his call of "Play on." But if the ball has been taken away from the player by another player, the field

umpire's call "Play on" shall hold good.
   11.5.5 The field umpire shall allow play to continue if a player in the act of kicking or handball, is swung off balance and his foot or hand does not connect with the ball.
   11.5.6 The field umpire shall allow play to continue if a player is bumped and the ball falls from his hands.
   11.5.7 The field umpire shall allow play to continue when a player's arm is knocked, causing him to drop the ball.
   11.5.8 The field umpire shall allow play to continue if a player has his arms pinned to his sides causing him to drop the ball.
   11.5.9 The field umpire shall allow play to continue if a player is pulled by one arm or swung causing the ball to fall from his hand.

Making your mark
One of the most distinctive
moments in Australian rules
football is the dramatic high jump
or mark as a player leaps to catch
a ball kicked by a teammate. A
good, clean catch gives the player a
free kick. Here the leaping player in
black has gone up to make a mark
but his opponent has prevented the
catch by punching the ball away.

Gray area

A tackled player must immediately dispose of the ball (ideally by kicking or handballing it to a teammate). If he does not get rid of the ball quickly and correctly, he is penalized. However, in an attempt to avoid losing possession, tackled players often fake an attempt to dispose of the ball, hoping that the umpire will be fooled into calling for a ball-up to continue play.

When tackled, players are supposed to give up the ball, but don't always do so.

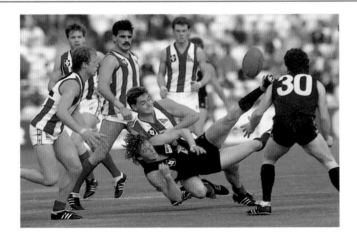

Losing control
When tackled, a player must be
allowed to kick or handball the ball
away—if he is still holding the ball.
So opponents usually try to force him
to drop the ball—for example, by
swinging him off balance, as here—
so that he loses possession.

12 Free Kicks

12.1 The spirit of the laws relating to awarding free kicks is:

12.1.1 The player who makes the ball his sole objective shall be given every opportunity to gain possession of the ball.

12.1.2 The player who has possession of the ball and is held by an opponent shall be given a reasonable time to kick or handball the ball.

12.1.3 The ball shall be kept in motion. The field umpire shall call "Play on" even though a free kick should have been awarded but by doing so would penalize the team offended against.

12.2 All breaches of the laws shall be penalized whether the ball is dead or in play. The field umpire shall sound his whistle for the awarding of a free kick. Unless otherwise specified, the player nearest to the opponent who commits a breach of the Laws shall receive the free kick.

12.2.1 If the field umpire has sounded his whistle for a free kick, he may cancel such a free kick by calling "Play on" if the side offended against will be penalized by enforcing the free kick.

Should the field umpire cancel a free kick he may reverse the decision if it is obvious that it is not to the advantage of the team concerned.

12.2.2 A player awarded a free kick must go back to the spot where the breach occurred before being allowed to kick or play the ball. If such a player kicks or plays the ball without complying to this law, the field umpire shall stop play and enforce compliance.

12.2.3 A free kick shall be awarded against a player who throws or hands the ball to another player, or to the advantage of play, while the ball is in play.

12.2.4 When a player who has taken a mark or been awarded a free kick is, in the opinion of the field umpire, unable to dispose

➡ *page 24*

continued from page 23

of the ball through accident or the deliberate action of an opponent, the field umpire shall award a free kick to the nearest player of the same team at the time the incident occurred. The kick shall be taken at the spot nearest to where the incident occurred.

12.2.5 If a player has been awarded a free kick or a mark, and before the kick is taken a further breach of the laws is made by a player on the same side as the first offender, the field umpire shall sound his whistle and direct the free kick to be taken by a teammate at the spot where the subsequent breach took place, if doing so will penalize the offending team. Where a subsequent breach is committed by a teammate of the player taking the kick, a free kick shall be given to the nearest opponent at the spot of the original free kick, if doing so will penalize the offending team.

12.2.6 If a breach of the laws is committed, regardless of the position on the field, the free kick is to be taken at the spot where the infringement occurred, or where the ball is at the time, whichever would be the greater penalty for the offending team.

12.2.7 A free kick shall be given if a player infringes any of the laws between the time the field umpire sounds his whistle and bounces the ball.

12.3 Free kicks for infringements concerning the field umpire bouncing the ball will be awarded against the player who:

12.3.1 Enters the center circle when the field umpire is in the act of bouncing the ball at the start of the match, the start of the quarter, and after a goal has been scored.

12.3.2 Interferes with an opponent from the time the ball has been bounced in the center circle until the ball subsequently makes contact with a player or the ground.

12.3.3 Unduly interferes with the bouncing of the ball by the field umpire or deliberately interferes with an umpire during the progress of the match.

12.4 A free kick will be awarded against a player who interferes with an opponent in the following manner:

12.4.1 Interferes with an opponent from the time the ball goes out of bounds, until the ball, after being thrown in by the

boundary umpire, makes contact with a player or the ground.

12.4.2 When a goal is kicked by a player, and while the ball is being kicked or is in transit a breach of the laws is made by an opponent, the field umpire shall give the "All clear" signal and the goal shall be registered; but in the event of a behind being scored the ball not having touched the ground or player, the player shall be given the option of another kick.

12.4.3 After the ball has been kicked and an infringement occurs, and the ball crosses the behind line on the full or hits the goalpost on the full, the option of another kick shall be given to the player who originally kicked the ball at the spot from where the kick originated. If the breach of the laws occurred before or during the act of kicking or handball, a free kick shall be taken by the player offended against, at the spot where the breach occurred, provided that the team offended against will not be penalized by the taking of such a free kick.

12.4.4 If a breach of the laws is made by a player of the attacking side, the field umpire shall not signal "All clear" but must award a free kick, to the nearest player of the defending team.

12.4.5 If a player is fouled immediately after scoring a goal or behind and after the field umpire has given the "All clear," the field umpire shall award such player a free kick at the spot where the offense took place. Another score may then be registered without the ball having been bounced in the center circle or kicked off.

12.4.6 If a breach of the laws is committed against a player who has disposed of the ball, or who is shepherding for a team-mate with the ball, and this occurs after the ball has been kicked or handballed, a penalty free kick shall be awarded to a player of the team offended against at the spot where the ball first touched the ground, a player, was marked or went out

Foul
See
12.4.7

of bounds. If the awarding of such a free kick will penalize the team offended against, the free kick shall be given to the player who originally kicked the ball.

12.4.7 Trips or kicks, attempts to trip or kick or sling an opponent, or when not in possession of the ball, kicks in a manner likely to cause injury to an opponent, or strikes or attempts to strike an opponent with either hand or arm or deliberately with the knee.

12.5 A free kick shall be awarded against a player who kicks the ball out of bounds in the following manner:

12.5.1 Kicks the ball out of bounds on the full. The free kick shall be taken at the spot where the ball went out of bounds.

12.5.2 When kicking off after a behind has been registered, the ball is kicked out of bounds without it having been touched by any player, a free kick shall be given at the spot where the ball went out of bounds.

12.5.3 Willfully kicks or forces the ball out of bounds without it being touched by another player.

12.6 A free kick shall be awarded against the player who checks or tackles an opponent in the following manner:

12.6.1 Catches hold of an opponent below the knee or by the neck or head, which includes the top of the shoulder.

12.6.2 Charges an opponent.

12.6.3 Pushes an opponent from behind in any way, except when legitimately going for a mark, a player may interfere with an opponent from behind.

12.6.4 Pushes, bumps or shepherds an opponent in the face, head, neck, or in the shoulder.

12.6.5 Pushes, bumps, or

Foul
See
12.6.1

Foul
See
12.6.3

shepherds an opponent who is in the air for a mark.

12.6.6 Shepherds an opponent when the ball is more than 5 m (16 ft) away or is out of play.

12.6.7 Deliberately holds back or throws an opponent after that opponent has kicked or handballed the ball. No free kick shall be given if the player, unable to release his hold at once, throws the opponent down.

12.7 A free kick shall be awarded against a player who interferes with play as follows:

12.7.1 If the ball is in transit toward goal from a free kick, mark, or field kick and an opponent shakes the goalpost, the field umpire shall give the player the option of another kick if in the umpire's opinion, the opponent's action could have affected the result.

12.7.2 If a teammate shakes the goalpost, the field umpire shall award a free kick to the nearest opponent at the spot from where the ball was kicked.

12.8 A free kick shall be awarded against a player who willfully wastes time by not allowing the ball to be brought into play prior to, or when directed to do so, by the field umpire.

12.9 A free kick shall be awarded against the team as follows:

12.9.1 Any official runner, trainer, medical officer, other approved team official, or replaced player who interferes with the ball, the play, or a player of the opposing team during the course of the game shall cause the field umpire to award a free kick to the nearest player of the team offended against at the spot of the infringement, or where the ball is at the time, whichever would be a greater penalty to the offending team. When a player is awarded a set kick at goal and an opposition player climbs on the shoulders of a teammate before the kick is taken, the mark shall be advanced to the center of the goal line and the player with the kick shall be permitted to kick from directly in front of goal.

12.9.2 A free kick shall be awarded against a player who carries the ball across the boundary line, and after a boundary umpire signals out of bounds, does not give the ball immediately to the boundary umpire or drop it directly to the ground.

12.9.3 A free kick shall be awarded against a player who touches the ball after it has passed outside the boundary line and been signaled out of bounds by the boundary umpire, except for a player of the team to receive the free kick when the ball has been kicked out on the full, kicked out directly from a kickoff from a behind, or willfully kicked or forced out without being touched by another player.

13 50-Meter Penalty

13.1 A 50-m (55-yd) penalty will be applied in instances where the actions of a player encroach over the mark, waste time, and/or delay the play.

13.2 When the umpire applies a 50-m penalty, he shall signal "time on." The player receiving the penalty shall not be permitted to play on. The mark shall then be advanced 50 m in a direct line with the center of the goal. The player receiving the penalty shall be given free access to take up a position behind the advanced mark. When the umpire is satisfied the player has taken up a correct position, he will instruct the timekeepers to stop adding time, irrespective of whether an opponent is standing on the mark.

13.3 A 50-m penalty shall have the same implication as a free kick.

13.4 If a free kick or mark has been awarded and a player of the opposing team runs through the 10-m protected area, unless accompanying or following an opponent within 5 m, a 50-m penalty shall be awarded.

13.5 Where a 50-m penalty advances the mark to the center of the goal line, the kick shall be taken from directly in front of the advanced mark.

13.6 Where a player has been awarded a mark or free kick and another player of the same team is unlawfully prevented from running past the spot of the mark or free kick, a 50-m penalty shall be awarded to the player originally awarded the mark or free kick.

13.7 Where a free kick is awarded for intentionally tripping, a 50-m penalty shall automatically apply.

13.8 To suit local requirements controlling bodies may reduce the distance of the penalty to 25 m (27 yds).

14 Play On

The field umpire shall call and indicate "Play on" and the ball shall immediately remain in play in any of the following circumstances:

14.1 When an umpire, or any other authorized official or player is struck by the ball while it is in play.

14.2 When the ball, having been kicked, is touched while still in transit.

14.3 When the ball is caught directly from a kick of another player less than 10 m (33 ft) away.

14.4 When the field umpire cancels a free kick.

14.5 When a player who has taken a mark or been awarded a free kick, attempts to run, handball, or kick other than over his mark.

15 Bouncing the Ball

15.1 The field umpire shall bounce the ball in the following circumstances:

15.1.1 At the start of the match, at the start of each quarter, and after each goal has been kicked, except when a breach of the laws has been penalized by the awarding of a free kick.

15.1.2 When in doubt as to which player has taken a mark.

15.1.3 When a player, in kicking off after a behind has been registered,

fails to correctly bring the ball into play, the ball to be bounced on the center of the kickoff line.

15.1.4 In a scrimmage where players are struggling in undue confusion for possession of the ball.

15.1.5 When the field umpire has bounced the ball and it goes over the goal, behind, or boundary line without having been touched by any player.

15.1.6 When a player claims a mark, the ball having been touched, and retains possession of the ball when held by an opponent, the field umpire will bounce the ball if he is satisfied that the player did not hear his call of "Play on."

15.1.7 When a goal umpire is unable to see whether the ball goes over the goal or behind lines, and cannot give a decision, the ball shall be bounced on the center of the kickoff line in front of the goal.

15.1.8 When there is simultaneous encroachment of players from opposing teams, into the center square prior to the ball being bounced.

16 Umpires: Duties and Instructions

17 Match-Time, Duties, and Responsibilities of Umpires and Timekeepers

18 Controlling Body

19 Doping Policy

20 Infectious Diseases

These laws are reprinted by permission of the Australian Football League who hold the copyright. The complete Laws of Australian rules football can be obtained from the AFL.

Possession
Gaining possession of the ball is crucial in Australian rules football and whenever a ball goes loose you will see players hurtling in to grab it before their opponents. But picking up a slippery, oval shaped ball on the run can be extraordinarily difficult and players often resort to kicking it instead.

Football
Essentials

This enormously popular American sport is as complex as it is popular. Sometimes compared to a warlike game of chess, this hard-hitting, physical sport involves sophisticated, well-rehearsed tactics and formations, adjusted strategically as a game progresses. Although "pickup" recreational games are also popular, they tend to be highly simplified versions of the game, since the playing conditions of organized leagues are almost impossible to reproduce.

The field (or gridiron)

Rectangular. 100 yards long plus two 10-yard end zones (bringing the total length to 120 yards). The field is 160 ft wide. Bounded by sidelines and end lines. Each yard is marked, and every five yards a white line extends across the field. Every 10 yards, the field is marked with a number, which increases from 10 to 50 on each side of the field.

The goals

Two goalposts are offset from each end line, at the center, connected by a horizontal crossbar, 18 ft 6 in long, 10 ft above the ground. The posts extend 30 ft above this bar and the goal is the vertical plane extending indefinitely above the crossbar and between the two posts.

Pylons

120 yds

Inbound yard markers

20-yd line

Goal

10 yds

Goal line

The ball

Oval, tan. An inflated rubber bladder enclosed in a pebble-grained leather case. Standard measurements are: long axis, 11 to 11¼ in; long circumference (around the middle), 28 to 28½ in; weight, 14 to 15 oz. There are 24 balls available for NFL games.

Side view

The gridiron game
Football field markings are very precise, with every yard marked along both sidelines and along two rows nearer to the center of the field. Markings along these interior rows are called hash marks, and every play must begin on or between them. For instance, if the previous play has ended with a player tackled to the far left of the playing field, the next play will begin on the left hash mark for the yard at which the player was tackled.

Armor
Football players are among the most heavily protected of all sportsmen and look almost like medieval knights when they enter the field. Underneath his shirt the player wears a full body jacket with massive shoulder pads, a complete pelvic guard, and hip pads.

Super Bowl
Each January, the two best teams in the National Football League meet in the Super Bowl to decide the season's champion. First played in 1967, the Super Bowl has been won most often by the Dallas Cowboys and San Francisco 49ers—five times each.

The players

NFL teams consist of 45 players, only 11 of which are allowed on the field at any one time. With few exceptions, players play either on offense or defense. There are also special team players (who may also play an offensive or defensive position) brought on to the field for plays involving kicks: kick-offs, punts, extra points, and field goals.

Dress

Helmet, shoulder pads, thigh pads, knee pads, trousers, jerseys, wristbands, gloves, stockings, and shoes. Jerseys feature the player's number and last name. Numbers generally provide a clue as to a player's position:
1–19 quarterbacks, punters, placekickers
20–49 running backs and defensive backs
50–59 centers and linebackers
60–79 offensive guards and tackles
80–89 wide receivers and tight ends
90–99 defensive linesmen
90–99 linebackers (if 50–59 unavailable).

Officials

A referee, umpire, head lineman, line judge, back judge, side judge, and field judge.

Target
The player with the ball is the only player who may be tackled.

Field goal
If a team gets close enough to their opponent's goal line on fourth down, the team's kicker may try to score a field goal by kicking the ball over the bar and between the posts.

Quarterback pass
Unlike rugby, a forward pass is allowed in football. It is usually the quarterback who makes it.

Short runs
Only occasionally does a runner break into the open for a long gain. But even short runs can be productive, helping an offense advance 10 yards in 4 plays.

COLLEGE FOOTBALL

Although the general principles of play resemble those of the NFL, there are a number of rule differences. In the NFL, a player on the ground with the ball may get up and run if he has not been touched by a member of the opposition. In college football, however, a play ends as soon as a knee of the player with the ball touches the ground—whether or not he has been touched. In the NFL, a player attempting to catch a pass must get two feet down in bounds in order for the catch to be valid (unless he is pushed out of bounds by a defender). In college football, only one foot needs to come down in bounds. In the NFL, kickoffs are made from the 30-yard line (unless the ball is moved due to a penalty). In college football, the ball is placed on the 35-yard line for a kickoff. Tied NFL games are resolved with a sudden death overtime (explained in Key Rules). In college football, tied teams each begin an offensive series from the opposition's 25-yd line. The game ends when one team gets more points out of its series than does the opposition.

HOW TO PLAY

Players run with the ball or pass it. An offensive team has four downs—that is, four plays or chances, to advance the ball 10 yards toward its opponent's goal line. If successful, the offense is awarded another four downs to go an additional 10 yards. And so on. The ultimate aim is to score touchdowns or field goals.

If a team fails to advance the ball 10 yards within the allotted four downs, possession of the ball reverts to the other team, which then begins its own offensive series. Usually, a team that has failed to go the 10 yards on its first three plays will not attempt a fourth. Rather, on fourth down, the offensive team will kick the ball downfield (a punt), forcing the opposition further away from the goal line. If a team has managed to get relatively close to the opponent's goal, they may choose to use their fourth down play to attempt a field goal.

Possession of the ball also changes from one team to another as a result of a *turnover*. A turnover occurs either when a player with the ball loses it and it is subsequently recovered (picked up or jumped on) by a member on the other team (a fumble) or when a quarterback's pass is caught by an opposing player (an interception). The team recovering a fumble or making an interception then begins an offensive series.

Starting

The winner of the toss chooses which goal to defend or to receive the ball.

One team then kicks off from its 30-yd line. The ball is placed on a kicking tee and kicked down the field toward the opposing team who then attempt to advance it in the other direction.

How to win

There are several ways to score. A touchdown (six points) results when a team advances the ball beyond its opponent's goal line, successfully controlling the ball in the end zone. Following a touchdown, the successful team receives the ball at its opponent's 2-yard line, where it has the option of attempting an extra point (1 pt) or a two-point conversion. An extra point is worth less, but it is easier to achieve. It consists of a kick of the ball through the goalposts, following the protocol for a field goal.

In control

Seven officials are responsible for keeping control of a football game. At the heart of the action is the referee, who positions himself behind the offense and maintains overall control of the game, announcing all calls.

NATIONAL FOOTBALL LEAGUE RULES

These rules are abridged and summarized.

Rule 1 The Field
See The field (page 26).

Rule 2 The Ball
See The ball (page 26).

Rule 3 Definitions

Rule 4 Game Timing

Rule 5 Players, Substitutes, Equipment
See The players and Dress (page 26).

Rule 6 Free Kick
Section 1 Putting Ball in Play
Article 1 A free kick called a kickoff puts the ball in play:
(a) at the start of each half;
(b) after a try; and
(c) after a successful field goal.
Article 2 A free kick also puts the ball in play:
(a) after a safety;
(b) following a fair catch when this method is chosen;
(c) when there is a replay for a short free kick; and
(d) when enforcement for a foul during a free kick is from the previous spot.
Article 3 A free kick may be

made from any point on or behind the offensive team's free kick line and between inbounds lines. A dropkick, placekick, or punt may be used.
Penalty: For illegal kick at free kick: loss of 5 yds from previous spot.
Article 4 The initial free kick lines during a given free kick shall be as follows (plus or minus any distance they might be moved because of a distance penalty enforced prior to the kick):
   For the kicking team:
(a) Kickoff—offensive 30
(b) Safety kick—offensive 20
(c) Fair-catch kick—the yard line through the mark of the catch.
   For the receiving team:
A yard line 10 yards in advance of the offensive team's free kick line.
Article 5 After the referee's whistle prior to a free kick:
(a) All receiving players (Team B) must be inbounds and behind their line until the kick.
(b) All kicking players (Team A) must be inbounds and behind the ball when kicked except the holder of the placekick may be beyond the line and the kicker may be beyond the line but his kicking foot may not be.
Penalty: For violation of free kick formation: the free kick is

made again. New free kick lines are set 5 yds nearer the offender's end line unless a half-distance penalty is being enforced.
Section 2 Ball in Play After Free Kick
Article 1 A free kick is short when it does not go to or across the receiving team's free kick line unless, before doing so, it is first touched by a player of the receiving team, or goes out of bounds.
Penalties:
(a) For the first short free kick: loss of 5 yds from the previous spot, and rekick must be made.
(b) For the second (or more) consecutive short free kick illegally touched:
the receiving team takes possession of the ball at the spot of illegal touch or recovery. If a free kick is to be made, new free kick lines are set.
Article 2 Free Kick Recovery
(a) If a free kick is recovered by the receiving team it may advance.
(b) If a free kick(legal or illegal) is recovered by the kicking team, the ball is dead. If the recovery is legal, the kicking team next puts the ball in play at the spot of recovery. Undue advance by the kicking team recovering (legal or illegal) is delay of game.

(c) If a free kick is simultaneously recovered by two opposing players, the ball is awarded to the receiving team.
Article 3 All general rules apply—when play continues after a free kick (loose ball) ends.
Article 4 No player of the kicking team may touch or recover a kickoff or safety kick before:
(a) it is touched by the receiving team (B) if that kicking team player has been out of bounds during the kick; or
(b) it has crossed the receiving team's restraining line, unless before doing so, it has first been touched by the receiving team.
Penalty: For illegal touching of a free kick by the kicking team: loss of 5 yds from the previous spot. New free kick lines are set if enforced.
Article 5 If there is a foul other than a personal foul (blocking) after a fair-catch signal, fair-catch interference, or an invalid fair-catch signal during a free kick, any enforcement, if made, is from the previous spot and the free kick must be made again.
Section 3 Free Kick Out of Bounds or in Touch
Article 1 The kicking team may not kick a free kick out of bounds between the goal lines.
Penalties:
(a) Receivers' ball 30 yds from

the spot of the kick or the team may elect the option of taking possession of the ball at the out-of-bounds spot.

(b) For the second (or more) consecutive onside kick out of bounds: receiving team takes possession of the ball at the out-of-bounds spot.

Article 2 Rule 11 governs if a free kick:

(a) goes out of bounds behind the receiving team's goal line;

(b) kickoff or safety kick becomes dead because the ball strikes the receiving team's goalpost; or

(c) is downed in the end zone.

Rule 7 Scrimmage
Section 1 Necessary Gain on Downs

Article 1 A new series (first-and-10) is awarded to the offensive team when the following conditions exist; subject, however, to the specific rules of enforcement (Rule 12).

(a) When, during a given series, the ball is declared dead in possession of offensive team while it is on, above, or across the necessary line, or unless a penalty places it there, or unless

a touchback for them results.

(b) When the ball is dead in the field of play in the offense's possession, after having been in the defensive team's possession during the same down.

(c) When a foul is made by the defense, except as otherwise specified, or when an impetus by them results in a touchback for the offensive team.

(d) When the kicking team recovers a scrimmage kick anywhere in the field of play after it first has been touched beyond the line by the receivers.

Article 2 The forward part of the ball in its position when declared dead in the field of play shall be taken as the determining point in measuring any distance gained. The ball shall not be rotated when measuring.

Article 3 If offensive team fails to advance ball to necessary line during a given series, it is awarded to defensive team for a new series at the spot:

(a) where dead at end of fourth down; or

(b) where it is placed because of a combination penalty or a touchback for defensive team.

Section 2 Position of Players at Snap

Article 1 The offensive team must have:

(a) seven or more players on its line at the snap.

(b) all players who are not on line, other than the snap receiver under center, must be at least 1 yd behind it at snap.

Penalty: For violation of snap formation: loss of 5 yds from previous spot.

Article 2 After the neutral zone starts, no player of either team at snap may:

(a) encroach upon it; or

(b) be offside.

Penalty: For encroachment, offside, or a neutral zone infraction: loss of 5 yds from previous spot. Number of down and necessary line remain the same.

Article 3 An offensive player who comes into game wearing an illegal number for the position he takes must report to the referee who in turn will report same to the defensive captain. The clock shall not be stopped and the ball may not be put in play until the referee takes his normal position.

Penalties:

(a) 5 yds for illegal substitution if player in above category enters the game and/or his team's huddle without reporting and later reports his player position status to the referee prior to snap.

(b) For failure to notify referee of change in eligibility or ineligibility status (when required) prior to snap: loss of 5 yds for illegal susbstitution.

Article 4 At the snap, a center, guard, or tackle of the offensive team may be anywhere on his line, but he may not be behind it unless he is at least 1 yd behind it and has informed the referee of his change of position to that of an eligible receiver.

Penalty: For center, guard, or tackle not on the line at the snap: loss of five yards from previous spot.

Article 5 At the snap, all offensive players must be stationary in their positions:

(a) without any movement of feet, head, or arms;

(b) without swaying of body; and

(c) without moving directly forward except that one player only and he, provided he is moving, parallel to, obliquely backward from, or directly backward from the line of scrimmage at snap.

Penalty: For player illegally in motion at snap: loss of five yards from previous spot. In case of doubt, this penalty shall be enforced.

Article 6 After a shift or huddle all offensive players after assuming a set position must come to an absolute stop. They also must remain stationary in their position without any

➡ *page 31*

Head to head

Players line up at the line of scrimmage—ready for action.

Line of scrimmage
Football is a game of stops and starts. Every new play begins with the players lined up along the line of scrimmage. Although the formation below is legal,

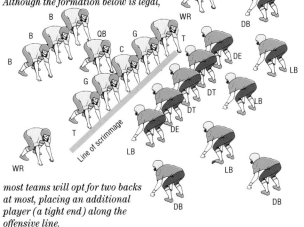

most teams will opt for two backs at most, placing an additional player (a tight end) along the offensive line.

Positions
Offense:

B	back
QB	quarterback
WR	wide receiver
C	center
T	tackle
G	guard

Defense:

LB	line backer
DE	defense end
DT	defense tackle
DB	defense back

Offside
A defensive player should not cross the line of scrimmage prior to the snap. If he does, he may return without incurring a penalty—provided that he has not made contact with any offensive player. If he makes contact or is across the line at the time of the snap, he is "offsides." His team is penalized 5 yards.

The snap
The most basic action is the "snap," which begins every play. The center snaps the ball back through his legs to the quarterback in one quick, continuous action, while every offensive player on the line of scrimmage remains completely motionless until the snap is complete. Below, the offense executes a running play, as the quarterback "hands off" to a back.

The snap

Center　　Quarterback　　Back

Special plays
Football is an elaborate game and teams prepare a series of carefully worked out "plays" beforehand. These include running plays such as: the "sweep" (the ball carrier is protected by two blockers as he runs wide around his linesmen); the "trap" (the offensive players leave a gap to fool their opponents); and the "quarterback sneak," which creates a gap for the quarterback to run through. There are also a wide variety of intricate passing plays. The defense too employs a wide variety of formations and strategies, attempting to anticipate and disrupt the plans of the offense.

A catch
In the NFL, a player must get two feet down in-bounds for a catch to be valid—unless he is pushed out of bounds by a defender, in which case an official must judge whether or not he would have got both feet down if it weren't for the push. These rules also apply to a defensive player who attempts to intercept a quarterback's pass and take possession of the ball for his own team's offense.

KEY RULES

• A game consists of four periods of 15 minutes each with a break at halftime. The clock stops running, however, after an incomplete pass, a change of possession, or after a player with the ball has gone out of bounds. These and other stoppages mean that a game usually lasts for around three hours. Teams change ends after each quarter, and a kickoff begins each half. Between the first and second, and third and fourth quarters the team with the ball retains possession (moving in the opposite direction). The second half (third quarter) begins with a kickoff from the team that received the first half kickoff.

• Football is a game of discrete plays. With the exception of kickoffs (and rare free kicks), each play begins with both teams placing their players across from each other along the line of scrimmage, an imaginary line running parallel to the end zones and running through the end of the ball nearest to the team in possession. Strict rules govern how teams position themselves along the line of scrimmage and who may move prior to the snap. *See Rule 7, Scrimmage (page 29).*

• Players are allowed to run with the ball or pass it. Forward passes are permitted, but only one is allowed to an offensive player per play, made from behind the line of scrimmage. A backward pass can occur at any time from any place on the field. *See Rule 8, Forward Pass, Backward Pass, Fumble (page 33).*

• In order for a touchdown to be scored, a ball must

"break the plane" of the end zone. That is, a player must be in possession of the ball anywhere beyond an imaginary straight edge rising up from the front part of the goal line. As soon as this requirement is met, the play is over and a touchdown is scored.

• Offensive players are allowed to use their arms or hands to block their opponents, but they are not allowed to hold on to them. Offensive holding generally results in a 10-yard penalty—the ball is moved back 10 yards from the original line of scrimmage. *See Rule 12, Player Conduct (page 37).*

• A player (either offensive or defensive) must not unfairly impede the attempts of an opponent to catch the ball. A violation of this rule by a defensive player results in a first down for the offensive team at the spot of the foul (if the foul occurred in the end zone, the ball is placed at the 1-yd line). A violation by an offensive player (who interferes with a defender attempting to intercept a pass) results in a loss of yardage. *See Rule 8, Section 2 Pass Interference (page 33).*

• A game tied after the conclusion of the fourth quarter is resolved with an overtime procedure known as sudden death. Another 15-minute quarter is begun, but the game ends as soon as one team scores in any manner. Following a coin toss, one team kicks off to the other. After this, play continues as before. If neither team scores during the overtime, the game is declared a tie. Playoff games, however, will continue until one team manages to score.

SKILLS

On a team, each player specializes in a specific position, since each position requires quite different skills. It is very rare for a football player to participate on both offense and defense.

The offense

The *quarterback* is a powerful thrower who directs the offense and can handle pressure. Although most plays are selected by the coaches, the quarterback must be able to look over the defense and determine whether a better play might be available, in which case he will call out coded instructions (an *audible*) directing his teammates to change the play. A play begins when the *center* passes, or snaps, the ball to the quarterback who then runs with it himself, hands it to a running back, or attempts to throw it to an eligible receiver. The running backs are either *halfbacks* (quick, agile, and evasive enough to dodge tackles) or *fullbacks* (strong enough to plow through tacklers). Fullbacks, in particular, must double as good blockers, helping lead the way for a halfback. *Wide receivers* are fast players who need sure hands to receive passes from the quarterback. Passes can also be caught by the running backs, the tight end, or in rare circumstances an *eligible* tackle. The *tight end* is generally a big player, capable of either blocking or catching passes. The biggest offensive players are the *guards* and *tackles,* who must hold back the opposition in order to create openings in the defense or to protect the quarterback.

The defense

The *defensive ends* head off runners attempting to break through or around the line. *Defensive tackles* are powerful, tenacious players who face the offense from the center of the defensive formation. *Linebackers* attempt to block a particular part of the field to put pressure on the quarterback. *Cornerbacks* guard a wide receiver and prevent him from making a catch. *Safeties* often join the cornerbacks on pass defense, although they also serve as the last line of defense.

Tackling
A defensive player attempts to, tackle any offensive player carrying the ball.

---

continued from page 29

movement of their feet, head or arms, or swaying of their body for a period of at least one second before snap.
Penalty: For illegal pause or motion after a shift: loss of 5 yds from previous spot. In case of doubt the penalty is to be enforced.
Article 7 No player may be out of bounds at the snap.
Penalty: For player out of bounds at snap: loss of 5 yds from the previous spot.
Section 3 Putting the Ball in Play
Article 1 The offensive team must put the ball in play by a snap at the spot where previous down ended, unless otherwise specifically provided for, unless a free kick is prescribed or is chosen after a fair catch.
Penalty: For not using a snap when prescribed: loss of 5 yds.
Article 2 When a foul occurs, the ball shall not be put in play again until the penalty has been:

(a) enforced;
(b) declined;
(c) offset;
(d) annulled by a choice; or
(e) disregarded.
Article 3 The snap may be made by any offensive player who is on the line but must conform to the following provisions:
(a) The snap must start with ball on ground with its long axis horizontal and at right angles to line; and
(b) The impulse must be given by one quick and continuous motion of hand or hands of snapper. The ball must actually leave or be taken from his hands during this motion.
(c) The snapper may not:
(1) move his feet abruptly from the start of snap until the ball has left his hands;
(2) have quick plays after the neutral zone starts if the referee has not had a reasonable time to assume his normal stance. The ball remains dead. No penalty unless for a repeated act after warning (delay of game).

Penalty: For illegally snapping ball: loss of 5 yds from spot of snap for false start.
Article 4 From the start of the neutral zone until the snap, no offensive player, if he assumed a set position, shall charge or move in such a way as to simulate the start of a play (false start).
Penalty: For false start: loss of 5 yds from spot of snap.
Article 5 Prior to the snap no defensive player shall enter the neutral zone and touch the ball.
Penalty: For actions interfering with the ball prior to or during the snap: loss of 5 yds for delay from the spot of snap.
Article 6 The snap must be to a player who was not on his line at the snap, unless it has first struck the ground. The play continues as after any other backward pass if the snap either:
(a) first touches the ground; or
(b) first touched or is caught by an eligible backfield receiver.
Penalty: For snapping to ineligible snap receiver: loss of

5 yds from the spot of snap.
Article 7 Ball is next put in play (snap) at inbounds spot by the team entitled to possession when:
(a) a loose ball is out of bounds between goal lines;
(b) a runner is out of bounds between goal lines;
(c) the ball is dead in a side zone;
(d) the ball is placed there as a result of an enforcement; or
(e) the mark of a fair catch is in a side zone.
Section 4 Dead Ball
Article 1 An official shall declare dead ball and the down ended:
(a) when a runner is out of bounds, cries "down," or falls to the ground and makes no effort to advance.
(b) any time a quarterback immediately drops to his knee (or simulates dropping to his knee) to the ground behind the line of scrimmage during the last two minutes of a half. The game

➡ *page 32*

continued from page 31

clock will not stop during this action.

(c) whenever a runner declares himself down by sliding feet first on the ground. The ball is dead at the spot of the ball at the instant the runner so touches the ground.

(d) when a runner is so held or otherwise restrained that his forward progress ends.

(e) when a runner is contacted by a defensive player and he touches the ground with any part of his body except his hands or feet, ball shall be declared dead immediately. The contact by the defensive player must be the cause of runner going down.

(f) when an opponent takes a ball (hand in hand) in possession of a runner who is down on the ground.

(g) when any forward pass (legal or illegal) is incomplete.

(h) when any legal kick touches receivers' goalposts or crossbar unless it later scores a goal from field.

(i) when any scrimmage kick crosses receivers' goal line from the impetus of kick and no attempt is made to run it out, or if it is lying loose in the end zone from the impetus of the kick.

(j) when any legal kick or a short free kick is recovered by the kickers, except one kicked from behind line which is recovered behind line (not a try-kick).

(k) when defense gains possession during a try, or a try-kick ceases to be in play.

(l) when a touchdown, touchback, safety, field goal, or try has been made.

(m) when any receiver catches after a fair-catch signal (valid or invalid) before kick is touched in flight by an opponent.

(n) when any official sounds his whistle, even though inadvertently.

(o) when any fourth down fumble by offensive team is recovered or caught by any offensive player other than the fumbling player.

Article 2 If a loose ball comes to rest anywhere in field and no player attempts to recover, official covering the play should pause momentarily before signaling dead ball (official's time-out). Any legal kick is awarded to receivers and any other ball to team last in possession. When awarded to a team behind the goal line, the ball is placed on its 1-yd line.

Article 3 If an official inadvertently sounds his whistle during a play, the ball becomes dead immediately:

(a) If during a run, it is the offensive team's ball at the spot of the ball at the time of the whistle.

(b) If during a backward pass or fumble, it is the offensive team's ball at the spot of the ball at the time of the whistle.

(c) If during a kick, it is the receiver's ball at the spot of the ball at the time of the whistle.

(d) If during a forward pass from behind the line, the ball reverts to the passers at the previous spot. It is an incomplete pass.

(e) If during a forward pass from beyond the line, the ball reverts to the passers at the spot of the pass. It is an illegal pass. The penalty is assessed from the spot of the pass.

(f) If during a forward pass not from the scrimmage, the ball reverts to the passers at the spot of the pass. The penalty is assessed from the spot of the pass.

Article 4 When the ball is dead, it is next put in play at spot designated by official so declaring it. This is usually the spot of the ball when his whistle sounded, but may be some other spot, when referee is informed by an official that the ball should have been dead at another spot or when the rules prescribe otherwise.

Article 5 The ball is not dead because of touching an official who is inbounds or because of a signal by an official other than a whistle.

Section 5 Possession of Ball after Out of Bounds

Article 1 If any legal kick, except for a free kick, is out of bounds between the goal lines, ball is next put in play at inbounds spot by the receivers, unless there is a spot of illegal touching nearer kickers' goal line.

Article 2 If it is a play from scrimmage, any possession by offensive team after an out of bounds during fourth down is governed by the location of the necessary line.

Article 3 If a runner is out of bounds between goal lines, the ball is next put in play by his team at inbounds spot.

Article 4 If a forward pass is out of bounds between the goal lines, the ball is next put in play by passing team as provided for an incompletion or for an illegal pass.

Article 5 If a backward pass is out of bounds between the goal lines, the ball is next in play at the inbounds spot by the team last in possession.

Article 6 A fumble by the offensive team cannot result in an advance by that team if the ball is not recovered in the field of play or end zone.

(a) A fumble that goes forward and out of bounds is to return to that team at the spot of the fumble.

(b) A fumble in the field of play that goes backward and out of bounds belongs to the offense at the out-of-bounds spot.

(c) A fumble in the field of play that goes forward into the opponent's end zone and over the end line or sideline results in the ball being given over to the defensive team and a touchback awarded.

(d) A fumble which occurs in a team's own end zone and goes forward into the field of play and out of bounds will result in a safety if that team provided the impetus that put the ball into the end zone. If the impetus was provided by the opponent, the play will result in a touchback.

(e) A fumble which occurs in a team's own end zone or in the field of play and the ball goes out of bounds in the end zone will result in a safety if that team provided the impetus that put

Staying ready
Unlimited substitutions are allowed from among the squad of 45 players and throughout the game players on the sideline need to stay ready.

the ball into the end zone. If the impetus was provided by the opponent, the play will result in a touchback.

Rule 8 Forward Pass, Backward Pass, Fumble
Section 1 Forward Pass
Article 1 The offensive team may make one forward pass from behind the line during each play from scrimmage provided the ball does not cross the line and return behind line prior to the pass.
(a) Any other forward pass by either team is illegal and is a foul by the passing team.
(b) When any illegal pass is intercepted, the ball may be advanced and the penalty declined.
(c) When illegal pass is caught by an offensive player, the ball is dead immediately.
Penalties:
a) For a forward pass not from scrimmage: loss of 5 yds from the spot of the pass. It is a safety when the spot of the pass is behind the passer's goal line.
b) For a second forward pass from behind line, or for a pass that was thrown after the ball returned behind the line: loss of down from the previous spot. (This is an offset foul).
c) For a forward pass from beyond the line: loss of down and 5 yds from the spot of the pass.
Article 2 A forward pass from behind the line may be touched or caught by any eligible player. (Pass in flight may be tipped, batted, or deflected in any direction by any eligible player at any time).
(a) Defensive players are eligible at all times.
(b) Offensive players who are on either end of the line (other than a center, guard, or tackle) are eligible.
(c) Offensive players who are at least (legally) 1 yd behind the line at the snap are eligible, except T-formation quarterback.
Article 3 an eligible receiver becomes ineligible if he goes out of bounds (prior to or during a pass) and remains ineligible until an eligible receiver or any defensive player touches the pass.
Article 4 An ineligible offensive player is one who:
(a) was originally ineligible;
(b) loses his eligibility by going out of bounds;
(c) fails to notify the referee of being eligible when indicated; or
(d) is a T-formation quarterback, who takes his stance behind center,

(1) receives a hand-to-hand pass or snap from him while moving backward;
(2) does not receive a hand-to-hand pass or snap from him and is not legally 1 yd behind the line of scrimmage; or
(3) ever receives a forward pass (handed or thrown) from a team-mate during a play from scrimmage.
Article 5 Any forward pass (legal or illegal) becomes incomplete and the ball is dead immediately if the pass strikes the ground, goes out of bounds, touches the goalpost of either team, or is caught by any offensive player after it has touched an ineligible offensive player before any touching by any eligible receiver. It is a foul if a forward pass (legal or illegal):
(a) first touches or is caught by an ineligible offensive player on or behind the line of scrimmage. Penalty: Loss of down at previous spot. (This foul offsets a foul by the defense).
(b) is first touched or caught by an ineligible offensive player beyond the line (including a T-formation quarterback). Penalty: Loss of 10 yds or loss of down from the previous spot. (This foul offsets a foul by the defense).
Article 6 A legal forward pass thrown from behind the line is complete and may be advanced if it is:
(a) caught by an eligible offensive player before any illegal touching by a teammate;
(b) caught by any offensive player after it is first touched by any eligible player; or
(c) intercepted by the defense (defense may also intercept and advance an illegal forward pass).

Section 2 Pass Interference/Ineligible Player Downfield
Article 1 There shall be no pass interference beyond line of scrimmage when there is a forward pass thrown from behind the line. This applies regardless of whether the pass crosses the line.
(a) The restriction for the offensive team begins with the snap.
(b) The restriction for the defensive team begins when the ball leaves the passer's hands.
Article 2 It is a foul when an ineligible offensive player (including a T-formation quarterback), prior to a legal forward pass:
(a) advances beyond his line, after losing contact with an

opponent at the line of scrimmage;
(b) loses contact with an opponent downfield after the initial charge and then continues to advance or move laterally; or
(c) moves downfield without contacting an opponent at the line of scrimmage.
The above restrictions end when the ball leaves the passer's hand.
Penalty: Ineligible offensive player downfield: loss of 5 yds from previous spot.
Article 3 It is not a foul for an ineligible receiver downfield when ineligible receivers:
(a) block an opponent at the line of scrimmage and drive him downfield, then lose the block and remain stationary;
(b) are forced behind their line;
(c) move laterally behind their line (before or after contact of their initial charge) provided they do not advance beyond their line until the ball leaves the passer's hands; or
(d) have legally crossed their line in blocking an opponent (eligible offensive player A1 may complete a pass between them and the offensive line).
Article 4 After the ball leaves the passer's hand, ineligible forward pass receivers can advance:
(a) from behind their line;
(b) from their own line; or
(c) from their initial charge position, provided they do not block or contact a defensive player until the ball is touched by a player of either team. Such prior blocking and/or contact is forward-pass interference.
When an ineligible lineman, who has legally crossed his line in blocking an opponent or a T-formation quarterback is touched by a forward-pass while beyond his line, enforcement is for Penalty (b) under 8.1.5 (loss of down or 10 yds).
Article 5 It is pass interference by either team when any player movement beyond the offensive line significantly hinders the progress of an eligible player or such player's opportunity to catch the ball during a forward pass. When players are competing for position to make a play on the ball, any contact by hands, arms, or body shall be

Center of attention
The quarterback directs the offense and is often the team's star player.

considered incidental unless prohibited. Prohibited conduct shall be when a player physically restricts or impedes the opponent in a manner that is visually evident and materially affects the opponent's opportunity to gain position or retain his position to catch the ball. If a player has gained position, he shall not be considered to have impeded or restricted his opponent in a prohibited manner if all of his actions are a bona fide effort to go to and catch the ball.
Provided an eligible player is not interfered with in such a manner, the following exceptions to pass interference will prevail:
(a) If both players are looking for the ball or if neither player is looking for the ball and there is incidental contact in the act of moving to the ball that does not materially affect the route of an eligible player, there is not interference. If there is any question whether the incidental contact materially affects the route, the ruling shall be no interference.
(b) Any eligible player looking for and intent on playing the ball who initiates contact however

➡ *page 34*

TACTICS
• • • • • •

Generally speaking, the offense may opt for either a passing play, in which the quarterback locates a receiver and attempts to throw the ball to him, or a running play, with a player carrying the ball as far

Pass interference
A defender must not impede an offensive player's attempt to catch a pass. At left, the defender has clearly made contact with the would-be receiver before the ball arrives and is in danger of being penalized for pass interference.

First line of defense
Defensive linesmen attempt to stop runners before they can break through the line. They also try to reach the quarterback on pass plays, tackling him before he can get the ball away (a sack). Even when they fail to reach the ball carrier, defensive linesmen can fulfill a valuable function, occupying the attention of more than one offensive lineman and preventing them from blocking the defender's teammates.

toward the end zone as possible before being tackled. Plays are very well-rehearsed. Generally, before each new play the quarterback forms a huddle with his teammates and passes on the coach's instructions for a particular plan of action. But it is up to the quarterback to make last minute changes whenever he senses that the defense have anticipated their intentions and have set up a formation to counteract them. He does this by calling out coded instructions on the field.

The defense's aim then is to break up offensive plays by tackling the ball carrier or intercepting passes, while also blocking the rest of the offense, preventing them from providing support for their ball carrier and progressing

severe, while attempting to move to the spot of completion or interception will not be called for interference.
(c) Any eligible player who makes contact, however severe, with one or more eligible opponents while looking for and making a genuine attempt to catch or bat a reachable ball will not be called for interference. The restriction for pass interference ends for both teams when the pass is touched.
(d) After a legal forward pass has been touched by an eligible player, any player may use his hands to push an opponent out of the way during an actual personal attempt to catch the ball, irrespective of his original eligibilty. This does not preclude a penalty against the offensive team for illegal touching prior to touching an eligible player.
(e) Pass interference by the defense or the offense is not to be called when the forward pass is clearly uncatchable by the

continued from page 33

up the field (an "audible"). The defense attempts to anticipate and disrupt offensive plays. The defense also attempts to secure possession of the ball, either by forcing and recovering a fumble or by intercepting a quarterback's pass. The defense itself relies on a variety of well-rehearsed maneuvers. One common tactic it to *blitz*, sending additional players after the quarterback to pressure him and perhaps tackle him before he can get the ball away. Such a tactic involves a certain amount of risk, since fewer defensive players are available to guard against the offense's receivers. Players involved in pass defense may play either in a *zone* (in which they guard a part of the field) or in *man-to-man* (in which they follow the movements of a specific receiver). Defense against running plays generally involves prevention of gaps in the line of scrimmage.

involved receiver and defender.
Penalties:
(a) Pass interference by offense: loss of 10 yds from previous spot.
(b) Pass interference by defense: first down for offensive team at the spot of any such foul. If the interference is also a personal foul, the usual distance penalty for such a foul is also enforced (from spot of foul). If the interference is behind the defensive goal line, it is first down for the offensive team on the defense's 1-yd line, or, if the previous spot was inside the 2-yd line, then halfway between the previous spot and the goal line.

Section 3 Fouls on Passes and Enforcement
Article 1 Intentional grounding will be called when a passer, facing an imminent loss of yardage because of pressure from the defense, throws a forward pass without a realistic chance of completion.
Penalty: For intentional grounding: loss of down and 10 yds from the previous spot, or if foul occurs more than 10 yds from line of scrimmage or where it is more advantageous to the defense, loss of down at spot of foul, or safety if passer is in his end zone when ball is thrown.
Article 2 If there is a foul by either team from the time of the snap until a forward pass from behind the line ends, the penalty is enforced from the previous spot.
Article 3 When the defense

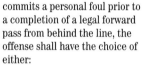

Flattened
When a runner is brought down by a lineman he certainly knows it. Linemen are the biggest men in football and are quite often 6 ft 8 in tall and weigh 275 lbs or more. Crunches like this are the reason why body padding is essential.

Hands off
Above, the offensive player running with the ball can ward off his opponents with his hands or arms. His teammates may also help by blocking opponents, but they may not use their hands or arms. Holding a defensive player will result in a 10-yd penalty if it is detected.

commits a personal foul prior to a completion of a legal forward pass from behind the line, the offense shall have the choice of either:
(a) the usual penalty—15 yds from the previous spot; or
(b) a 15-yd penalty enforced from the spot where the ball is dead.
Article 4 When the offense commits a personal foul prior to an interception of a legal forward pass from behind the line, the defense will have a 15-yd penalty enforced from the spot where the ball is dead.
Article 5 If there is a foul by the defense from the start of the snap until a legal forward pass ends, it is not offset by an incompletion by the offensive team.

Section 4 Backward Pass and Fumble
Article 1 A runner may pass backward at any time.
(a) An offensive player may catch a backward pass or recover it after the pass touches the ground and advance.
(b) A defensive player may catch a backward pass or recover it after the pass touches the ground and advance.
Article 2 Any player of either team may recover or catch and advance a fumble:
(a) before the fumble strikes the ground; or
(b) after the fumble strikes the ground.
Article 3 If a backward pass goes

out of bounds between the goal lines, the ball is next put in play at the inbounds spot by the team in last possession. The ball is dead.
Article 4 When a foul occurs during a backward pass or fumble, the basic spot of enforcement is the spot of the fumble or the spot of the backward pass. If the offensive team fouls behind the spot of the fumble or backward pass, the spot of enforcement is the spot of the foul.

Rule 9 Scrimmage Kick
Section 1 Kick from Scrimmage
Article 1 The kicking team, behind the scrimmage line, may:
(a) punt;
(b) dropkick; or
(c) placekick.
Penalty: For a punt, dropkick, or placekick not kicked from behind the line of scrimmage: 10 yds from the spot of the kick.
Article 2 If the receivers recover any kick, they may advance.
Article 3 During a kick from scrimmage, only the end men as eligible receivers on the line of scrimmage at the time of the snap, are permitted to go beyond the line before the ball is kicked.
Penalty: Loss of 5 yds from the previous spot for leaving before the ball is kicked.
Article 4 No player of the kickers may illegally touch a scrimmage kick before it has been touched by a receiver (first touching).
Penalty: For illegal touching of a

scrimmage kick: receivers' ball at any spot of illegal touching or possession. Officials' time-out when the ball is declared dead. This illegal touch does not offset a foul by the receivers during the down.
Article 5 No player of the kicker's team, who has been out of bounds, may touch or recover a scrimmage kick beyond the line until after it has been touched by B.
Penalty: Loss of 5 yds from previous spot.
Article 6 A ball is dead if the kickers recover a kick made from behind the line (other than one recovered on or behind the line unless a try-kick).
Article 7 If a kick from behind the line is touched in the immediate vicinity of the neutral zone or behind A's line by B, such touching does not make A eligible to recover the kick beyond the line.
Article 8 Any touching behind the line by a kicking team player is legal, even if the kick crosses the line and returns behind the line before touching a receiver beyond the line.
Article 9 When a legal kick is simultaneously recovered anywhere by two eligible opposing players, or if it is lying on the field of play with no player attempting to recover, it is awarded to the receivers.
Article 10 Ordinarily there is no distinction between a player touching a ball or being touched

by it.
Article 11 During a kick a kicking team player, after he has crossed his scrimmage line, may use his hands to ward off, push, or pull aside a receiver who is legally or illegally attempting to obstruct him.
Article 12 When a scrimmage kick from behind the line is recovered by the kicking team behind the line, the kicking team may advance.
Article 13 When a kick from scrimmage, or unsuccessful field goal crosses the receivers' goal line from the impetus of the kick it is a touchback unless:
(a) there is a spot of illegal touching by the kickers outside the receivers' 20-yd line; or
(b) the receivers after gaining possession, advance with the ball into the field of play; or
(c) kickers recover in end zone after receivers first touch ball in field of pay.
Ruling: Touchdown for kickers; or
(d) kickers recover in end zone after receivers first touch ball in end zone.
Ruling: Touchdown for kickers; or
(e) the ball goes out of bounds in the field of play after being touched by a receiver.
Ruling: Receiving team's ball at inbounds spot.
Article 14 If a scrimmage kick touches the receivers' goalposts

➡ *page 36*

continued from page 35

or crossbar either before or after touching a player of either team, it is a touchback unless it later scores a field goal.

Article 15 If a scrimmage kick touches the kickers' goalpost or crossbar (irrespective of where it was made from, or how it occurred), it is a safety. Goalpost is out of bounds.

Article 16 For a scrimmage kick out of bounds between goal lines, see Rule 7, Article 5, Section 1.

Article 17 If there is a foul from the time of the snap until a legal scrimmage kick ends, enforcement is from the previous spot. This includes a foul during a run prior to the legal kick and running into or roughing the kicker. If the offensive team commits a foul in its own end zone, it is a safety.

Rule 10 Fair Catch
Section 1 Fair Catch
Article 1 A fair-catch signal is valid beyond the line while kick is in flight when one arm is fully extended above the head and waved from side to side.
Penalty: For invalid fair-catch signal: snap by receivers 5 yds behind the spot of the signal.

Article 2 If a receiver signals (valid or invalid) for a fair catch during any kick except one which does not cross the line, the ball is dead when caught by any receiver. If the catcher did not signal, the ball is put in play by the receivers at the spot of the catch.

Article 3 If a player signals (valid or invalid) for a fair catch, he may not until the ball touches a player:
(a) block; or
(b) initiate contact with one of the kickers.
Penalty: For illegal block after a fair-catch signal: snap by receivers 15 yds from the spot of the foul. (Personal Foul).

Article 4 During any kick (except one which fails to cross the scrimmage line), if any receiver could reach the kick in flight, no player of the kickers shall interfere with either:
(a) the receiver;
(b) the ball; or

A score
Here the referee signals a score.

(c) the receiver's path to the ball.
Penalty (a): For fair-catch interference following a signal: loss of 15 yds from the spot of the foul. Fair catch also awarded irrespective of a catch.
Penalty (b): For interference with the opportunity to make a catch (no prior signal made): loss of 15 yds from the spot of the foul and offended team is entitled to put the ball in play by a snap from scrimmage.

Article 5 After a receiver has made a fair catch following a valid signal, an opponent:
(a) may not tackle him;
(b) may not block him; and
(c) must avoid contact with him.
Penalty: For illegal contact with the maker of a fair catch: loss of 15 yds from the mark of the catch (snap or free kick).

Article 6 When a fair catch is declared for a team, the captain must choose (and his first choice is not revocable) either:
(a) A fair-catch kick (punt, dropkick, or placekick without "tee"), or
(b) A snap to next put the ball in play.

Rule 11 Scoring
Section 1 Value of Scores
Article 1 The team that scores the greater number of points during the entire game is the winner. Points are scored as follows:

(a) Touchdown	6 points
(b) Field goal	3 points
(c) Safety	2 points
(d) Successful try after touchdown	1 or 2 points

Article 2 To insure a winner in all National Football League games the sudden-death method of deciding a tie game is Rule 16.
Section 2 Touchdown
Article 1 It is a touchdown:
(a) when a runner advances from the field of play and the ball touches the opponents' goal line (plane); or
(b) while inbounds any player

catches or recovers a loose ball on or behind the opponents' goal line.   *Just scored.*
Section 3 Try
Article 1 After a touchdown, the scoring team is allowed a try. This try is an attempt to score one or two additional points, during one scrimmage down with the spot of snap:
(a) anywhere between the inbounds lines and
(b) which is also 2 or more yds from the defensive team's goal line.
During this try:
(a) if a try-kick is good, one point is scored. If a kick cannot score, the ball becomes dead as soon as failure is evident.
(b) if a try results in what would ordinarily be a touchdown by the offense, two points are awarded. If a touchdown is not scored, the try is over at the end of play or if there is a change of possession.
(c) if there is no kick and the try results in what would ordinarily be a safety by the defense, one point is awarded to the offensive team.
Article 2 The try begins when the referee sounds his whistle for play to start.
Article 3 During a try:
(a) if any play or a foul by the offense would ordinarily result in a touchback or loss of down, the try is unsuccessful and there shall be no replay.
(b) if any play or a foul by the defense would ordinarily result in a safety, one point is awarded to the offensive team.
(c) if a foul by the defense does not permit the try to be attempted, the down is replayed and the offended team has the option to have the distance penalty assessed on the next try or on the ensuing kickoff.
(d) if the defensive team commits a foul and the try is attempted and is unsuccessful, the offensive team may either accept the penalty yardage to be assessed or decline the distance penalty before the down is replayed.
(e) all fouls committed by the defense on a successful try will result in the distance penalty being assessed on the ensuing kickoff or retry B1.
(f) if there is a false start, encroachment, or a neutral-zone infraction, which normally causes

play to be whistled dead during ordinary scrimmage plays, they are to be handled the same way during try situations.
Article 4 If fouls are signaled against both teams during a try, it must be replayed.
Article 5 During a try the defensive team can never score. When it gains possession, the ball is dead immediately.
Article 6 After a try the team on defense during the try shall receive.

Section 4 Safety
Article 1 When an impetus by a team sends the ball in touch behind its own goal, it is a safety if the ball is either:
(a) dead in the end zone in its possession; or
(b) out of bounds behind the goal line.
Article 2 It is a safety when the offense commits a foul (anywhere) and the spot of enforcement is behind its own goal line.
Article 3 After a safety, the team scored upon must next put the ball in play by a free kick (punt, dropkick, or placekick). No tee can be used.
Section 5 Field Goal
Article 1 A field goal is scored when all of the following conditions are met:
(a) The kick must be a placekick or dropkick made by the offense from behind the line of scrimmage or from the spot of a fair catch (fair-catch kick).
(b) The ball must not touch the ground or any player of the offensive team before it passes through the goal.
(c) The entire ball must pass through the goal. In case wind or other forces cause it to return through the goal, it must have struck the ground or some object or person before returning.
Article 2 All field goals attempted and missed when the spot of the kick is beyond the 20-yd line will result in the defensive team taking possession of the ball at the spot of the kick. On any field goal attempted and missed when the spot of the kick is on or inside the 20-yd line, the ball will revert to the defensive team at the 20-yd line.
Article 3 On a free kick following a fair catch all general rules apply as for a field-goal attempt

from scrimmage. The clock starts when the ball is kicked.

Article 4 No artificial media shall be permitted to assist in the execution of a field goal and/or try after touchdown attempt.

Article 5 After a field goal, the team scored upon will receive.

Section 6 Touchback

Article 1 When an impetus by a team sends a ball in touch behind its opponents' goal line, it is a touchback:

(a) if the ball is dead in the opponents' possession on their end zone;

(b) if the ball is out of bounds behind the goal line if the impetus was a scrimmage kick unless there is a spot of first touching by the kickers outside the receivers' 20-yd line or if the receivers after gaining possession advance with the ball into the field of play; or

(d) if any legal kick touches the receivers' goalposts or crossbar other than one which scores a field goal.

Article 2 It is a touchback:

(a) when the kickers interfere with a fair catch behind the receivers' goal line; or

(b) when the kickers first touch a scrimmage kick behind the receivers' goal line.

(c) when a kicking team player illegally recovers or catches a punt inside the receiver's 5-yd line and carries the ball across the defender's goal line or his body touches the end zone.

Article 3 When the spot of enforcement for a foul by the defense is behind the offensive goal line, the distance penalty is enforced from the goal line.

Article 4 After a touchback, the touchback team next snaps from its 20 (any point between the inbounds lines and the forward point of the ball on that line).

Rule 12 Player Conduct
Section 1 Use of Hands, Arms, and Body

Article 1 No offensive player may:

(a) assist the runner except by individually blocking opponents for him.

(b) use interlocking interference. Interlocked

interference means the grasping of one another by encircling the body to any degree with the hands or arms; or

(c) push the runner or lift him to his feet.

Penalty: For assisting runner or interlocked interference: loss of 10 yds.

Article 2 A runner may ward off opponents with his hands and arms, but no other offensive player may use them to obstruct an opponent, by grasping with hands or encircling with arm in any degree any part of body, during a block.

Article 3 No player on offense may push or throw his body against a teammate either:

(a) in such a way as to cause him to assist runner;

(b) to aid him in an attempt to obstruct an opponent or to

recover a loose ball;

(c) to trip an opponent; or

(d) in charging, falling, or using hands on the body into the back from behind above the waist of an opponent.

Penalty: For holding, illegal use of hands, arms, or body of offense: loss of 10 yds.

Article 4 A defensive player may not tackle or hold any opponent other than a runner. Otherwise, he may use his hands, arms, or body only to defend or protect himself against an obstructing opponent in an attempt to reach a runner. On a punt, field-goal attempt, or try-kick attempt, a defensive player (B1) may not grab and pull an offensive player out of the way which allows another defensive player(s) (B2) to shoot the gap (pull and shoot) in an attempt to block the kick, unless the defensive player (B1) is advancing toward the kicker.

Penalty: For illegal contact, illegal cut, or holding by the defense: loss of 5 yds and automatic first down.

Section 2 Personal Fouls

Article 1 All players are prohibited from:

(a) striking with the fists;

(b) kicking or kneeing; or

(c) striking, swinging, or clubbing to the head, neck, or face with the heel, back, or side of the hand, wrist, forearm, elbow, or clasped hands.

Penalty: For fouls in (a), (b), and (c): loss of 15 yds. If any of the above acts is

judged by the official(s) to be flagrant, the offender may be disqualified as long as the entire action is observed by the official(s).

Articles 2–14 define personal fouls in detail.

Section 3 Unsportsmanlike Conduct

Article 1 There shall be no unsportsmanlike conduct. This applies to any act that is contrary to the generally understood principles of sportsmanship. Such acts specifically include, among others:

(a) The use of abusive, threatening, or insulting language or gestures to opponents, teammates, officials, or representatives of the League.

(b) The use of baiting or taunting acts or words that engender ill will between teams.

(c) Unnecessary physical contact with a game official.

Penalty: (a), (b), and (c): loss of 15 yds from succeeding spot or whatever spot the referee, after consulting with the crew, deems equitable.

Article 2 The defense, when near its goal line, shall not commit successive or continued fouls (half-distance penalties) to prevent a score.

Penalty: For continuous fouls to prevent a score: if the violation is repeated after a warning, the score involved is awarded to the offensive team.

Article 3 A player or substitute shall not interfere with play by any act which is palpably unfair.

Penalty: For a palpably unfair act: offender may be disqualified. The referee, after consulting his crew, enforces any such distance penalty as they consider equitable and irrespective of any other specified code penalty. The referee could award a score.

These rules are reprinted by permission of the National Football League. For a complete copy of the rules, including Rules 13–18, as well as various exceptions to the rules, contact the NFL.

Field marshal
A quarterback typically has a number of options on a pass play and will try to find the receiver with the best chance of catching his pass. Skilled quarterbacks will often seem to follow a particular receiver with their eyes— drawing defenders toward that receiver—but then turn and throw to another receiver at the last moment.

Rugby League
Essentials

Played mostly in Australia, New Zealand, and the north of England, this physical, fast-moving game originated as a professional offshoot of the then-amateur Rugby Football Union (see next chapter). Fans of football will notice similarities between the two games, but in general Rugby League features fewer stoppages of play, fewer set plays, and a wide-open style of play that—to the uninitiated observer—borders on chaos.

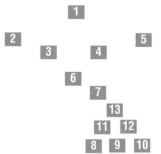

Headgear
More and more Rugby League players wear a helmet to protect their head and ears. Protective clothing may be worn if it contains nothing of a rigid nature.

The field and goals
Grass. Maximum length of 100 m (109 yds) and width of 68 m (74 yds). Goalposts at least 4 m (14 ft) high, 5.5 m (18 ft) apart, joined by a crossbar 3 m (10 ft) above the ground.

Unfamiliar terms
The sidelines are called the "touchlines" (touch means out of bounds) and the end zone is called the "in-goal."

Touch-in-goal line
In-goal
Dead-ball line
Goal line
Touch-in-goal
Touch
10 m
10 m
Touchline
Halfway line
5.5 m
40 m line
30 m line
20 m line
10 m line
100 m maximum
4 m minimum
3 m
11 m maximum
5 m minimum

Below, Central park in Wigan, England.

The teams
Two teams of 13 players, with a maximum of four replacements. Positions are as follows:
Backs
1   Fullback
2   Right wing
3   Right center
4   Left center
5   Left wing
6   Stand-off half or five-eighth
7   Scrum-half
Forwards
8   Prop
9   Hooker
10 Front row
11 Second row
12 Second row
13 Loose forward

Although some teams now assign individual numbers, players used to wear the number of their position (depicted above).

Officials
A referee and two touch (i.e., sideline) judges, plus in-goal (i.e., end zone) judges at the professional level.

Flying tackle
Rugby League is as physical as any game. Here, tackle involves a player launching himself sideways at an opponent who is running with the ball.

The ball
Oval, inflated, with an outer casing of leather or approved material. It must be between 27 and 29 cm (approx. 11 in) long, have a longest circumference of 73–75 cm (approx. 29 in), a width of 58–61 cm (approx. 24 in) and a weight of 380–440 g (approx. 14 oz).

HOW TO PLAY

Both teams attempt to gain possession of the ball in order to have a chance at scoring points in any of four ways (described below). Attacking players can run with the ball, kick it in any direction, or pass it sideways or behind—but never forward. Defenders attempt to stop the player with the ball by tackling him.

Starting

The team that loses a coin toss begins play by kicking off from the center of the halfway line. The kickoff is a placekick, which means that the ball is positioned on the ground on one end before it is kicked. The ball must travel at least 10 m (33 ft) forward and all players must stand at least 10 m away from the kicker until after the kick.

How to Win

A *try* (worth four points) is scored when a player grounds the ball (places it on the ground) in his opponent's in-goal. Following a try, the successful team attempts to kick the ball through its opponent's goalposts for a *conversion goal* (2 points). In addition, after a penalty, a team may choose to attempt a *penalty goal*, again trying to kick the ball

through the goalposts (another 2 points). Finally, a player who kicks the ball through the goalposts during the course of play scores a *drop goal* (1 point). The team with the most points wins.

Dress

A numbered jersey, shorts, socks, and cleats. Players must not wear anything dangerous to other players.

How to hold the ball

The ball should be carried in complete control, either in both hands or against the chest—not tucked under the arm, as some inexperienced players do. Holding with both hands allows a player to pass the ball quickly and accurately if he is about to be tackled. Holding the ball with one arm against the chest allows a runner one free hand to generate momentum and fend off tackles. This kind of grip (demonstrated in the photo) is typically used when a player is running in the clear.

KEY RULES

• A game is 80 minutes long, with a halftime break of five minutes, although time is extended to allow for injuries, conversion, or penalty kicks. Teams change ends at halftime.

• After points have been scored, the scoring team restarts play with a placekick from the halfway line. However, the restart is a placekick from the center of the 20-m line if a player: sends the ball over the opposition's dead-ball or touch-in-goal line; infringes the rules in the opposition's in-goal area; or catches a kick in general play from the opposition while in his own in-goal. It is a dropkick from the 20-m line if the ball crosses the dead-ball or touch-in-goal line from a penalty kick.

(A dropkick is when the ball is dropped on the ground and kicked immediately as it rebounds.) It is a dropkick from the goal line if a player: sends the ball over his own dead-ball or touch-in-goal line; does this from a kickoff at the halfway line; commits a breach or is tackled in his own in-goal area or kicks the ball into touch from his own in-goal area.

• A player may be tackled by one or more opponents only when he is in possession of the ball. He is said to be "tackled" when he is held by his opponent(s) and the ball, his hand, or his arm holding the ball touches the ground. In Rugby League, a team is allowed to be tackled five times in succession, but on the sixth tackle they lose possession to

the opposition. *See Section 2, The Tackle (page 40).*

• Until this loss of possession, a tackled player is released to immediately "play the ball." For this one opponent marks him and another player from each team (acting halfbacks) positions himself immediately behind his own tackled player/marker. The tackled player then places the ball on the ground and plays it backward with his foot. *See Section 3, The Play-the-Ball (page 40).*

• Minor offenses are penalized by the formation of a *scrum* to reestablish possession of the ball. This happens if a player fumbles the ball and knocks it forward (a "knock-on"), passes it forward, or accidentally

becomes offside. *See Section 5, The Scrum (page 41).*

• Serious infringements are penalized with a penalty kick awarded to the opposition. The kicking team may punt, dropkick, placekick, or tap the ball from the point where the offense took place. *See Section 6, The Penalty (page 41).*

• A try is only scored if a player *grounds the ball* (i.e., touches the ball to the ground) in his opponents in-goal. A try is not scored if a player with the ball runs through his opponents' in-goal without grounding the ball. *See Section 7.3, How a Try Is Scored (page 44).*

RUGBY LEAGUE THE RULES
· · · · · · · · ·

Section 1 Start of Play

See Starting page 39.

Section 2 The Tackle

2.1 The Tackle

2.1.1 A player in possession may be tackled by any number of opposing players.

2.1.2 It is illegal to tackle or obstruct a player who is not in possession.

2.1.3 A player in possession is tackled:

a) When he is held by one or more opposing players and the ball or the hand or arm holding the ball comes into contact with the ground.

b) When he is held by one or more opposing players in such a manner that he can make no further progress and cannot part with the ball.

c) When being held by an opponent and the tackled player makes it evident he has succumbed to the tackle and wishes to be released in order to play the ball.

d) When he is lying on the ground and an opponent places a hand on him.

2.1.4

a) A tackle is not effected if the player in possession is brought to the ground and the hold on the player in possession is broken before he is grounded.

b) The referee should be sure in his own mind that the tackle was indeed broken and the tackler had not released the player having thought the tackle was completed.

2.1.5 A tackler must not use any special holds or throws that are likely to cause injury.

2.1.6 Bringing a player to the ground by pulling him over the outstretched leg is permissible provided both arms make contact with the opponent before the leg.

2.1.7 A tackler must not use his knees in making a tackle.

2.1.8 Where opponents, while making a tackle, attempt to push, pull, or carry the player in possession, the tackled player's colleagues may lend their weight in order to avoid losing ground. Immediately this happens the referee should call "Held."

2.1.9 Once a player in possession has been tackled it is illegal for any player to move or try to move him from the point where the tackle is effected.

2.1.10 When a tackled player is tackled within easy reach of the

Dangerous tackle
Tacklers are not allowed to use any holds or throws that might cause injury, so this kind of tackle in which the tackler has grabbed his opponent by the neck is definitely out of order. See Rule 2.1.5.

goal line he should be penalized if he makes a second movement to place the ball over the line for a try.

2.1.11 If an attacking player in possession is brought down near the goal line and the ball is not grounded, it is permissible to place the ball over the line for a try. In this case the tackle has not been completed.

2.1.12 A player in possession shall not deliberately or unnecessarily allow himself to voluntarily fall to the ground when not held by an opponent.

2.1.13 If a player drops on a loose ball, he shall not remain on the ground waiting to be tackled if he has time to regain his feet and continue play.

2.1.14 If a tackled player slides along the ground because of his momentum, the tackle is effected where his slide ends.

2.1.15 If any doubt arises as to a tackle, the referee should give a verbal instruction to "play on" or shout "held" as the case may be.

2.1.16 If there is no acting halfback, it is permissible for a player to dive behind the tackled player to drop on the ball after he has played it. He should then immediately try to regain his feet and play on.

2.2 Sixth Tackle

2.2.1 A team in possession of the ball shall be allowed five successive play-the-balls.

2.2.2 If tackled for a sixth time the referee will rule a handover.

2.2.3 If an infringement occurs by the team in possession after the fifth play-the-ball, the referee will rule a handover.

2.2.4 A handover play-the-ball

will not be counted in the tackle count.

2.2.5 If the ball is kicked out on the full after the fifth tackle the handover takes place at the point from where the ball was kicked.

2.2.6 If the ball is kicked out after landing in the field of play after the fifth tackle a scrum will be formed. The scrum shall be formed 20 m (22 yds) in from where the ball crosses the touchline and no closer than 10 m to the goal line.

2.2.7 The referee will indicate the fifth tackle by raising one arm vertically with fingers and thumb outstretched.

2.2.8 He will indicate the sixth tackle by blowing his whistle and signaling the player to release the ball for his opponents to play the ball.

2.3 Zero Tackle

2.3.1 When a player gathers the ball from an opposition kick in general play and does not subsequently pass or kick the ball himself, the initial kick will be a zero tackle.

2.3.2 If a player knocks on and an opponent gathers the ball and is tackled before gaining any territorial advantage the play-the-ball will not be counted as a tackle in the tackle count.

2.3.3 A tackled player shall not intentionally lose the ball.

2.3.4 If after being tackled a player accidentally loses possession, a scrum shall be formed, except after the fifth play-the-ball.

2.3.5 A player in possession brought to his knees or brought to the ground on his back may

still pass the ball provided he has not made it evident he has succumbed to the tackle.

2.4 Stealing the Ball

2.4.1 Once a tackle has been completed, no player shall take or attempt to take the ball from the tackled player.

2.4.2 If more than one player makes no effort to complete a tackle of the player in possession but simply hold him so that a colleague can take the ball from him, they should be penalized.

2.4.3 In tackles involving only one tackler, it is permissible to steal the ball prior to the tackle being effected. In tackles involving two or more tacklers, the ball cannot be intentionally stolen.

Section 3 The Play-the-Ball

3.1 Playing the Ball

3.1.1 The tackled player shall be immediately released and shall not be touched until the ball has been played.

3.1.2 If any doubt arises as to which player should play the ball (disputed possession) the referee should nominate the team in possession.

3.1.3 In the case of a player lying on the ground and not holding the ball with both hands or arms, circumstances may arise where there is some doubt as to whether he is "in possession."

3.1.4 If he is holding the ball with a hand or arm to some part of his person then he is "in possession."

3.1.5 The tackled player shall without delay regain his feet where he was tackled.

3.1.6 No part of the tackled player's person other than his feet should be in contact with the ground when he releases the ball.

3.1.7 One opponent may take up a position immediately opposite the tackled player, known as the "marker."

3.1.8 The tackled player shall lift the ball clear of the ground, face his opponents' goal line and drop or place the ball in front of his foremost foot.

3.1.9 The ball must be played backward with the foot and it is clear of the ruck when it passes

Below: see 3.1.9

behind the heel of the tackled player.

3.1.10 The marker is not allowed to strike for the ball.

3.1.11 A player from each team, to be known as the acting halfback, may stand immediately and directly behind his own player taking part in the play-the-ball.

3.1.12 He must remain in this position until the ball has come clear of the two players in the play-the-ball movement.

3.1.13 Players of the side not in possession other than the marker and the acting halfback are out of play if they fail to retire 10 m (33 ft) from the point at which the ball is played or to their own goal line. They should only be penalized if they intentionally interfere with the play.

3.1.14 Players of the side in possession other than the player playing the ball and the acting halfback are out of play if they fail to retire 5 m (16 ft) from the point at which the ball is played or to their own goal line.

3.1.15 If the interference with play is accidental, a scrum should be formed.

3.1.16 Having retired the distance required, a player may not advance until the ball has cleared the ruck.

3.1.17 A player who is out of play may take part in the game when the advantage gained by not retiring has been lost.

3.1.18 The play-the-ball must be performed as quickly as possible.

3.1.19 Any player who intentionally delays the bringing of the ball into play shall be penalized.

3.1.20 If part of the tackled player is on or over the goal line but the ball is in the field of play, the tackled player shall play-the-ball where the ball lies.

3.1.21 If a player is tackled in an upright position bestriding the goal line he is deemed to be tackled in the in-goal area.

Section 4 The Knock-On and Forward Pass

4.1 Knock-On

4.1.1 Play shall stop after a knock-on and a scrum formed, except after the fifth tackle.

4.1.2 The referee should allow play to proceed long enough after the knock-on to allow the opposing team the advantage of gaining possession.

4.1.3 An opponent may charge down a kick and this is not a knock-on.

Knock-on.

4.1.4 A player shall be penalized if he deliberately knocks on.

4.1.5 If after an accidental knock-on the player knocking on regathers or kicks the ball before it hits the ground, goalpost, or an opponent, play shall be allowed to proceed.

4.1.6 If a player knocks on in the field of play, and the ball goes into the in-goal area before being touched down by that player or a colleague, play is restarted with a scrum.

4.2 Forward Pass

4.2.1 A player shall be penalized if he deliberately passes the ball forward.

4.2.2 If the ball is passed correctly and then bounces forward or is blown forward by the wind there is no infringement and play should continue.

4.2.3 The direction of a pass is relative to the player making it and not to the actual path relative to the ground.

4.2.4 A player running toward his opponents' goal line may pass the ball to a colleague who is behind him but because of his momentum the ball travels forward relative to the ground. This is not a forward pass as the player has not passed the ball forward in relation to himself. A good example is a high lobbed pass made by a running player.

4.2.5 If the referee forms the opinion that a forward pass was not deliberate he will restart play with a scrum.

4.2.6 It is illegal to head the ball in a forward direction.

Section 5 The Scrum

5.1 Formation of Scrum

5.1.1 A scrum is formed to restart play when play is not being restarted with a kickoff, drop out, penalty kick, or play-the-ball.

5.1.2 A maximum of six forwards will be used to form a scrum in a 3-2-1 formation.

5.1.3 A minimum of three forwards can form a scrum if a team is depleted.

5.1.4 It is an infringement

resulting in a penalty if there are more than seven backs when a scrum is formed.

5.1.5 The front row is made up of three forwards who interlock arms and bend forward from the hip. The forward in the center (hooker) must bind with his arms over the shoulders of the prop and front row forward.

5.1.6 Two second row forwards bend from the hip, interlock arms and place their heads in the gaps between the front row forwards.

5.1.7 The loose forward bends from the hip and places his head in the gap between the second row forwards.

5.1.8 All forwards with their bodies bent brace themselves and interlock against the opposing team's forward pack. This forms a tunnel between the front row forwards.

5.1.9 Scrums shall be formed where an infringement occurs, but no closer than 20 m (22 yds) to the touchline or 10 m (33 ft) to the goal line.

5.1.10 Scrums shall be formed at right angles to the touchline.

5.1.11 The forwards take the weight and hold the scrum on the mark until the ball has been put in.

5.1.12 The non-offending team will have the loose head and put-in except when a mutual infringement occurs; in this case the attacking team have the loose head and put-in. If the infringement occurs on the halfway line the last team in possession shall have the loose head and put-in.

5.1.13 The ball must be held horizontally and put into the scrum on the referee's side by rolling it along the ground between the outside feet of the two prop forwards. The outside feet must also be the forward-most foot of the two props.

5.1.14 The ball should be put into the scrum without delay when the scrum has been formed correctly and the halfback shall retire behind his last row of forwards.

5.1.15 The opposing halfback shall retire behind his last row of forwards. The rest of his team shall retire at least 5 m (16 ft) behind this last row of forwards.

5.1.16 When the ball is in the scrum, it can only be played at with the foot.

5.1.17 The hooker can strike for the ball with either foot once the ball is in the tunnel.

5.1.18 The prop must keep both feet on the ground and may

only strike for the ball after the hooker.

5.1.19 No player shall willfully collapse a scrum.

5.1 20 The ball is out of the scrum when it emerges from between and behind the inner feet of the second rowers.

5.1.21 Any forward can detach himself from the scrum to gather or kick the ball when the ball has emerged from the scrum correctly, even if the scrum has wheeled.

5.1.22 Forwards must not butt violently when coming together to form a scrum.

5.2 Held Up In-Goal

5.2.1 If an attacking player is held up in his opponents' in-goal and is unable to ground the ball, play is restarted with a scrum 10 m (33 ft) from the goal line opposite where the player was held. The loose head and put-in shall be awarded to the team in possession and unable to ground the ball.

5.2.2 If the player is held up in-goal after the fifth tackle play will restart with a hand over 10 m (33ft) out from the goal line in line with the tackle.

Section 6 The Penalty

6.1 When Penalties Are Awarded

6.1.1 A penalty shall be awarded against a player who deliberately breaks the rules provided that the awarding of the penalty will not disadvantage the opposing team.

6.1.2 The advantage to the opposing team must be apparent if the referee is to allow play to proceed.

6.1.3 Any player can ask the referee the reason why a penalty has been awarded provided he does so respectfully.

6.2 Where Penalties Are Awarded

6.2.1 Unless stated the mark is where the offense occurred. The mark is moved in the following circumstances:

6.2.2 If misconduct occurs in-touch, the penalty is awarded 10 m (33 ft) in field opposite where the offense occurred.

6.2.3 Where a kicker is interfered with after a kick, the mark is where the ball lands or is caught in the field of play. If the ball crosses the touchline on the full, or crosses the goal line on the full, the penalty is awarded 10 m (33 ft) in field from where the ball crossed the line.

➡ *page 44*

SKILLS AND TACTICS

All players need speed, power, and endurance. As with any game, the best strategy is one that takes into account the opposition's strengths, and combats these by placing its players in the most strategic positions.

Tackling—Players use a mix of force and determination to overcome opponents who are often traveling at top speed with a tight grip on the ball.

Kicking—Accuracy is always vital, whether kicking for field position or attempting goals. A good placekicker who can kick at goal or convert tries with a high degree of success is an invaluable member of a team.

Handling—Accurate passing and catching help a team in possession of the ball to advance it toward tries and other scoring opportunities. Drop the ball and you give it to the opposition. When passing, the ball generally should be projected with the points horizontal, so that it flies through the air like a torpedo rather than spinning wildly.

Quick break
Many scoring situations are set up when the scrum-half picks up the ball from a scrum and makes a break past the opposing winger.

On the wing
Wingers need speed, stamina, and agility for quick breaks rather than the brute strength of the forwards.

Vital support
It is essential for anyone running with the ball to pass it before he is tackled. Players always follow a teammate with the ball ready for a timely pass.

Straight punt
The straight punt is the most common of all kicks in Rugby League. The aim is to send the ball far upfield to gain ground—or else to find touch (i.e. kick it out of bounds) from a penalty. Typically a standoff half may punt the ball far up the field to clear the ball after a scrum close to his own goal line.

Placekick
Placekicks are used to start the game, to kick for goal, or for an attempt to convert a try. Above, a player prepares to hold the ball so that a team-mate may kick it.

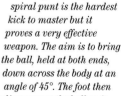

Spiral punt
Above left and left, the spiral punt is the hardest kick to master but it proves a very effective weapon. The aim is to bring the ball, held at both ends, down across the body at an angle of 45°. The foot then slices across the ball as it kicks, sending it spinning wildly far down the field, making it very difficult to catch.

Power play
Since a player doesn't have to release the ball until he is brought down to the ground, the strength to break tackles and gain extra yards is an invaluable attribute for a forward.

Bring him down
Two players or more are often needed to bring down a strong player once he has found his stride.

Tackling techniques
A tackle high on the body stands less chance of success because the player with the ball can fend it off with his hand. In this picture, the tackler on the right stands a much better chance of bringing down his opponent.

Time to pass
This player has timed his pass perfectly, getting the ball cleanly away to a teammate just as he is about to be brought down. The important thing to remember when passing under pressure is that the ball must not go forward (see Section 4.2 on page 41 for a description of what constitutes a forward pass).

A classic tackle
In a flying tackle the defender launches himself into the air clasping the runner around the thighs and stopping the forward motion of his legs. It is the runner's own momentum that brings him down.

GRAY AREA

To keep the game moving, the play-the-ball rule discourages players from holding on to tackles for too long. But just what is "too long"? Since this involves a subjective call by the referee, there are often disputes.

Passing
The perfect pass travels straight through the air with the ball propelled horizontally. The player grips the ball firmly around the middle with out-stretched fingers forming a cradle underneath. The passer's fingers guide the ball toward his teammate as he lets go of it. As the ball leaves the hands, the arms follow through in the same direction.

continued from page 41

6.2.4 Any offense in the in-goal that results in a penalty being awarded, the penalty is awarded 10 m (33 ft) in the field opposite where the offense occurred.

6.3 Further Misconduct

In cases of further offenses, the mark shall be advanced once by 10 m (33 ft), toward the offending team's goal line.

6.4 Breaches by the Kicker's Team

In cases of a breach by the kicker's team, a scrum is formed where the penalty kick was awarded.

6.5 Breaches by Opposing Teams

In cases of a breach by the opposing team another penalty shall be awarded opposite where the breach occurred, 10 m (33 ft) from where the original penalty was awarded.

6.6 How Penalty Kicks Are Taken

6.6.1 A player may take a penalty kick by punting, drop-kicking, or placekicking the ball from the mark or behind the mark provided it is parallel with the touchline.

6.6.2 The ball may be kicked in any direction, after which it is in play, except when kicking for goal. If the kicker advises the referee that he is kicking for goal from a penalty it is an offense to do otherwise.

Placekick

Dropkick

Punt

6.6.3 A penalty from a scrum is a differential penalty, which a goal cannot be scored from. If the penalty is for foul play or offensive language, a normal penalty is awarded.

6.6.4 The differential penalty applies to all players in the team including those outside the scrum.

6.7 Position of Players

6.7.1 All players from the kicker's team must remain behind the ball when it is kicked from a penalty kick.

6.7.2 The opposing players shall position themselves at least 10 m (33 ft) from the point where the penalty was awarded.

6.7.3 Opposing players who have not retired 10 m (33 ft) at a penalty kick should only be penalized if they interfere with play.

6.7.4 Opposing players shall not interfere with or distract the attention of the kicker at a penalty kick.

6.7.5 Opposing players may only advance after the ball has been kicked.

6.8 Finding Touch

6.8.1 From a penalty kick, if the ball is kicked into touch without touching any other player, the kicking team shall restart play with a free kick 10 m (33 ft) in the field of play opposite where the ball crossed the line.

6.8.2 If the ball touches an opposing player and goes into touch, a scrum shall be packed 20 m (22 yds) in field from where the ball crossed the line. The kicker's team has the loose head and the put-in.

6.8.3 Play is restarted with a 20 m (22-yd) dropkick if the ball is kicked dead in the opponents' in-goal from a penalty kick.

6.9 Free Kick

6.9.1 The ball may be kicked in any direction in any manner when bringing it into play after finding touch.

6.9.2 Opposing players shall retire 10 m (33 ft) from the free kick.

6.9.3 In the event of a breach by the opposing team a penalty kick shall be awarded opposite where the breach occurred and 10 m (33 ft) from the free kick.

6.9.4 In the event of a breach by the kicker's team, a scrum shall be packed 20 m (22 yds) from the touch line opposite where the free kick was to be taken.

6.10 No Delay

6.10.1 No player shall

deliberately delay the taking of a penalty kick.

6.11 Infringement by Kicker's Team

6.11.1 If the penalty kick is not taken as stated or if a player from the kicker's team infringes, a scrum shall be formed at the mark, not closer than 20 m (22 yd) from the touchline.

6.12 Offense Against Try Scorer

6.12.1 If a player fouls an opponent who is touching down for a try, an eight-point try is awarded, i.e., a penalty kick at goal shall be taken from in front of the posts after the attempt to convert the try.

6.12.2 After an eight-point try, play is restarted with a kickoff from the center of the halfway line.

6.13 Drop Goal Foul Play on Kicker

6.13.1 If a player attempting a drop goal is fouled, a penalty kick shall be awarded in front of the goalposts.

6.13.2 If he is successful with the drop goal, a kick at goal must be taken from the penalty kick. Play is then restarted from the center of the halfway line.

6.13.3 If the drop goal is unsuccessful, the penalty kick can be taken in any manner.

6.14 The Mark

6.14.1 As the mark cannot be marked on the ground, a player who punts or drop-kicks may deviate slightly from it, provided no advantage is gained from it.

6.14.2 Where a player is taking a kick at goal and moves the ball back from the point where the penalty was awarded, the point where the kick is taken becomes the new mark. Opposition players must be at least 10 m (33 ft) from where the kick is being taken from.

Section 7 Scoring Points

7.1 Points Value of a Try, Goal, and Field Goal

7.1.1 A try is worth four points.

7.1.2 A conversion or penalty goal is two points.

7.1.3 A field goal is one point.

7.2 Winning the Game

7.2.1 The game shall be decided by the team scoring the higher number of points. If both teams have the same number of points, the game is drawn.

7.3 How a Try Is Scored

7.3.1 A try is scored when a player grounds the ball in his opponents' in-goal. The ball must be grounded before the player or the ball crosses the touch in-goal or dead-ball line.

7.3.2 A player may pick up the ball in his opponents' in-goal, in order to ground it in a more advantageous position.

7.3.3 A try is scored when opposing players ground the ball simultaneously in the in-goal area.

7.3.4 A try is scored when a tackled player's momentum carries him into the opponents' in-goal where he grounds the ball.

7.3.5 A try is scored by grounding the ball on the goal line. A try is not scored by grounding the ball at the foot of the goalposts in the field of play.

7.3.6 When the ball is not grounded correctly play is allowed to continue unless the ball has been knocked on or has gone dead.

7.3.7 A referee should not disallow a try because a player who correctly grounds the ball fails to retain it.

7.3.8 The referee should not disallow a try because he was not in a position to see the grounding of the ball.

7.3.9 When the ball is in the scrum, a try cannot be scored by grounding it.

7.3.10 When the ball is at the base of the scrum, it is permissible for a player to pick it up and bore through his own forwards to ground the ball for a try.

7.4 Penalty Try

7.4.1 The referee can award a penalty try if, in his opinion, a try would have been scored, except for the unfair play of a defender.

7.4.2 A penalty try is awarded between the goalposts.

7.5 Touching Referee (Etc.)

7.5.1 If play is effected following an attacking player coming into contact with the referee, touch judge or spectator in the opposition's in-goal area, a try is awarded.

7.6 Where Try Is Awarded

7.6.1 Where the ball is grounded as in 7.3.1 and 7.3.2, and 7.3.3.

7.6.2 Where the ball first crosses the goal line if scored as per 7.3.4.

7.6.3 In-between the goalposts if a penalty try is to be awarded.

7.6.4 Where contact took place if scored as per 7.5.1.

7.7 Referee Is the Sole Judge

7.7.1 A try can only be awarded by the referee. The referee can take advice from the touch judge before making a decision.

7.7.2 To award a try, the referee points to the spot where

the ball was grounded and blows his whistle.

7.7.3 Before awarding the try the referee should look at the two touch judges to ensure that they are not reporting a prior incident.

7.7.4 When approved by the controlling authority of any competition, ingoal judges, and the use of audiovisual electronic aids may be used to assist the referee in the decision making process.

7.8 How a Goal Is Scored

7.8.1 A goal is scored if the ball passes over the opponents' crossbar and between the uprights after being kicked on the full by a player (and not being touched in flight by any other player) in any of the following circumstances:

7.8.2 By a placekick after a try has been scored and counts as two points.

7.8.3 By a placekick or a dropkick when a penalty has been awarded and counts as two points.

7.8.4 If, after completely passing over the crossbar the ball is blown back, a goal is still allowed.

7.8.5 When a kick at goal is being taken, a teammate of the kicker is allowed to hold the ball in position by placing a hand on it.

7.9 No Goal from Kickoff

7.9.1 A goal cannot be scored from a kickoff or drop-out, or from a dropkick when bringing the ball into play by a free kick, or from a differential penalty.

7.10 How a Drop Goal Is Scored

7.10.1 By a dropkick during general play from any position in the field of play, over the crossbar and between the uprights. A drop goal counts as one point.

7.11 Where Kicks at Goal Are Taken

7.11.1 A kick at goal after a try may be taken from any point opposite where the try is scored and parallel to the touchline.

7.11.2 A kick at goal from a penalty may be taken from the mark or from any point opposite the mark and parallel to the touchline.

7.11.3 A referee should ensure that a kick at goal is taken from the correct position. If the kick is taken from the incorrect position, no goal shall be allowed and the kick shall not be retaken.

7.12 Players' Positions

7.12.1 When a kick at goal is being taken following a try, the opposing players shall stand within their own in-goal area.

7.12.2 Players from the kicker's team must be behind the ball.

7.12.3 When a penalty kick at goal is being taken, the opposing players shall retire to their goal line or not less than 10 m (33 ft) from the mark.

7.13 Illegal to Distract the Kicker

7.13.1 It is illegal to attempt to distract the attention of the kicker.

7.14 Goalposts

7.14.1 For the purpose of judging a kick at goal, the goalposts are assumed to extend indefinitely upward.

7.15 Judging Kicks at Goal

7.15.1 If a touch judge believes a goal has been kicked he shall raise his flag above his head.

7.15.2 If a touch judge believes the kick at goal is unsuccessful he shall wave his flag in front of him.

7.15.3 If both touch judges are in agreement, their decision shall be final.

7.15.4 In the event of a disagreement, the referee shall decide.

7.16 Wasting Time

7.16.1 If a player wastes time when kicking at goal, the referee may caution him or, in extreme cases, dismiss him. The kick should not be cancelled, but extra time should be allowed.

7.17 Colleague Holds Ball

7.17.1 When a placekick is being taken, it is permissible for a colleague of the kicker to hold the ball in position by placing a hand on it.

7.18 Pretending to Kick at Goal

7.18.1 It shall count as misconduct for a player to pretend to kick at goal from a penalty kick and then deliberately kick it elsewhere. Such misconduct shall result in a

penalty being awarded against the kicker.

Section 8 Offside

8.1 When Players Are Offside

8.1.1 A player is offside if the ball touches, is touched, held, or kicked by one of his own team behind him.

8.1.2 A player cannot be offside in his own in-goal.

8.1.3 When the referee is satisfied that accidental offside has taken place, a scrum should be packed where the accidental offside took place.

8.2 Out of Play

8.2.1 An offside player shall not take any part in the game or attempt in any way to influence the course of the game.

8.3 Players to Retire 10 Meters

8.3.1 An offside player shall not encroach within 10 m (33 ft) of an opponent waiting for the ball.

8.3.2 An offside player shall retire 10 m (33 ft) from an opponent who first secures possession of the ball.

8.4 Player Placed Onside

8.4.1 An offside player is placed onside in the following circumstances:

a) An opposing player runs 10 m (33 ft) or more with the ball.

b) An opposing player touches the ball but does not retain it.

c) A teammate in possession of the ball runs in front of him.

d) A teammate kicks or knocks the ball forward and takes up a position in front of him in the field of play.

e) If he

retires behind the point where the ball was last touched by one of his teammates.

8.4.2 Players who are out of play are not put onside in the manner described above.

8.5 Catcher Claims Opponent Offside

8.5.1 A player who catches the ball near an offside opponent must not go out of his way to make interference by the offside player inevitable.

8.5.2 If the catcher deliberately and unnecessarily runs into the offside player then play should proceed.

8.6 Accidental Offside

8.6.1 If the touch judge considers that any interference caused by an offside player is accidental, play should be restarted with a scrum.

Section 9 Touch and Touch-in Goal

Section 10 Obstruction

Section 11 Player's Misconduct

These rules are reprinted by permission of the Rugby Football League. A complete copy of the International Rules of Rugby League can be obtained from the League.

Aggressive double tackle

Rugby Union
Essentials

The original version of rugby traces its roots to a pupil at England's Rugby School who, in 1823, broke the rules in a soccer game by picking up the ball and running with it. Today, this physical, fast-paced game enjoys widespread popularity.

Officials
A referee and two touch (i.e., sideline) judges.

The ground
Grass covered, clay, or sand. There are only maximum —not minimum— distance requirements.

Not exceeding 22m

Dead-ball line

In-goal area

Goal line

22-meter line

10-meter line

5 m

Touchline

10 m

10-meter line

15 m

10 m

Halfway line

10-meter line

Touchline

Not exceeding 100m

22-meter line

22 m

Not exceeding 22m

Goal line

In-goal area

5 m

Dead-ball line

Touch-in-goal line

At least 3.4 m (11 ft)

3 m (10 ft)

5.6 m (18 ft)

The goals
Two goalposts at each end, at least 3.4 m (11 ft) high. The posts are placed 5.6 m (18 ft) apart and are joined by a crossbar, 3 m (10 ft) above the ground.

⑮

⑪ ⑩ ⑫ ⑬ ⑭

⑨

⑥ ⑧ ⑦

④ ⑤

① ② ③

Team numbers and positions on the field:
1–8 forwards (also see positions, p. 50)
9 and 10 halfbacks
12 and 13 centers
11 and 14 wing three-quarters
15 fullback

Francois Pienaar, captain of South Africa's 1996 World Cup–winning team.

Dress
Jerseys, shorts, and undergarments, socks, and shoes. Players may also wear mouth- guards and shin guards. They must not wear anything that might cause injury to other players. Cleats are allowed provided they adhere to specifications.

The World Cup

Major event
Below, teams from Ireland, France, Wales, England, and Scotland play for the Five Nations Championship.

Scrum time
Above, the scrum is one of the key parts of a rugby game, occupying much of the playing time.

The players
Two teams of 15 players.

The ball
Oval, with four panels. Its length must be 280–300 mm (approx. 11 in); its circumference must be 760–790 mm (approx. 30 in) and its weight, 400–440 g (approx 15 oz). At the start of play the pressure should be 0.67–0.70 kg/sq. cm.

GILBERT

HOW TO PLAY

Each team contests possession of the ball in an attempt to touch it down in their opponent's in-goal (a try) or to kick it over the crossbar and between the extended lines of the posts (a goal). Players may carry, kick, or pass the ball. They may also take part in a scrummage, ruck, maul, and line-out, all unique features of the Rugby Union game.

Starting

Captains toss for the right to kick off or the choice of ends. A player from the team kicking off placekicks the ball from the center of the halfway line. This kick must reach the opponents' 10-meter line, unless first played by an opponent. The kicker's team must be behind the ball and the opposing team must be on or behind the 10-meter line at the start of play. *See Law 10, Kickoff (page 48).*

How to win

A try scores five points. Following a try, the scoring team attempts a conversion goal (two points). Three points are scored for either a goal made from a penalty kick or for a goal made during the course of play. If a goal is attempted during the course of play, it is done via a placekick (the ball is kicked from a spot on the ground) or a dropkick (a player drops the ball onto his foot). No goal can be scored from a free kick. The team with the most points wins.

KEY RULES

• A game consists of two halves of 40 minutes each (international matches) with halftime break of not more than 10 minutes.

• The ball may be *carried* or *kicked* in a forward direction, but it may only be *passed* to the side or backward.

• When a player is tackled, he must release the ball immediately. Both teams will try to gain possession of it.

• A *ruck* is formed when one or more players from each team, all on their feet and binding with one another, close around the ball. A *maul* occurs when players bind in a similar manner around a player who is in possession of the ball. *See Law 21, Ruck, and Law 22, Maul (page 53). Also see Law 20 (6) (a), Binding of Players (page 52).*

• If neither team manages to gain possession with either of these methods, a *scrummage* is ordered. This is formed by the forwards from each team binding together in a precise formation. First, the hooker and props bind (i.e., link) together in a fashion prescribed by the rules. These players keep a clear tunnel between their feet. The players behind them then link up with each other using at least one arm and hand. Finally, both teams' players come together to complete the scrum formation. The ball is put in by the scrum-half, who then plays the ball as it emerges from the scrummage. He puts the ball in so that it travels along the imaginary middle line between the two front rows. The hookers must be the first ones to touch the ball with their feet, otherwise the ball is put in again. *See Law 20, Scrummage (page 51).*

• A *fair catch* is made by a player who, within his own 22-meter area, manages to catch the ball cleanly from an opponent's kick, exclaiming "Mark!" as he does so. This player is then awarded a free kick. *See Law 16, Fair Catch (Mark) (page 49).*

• If the ball is in touch (i.e., if it or the player carrying it goes out of bounds by touching the touchline or the ground beyond it), play must be restarted with a line-out. At least two players from each team form a single line parallel to the other team's line, one meter apart from it, and at right angles to the touchline. The line-out stretches from 5 meters to 15 meters from the touchline. The player throwing in the ball does so from outside the field of play. The players in the line-out try to catch the ball cleanly or guide it toward a teammate in order to gain possession for their team. *See Law 23, Touch and Line-Out (page 53.)*

Just for kicks
Because it is difficult to kick the strangely shaped rugby ball accurately, each team turns to a specialist for penalties and goal kicks. Here, Scotland's specialist (who is also one of the team's fullbacks) attempts a kick.

Nice try
The ultimate aim of most moves on the field is to get the ball over the opposing team's goal line and touch it down for a try, which scores a team five points.

RUGBY UNION THE LAWS

These laws are abridged and summarized. P.K. and F.K. stand for the Penalty Kick and Free Kick provisions for infringements of the laws.

Laws 1–6
These laws are covered on page 47.

Law 7 Mode of Play
A match is started by a kickoff, after which any player who is onside, and provided he does so in accordance with these laws, may at any time:

• catch or pick up the ball and run with it;
• pass, throw, or knock the ball to another player;
• kick or otherwise propel the ball;
• tackle, push, or shoulder an opponent holding the ball;
• fall on the ball;
• take part in a scrummage, ruck, maul, or line-out;
• ground the ball in in-goal.

Law 8 Advantage
The referee shall not whistle for an infringement during play that is followed by an advantage gained by the non-offending team. An advantage must be either territorial or such possession of the ball as constitutes an obvious tactical advantage. A mere opportunity to gain advantage is not sufficient.
Notes:
(i) The referee is given a wide discretion as to what constitutes an advantage and is not limited to a territorial advantage. The referee is the sole judge of whether an advantage has been gained.
ii) Neither team may gain an advantage from the following circumstances:
   (a) when the ball or a player carrying it touches the referee (Law 9 (1));
   (b) when the ball emerges from either end of the tunnel at a scrummage not having been played (Law 20, note (xiv)).
iii) When any irregularity of play not provided for in the laws occurs, a scrummage shall be formed where the irregularity

International referee Derek Bevan

occurred. In deciding which team should put in the ball, the referee should apply Law 20 (7).

Law 9 Ball or Player Touching Referee
(1) If the ball or a player carrying it touches the referee in the field of play, play shall continue unless the referee considers either team has gained an advantage, in which case he shall order a scrummage. The team that last played the ball shall put it in.
(2) (a) If the ball in a player's possession or a player carrying it touches the referee in his opponents' in-goal, play shall continue unless the referee considers an advantage has been gained by that player's team, in which case a touchdown shall be awarded at the place where the referee was touched.
(b) If the ball in a player's possession or a player carrying it touches the referee in this opponents' in-goal, play shall continue unless the referee considers an advantage has been gained by that player's team in which case a try shall be awarded at the place where the referee was touched.
Notes:
(i) If the ball, while in play in in-goal at either end but not held by a player, touches the referee, a touch judge, or a spectator, a touchdown shall be awarded provided that a touchdown would otherwise have been obtained or the ball would have gone into touch-in-goal or on or over the dead-ball line.
(ii) If the ball while in play in in-goal at either end, but not held by a player, touches the referee, a touch judge, or a spectator, a try shall be awarded at that place provided an attacking player would otherwise have scored it.

Law 10 Kickoff
Kickoff is (a) a placekick taken from the center of the halfway line by the team that has the right to start the match or by the opposing team on the resumption of play after the halftime interval or (b) a dropkick taken at or from behind the center of the halfway line by the defending team after the opposing side has scored.
(1) The ball must be kicked from the correct place and by the

correct form of kick; otherwise it shall be kicked off again.
(2) The ball must reach the opponents' 10-meter line, unless first played by an opponent; otherwise it shall be kicked off again, or a scrummage formed at the center, at the opponents' option. If it reaches the 10-meter line and is then blown back, play shall continue.
(3) If the ball is kicked directly into touch, the opposing team may accept the kick, have the ball kicked off again, or have a scrummage formed at the center.
(4) If the ball crosses the opposing team's goal line from a kickoff, without touching or being touched by a player, the opposing team has the option of grounding the ball, making it dead, or playing on. If the opposing team grounds the ball or makes it dead or the ball becomes dead by touch-in-goal or by touching or crossing the dead-ball line, they will have the option of either having a scrummage formed at the center of the halfway line, with the put-in, or having the other team kick off again.
(5) The *kicker's team* must be behind the ball when kicked; otherwise a scrummage shall be formed at the center.
(6) The *opposing team* must stand on or behind the 10-meter line. If they are in front of that line or if they charge before the ball has been kicked, it shall be kicked off again.

Law 11 Method of Scoring
Try. A try is scored by first grounding the ball in the opponents' in-goal.
   A penalty try shall be awarded if one would probably have been scored but for foul play by the opposing team.
   Goal. A goal is scored by kicking the ball over the opponents' crossbar and between the goalposts from the field of play by any placekick or dropkick, except a kickoff, drop-out or free kick, without touching the ground or any player of the kicker's team.
   A goal is scored if the ball has crossed the bar notwithstanding a prior offense of the opposing team.
   A goal is scored if the ball has crossed the bar, even though it may have been blown backward afterwards, and whether it has touched the crossbar or either goalpost or not.
   A goal may be awarded if the ball is illegally touched by any

player of the opposing team and if the referee considers that a goal would otherwise probably have been scored. *For scoring values, see How to win (page 47).*

Law 12 Try and Touchdown
Grounding the ball is the act of a player who
   (a) while holding the ball in his hand (or hands) or arm (or arms) brings the ball in contact with the ground, or
   (b) while the ball is on the ground either
• places his hand (or hands) or arm (or arms) on it with downward pressure, or
• falls upon it and the ball is anywhere under the front of his body from waist to neck inclusive.

A. Try
(1) A player who is onside scores a try when
• he carries the ball into his opponents' in-goal, or
• the ball is in his opponents' in-goal,
and he first grounds it there.
(2) The scoring of a try includes the following cases:
(a) if a player carries, passes, knocks, or kicks the ball into his in-goal and an opponent first grounds it;
(b) if, at a scrummage or ruck, a team is pushed over its goal line and before the ball has emerged it is first grounded in in-goal by an attacking player;
(c) if the momentum of a player, when tackled, carries him into his opponents' in-goal and he first there grounds the ball;
(d) if a player first grounds the ball on his opponents' goal line or if the ball is in contact with the ground and a goalpost; and
(e) if a tackle occurs in such a position that the tackled player while complying with the law is able to place the ball on or over the goal line.
(3) If a player grounds the ball in his opponents' in-goal and picks it up again, a try is scored where it was first grounded.
(4) A try may be scored by a player who is in touch or in touch-in-goal provided he is not carrying the ball.

B. Penalty Try
A penalty try shall be awarded between the posts if but for foul play by the defending team
• a try would probably have been scored, or
• it would probably have been scored in a more favorable position than that where the ball was grounded.

C. Touchdown
(1) A touchdown occurs when a

player first grounds the ball in his in-goal.

(2) After a touchdown, play shall be restarted either by a drop-out or a scrummage.

D. Scrummage after Grounding in Case of Doubt

Where there is doubt as to which team first grounded the ball in in-goal, a scrummage shall be formed 5 m (16 ft) from the goal line opposite the place where the ball was grounded. The attacking team shall put in the ball.

Law 13 Kick at Goal after a Try

(1) After a try has been scored, the scoring team has the right to take a placekick or dropkick at goal on a line through the place where the try was scored.

(2) If a kick is taken:

(a) it must be taken without undue delay;

(b) any player including the kicker may place the ball;

(c) the kicker's team, except a placer, must be behind the ball when kicked;

(d) if the kicker kicks the ball from a placer's hands without the ball being on the ground, the kick is void;

(e) the opposing team must be behind the goal line until the kicker begins his run or offers to kick when they may charge or jump with a view to preventing a goal.

(3) Neither the kicker nor a placer shall willfully do anything that may lead the opposing team to charge prematurely. If either does so, the charge shall not be disallowed.

Penalty:

• For an infringement by the kicker's team—the kick shall be disallowed

• For an infringement by the opposing team—the charge shall be disallowed. If, however, the kick has been taken successfully, the goal shall stand. If it was unsuccessful, the kicker may take another kick under the original conditions without the charge and may change the type of kick.

Law 14 In-Goal

In-goal is the area bounded by a goal line, touch-in-goal lines, and dead-ball line. It includes the goal line and goalposts but excludes touch-in-goal lines and dead-ball line.

Touch-in-goal occurs when the ball or a player carrying it touches a corner post or a touch-in-goal line or the ground or a person or object on or beyond it. The flag is not part of the corner post.

Five-Meter Scrummage

(1) A 5-meter scrummage is a scrummage formed 5 m (16 ft) from the goal line opposite the place where the ball became dead in in-goal, but no closer than 5 m from the touchline. The attacking team shall put in the ball.

(2) If a player carrying the ball in in-goal is so held that he cannot ground the ball, the ball becomes dead.

(3) A 5-meter scrummage shall be formed:

(a) if a defending player heels, kicks, carries, passes, or knocks the ball into his in-goal, and it there becomes dead without an infringement having occurred; except where

• a try is scored, or

• he willfully knocks or throws the ball from the field of play into touch-in-goal or over his dead-ball line or,

(b) if a defending player carrying the ball in the field of play is forced into his in-goal and he then touches down; or

(c) if at a scrummage or ruck a defending team, with the ball in its possession, is pushed over its goal line and before the ball has emerged first grounds it in in-goal.

Drop-Out

(4) Except where the ball is knocked on or thrown forward in the field of play or in-goal, if an attacking player kicks, carries, passes, or charges down the ball from an opponent's kick and it travels into his opponent's in-goal, either directly or having touched a defender who does not willfully attempt to stop, catch, or kick it, and it is there:

• grounded by a defending player, or

• goes into touch-in-goal or over the dead-ball line

a drop-out shall be awarded.

Penalties:

(a) A penalty try shall be awarded when by foul play in in-goal the defending team has prevented a try that otherwise would probably have been scored.

(b) A try shall be disallowed and a penalty kick awarded, if a try would probably not have been gained but for foul play by the attacking team.

(c) For foul play in in-goal while the ball is out of play the penalty kick shall be awarded at the place where play would otherwise have restarted and, in addition, the player shall either be ordered off or cautioned that he will be sent off if he repeats the offense.

(d) For willfully charging or

obstructing in in-goal a player who has just kicked the ball the penalty shall be

• a penalty kick in the field of play 5 m (16 ft) from the goal line opposite the place of infringement, or, at the option of the non-offending team,

• a penalty kick where the ball alights as provided under law 26 (3) Penalty (ii) (b).

(e) For other infringements in in-goal, the penalty shall be the same as for a similar infringement in the field of play except that the mark for a penalty kick or free kick shall be in the field of play 5 m(16 ft) from the goal line opposite the place of infringement and the place of any scrummage shall be 5 m from the goal line opposite the place of infringement but not within 5 m of the touchline.

Law 15. Drop-Out

A drop-out is a dropkick awarded to the defending team.

(1) The dropkick must be taken from anywhere on or behind the 22-meter line; otherwise the ball shall be dropped out again.

(2) The dropkick must be taken without delay.

Penalty:

Penalty kick on the 22-meter line.

(3) The ball must cross the 22-meter line; otherwise the opposing team may have it dropped out again, or have a scrummage formed at the center of the 22-meter line. If it crosses the 22-meter line and is then blown back, play shall continue.

(4) If the ball is kicked directly into touch, the opposing team may accept the kick, have the ball dropped out again, or have a scrummage formed at the center of the 22-meter line.

(5) The kicker's team must be behind the ball when kicked. However, retiring players of the kicker's team who are in front of the ball will not be penalized if their failure to retire is due to the rapidity with which the kick has been taken but they must not stop retiring and must not enter the game until they have been made onside by an action of their own team as required by Law 25 (1).

Penalty:

Scrummage at the center of the 22-meter line and the opposing team shall put in the ball.

(6) The opposing team must not charge over the 22 meter line; otherwise the ball shall be dropped out again.

(7) When the ball has been made dead by the attacking team by a

kick, other than an unsuccessful kick at goal, which goes into touch-in-goal or on or over the dead-ball line, the defending team will have the option of a drop-out or of a scrummage. If a scrummage is chosen, the scrummage will be ordered at the place from where the ball was kicked but not less than 5 m (16 ft) from the touchline.

Law 16 Fair Catch (Mark)

(a) A player makes a fair catch when, in his 22-meters area or in his in-goal, he cleanly catches the ball direct from a kick, other than from a kickoff, by one of his opponents and at the same time he exclaims "Mark!" A fair catch may be obtained even though the ball on its way touches a goalpost or crossbar.

(b) A free kick is awarded for a fair catch.

(1) The free kick must be taken by the player making the fair catch, unless he is injured in so doing. If he is unable to take the kick within one minute a scrummage shall be formed at the mark. His team shall put in the ball.

(2) If the mark is in in-goal, any resultant scrummage shall be 5 m (16 ft) from the goal line on a line through the mark.

Law 17 Knock-On or Throw-Forward

A knock-on occurs when the ball travels forward toward the direction of the opponents' dead-ball line after:

• a player loses possession of it, or

• a player propels or strikes it with his hand or arm, or

• it strikes a player's hand or arm and touches the ground or another player before it is recovered by the player.

A throw-forward occurs when a player carrying the ball throws or passes it in the direction of his opponents' dead-ball line. A throw-in from touch is not a throw-forward. If the ball is not thrown or passed forward but it bounces forward after hitting a player or the ground, it is not a throw-forward.

(1) The knock-on or throw-forward must not be intentional.

Penalty:

Penalty kick at the place of infringement or in accordance with Law 14 Penalty (e). A penalty try may be awarded.

(2) If the knock-on or throw-forward is unintentional, a

➡ *page 51*

POSITIONS AND SKILLS

Forwards: The *front row* consists of the *props* and the *hooker*. The hooker is responsible for controlling the ball with his feet in a scrum. The props are big, strong players who assist the hooker by channeling the force of their own pack as well as withstanding the pressure of the opposition. The *locks* add power of the scrum. Generally tall players, they are also often relied on to secure possession at the line-out. The *back row* is made up of two *flankers* and the *number eight*. Flankers are good tacklers who are also the key players in a maul or line-out. The number eight must have the stamina, strength, and awareness to control the ball when it is channeled back through the scrum.

Other positions: The *scrum-half* works together with the *fly-half* to link the forwards and the backs. These two have tactical control over the game, deciding whether to kick, pass, or run the ball once the forwards have gained possession. Both must be quick and cunning, able to kick and pass well. The *center three-quarters* play either in attack, setting up scoring opportunities for the wingers, or in defense, tackling and blocking the attacks of the opposition's three-quarters. The *wing three-quarters* receive the ball from the center and must be swift runners able to evade opponents. The *full-back* is the last line of defense and must be able to kick to touch (i.e., out of bounds) accurately.

TACTICS

The forwards attempt to control the ball through a series of "set pieces," (e.g., scrums and line-outs). If successful, they generally release the ball to the backs for an attack. Alternatively, if forwards are a particularly strong unit, they may head the attack themselves, keeping possession of the ball rather than passing it to the backs, and shifting play toward their opponents' in-goal directly via scrums, mauls, and line-outs.

Training session
A second row forward (a lock) practices jumping in the line-out, supported by the props.

Coming together
As required by rule, players use the entire arm and hand to bind together in a scrum. They do so both to ensure maximum power and a safe encounter.

Number eight
The number eight is the back row of the scrum. His task is to control the ball as it comes out of the scrum, directing the ball to the scrum-half waiting behind.

In control
Not all rugby players are big. The fly-half needs to be agile and very good at ball handling, kicking, and passing. The fly-half is the team's mid-field general; his chief task is to set the three-quarters in motion. He controls not only the direction but also the pace of their movements, and it is important for him to be able to switch direction quickly to surprise the opposition.

Hard ruck
When a player goes down with the ball, players pile on in a loose scrum or ruck in an attempt to drive over the top and gain possession of the ball.

Last hope
The fullback often serves as the team's specialist kicker. It is very useful to have a man at the back who can sweep up the ball and kick it far upfield.

Key link
The scrum-half is the essential link between the fowards and the backs. He must quickly take the ball as it is cleared by the forwards from a scrum, line-out, or ruck and then clear it to the three-quarters line.

Three-quarters line
There is nothing more exciting than a swift three-quarters line movement. The ball is fed out rapidly along the line from player to fast moving player.

On the run
The wingers are the team's speed kings, able to outpace and outmaneuver the opposition on a penetrating run upfield.

Scrum-halfs *are typically small and agile. You will often see them diving full length to get the ball quickly away from a scrum and out to the three-quarters line.*

---

continued from page 49

scrummage shall be formed either at the place of infringement or, if it occurs at a line-out, 15 m (16 yds) from the touchline along the line of touch unless:
• the ball is knocked on by a player who is in the act of charging down the kick of an opponent but is not attempting to catch the ball, or
• the ball is knocked on one or more times by a player who is in the act of catching or picking it up or losing possession of it and is recovered by that player before it has touched the ground or another player.

Law 18. Tackle, Lying with, on, or Near the Ball
A tackle occurs when a player carrying the ball in the field-of-play is held by one or more opponents so that while he is so held he is brought to the ground or the ball comes into contact with the ground. If the ball carrier is on one knee, or both knees, or is sitting on the ground, or is on top of another player who is on the ground, the ball carrier is deemed to have been brought to the ground.
(1) (a) A tackled player must immediately pass the ball or

release the ball and get up or move away from the ball.
(b) Any player who tackles an opponent and, in doing so, goes to ground in the same way as the tackled player, must immediately release the tackled player and get up or move away from the tackled player and the ball. He must not play the ball until he is on his feet.
(c) After a tackle any other player must be on his feet when he plays the ball.
(d) A player who goes to the ground and gathers the ball or with the ball in his possession but who is not tackled must immediately get up on his feet with the ball or pass the ball or release the ball, and get up or move away from the ball.
(2) It is illegal for any player:
(a) to prevent a tackled player from passing or releasing the ball, or getting up or moving away after he has passed or released it;
(b) to pull the ball from a tackled player's possession or attempt to pick up the ball before the tackled player has released it;
(c) while lying on the ground after a tackle to play or interfere with the ball in any way or to tackle or attempt to tackle an opponent carrying the ball;
(d) to willfully fall on or over a

player lying on the ground with the ball in his possession;
(e) to willfully fall on or over players lying on the ground with the ball between them or in close proximity; or
(f) while lying on the ground in close proximity to the ball to prevent an opponent from gaining possession of it.
Note:
(viii) Close proximity means within 1 m (3 ft).
(3) A player must not fall on or over the ball emerging from a scrummage or ruck.
Penalty:
Penalty kick at the place of infringement.
(4) A try may be scored if the momentum of a player carries him into his opponents' in-goal even though he is tackled.

Law 19 Lying with, on, or Near the Ball
The requirements of this law are now incorporated into Law 18.

Law 20 Scrummage
A scrummage, which can take place only in the field of play, is formed by players from each team closing up in readiness to allow the ball to be put on the ground between them but is not to be formed within 5 m (16 ft) of

the touchline.
The middle player in each front row is the hooker, and the players on either side of him are the props.
The middle line means an imaginary line on the ground directly beneath the line formed by the junction of the shoulders of the two front rows.
If the ball in a scrummage is on or over the goal line the scrummage is ended.
Forming a Scrummage
(1) A team must not willfully delay the forming of a scrummage (F.K.).
(2) Every scrummage shall be formed at the place of infringement or as near thereto as is practicable within the field of play. It must be stationary with the middle line parallel to the goal lines until the ball has been put in.
Before commencing engagement, each front row must be in a crouched position with heads and shoulders no lower than their hips and so that they are not more than one arm's length from the opponents' shoulders.
In the interest of safety, each front row should engage in the

➡ *page 52*

continued from page 51

sequence of crouch, then pause and only begin on the call "Engage" given by the referee (F.K.).

Notes:

(i) To the extent that it is necessary, the scrummage is to be moved from the place of infringement so that the scrummage is formed in the field of play and the feet of all the defending players in the scrummage are in the field of play.

(ii) When the place of infringement is within 5 m (16 ft) of a touchline the scrummage is to be formed 5 m from that touchline.

(iii) The referee shall mark the place of engagement with his foot before the scrummage is formed.

(iv) A crouched position is the extension of the normal stance by bending the knees sufficiently to step into the engagement without a charge.

(3) It is dangerous play for a front row to form down some distance from its opponents and rush against them. (P.K.).

Note:

(v) The referee should not call the front rows to engage until the ball is in the hands of the player putting in the ball and is available to be put in immediately. This call is not a command, but an indication that the front rows may engage when ready.

(4) **Experimental Variation:**
A maximum of eight players from each team shall be required to form a scrummage and the number of these players shall not be increased while the scrummage is taking place. These players shall remain bound in the scrummage until it ends. Each front row of a scrummage shall have three players in it at all times. The head of a player in the front row shall not be next to the head of a player of the same team (P.K.).

Exception:

(a) when for any reason the number of players in a team is reduced to less than 15 players, the number of players of each team in the scrummage may be similarly reduced. Any reduction must not be such that the number of players for any team in the scrummage is less than five;

(5) (a) While a scrummage is forming:
• the shoulders of each player in

the front row must not be lower than his hips,
• all players in each front row must adopt a normal stance,
• both feet must be on the ground and not crossed,
• the hookers must be in a hooking position,
• a hooker's foot must not be in front of the forward feet of his props (F.K.).

(b) While the scrummage is taking place, players in each front row must have their weight firmly on at least one foot and be in a position for an effective forward shove and the shoulders of each player must not be lower than his hips (F.K.).

Notes:

(vi) The restriction on the crossing of the feet of the players in the front rows refers only to the feet of individual players. The feet of all players in the front rows must be in a position for an effective forward shove.

(vii) A hooking position is where a hooker in the scrummage has both feet on the ground, the weight retained firmly on one foot and in a position to hook or strike the ball.

(viii) A flank forward in the second or third row of a scrummage may pack at an angle provided he is properly bound. If the ball is emerging from the back of the scrummage and he moves outward, thereby preventing an opponent from advancing around the scrummage, a penalty kick should be awarded.

(ix) In the event of the scrummage collapsing the referee should whistle immediately so that players do not continue to push. The referee should also whistle immediately if any player in the scrummage is lifted off his feet or is forced upward out of the scrummage.

(x) The scrummage is ended:
• if the ball in the scrummage is on or over the goal line
• when the ball emerges from the scrummage
• if, in the scrummage, a player whose feet are the "hindmost" feet in that scrummage, has the ball at his feet, unbinds, and picks up the ball.

Binding of Players

(6)(a) The players of each front row shall bind firmly and continuously while the scrummage is forming, while the ball is being put in, and while it is in the scrummage (P.K.).

(b) The hooker may bind either over or under the arms of his props but, in either case, he must

bind firmly around their bodies at or below the level of the armpits. The props must bind the hooker similarly. The hooker must not be supported so that he is not carrying any weight on either foot (P.K.).

(c) The outside (loose-head) prop must either (i) bind his opposing (tight-head) prop with his left arm inside the right arm of his opponent, or (ii) place his left hand or forearm on his left thigh.

The tight-head prop must bind with his right arm outside the left upper arm of his opposing loose-head prop. He may *grip* the jersey of his opposing loose-head prop with his right hand but only to keep himself and the scrummage steady and he must not exert a downward pull (P.K.).

(d) All players in a scrummage, other than those in a front row, must bind with at least one arm and hand around the body of another player of the same team. The player whose feet are the "hindmost" feet in the scrummage must bind with at least one arm on to one of his locks (P.K.).

(e) No outside player other than a prop may hold an opponent with this outer arm (F.K.).

Putting the Ball into the Scrummage

(7) When an infringement occurs the team not responsible shall put in the ball. In other circumstances, unless otherwise provided, the ball shall be put in by the team that was moving forward prior to the stoppage or, if neither team was moving forward, by the attacking team.

(8) The ball shall be put in without delay as soon as the two front rows have closed together. A team must put in the ball when ordered to do so and on the side first chosen (F.K.).

(9) The player putting in the ball shall:

(a) stand 1m (3 ft) from the scrummage on the middle line between the two front rows (F.K.);

(b) hold the ball with both hands over the middle line between the two front rows at a level midway between his knees and ankles (F.K.);

(c) from that position put in the ball
• without any delay or without feint or backward movement, i.e., with a single forward movement, and
• at a quick speed straight along the middle line so that it first touches the ground immediately

beyond the width of the nearer prop's shoulders (F.K.).

(10) Play in the scrummage begins when the ball leaves the hands of the player putting it in.

(11) If the ball is put in and it comes out at either end of the tunnel, it shall be put in again, unless a free kick or penalty kick has been awarded. If the ball comes out otherwise than at either end of the tunnel and if a penalty kick has not been awarded play shall proceed.

Notes:

(xiv) Advantage applies as soon as the ball has been put into the scrummage and played.

Restrictions on Front Row Players

(12) All front row players must place their feet so as to allow a clear tunnel. A player must not prevent the ball from being put into the scrummage, or from toughing the ground at the required place (F.K.).

(13) No front row player may raise or advance a foot until the ball has left the hands of the player putting it into the scrummage (F.K.).

(14) When the ball has touched the ground, any foot of any player in either front row may be used in an attempt to gain possession of the ball subject to the following:

players in the front row must not at any time during the scrummage willfully:

(a) raise both feet off the ground at the same time (P.K.); or

(b) adopt a position or take any action, by twisting or lowering the body or by pulling on an opponent's dress, which is likely to cause the scrummage to collapse (P.K.); or

(c) lift an opponent off his feet or force him upward out of the scrummage (P.K.); or

(d) kick the ball out of the tunnel in the direction from which it is put in. (F.K.)

Restrictions on Players

(15) Any player who is not in either front row must not play the ball while it is in the tunnel. (F.K.).

(16) A player must not:

(a) return the ball into the scrummage (F.K.); or

(b) handle the ball in the scrummage except in the act of obtaining a "push-over" try or touchdown (P.K.); or

(c) pick up the ball in the scrummage by hand or legs (P.K.); or

(d) wilfully collapse the scrummage (P.K.); or

(e) willfully fall or kneel in the scrummage (P.K.); or
(f) attempt to gain possession of the ball in the scrummage with any part of the body except the foot or lower leg (F.K.).
(17) (a) The player putting in the ball and his immediate opponent must not kick the ball while it is in the scrummage (F.K.).
(b) Neither of the players referred to in (a) should take any action while the ball is in the scrummage to convey to the opponents that the ball is out of the scrummage (F.K.).
(18) A scrummage must not be wheeled beyond a position where the middle line becomes parallel to the touchline. The scrummage will be reformed at the site of the stoppage, the ball to be put in by the side that has gained possession or otherwise by the same team.
Penalty:
(a) For an infringement of paragraphs (1), (2), (5) and (6)(e), (9), (9), (12), (13), (14)(d), (15), (16)(a) and (f), and (17)(a) and (b), a free kick at the place of infringement.
(b) For an infringement of paragraphs (3), (4), (6)(a)(b)(c) and (d), (14)(a)(b) and (c), or (16) (b)(c)(d) and (e), a penalty kick at the place of infringement.
For Offside at Scrummage see Law 24 B.

Law 21 Ruck
A ruck, which can take place only in the field of play, is formed when the ball is on the ground and one or more players from each team are on their feet and in physical contact, closing around the ball between them.
Rucking is the act of a player who, in a ruck, is using his feet to retrieve or retain the ball without contravening Law 26.
If the ball in a ruck is on or over the goal line the ruck is ended.
(1) A player joining a ruck must have his head and shoulders no lower than his hips. He must bind with at least one arm around the body of a player of his team in the ruck.
Penalty:
Free kick at the place of infringement (F.K.).
Notes:
(i) The placing of a hand on another player is not binding. Binding involves the whole arm, from hand to shoulder.
(2) A player must not:
(a) return the ball into the ruck;
(b) take any action while the ball is in the ruck to convey to the

opponents that the ball is out of the ruck;
Penalty:
Free kick at the place of infringement (F.K.).
(c) or handle the ball in the ruck except in the act of securing a try or touchdown; or
(d) pick up the ball in the ruck by hand or legs; or(e) willfully collapse the ruck; or
(f) jump on top of other players in the ruck; or
(g) willfully fall or kneel in the ruck; or
(h) while lying on the ground interfere in any way with the ball in or emerging from the ruck. He must do his best to roll away from it.
Penalty:
For (c) to (h), a penalty kick at the place of infringement (P.K.).
For Offside at Ruck see Law 24 C.
Note:
(ii) Players' safety is of primary importance and players should ruck for the ball and not the players on the ground. Players rucking for the ball should attempt to step over other players lying on the ground and should not intentionally step on them. Players must ruck in close proximity to the ball.
(3) When the ball in the ruck becomes unplayable a scrummage shall be ordered and the ball put in by the team moving forward immediately prior to the stoppage. When neither team was moving forward or when the referee is unable to determine which team was moving forward, the ball shall be put in by the team moving forward immediately before the formation of the ruck and if no team was moving forward by the attacking team.

Law 22 Maul
A maul, which can take place only in the field of play, is formed by one or more players from each team on their feet and in physical contact closing round a player who is in possession of the ball.
A maul ends when the ball is on the ground or the ball or a player carrying it emerges from the maul or when a scrummage is ordered.
If the ball in a maul is on or over the goal line the maul is ended.
(1) A player joining a maul must have his head and shoulders no lower than his hips.
Penalty:
Free kick at the place of infringement (F.K.).
(2) A player must not:

(a) jump on top of players in a maul;
(b) willfully collapse a maul;
(c) attempt to drag an opponent out of a maul;
Penalty:
Penalty kick at the place of infringement (P.K.).
(d) take any action while the ball is in the maul to convey to the opponents that the ball is out of the maul.
Penalty:
Free kick at the place of infringement.
(3) A player is not in physical contact unless he is caught in or bound to the maul and not merely alongside it.
(4) (a) When a maul remains stationary or stops moving forward or the ball in a maul becomes unplayable, a scrummage shall be ordered and the ball shall be put in by the team not in possession at the commencement of the maul, except where the referee is unable to determine which team was in possession then the ball shall be put in by the team which was moving forward prior to the stoppage, or if neither team was moving forward by the attacking team.
(b) If a player catches the ball direct from a kick by an opponent other than from a kickoff or from a drop-out, and is immediately held by an opponent so that a maul ensues and the maul remains stationary or stops moving forward or the ball becomes unplayable, his team shall put in the ball at the ensuing scrummage. *For Offside at Maul see Law 24 C.*

Law 23 Touch and Line-Out
A. Touch
(1) The ball is in touch
• when it is not being carried by a player and it touches a touchline or the ground or a person or object on or beyond it, or
• when it is being carried by a player and it or the player carrying it touches a touchline or the ground beyond it.
(2) If the ball is not in touch and has not crossed the plane of the touchline, a player who is in touch may kick the ball or propel it with his hand but not hold it.
(3) The ball is deemed to have been kicked directly into touch if, from a kick, it is in touch without having pitched on the playing area or without having touched or been touched in flight by a player or the referee.
Notes:

(i) (a) If the ball is kicked directly into touch from a kickoff and the opposing team elects to accept the kick, the line-out shall be formed.
• at the halfway line, or
• where the ball went into touch if that place be nearer to kicker's goal line.
(b) If the ball is kicked directly into touch from a drop-out and the opposing team elects to accept the kick, the line-out shall be formed where the ball went into touch.
(ii) On or beyond the touchline or touch-in-goal line refers to all areas except the playing area.
(iii) It is not touch or touch-in-goal when a player with both feet in the playing area catches the ball, even though the ball before being caught has crossed the touchline or touch-in-goal line. Such a player may deflect or tap the ball in the playing area provided it is not propelled forward. If a player jumps and catches the ball his feet must land in the playing area.
B. Line-Out
The line of touch is an imaginary line in the field of play at right angles to the touchline through the place where the ball is to be thrown in.
Formation of line-out
(1) A line-out is formed by at least two players from each team lining up in single lines parallel to the line of touch in readiness for the ball to be thrown in between them. The team throwing in the ball shall determine the maximum number of players from either team who so line up. Such players are those "in the line-out" unless excluded below (F.K.).
(2) Each team must line up half a meter (1 ½ ft) on its side of the line-of-touch so as to leave a clear space of 1 m (3 ft) between the two lines of players (measured between the shoulders of the players, standing upright) (F.K.).
(3) The line-out stretches from 5 m (16 ft) from the touchline from which the ball is being thrown in to a position 15 m (16 yds) from that touchline (F.K.).
(4) Any player of either team who is further than 15 m (16 yds) from the touchline when the line-out begins is not in the line-out (F.K.).
Note:
(vi) If, at a formed line-out, the team throwing in the ball line up

➡ *page 55*

Line-out

If the ball goes into "touch" (out of bounds), play is restarted with a line-out. The opposing forwards stand in two lines and jump to catch the ball as it is thrown. The maximum number of players in the line-out is determined by the team making the throw.

Jump ball

Line-outs are one of the main ways of gaining possession of the ball. As players jump for the ball, they try to either catch it, deflect it to the scrum-half, or knock it back to another player in the line-out.

The target

In any line-out there is usually one target jumper. As soon as he catches the ball, the players in front of him close ranks to protect him.

Up for grabs

In contrast to a scrum, where the team putting in the ball has the best chance of gaining possession, in a line-out each team has an equally good chance. The result is often a chaotic scramble for the ball.

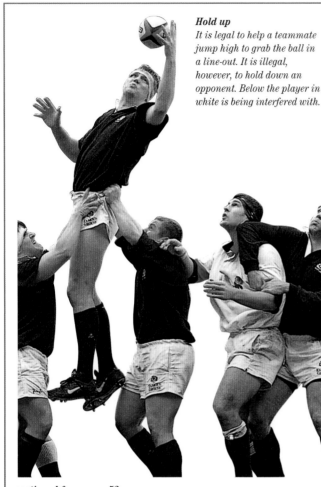

Hold up
It is legal to help a teammate jump high to grab the ball in a line-out. It is illegal, however, to hold down an opponent. Below the player in white is being interfered with.

continued from page 53

less than the normal number, their opponents must be given a reasonable opportunity to conform. Opposing players who are retiring for that purpose must do so directly and without delay to a line 10 m (33 ft) behind the line of touch. Loiterers must be penalized. Subject to this, when the line-out is ended players so retiring may rejoin play, even if they have not reached the 10 m line.

Throwing in the Ball

(5) When the ball is in touch the place at which it must be thrown in is as follows:

(a) When the ball goes into touch from a penalty kick; or from a kick including a free kick awarded within 22 m (24 yds) of the kicker's goal line, at the place where it touched or crossed the touchline, except as otherwise provided;

(b) when the kicker has received the ball outside his 22-meter line and retreated behind that line before kicking, and on other occasions when the ball is kicked directly into touch, after having been kicked otherwise than as stated in (a), opposite the place from which the ball was kicked or at the place where it touched or crossed the touchline if that

place be nearer to the kicker's goal line;

(c) when a quick throw-in is taken, from any point along the touchline between where the ball went into touch and the goal line of the team throwing in the ball;

(d) otherwise when the ball is in touch, at the place where the ball touched or crossed the touch-line.

(6) (a) When kicked into touch from a penalty kick, the ball will be thrown in at the line-out by the team that kicked the ball into touch.

(b) Otherwise the ball is to be thrown in by an opponent of the player whom it last touched, or by whom it was carried before being in touch.

(c) In the event of doubt as to which team should throw in the ball, the attacking team shall do so.

(7) The ball may be brought into play at a formed line-out or by a quick throw-in which can only be taken before the line-out has formed.

If a quick throw-in occurs after the line-out has formed, it is void and the ball is brought into play at the formed line-out by the same team.

(8) At a formed line-out the player throwing in the ball must:

• not put any part of either foot in the field of play.

• throw the ball in at the place indicated in (5) so that it first touches the ground or touches or is touched by a player at least 5 m (16 ft) from the touchline along the line of touch; otherwise the opposing team shall have the right, as its option, to throw in the ball or to take a scrummage 15 m (16 yds) from the touchline.

(9) (a) At a quick throw-in, the ball that went into touch must be used and, after going into touch and being made dead, unless it has been touched only by the player throwing it in, the ball shall be thrown in at the place indicated in (5) by the same team.

(b) At a quick throw-in, the ball must be thrown straight along the line of touch so that it first touches the ground or touches or is touched by a player at least 5 m (16 ft) from the touchline along the line of touch, otherwise the opposing team shall have the right, at its option, to throw in the ball or to take a scrummage 15 m (16 yds) from the touchline at the place where the quick throw-in occurred;

(c) At a quick throw-in a player must not prevent the ball from being thrown 5 m (16 ft) (F.K.).

(10) If, on the second occasion, the ball is not thrown in correctly, a scrummage shall be formed and the ball shall be put in by the team which threw it in on the first occasion.

Beginning and End of Line-Out

(11) The line-out begins when the ball leaves the hands of the player throwing it in.

(12) The line-out ends when

• a ruck or maul is taking place and all feet of players in the ruck or maul have moved beyond the line of touch, or

• a player carrying the ball leaves the line-out, or

• the ball has been passed, knocked back, or kicked from the line-out, or

• the ball is thrown beyond a position 15 m (16 yds) from the touchline, or

• the ball becomes unplayable.

Peeling-Off

"Peeling-off" occurs when a player (or players) moved from his position in the line-out for the purpose of catching the ball when it has been passed or knocked back by another of his team in the line-out.

(13) When the ball is in touch players who approach the line of touch must always be presumed to do so for the purpose of forming the line-out. Before the

ball leaves the hands of the player throwing it in, the players in the line-out must not leave it but may change their position along the line of touch. After the ball has been thrown in such players must not leave the line-out except in a peel-off movement (F.K.).

(14) In a peeling-off movement a player must move parallel and close to the line-out (F.K.).

Restrictions on Players in Line-Out

(15) **Experimental Variation:** When a line-out is taking place, any player in the line-out must not

(a) stand within 5 m (16 ft) of the touchline or prevent the ball from being thrown 5 m (F.K.); or

(b) be offside (P.K.); or

(c) use an opponent as a support to enable him to jump for the ball (P.K.); or

(d) hold, push, charge, obstruct, or grasp an opponent not holding the ball, except when a ruck or a maul is taking place (P.K.); or

(e) charge an opponent except in an attempt to tackle him or to play the ball (P.K.); or

(f) use any player of his team as a support to enable him to jump for the ball (F.K.); or

(g) lift a player of his team (F.K.); or

(h) support any player of his team before this player has jumped for the ball (F.K.); or

(i) hold a supported player below the waist (P.K.).

(16) **Experimental Variation:** A player jumping for the ball must do so with either both hands or his inside arm to catch or deflect the ball. When a player plays the ball with both hands above his head, he is allowed to use either hand (F.K.).

(17) Except when jumping for the ball or peeling off, a clear space of 1 m (3 ft) must be left between the two lines of players until the ball has touched or has been touched by a player or has touched the ground (F.K.).

Note:

(xv) The act of jumping for the ball may include a step or steps in any direction provided it takes the jumper up to but not across the line of touch.

(18) A player in the line-out may move into the space between the touchline and the 5-m mark only when the ball has been thrown beyond him, and if he does so, he must not move toward his goal line before the line-out ends, except in a peeling-off movement (F.K.).

➡ *page 56*

continued from page 55

(19) Until the line-out ends, no player may move beyond a position 15 m (16 yds) from the touchline except as allowed when the ball is thrown beyond that position, in accordance with the Exception following Law 24 D(1)(c) (P.K.).

Note:

(xvi) If the ball in a line-out becomes unplayable, otherwise than as a result of an infringement for which a penalty is prescribed, a scrummage should be ordered.

(20) A player participating in the line-out as defined in Law 24 D may run into a gap in the line-out and take the ball provided he does not charge or obstruct an opponent in the line-out (P.K.).

Restrictions on Players not in Line-Out

(21) Players of either team who are not in the line-out may not advance from behind the line-out and take the ball from the throw-in, except only a player advancing at a long throw-in (P.K.) on offside line.

Penalty:

(a) For an infringement of paragraphs (1), (2), (3), (4), (9)(c), (13), (14), (15)(a), (b), (g), or (h), (16), (17), or (18) a free kick 15 m (16 yds) from the touchline along the line of touch.

(b) For an infringement of paragraphs (15)(b), (c), (d), (e) or (i), (19), or (20), a penalty kick 15 m (16 yds) from the touchline along the line of touch.

(c) For an infringement of paragraph (21), a penalty kick on the offending team's offside line (as defined in Law 24 D) opposite the place of infringement, but not less than 15 m (16 yds) from the touchline.

Place of Scrummage

Any scrummage taken or ordered under this Law or as the result of any infringement in a line-out shall be formed 15 m (16 yds) from the touchline along the line of touch.

Note:

(xvii) If a player repeatedly infringes, he must be dealt with under Law 26(2). *For Offside at Line-Out, see Law 24 D.*

Law 24 Offside

Offside means that a player is in a position in which he is out of the game and is liable to penalty.

In general play the player is in an offside position because he is in front of the ball when it has been last played by another player of his team.

In play at a scrummage, ruck, maul, or line-out the player is offside because he remains or advances in front of the line or place stated in, or otherwise infringes, the relevant sections of this Law.

A. Offside in General Play

(1) A player is in an offside position if the ball has been
• kicked, or
• touched, or
• is being carried
by one of his team behind him.

(2) There is no penalty for being in an offside position unless:

(a) the player plays the ball or obstructs an opponent; or

(b) he being within 10 m (33 ft) of an opponent waiting to play the ball or of the place where the ball pitches, does not retire without delay and without interfering with the opponent, or

(c) he, on all other occasions, moves toward the opponents waiting to play the ball or to the place where the ball pitches, before he is put onside.

Exceptions:

(i) When an offside player cannot avoid being touched by the ball or by a player carrying it, he is "accidentally offside." Play should be allowed to continue unless the infringing team obtains an advantage, in which case a scrummage shall be formed at that place.

(ii) A player who receives an unintentional throw-forward is not offside.

Penalty:

Penalty kick at the place of infringement, or, at the option of the non-offending team, a scrummage at the place where the ball was last played by the offending team. If the latter place is in in-goal, the penalty kick shall be taken or the scrummage shall be formed 5 m from the goal line, on a line through the place.

For an infringement of (2)(c) by more than one player, the place of infringement will be that of the offside player closest to the player waiting for the ball or where the ball pitches.

Notes:

(i) A penalty for offside should not be given at once if the non-offending team gains an advantage or if it appears likely to gain an advantage; but if the expected advantage is not gained, the penalty should in all cases be awarded even if it is necessary to bring play back for that purpose to the place of infringement.

(ii) When a player knocks on and offside player or the same team next plays the ball, a penalty for

offside should not be awarded unless the offside deprives the non-offending team of an advantage.

(iii) A player can be offside in his in-goal.

(iv) If a player hands the ball to another player of his team in front of him, the second player is offside. A scrummage for "accidental offside" should be awarded unless it is considered the player was willfully offside in which case a penalty kick should be awarded.

(v) The referee should whistle at once if an offside player who cannot be placed onside charges within 10 m (33 ft) of an opponent waiting to receive the ball. Delay may prove dangerous to the latter player. Where there is no opponent waiting to play the ball but one arrives as the ball pitches, an offside player who is near such an opponent must not obstruct or interfere with him in any way whatsoever before he is put onside.

(vi) If an attacking player kicks the ball which is misfielded by an opponent and the ball is then played by another attacking player in an offside position within 10 m (33 ft) of the opponent, a penalty kick should be awarded.

(vii) If an attacking player kicks the ball which is charged down by an opponent and another attacking player within 10 m (33 ft) of the opponent then plays the ball, play should be allowed to continue. The opponent was not "waiting to play the ball" and the second attacking player is therefore onside under Law 25 (2).

(viii) Law 24 A(2)(b) and (c) also apply where the ball has struck a goalpost or crossbar. Offside players must not approach or remain within 10 m (33 ft) of an opponent waiting to play the ball or the place where the ball pitches.

B. Offside at Scrummage

The term "offside line" means a line parallel to the goal lines through the hindmost foot of the player's team in the scrummage.

While a scrummage is forming or is taking place:

(1) A player is offside if

(a) he joins it from his opponent's side, or

(b) he, not being in the scrummage nor the player of either team who puts the ball in the scrummage,

• fails to retire behind the offside line or to his goal line whichever is the nearer, or

• places either foot in front of the offside line while the ball is in the scrummage.

(2) A player is offside if:

(a) he being the player in a scrum-half position whose team has won the ball, places both feet in front of the ball while it is still in the scrummage; or

(b) he being the immediate opponent of the player in a scrum-half position whose team has won the ball, places either foot in front of the ball while it is still in the scrummage.

(3) A player is offside if he, being the immediate opponent of the player putting in the ball, moves to the opposite side of the scrummage or moves away from the scrummage and is in front of the scrummage offside line. (P.K.).

Penalty:

Penalty kick on the offside line.

Notes:

(ix) Players must retire without delay to the scrummage offside line when a scrummage is forming. Loiterers must be penalized.

(x) Any player of either team may at a particular scrummage be the player who puts in the ball or who takes up position as scrum-half when his opponent is putting in the ball; but such player is at that scrummage the only player of his team who has the benefit of Law 24 B(2).

C. Offside at Ruck or Maul

The term "offside line" means a line parallel to the goal lines through the hindmost foot of the player's team in the ruck or maul.

(1) Ruck or Maul Other Than at Line-Out

While a ruck or maul is taking place (including a ruck or maul which continues after a line-out has ended) a player is offside if he:

(a) joins it from his opponents' side; or

(b) joins it in front of the hindmost player of his team in the ruck or maul; or

(c) does not join the ruck or maul but fails to retire behind the offside line without delay; or

(d) unbinds from the ruck or leaves the maul and does not immediately retire behind the offside line, or once he is on side, if he rejoins the ruck or maul in front of the hindmost player of his team in the ruck or maul; or

(e) advances beyond the offside line with either foot and does not join the ruck or maul.

Penalty: Penalty kick on the offside line.

(2) Ruck or Maul at Line-Out

The term "participating in the

line-out" has the same meaning as in Section D of this Law. A player participating in the line-out is not obliged to join or remain in the ruck or maul and if he is not in the ruck or maul he continues to participate in the line-out until it has ended.

While a line-out is in progress and a ruck or maul takes place, a player is offside if he:

(a) joins the ruck or maul from his opponents' side; or

(b) joins it in front of the hindmost player of his team in the ruck or maul; or

(c) being a player who is participating in the line-out and is not in the ruck or maul, does not retire to and remain at the offside line defined in this section.

Penalty:

Penalty kick 15 m (16 yds) from the touchline along the line of touch.

(d) or being a player who is not participating in the line-out, remains or advances with either foot in front of the offside line defined in Section D of this Law.

Penalty:

Penalty kick on the offending team's offside line opposite the place of infringement, but not less than 15 m (16 yds) from the touchline.

Note:

(xi) When the line-out has ended but the ruck or maul is still taking place, a player is offside if he infringes Section (1) of these Laws.

D. Offside at Line-out

The term "participating in the line-out" refers exclusively to the following players:

• those players who are in the line-out, and

• the player who throws in the ball, and

• his immediate opponent who may have the option of throwing in the ball, and

• one other player of either team who takes up position to receive the ball if it is passed or knocked back from the line-out.

All other players are not participating in the line-out.

The term "offside line" means a line 10 m (33 ft) behind the line of touch and parallel to the goal lines or, if the goal line be nearer than 10 m (33 ft) to the line of touch, the "offside line" is the goal line.

Offside While Participating in Line-Out

(1) A participating player is offside if:

(a) before the ball has touched a player or the ground he willfully

remains or advances with either foot in front of the line of touch, unless he advances while jumping for the ball, provided that the jump is made from his side of the line of touch; or

(b) after the ball has touched a player or the ground, if he is not carrying the ball, he advances with either foot in front of the ball, unless he is lawfully tackling or attempting to tackle an opponent who is partcipating in the line-out. Such tackle or attempt to tackle must, however, start from his side of the ball; or

(c) before the line-out ends he moves beyond a position 15 m (16 yds) from the touchline.

Exception:

Players of the team throwing in the ball may move beyond a position 15 m from the touchline for a long throw-in to them. They may do so only when the ball leaves the hands of the player throwing it in and if they do so their opponents participating in the line-out may follow them. If players so move and the ball is not thrown to or beyond them they must be penalized for offside.

Penalty:

Penalty kick 15 m from the touchline along the line of touch (P.K.).

Notes:

(xii) Players who advance beyond the offside line or who move beyond a position 15 m from the touchline in the expectation of a long throw-in must be penalized, if for any reason the ball is not thrown beyond that position.

(xiii) A player who has jumped unsuccessfully for the ball and crossed the line of touch should not be penalized if he retires immediately to an onside position.

(2) The player throwing in the ball and his immediate opponent must:

(a) remain within 5 m of the touchline; or

(b) retire to the offside line; or

(c) join the line-out after the ball has been thrown in 5 m; or

(d) move into position to receive the ball if it is passed or knocked back from the line-out provided no other player is occupying that position at that line-out. If they do not they are offside.

Penalty:

Penalty kick 15 m from the touchline along the line of touch.

Notes: (xv) If a player other than the wing three-quarter throws in the ball from touch, the wing three-quarter must retire to the offside line, or join the line-out.

Offside While Not Participating in Line-Out

(3) A player who is not participating is offside if before the line-out has ended he advances or remains with either foot in front of the offside line.

Exception:

Players of the team throwing in the ball who are not participating in the line-out may advance for a long throw-in to them beyond the line-out. They may do so only when the ball leaves the hands of the player throwing in the ball and, if they do, their opponents may advance to meet them. If players so advance for a long throw-in to them and the ball is not thrown to them they must be penalized for offside.

Players Returning to "Onside" Position

(4) A player is not obliged, before throwing in the ball, to wait until players of his team have returned to or behind the line-out but such players are offside unless they return to an onside position without delay.

Penalty:

Penalty kick on the offending team's offside line (as defined in Section D of this Law) opposite the place of infringement but not less than 15 m from the touchline.

Note:

(xvii) Scrummage, Ruck, Maul and Line-Out—where these Laws state a line which determines the offside position such line stretches continuously from touchline to touchline.

Law 25 Onside

Onside means that a player is in the game and not liable to penalty for offside.

Player Made Onside by Action of His Team

(1) Any player who is offside in general play and who is not infringing Law 24(A)(2) becomes onside as a result of any of the following actions of his team:

• when the offside player has retired behind the player of his team who last kicked, touched, or carried the ball, or

• when one of his team carrying the ball has run in front of him, or

• when one of his team has run in front of him after coming from the place or from behind the place where the ball was kicked.

In order to put the offside player onside, this other player must be in the playing area, but he is not debarred from following up in touch or touch-in-goal.

Note:

(i) An offside player who is

within 10 m (33 ft) of an opponent waiting to play the ball or the place where the ball pitches must retire and continue to do so up to 10 m until he is put onside. If he does not do so, he must be penalized.

Player Made Onside by Action of Opposing Team.

(2) Any player who is offside in general play, except an offside player within 10 m of an opponent waiting to play the ball or the place where the ball pitches, becomes onside as a result of any of the following actions:

• when an opponent carrying the ball has run 5 m (16 ft), or

• when an opponent kicks or passes the ball, or

• when an opponent intentionally touches the ball and does not catch or gather it.

An offside player within 10 m (33 ft) of an opponent waiting to play the ball or the place where the ball pitches cannot be put onside by any action of his opponents.

Any other offside player in general play is always put onside when an opponent plays the ball.

Player Retiring at Scrummage, Ruck, Maul, or Line-Out

(3) A player who is in an offside position when a scrummage, ruck maul, or line-out is forming or taking place and is retiring as required by Law 24 (Offside) becomes onside:

• when an opponent carrying the ball has run 5 m (16 ft), or

• when an opponent has kicked the ball.

An offside player in this situation is NOT put onside when an opponent passes the ball.

Law 26 Foul Play

Foul Play is any action by a player that is contrary to the letter and spirit of the game and includes obstruction, unfair play, misconduct, dangerous play, unsporting behavior, retaliation, and repeated infringements.

Obstruction

(1) It is illegal for any player:

(a) who is running for the ball to charge or push an opponent also running for the ball, except shoulder to shoulder;

(b) who is in an offside position willfully to run or stand in front of another player of his team who is carrying the ball, thereby preventing an opponent from reaching the latter player;

(c) who is carrying the ball after if has come out of a scrummage,

➡ *page 58*

Forward play

Number eight break

1 Occasionally the number eight, instead of heeling the ball out to the scrum half, unbinds from the pack and picks up the ball himself.

2 He runs directly at the opposing forwards on the blind side of the scrum. He inevitably runs into opposition but his aim is to drive as far as he can to gain valuable ground before being brought down.

Stopper

One of the key roles of a flanker is to break away rapidly when the opposition gains possession and make a quick tackle.

Mutual support

When a player is running with the ball his teammates must be ready to receive the ball as soon as he is tackled.

Getting it away

When a player is tackled, he must get the ball away to a team-mate before hitting the deck—taking care not to throw it forward.

Big man

The prop forwards are usually the biggest players on the team: they have to support the hooker and drive the scrum forward. But they must also be able to run with the ball.

---

continued from page 57

ruck, maul, or line-out, to attempt to force his way through the players of his team in front of him;
(d) who is an outside player in a scrummage to prevent an opponent from advancing around the scrummage.
Penalty:
Penalty kick at the place of infringement. A penalty try may be awarded.
Notes:
(i) There are no circumstances in which a player carrying the ball can be penalized for obstruction.
Unfair Play, Repeated Infringements
(2) It is illegal for any player:
(a) deliberately to play unfairly or willfully infringe any law of the game;
(b) willfully to waste time;
(c) willfully to knock or throw the ball from the playing area into touch, touch-in-goal or over the

dead-ball line;
(d) to infringe repeatedly any law of the game.
Penalty:
Penalty kick at the place of infringement. A penalty try may be awarded if the offense prevents a try which otherwise would have been probably scored.
For offences under 2(d) a player may be cautioned and, if he repeats the offense, must be ordered off.
Misconduct, Dangerous Play
(3) It is illegal for any player:
(a) to strike an opponent;
(b) willfully or recklessly to hack or kick an opponent or to trip him with the foot or to trample on an opponent lying on the ground;
(c) to tackle early, or late or dangerously, including the action known as "a stiff arm tackle"
(d) who is not running for the ball willfully or recklessly to charge or obstruct an opponent who has just kicked the ball;

(e) to hold, push, charge, obstruct, or grasp an opponent not holding the ball except in a scrummage, ruck, or maul;
(Except in a scrummage or ruck the dragging away of a player lying close to the ball is permitted. Otherwise pulling any part of the clothing of an opponent is holding.)
(f) in the front row of a scrummage to form down some distance from the opponents and rush against them;
(g) in the front row of a scrummage willfully to lift an opponent off his feet or force him upward out of the scrummage;
(h) willfully or recklessly to cause a scrummage, ruck, or maul to collapse;
(i) while the ball is out of play to molest, obstruct, or in any way interfere with an opponent or be guilty of any form of misconduct;
(j) to commit any misconduct on

the playing enclosure that is prejudicial to the spirit of good sportsmanship.
Penalty:
A player guilty of misconduct or dangerous play shall either be ordered off or else cautioned that he will be ordered off if he repeats the offense. For a similar offense after caution, the player must be ordered off.
In addition to a caution or ordering off a penalty try or a penalty kick shall be awarded as follows:
(i) If the offense prevents a try which would otherwise probably have been scored, a penalty try shall be awarded.
(ii) The place for a penalty kick shall be:
(a) For offenses other than under paragraphs (d) and (i), at the place of infringement;
(b) For an infringement under (d) the non-offending team shall have the option of taking the kick

Back play

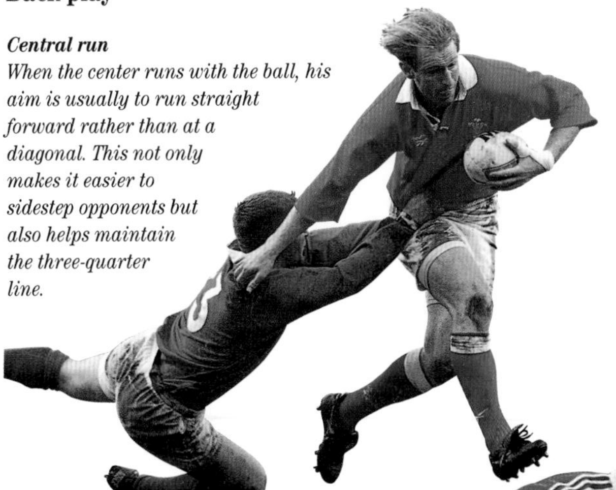

Central run
When the center runs with the ball, his aim is usually to run straight forward rather than at a diagonal. This not only makes it easier to sidestep opponents but also helps maintain the three-quarter line.

Away in time
It is crucial that a three-quarter gets the ball away to a teammate before he is tackled. Ideally, he will get it away before he has even slowed down so that the line's momentum is maintained.

The three-quarters
The back division of a rugby team is seven players: the scrum-half who links the forwards and backs; the fly-half who initiates movements in the three-quarter line; the two center three-quarters and the wing three-quarters, who are the team's main try scorers; and the fullback, who is often the last line of defense.

Offensive defense
Center three-quarters must be strong tacklers. Timing and strength are essential, but here the player not only stops his opponent but drives him backward, gaining the initiative.

at the place of infringement or where the ball alights, and if the ball alights.
• in touch, the mark is 15 m (16 yds) from the touchline on a line parallel to the goal lines through the place where it went into touch, or
• within 15 m from the touch-line, it is 15 m from the touchline on a line parallel to the goal lines through the place where it alighted, or
• in in-goal, touch-in-goal, or over or on the dead-ball line, it is 5 m from the goal line on a line parallel to the touchline through the place where it crossed the goal line or 15 m from the touchline whichever is the greater. When the offense takes place in touch the "place of infringement" in the optional penalty award is 15 m from the touchline opposite to where the offense took place:

If the offense takes place in touch-in-goal, the "place of infringement" in the optional penalty award is in the field of play 5 m (16 ft) from the goal line and 15 m (16 yds) from the touchline;
(c) For an offense under (i), at any place where the ball would next have been brought into play if the offense had not occurred, or, if that place is on the touchline, 15 m from that place, on a line parallel to the goal lines.
(iii) For an infringement in in-goal, a penalty kick is to be awarded as provided for under Law 14 Penalties.
(iv) For an offense under Law 26(3)(i), the penalty kick is to be taken at whichever is the place where play would restart, that is
• at the 22-meter line (at any point the non-offending team may select), or

• at the center of the halfway line, or
• if a scrummage 5 m (16 ft) from the goal line would otherwise have been awarded, at that place or 15 m from the touchline on a line 5 m from and parallel to the goal line, whichever is the greater.
(v) For an offense that occurs within the playing enclosure and is not otherwise covered in the foregoing, the penalty kick shall be awarded in the playing area 15 m (16 yds) from the touchline and opposite to where the offense took place.
(4) It is illegal for a team to adopt ploys known as:
(a) The Flying Wedge; and
(b) The Cavalry Charge
as described in Notes (xii) and (xiii).
Penalty:
Penalty kick at the place of the original infringement.

Notes:
(iii) "Playing the man without the ball" and all forms of dangerous tackling including early, late, and stiff arm "tackling" or tackling or attempting to tackle a player around the neck or head or above the line of the shoulders must be punished severely. Players who willfully resort to this type of foul play must be ordered off the field. Advantage should be played, but a penalty try must be awarded if the dangerous tackle prevents a probable try (P.K.).
(iv) It is for the referee to decide what constitutes a dangerous tackle, having regard to the circumstances, e.g., the apparent intentions of the tackler, or the nature of the tackle, or the defenseless position of the player being tackled or knocked over, which may be the cause of

➡ *page 60*

continued from page 59

serious injury.

(v) The following actions constitute dangerous play:

(a) If a player charges or knocks down an opponent carrying the ball without any attempt to tackle him;

(b) If a player taps or pulls the foot or feet of another player who is jumping in a line-out;

(c) If a player attempts to tackle a player who, when fielding a kick in open play, is off the ground jumping for the ball.

(vi) A player shall not "take the law into his own hands" nor willfully do anything that is dangerous to an opponent even if the latter is infringing the laws.

(vii) If a player is obstructed after kicking the ball and the ball strikes a goalpost, the optional penalty should be awarded where the ball alights after bouncing off the post.

(viii) If a penalty kick has been awarded and, before the kick has been taken, the offending team infringes Law 26(2)(i), the referee should:

(a) caution or order off the player guilty of misconduct; and

(b) in addition advance the mark for the penalty kick 10 m (33 ft), this to cover both the original infringement and the misconduct.

(ix) If a penalty kick is awarded to a team and before the kick is taken, a player of that team infringes Law 26(3)(i) the referee should:

(a) caution or order off the player guilty of misconduct; and

(b) declare the penalty kick void; and

(c) award a penalty kick against the team last guilty of misconduct.

(x) The referee should note that:

(a) Repeated infringement is a question of fact and not a question of whether the offender intended to infringe;

(b) If the same player has to be penalized repeatedly he should be dealt with under Law 26(2)(d);

(c) Foul play must not be condoned;

(d) Repeated infringements arise mainly in connection with scrummages, offside and line-outs, tackles, rucks, and mauls. If a player has been penalized for infringing one of these laws several times in the same match, he should be cautioned and, if he repeats the offense, ordered off;

(e) It is a question for the referee whether or not a series of the same offenses by different players of a team amounts to repeated infringement. If he considers that it does, he should give a general warning to that team and, if the offense is repeated, he must order the next offending player off the field;

(f) In deciding the number of offenses that should constitute "repeated infringement," as indicated in (d) and (e) above, the referee should always apply a strict standard in representative and senior matches. On the third occasion a caution must be given.

In the case of junior or minor matches where ignorance of the laws and lack of skill may account for many infringements, a less strict standard may be applied.

(xi) The International Board and the Unions in membership with it willfully support referees in the strict and uniform enforcement of the law as to repeated infringements.

(xii) Flying Wedge.

This move usually occurs close to the opponent's goal line when a penalty kick or a free kick is awarded to the attacking team, and is initiated by a player either tapping the ball to himself or receiving a short pass, and then driving toward the goal line with his colleagues binding on to either side of him in a V or wedge formation. Frequently the player is isolated illegally by those of his own team in front of him. The dangers inherent in this formation are not for those initiating the move but for those trying to stop it.

(xiii) The Cavalry Charge.

A cavalry charge usually occurs when a penalty kick or free kick is awarded to the attacking team close to the opponents' goal line. Players of the attacking team line up behind the kicker, spacing themselves across the field in gaps of a meter or two. On a signal from the kicker they begin to charge forward. Only when they are close to the kicker does he tap kick the ball and pass it to one of them. The defending team has to remain behind a line 10 m (33 ft) from the mark of their own goal line (if nearer) until the ball has been kicked. The move is potentially dangerous.

Players Ordered Off

A player who is ordered off shall take no further part in the match.

Law 27 Penalty Kick

A penalty kick is a kick awarded to the non-offending team as stated in the laws.

It may be taken by any player of the non-offending team and by any form of kick provided that the kicker, if holding the ball, must propel it out of his hands or, if the ball is on the ground, he must propel it a visible distance from the mark.

(1) The non-offending team has the option of taking a scrummage at the mark and shall put in the ball.

(2) When a penalty kick is taken the following shall apply:

(a) the kick must be taken without undue delay;

(b) the kick must be taken at or behind the mark on a line through the mark and the kicker may place the ball for a place-kick. If the place prescribed by the laws for the award of a penalty kick is within 5 m (16 ft) of the opponents' goal line, the mark for the penalty kick or a scrummage taken instead of it shall be 5 m from the goal line on a line through that place;

(c) the kicker may kick the ball in any direction and he may play the ball again, without any restriction, except that if he has indicated to the referee that he intends to attempt a kick at goal or has taken any action indicating such intention he must not kick the ball in any other way. A player kicking for touch may only punt or drop-kick the ball. Any indication of intention is irrevocable;

(d) the kicker's team, except the placer for a placekick, must be behind the ball until it has been kicked. However, retiring players of the kicker's team who are in front of the ball will not be penalized if their failure to retire is due to the rapidity with which the kick has been taken but they must not stop retiring and must not enter the game until they have been made onside by an action of their own team as required by Law 25 (1);

(e) the opposing team must run without delay (and continue to do so while the kick is being taken and while the ball is being played by the kicker's team) to or behind a line parallel to the goal lines and 10 m (33 ft) from the mark, or to their own goal line if nearer to the mark. If a kick at goal is taken they must there remain motionless with their hands by their sides until the kick has been taken.

Retiring players will not be penalized if their failure to retire 10 m (33 ft) is due to the rapidity with which the kick has been taken, but they must not stop retiring and must not enter the game until they have retired 10 m (33 ft) back from where the penalty kick was awarded, or until one of their own team who was at least 10 m (33 ft) from the mark has run in front of them.

(f) the opposing team must not willfully resort to any action which may delay the taking of a penalty kick. This includes actions such as willfully carrying, throwing or kicking the ball away out of the reach of the kicker or interfering with him;

Penalty:

• For an infringement by the kicker's team—a scrummage at the mark.

• For an infringement by the opposing team—a penalty kick 10 m (33 ft) in front of the mark or 5 m (16 ft) from the goal line whichever is the nearer, on a line through the mark. Any player of the non-offending team may take the kick.

Notes:

(i) The kick must be taken with the ball which was in play unless the referee decides that the ball is defective.

(ii) the use of sand, sawdust, or an approved kicking tee is permitted for placing the ball.

(iii) A player taking a penalty kick may not bounce the ball on his knee. The kick must be made with the foot or lower leg. If a player fails to kick the ball, a scrummage should be ordered.

(iv) In addition to the general provision regarding waste of time, the kicker is bound to kick without delay, under penalty.

The instructions in the second paragraphs of note (i) on Law 13 apply also in the case of a penalty kick.

Even without a caution, if the delay is clearly a breach of law the kick should be disallowed and a scrummage ordered.

(vi) If the kicker appears to be about to take a kick at goal, the referee may ask him to state his intention.

(vii) If the kicker is taking a kick at goal, all players of the opposing team must remain passive from the time the kicker commences his run until the kick has been taken.

(viii) When a penalty kick is taken in in-goal, a penalty try shall be awarded if a defending player by foul play prevents an opponent from first grounding the ball.

(ix) If, from a penalty kick taken in in-goal, the ball travels into touch-in-goal, or over the dead-ball line, a 5-m scrummage should be ordered, the attacking team to put in the ball.

(x) If the kicker takes a dropkick and a goal results, the goal stands even though the kicker has not indicated to the referee an intention to kick at goal.

(xi) If, notwithstanding a prior infringement by the opposing team, a goal is kicked, the goal should be awarded instead of a further penalty kick.

(xii) The referee should not award a further penalty if he is satisfied that the reason for such further penalty has been deliberately contrived by the kicker's team, but should allow play to continue. If the referee awards a further penalty, the penalty kick should not be taken before the referee has made the mark indicating the place of the penalty.

Law 28 Free Kick

A free kick is a kick awarded for a fair catch or to the non-offending team as stated in the laws. A goal may not be scored from a free kick.

The team awarded a free kick may not score a dropped goal until after the ball next becomes dead or an opposing player has played the ball or has tackled an opponent or a maul has been formed.

A free kick awarded for an infringement may be taken by any player of the non-offending team.

A free kick may be taken by any form of kick, unless kicking for touch, provided that the kicker, if holding the ball must propel it out of his hands, or, if the ball is on the ground he must propel it a visible distance from the mark.

(1) The team awarded a free kick has the option of taking a scrummage at the mark and shall put in the ball.

(2) When a kick is taken, it must be taken without undue delay.

(3) and (4) *As with Law 27 (2b).*

(5) The kicker may kick the ball in any direction and he may play the ball again without restriction. A player kicking for touch may only punt or drop-kick the ball.

(6) *As with Law 27 (2d).*

(7) The opposing team must not willfully resort to any action that may delay the taking of a free kick. This includes actions such as willfully carrying, throwing, or kicking the ball away out of reach

of the kicker.

(8) The opposing team must retire without delay to or behind a line parallel to the goal lines and 10 m (33 ft) from the mark or to their own goal line if nearer to the mark, or 5 m (16 ft) from their opponents' goal line if the mark is in in-goal. Having so retired, players of the opposing team may charge with a view to preventing the kick, as soon as the kicker begins his run or offers to kick.

Retiring players will not be penalized if their failure to retire 10 m is due to the rapidity with which the kick has been taken, but they must not stop retiring and must not enter the game until they have retired 10 m back from where the free kick was awarded, or until one of their own team who was at least 10 m from the mark has run in front of them.

(9) If, having charged fairly, players of the opposing team prevent the kick being taken, it is void.

(10) Neither the kicker nor the placer shall willfully do anything which may lead the opposing team to charge prematurely. If either does so, the charge shall not be disallowed.

Penalty:

• For an infringement by the kicker's team or for a void kick— a scrummage at the mark and the opposing team shall put in the ball.

If the mark is in-goal, the scrummage shall be awarded 5 m (16 ft) from the goal line on a line through the mark.

• For an infringement by the opposing team—a free kick 10 m (33 ft) in front of the mark or 5 m (16 ft) from the goal line whichever is nearer on a line through the mark. Any player of the non-offending team may take the kick.

Notes:

(i) *As with Law 27 (2), note (i).*

(ii) *As with Law 27 (2), note (iii).*

(iii) The kicker may not feint to kick and then draw back. Once he makes any movement to kick, the opponents may charge.

(iv) *As with Law 27 (2), note (iv).*

(v) The referee shall see that the opposing players do not gradually creep up and that they have both feet behind the 10-meter line, otherwise he shall award a penalty in accordance with the penalty provisions of Law 28.

(vi) If the kick is taken from behind the goal line, the ball is in play if an opponent legitimately plays it before it crosses the goal

line, and a try may be scored.

(vii) *As with Law 27 (2), note (viii).*

(viii) *As with Law 27 (2), note (ix).*

(ix) If opponents lawfully charge down a free kick in the playing area, play should be allowed to continue.

(x) If a free kick has been awarded in the field of play and the player retires to his in-goal to take the kick and his opponents having lawfully charged prevent the kick from being taken, a scrummage shall be awarded 5 m (16 ft) from the goal line on a line through the mark.

(xi) If a free kick has been awarded in in-goal and the opponents having lawfully charged prevent the kick from being taken, a scrummage shall be awarded 5 m (16 ft) from the goal line on a line through the mark.

(xii) If the referee is satisfied that the reason for a free kick under the penalty provisions has been contrived, he should allow play to continue. If the referee

awards a further penalty, the free kick should not be taken before the referee has made the mark indicating the place of the free kick.

These laws are reprinted by permission of the International Rugby Football Board. For a complete copy of the Laws of the Game of Rugby Football, including Laws 1–6, various accompanying notes and Under–19 Variations, contact the IRFB.

Field hockey

Essentials

Although primarily a women's game in the United States, this sport is played by both men and women internationally. Fast and even dangerous, it requires skill, energy, and teamwork.

Crossbar not to exceed sideways beyond goalposts
2 in wide, 3 in deep

7 ft

4 yds

2 in wide, 3 in deep

Front face must touch outer edge of back line

Back line

25 yds

5 yds

5 yds

16 yds

4 yds

25 yds line

Sideline

Center line

100 yds

Penalty spot

Shooting circle

5 yds

7 yds

60 yds

The goals

The goalposts and crossbar are white and rectangular, with a loosely fitted net. The whole structure is positioned at the center of each back-line.

The ball

Spherical, hard, of any material. Must weigh between $5\frac{1}{2}$ and $5\frac{3}{4}$ oz and have a circumference of $8\frac{13}{16}$ –$9\frac{1}{4}$ in (224–235 mm). Usually white.

The stick

Must weigh between 12 and 28 ounces and be able to pass through a 5.1 cm (interior diameter) ring. It has a curved wooden head no more than 4 in in length (measured from the lowest part of the flat face) and a flat face on the left hand side only.

The field

A grass or artificial surface, rectangular, 100 yards long and 60 yards wide. Flagposts between 4 and 5 ft high are placed at each 25 yds line and at each corner of the field.

Teams

Each of two teams fields 11 players. Substitution of one player for another is freely allowed.

Officials

Two umpires.

Hockey sticks
Most adults use a stick around three feet long. Only one side of the wooden head is flat; the flat side is the one used to strike the ball.

Dress

Shirt and shorts or a skirt. Players of the same team wear uniform clothing, except for the goalie, who wears (over any protection) a jersey of a color different from that worn by his or her teammates and the opposition.

Shin protection
For most of the players no special clothing is needed. However, players usually wear plastic or foam shin guards beneath their socks.

Saving the goalkeeper
Hockey balls are very hard and so goalies wear protective clothing, including helmet, pads, hand protectors, and shin guards.

Team extras
Each team is allowed 11 players on the field at any one time, but up to five substitutes may swap with players on the field throughout a match.

How to play

Both teams fight for possession of the ball using sticks, hoping to hit it down the field into the opposition's goal while blocking the opposition's attempts to do the same.

Starting

The winner of the toss chooses between possession of the ball at the start of the game and which end to attack first. The first pass is made from the center of the field by a player of the team that has possession of the ball. All the opposing team's players must be at least 5 yds away from the ball, and all players must be in their own half of the field. The pass is made back into the player's own half to a team member who hits it in an attacking direction.

How to win

The team scoring the highest number of goals by shooting the ball into the opposition's goal, from somewhere inside the shooting circle, wins the game.

Key rules

• A game consists of two halves of 35 minutes, with a half-time interval of five to 10 minutes.

• Goals can only be scored from shots taken inside the scoring circle.

• A number of rules are concerned with maintaining a high level of safety. Players must not play the ball with their sticks any higher than shoulder height, or raise their sticks in a dangerous manner when approaching the ball. It is also against the rules to kick, charge, or hold an opponent, or to use the stick to prevent an opponent from playing the ball. *See Rule 13, Conduct of Play (page 65).*

• The penalty incurred by an infringement of the rules depends on where it occurred and how serious it was. Generally, the penalty is a free hit to the opposition, but if, a defender intentionally prevents a goal from being scored, the opposition will be awarded a penalty stroke, in which an attacking player gets to take an unobstructed shot at the goalie. Another penalty is the penalty corner—for unintentional offenses inside the defender's own circle, or for intentional offenses within the 25-yards area but outside the circle. Here, an attacking player gets to put the ball into play from the opposition's back line. Goals cannot be scored directly from a penalty corner. *See Rule 14, Penalties (page 65)*

• In cases of extreme misconduct, the umpire may suspend a player for a period of time not less than five minutes. During this period, the player's team must play with one fewer person on the field. If the suspended player is the goalie, another player takes up that position, but the team must still have one fewer person on the field.

• Called a "bully" internationally, a *face-off* is used when both teams breach the rules simultaneously, or when play has to be stopped due to injury or other unforeseen circumstances. Two players (one from each team) face one another with their own back line to their right and the ball on the ground between them. The players tap their sticks on the ground and then against each other's sticks alternately three times, after which both are free to try and play the ball. *See Rule 10.4, Bully (page 64).*

Grass surface kings
In the past, international hockey used to be dominated by teams such as India and Pakistan who were masters on grass surfaces. Now that the international game is more often played on artificial surfaces, such countries have lost their dominance. Artificial surfaces create a far faster, more accurate game with fewer errors in ball control and passing.

FIELD HOCKEY THE RULES

I: Field and Equipment Section

Rule 1 Field of play
Rule 2 Goals
Rule 3 The ball
Rule 4 The stick
Rule 5 Player' dress and equipment *See page 62.*

II: Teams, Captains, and Umpires

6. Teams

6.1 A game shall be played between two teams of not more than 16 players each, but not more than 11 players of each team shall be on the field at the same time. Each team is permitted to substitute from the maximum of 16 players.

6.2 Substitution:

a. no limit to the number of players who may be substituted at the same time nor to the number of times any player may substitute or be substituted.

b. substitution of a player may be made only after a player from the same team has left the field.

c. time shall not be stopped for substitutions except for goalkeepers.

d. substitutes shall not be permitted for suspended players during their suspension.

e. after completing a suspension, a player may be substituted without first returning to the field.

f. players leaving or entering the field shall do so at the center line or such other place on the side of the field decided by the umpires before the game.

6.3 Each team must have one goalkeeper on the field:

a. an incapacitated or suspended goalkeeper shall be replaced immediately by another goalkeeper.

b. where no substitute goalkeeper is available, the field player replacing the goalkeeper must wear protective headgear and a shirt of a color different from those of either team and shall be permitted to put on, without time-wasting, other protective equipment.

c. during the suspension of a goalkeeper, the team must have one less player on the field.

6.4 During play only players and umpires may be on the field unless authorized by the umpire.

7. Captains

7.1 Each team must have a captain on the field who must wear a distinctive armband.

7.2 Captains shall:

a. toss a coin; the winner shall have choice of ends or possession of the ball to start the game.

b. indicate to the umpires any replacement captain.

c. be responsible for the substitution of players.

d. be responsible for the behavior of all their team players.

8. Umpires

Two umpires shall control the game and apply the rules; they are the sole judges of fair play. Players and substitutes, whether on or off the field, including any period of temporary or permanent suspension, are under the jurisdiction of the umpires.

8.1 Umpires shall be:

a. primarily responsible for the decisions in their half of the field, for the whole of the game without changing ends.

b. responsible for ensuring that the full or agreed time is played and for indicating the end of the first half and of the game if time is prolonged for completion of the penalty corner.

c. solely responsible for decisions on the ball going out of play for the full length of their nearer sideline and back line.

d. solely responsible for decisions on corners, penalty corners, penalty strokes, and goals in their own half and free hits in their own circle.

e. responsible for keeping a written record of goals scored and warnings/suspensions.

f. debarred from coaching during a game and during half-time.

8.2 Umpires shall blow the whistle to:

a. start/end each half of the game.

b. enforce a penalty.

c. start/end a penalty stroke.

d. indicate, when necessary, that the ball has passed wholly outside the field.

e. signal a goal.

f. restart the game after a goal has been scored or awarded.

g. restart the game after a penalty stroke in which a goal was not scored or awarded.

h. stop the game for any other reason and restart after such a stoppage.

III: Application of the Rules of the Game

9. Duration of Play

Two periods of 35 minutes each unless otherwise agreed:

a. halftime: 5 to 10 minutes as agreed: teams change ends.

b. each half starts when the umpire blows the whistle for the pass.

10. To Start and Restart the Game

10.1 Center pass:

a. played from the center of the field.

b. a push or hit may be played in any direction; all players other than the player making the pass shall be in their half of the field.

c. made at the start of the game, by a player of the team which did not choose ends.

d. after halftime, by a player of the team that did not start the game.

e. after a goal, by a player of the team against which the goal was scored or awarded.

10.2 Center pass and putting the ball back into play:

a. all opponents at least 5 yds from the ball.

Mandatory Experiment

a. no player of either team, other than the taker, shall be within 5 yds of the ball when the ball is put back into play from within the 25-yards area; no player of the opposing team shall be within 5 yds of the ball when the ball is put back into play from between the 25-yards lines.

b. the ball to be pushed or hit.

c. the ball must move at least 1 yd.

d. after playing the ball, the player may not do so again nor remain or approach within playing distance of it until it has been played by another player.

e. the ball shall not be raised intentionally or such as to be dangerous or lead to dangerous play.

10.3 Ball outside the field:

When the ball passes completely over the sideline or back line it shall be out of play and it or another ball shall be used to restart play.

10.3.1 Over the sideline:

a. on the sideline close to where the ball went out of play

b. the player playing the ball is not required to be wholly inside or outside the sideline

c. taken by a player of the opposing team.

10.3.2 Over the back line: by the attack when no goal is scored:

a. up to 16 yds from and opposite where, or close to where, it crossed the back line, in line parallel to the sideline.

b. taken by a defender.

10.3.3 Over the back line unintentionally by the defense when no goal is scored:

a. on the back line up to 5 yds from the corner flag nearest to where the ball crossed the back line.

Mandatory Experiment

a. on the sideline 5 yds from the corner flag nearest to where the ball crossed the back line.

b. taken by an attacker.

10.3.4 Over the back line: intentionally by the defense when no goal is scored:

a. on the back line from a spot 10 yds from the nearer goalpost on whichever side the attacking team prefers.

b. taken by an attacker. That is, a penalty corner.

10.4 Bully (or Face-Off):

10.4.1 The game shall be restarted with a bully when:

a. the ball in play has to be replaced.

b. there is a simultaneous breach of the rules by both teams.

c. the ball is lodged in a goalkeeper's pad or player's or umpire's clothing.

d. when time has been stopped for an injury or any other reason and there has been no offense.

10.4.2 The bully:

a. on a spot chosen by the umpire but not within 16 yds of the back line.

b. a player of each team

The Face-Off (or "Bully")

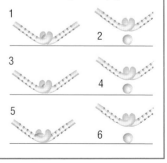

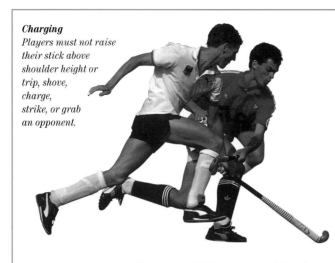

Charging
Players must not raise their stick above shoulder height or trip, shove, charge, strike, or grab an opponent.

shall face one another with their own back line to their right.

c. ball shall be on the ground between the two players.

d. the two players tap the ground with their stick to the right of the ball then the flat face of the opponent's stick over the ball, three times alternately, after which either player may play the ball to put it into play.

e. all other players at least 5 yds away until the ball is in play.

11. Scoring a Goal

a. a goal is scored when the ball is played in the circle by an attacker and does not go outside the circle before passing completely over the goal line and under the crossbar.

b. the ball may be played by or touch the stick or body of a defender before or after being played in the circle by an attacker.

c. after a stoppage of play inside the circle, the ball must again be played from inside the circle by an attacker before a goal can be scored.

d. a goal shall be awarded if a goalkeeper breaches the Penalty Stroke Rules preventing a goal being scored.
e. the team scoring the greater number of goals shall be the winner.

12. Offside

12.1 Players are in an offside position if, at the moment the ball is passed or played to them by a member of their team, they are:

a. in their opponents' 25-yard area and

b. in front of the ball and

c. nearer the back line than two opponents.

12.2 Players so positioned are not committing an offense unless the ball is passed to them or they gain an advantage for their team. Players level with the second defender (i.e., the one furthest from the goal) are NOT offside. Players off the field next to the 25-yards area or behind their opponents' back line can be in offside positions.
Mandatory Experiment
There is no offside.

13. Conduct of Play

Unless played with consideration for others, hockey can be a dangerous game. These Rules prohibit or explain actions which affect the safety of all players. Players shall not:

13.1.1 Use of the stick and playing equipment.

a. play the ball intentionally with the back of the stick.

b. take part in or interfere with the game unless they have their stick in their hand.

c. play the ball above shoulder height with any part of the stick.

d. lift their sticks over the heads of players.

e. raise their sticks in a manner that is dangerous, intimidating, or hampering to other players when approaching, attempting to play or playing the ball.

f. play the ball dangerously

or in such a way as to be likely to lead to dangerous play. A ball is dangerous when it causes legitimate evasive action by players.

g. hit, hook, charge, kick, shove, trip, strike at, or grab another player or their stick or clothing.

h. throw any object or piece of playing equipment on to the field, at the ball, at another player, or at an umpire.

13.1.2 Use of body, hands, feet

a. stop or catch the ball with the hand.

There is nothing to prevent players using their hands to protect themselves from dangerously raised balls.

b. intentionally stop, kick, propel, pick up, throw, or carry the ball with any part of their bodies.

It is not an offense if the ball hits the foot or body of a player unless that player:
•has moved into the path of the ball, or
•made no effort to avoid being hit, or
•was positioned with the clear intention of stopping the ball, or
•gains undue benefit.
Players should not be penalized when the ball is played at them from a short distance.

c. use the foot or leg to support the stick in a tackle.
Mandatory Experiment

d. intentionally enter their opponents' goal, or stand on their opponents' goal line.

e. intentionally run behind either goal.

13.1.3 Raised ball

a. intentionally raise the ball from a hit except for a shot at goal.

b. intentionally raise the ball so that it lands directly in the circle.

Not every ball entering the circle off the ground is forbidden. A ball that bounces into or lands in the circle after a short distance must be

judged solely on the intent or danger.

A ball raised over a player's stick or body when on the ground, even in the circle, must be judged solely on danger.

c. approach within 5 yds of a player receiving a falling raised ball until it has been played and is on the ground.

d. raise the ball at another player.

13.1.4 Obstruction
obstruct an opponent from attempting to play the ball by:
•moving or interposing themselves or their sticks.
•shielding the ball with their sticks or any part of their bodies.
•physically interfering with the sticks or bodies of opponents.

13.1.5 Time-Wasting
delay play by time-wasting.
13.2 Goalkeepers may, when the ball is inside their own circle:

a. use their stick, kickers, or pads to propel the ball, or any part of their bodies including the hands to stop but not propel or lie on the ball, provided such action is not dangerous or likely to lead to dangerous play.

A goalkeeper lying on the ball should be considered under the obstruction rule.

b. stop or deflect the ball with the stick above their shoulder unless dangerous or likely to lead to dangerous play.

c. deflect the ball over the crossbar or around the goal-posts with the face of the stick or off any part of the body.
13.3 If the ball

a. strikes an umpire or any loose object on the field, including any piece of playing equipment dropped unintentionally, the game shall continue.

14. Penalties

Advantage: a penalty shall be awarded only when a player or team has been clearly disadvantaged by an opponent's offense.
14.1 A free hit shall be awarded for:

a. an offense by an attacker within the opponents' 25-yards area.

b. an unintentional offense by the defense outside their circle within their own 25-yards area.

Player (2) is playing the ball. Player (1) is offside on three counts.

➡ *page 68*

POSITIONS AND SKILLS

A team assigns players to one of four positions: forward, midfielder, defender, and goalkeeper—although these roles are flexible enough to meet the demands of whatever strategy is chosen. All players require stick control and co-ordination to receive the ball, bring it under control, and then

Swivel stick
The ball can only be played with the left face of the stick so players must be adept at turning the stick to hit a ball on their left-hand side.

Dribble masters
Players from Asia used to dazzle opponents with their dribbling skills on grass surfaces. But long dribbles are relatively rare on the modern artificial surfaces that many international matches are played on.

pass or dribble it quickly and accurately.

Forwards must be able to shoot well—and quickly—to take advantage of any opportunity to score. Midfielders are very much team players, supporting both the attack and the defense as needed. They must constantly be aware of other players' positions on the field. Stamina, anticipation, and passing skills are all important. Defenders remain largely toward the back of their end of the field.

Marking (hanging close to an opponent and hampering efforts to play the ball) and tackling the ball are the basic elements of defensive play. The goalkeeper requires particular skills. Any part of the body or the stick may be used to stop the ball, so this player needs to be extremely agile, quick, and able to concentrate at all times. The goalkeeper is also responsible for coordinating the team's defense, surveying the game, and calling instructions out to the players in front of him.

TACTICS

There are two systems commonly used to position players on the field. The 5-3-2-1 configuration (5 forwards, 3 midfielders, 2 defenders and a goalkeeper) is the first. Another is the "sweeper" variation, which uses this configuration: 3-3-3-1. It is so named for one of the defenders who is positioned behind the other two (but in front of the goalkeeper) in order to "sweep" up any balls or opponents that get through the defense.

Lay down
One way of robbing an opponent of the ball is to slam down the stick in front of him. Such a tackle can be hard on the knuckles.

Left-hand dribble
Skillful players can often carry the ball past a defender by reversing the stick.

Jab tackle
A jab tackle is made when an opponent is still in front. The idea is to surprise the opponent by twisting the stick so that the back faces the ground and then jab it at the ball.

From the left
Tackling from the left side can be really awkward but if it has to be done, hold the stick in the left hand and twist the grip to point the toe downwards. Then use the toe to drag the ball away.

Open-side tackle
An open-side tackle is a conventional tactic. Often the best technique is to run with the dribbler until an error is made.

GRAY AREAS

Penalties for fouls vary greatly, depending not only on where they are committed, but also whether they are committed intentionally or not. An umpire is responsible, therefore, for making an often difficult distinction in an instant.

In an attempt to help the flow of the game (which is often interrupted by whistles), some governing bodies are experimenting with doing away with the offside rule.

Getting some stick
The sheer speed of field hockey and the force with which the sticks are often swung around means that injuries are frequent. The problem for the umpire is to decide whether a blow was deliberate or not.

Reverse-side tackle
With the reverse-side tackle, the idea is to trap the ball against the turf so that the attacker's momentum carries him past the ball.

Pushover
One of the most dynamic passing strokes is the "slap push." This involves a long swing at the ball with the right hand some way down the stick.

Dangerous play

Charging

Tripping

continued from page 65

c. any offense by any player between the 25-yards lines.

14.2 A penalty corner shall be awarded for:

a. an intentional offense by the defense within their 25-yards area but outside the circle.

b. an intentional offense by a defender in the circle which neither prevents a goal being scored nor deprives an attacker of actual or likely possession of the ball.

c. an unintentional offense by the defense in their circle that does not prevent the probable scoring of a goal

d. the defense intentionally playing the ball over their back line.

14.3 A penalty stroke shall be awarded for:

a. an intentional offense by a defender in the circle to prevent a goal being scored or to deprive an attacker of actual or likely possession of the ball.

b. an unintentional offense by a defender in the circle that prevents the probable scoring of a goal.

c. persistent early breaking off the back line by defenders at penalty corners.

14.4 If there is another offense before the awarded penalty has been taken, the penalty may be progressed up to 10 yds (9 m), upgraded, and/or dealt with as misconduct or reversed if committed by the previously benefiting team.

15. Procedures for Penalties
15.1 Free hit

a. more than 5 yds from the circle: close to where the offense occurred. "Close to" allows the free hit to be taken within playing distance of where the offense occurred. It is intended that no undue advantage be gained but the flow of the game be maintained.

b. outside the circle: to the defense within 16 yds (14.6 m) of the back line up to 16 yds from the back line in line with the offense, parallel to the sideline.

c. inside the circle: to the defense: anywhere within the circle or, outside it, up to 16 yds from the back line in line with the offense, parallel to the sideline.

d. within 5 yds (4.5 m) of the circle: to the attack: close to where the offense occurred: all players of both teams other than the taker to be at least 5 yds from the ball.

e. the ball must be stationary.

f. the striker shall push or hit the ball: it must move at least a yard before another player of the same team is allowed to play the ball.

g. the ball shall not be raised intentionally or in such a way as to be dangerous or likely to lead to dangerous play.

h. after playing the ball, the striker may not play the ball again or approach within playing distance of it until it has been played by another player.

i. no player of the opposing team shall be within 5 yds of the ball.

If a player is standing within 5 yds of the ball in order to gain an advantage, the free hit need not be delayed.

Mandatory Experiment

i. no player of either team, other than the taker, shall be within 5 yds of the ball for free hits taken inside the 25-yards area; no player of the opposing team shall be within 5 yds of the ball for free hits taken between the 25-yards lines.

15.2 Penalty corner:
15.2.1

a. an attacker shall push or hit the ball, without intentionally raising it, from a spot on the back line 10 yds from the goalpost on whichever side the attacking team prefers.

b. the player taking the hit must have at least one foot outside the field.

c. no other player shall be within 5 yds of the ball.

d. the remaining attackers shall be on the field with sticks, hands, and feet not touching the ground inside the circle.

e. not more than five defenders including the goalkeeper shall be behind the back line with their sticks, hands, and feet not touching the ground inside the circle.

f. the remaining defenders shall be beyond the center line.

g. until the ball has been played, no attacker other than the one taking the hit may enter the circle, nor may a defender cross the center line or back line.

h. the attacker taking the hit may not play the ball again nor remain or approach within playing distance of it until it has been played by another player.

i. no shot at goal shall be made until the ball be stopped or come to rest on the ground outside the circle.

j. the ball may be passed or deflected by the attackers but if it remains within 5 yds of the circle must be stopped or come to rest on the ground outside the circle before a shot at goal is made.

k. if the first shot at goal is a hit, the ball must cross the goal line at a height of not more than 18 in (the height of the backboard) for a goal to be scored, unless it touches the stick or body of a defender during its travel toward goal.

l. for flicks, deflections and scoops, and second and subsequent hits at goal, the ball may be raised to any height subject to there being no danger.

m. the attacker putting the ball into play may not score directly even if the ball is played into goal by a defender.

n. if the ball travels more than 5 yds (4.5 m) from the circle, the penalty corner rules no longer apply.

15.2.2 The penalty corner may be given again when:

a. defenders stand with feet, hands, and/or sticks touching the ground inside the circle.

b. defenders are within 5 yds of the ball before it is played.

c. defenders cross the back line or center line before the ball is played.

Free hit
During a free hit no opponent may be within 5 yards of the ball.

Attackers entering the circle before the ball is played should be penalized by a free hit.

Mandatory experiment

15.2.3 At halftime and fulltime the game shall be prolonged to permit completion of a penalty corner. For this purpose the penalty corner shall be considered completed when:

a. a goal is scored

b. an attacker breaches any rule

c. a defender commits a breach of a rule except that if another penalty corner or penalty stroke is awarded the game shall be prolonged again to permit completion of the penalty

d. the ball travels more than 5 yards from the circle

e. the ball is played out of the circle over the back line by an attacker or unintentionally by a defender

f. the ball goes out of the circle over the circle line again (i.e., for the second time after the initial injection from the back line)

15.3 Penalty stroke

15.3.1 Taking:

a. time shall be stopped when a penalty stroke is signaled and restarted when the whistle is blown for resumption of play.

b. the player taking the stroke shall stand close to and behind the ball prior to commencing the stroke.

c. all players, other than the defending goalkeeper, shall stand beyond the nearer 25-yards line, on the field, and shall not influence the situation.

d. the defending goalkeeper shall continue to wear protective headgear.

e. the defending goalkeeper shall stand with both feet on the goal line and shall not leave the goal line or move either foot until the ball has been played.

f. the player may not take the stroke until the controlling umpire confirms that both the stroke taker and the goalkeeper are ready and has blown the whistle.

g. the ball may be pushed, flicked, or scooped from the penalty spot.

h. the ball may be raised to any height.

i. the player may touch the ball only once and subsequently shall not approach either the ball or the goalkeeper.

j. in the process of taking the stroke, the player may take one step forward but the rear foot may not pass the front one until the ball has been played.

k. the player may not feint at playing the ball.

l. the defending goalkeeper shall not remove unnecessarily any protective equipment in order solely to gain time.

m. a penalty goal may be awarded by the umpire without the ball crossing the goal line when a goalkeeper breaches the rules to prevent a goal being scored.

15.3.2 Ending:

a. a goal is scored or awarded.

b. the ball comes to rest inside the circle, lodges in the goalkeeper's pad, is caught by the goalkeeper, passes outside the circle or the stroke-taker breaches the rules and a goal is not scored or awarded.

15.3.3 Restarting the game after a penalty stroke:

a. if a goal was scored or awarded: by a center pass.

b. if a goal was not scored or awarded: a push or a hit by a defender 16 yds in front of the center of the goal line.

15.3.4 Penalties:

a. free hit: for an offense by the stroke-taker, taken 16 yds in front of the center of the goal line.

b. goal awarded: for a breach of the rules by the goalkeeper that prevents a goal being scored.

c. penalty stroke: may be taken again for an offense by any player of either team.

15.4 Personal penalties:

a. for rough or dangerous play, misconduct, or any intentional offense, the umpire may award the appropriate penalty and may:

• caution the offending player.

• warn the offending player: green card.

• temporarily suspend the offending player for a minimum of five minutes of playing time: yellow card.

• permanently suspend the offending player: red card.

b. temporarily suspended players shall remain in a designated place until permitted by the umpire who suspended them to resume play.

c. temporarily suspended players may rejoin their team at halftime, then return to the designated place to complete their suspension.

d. permanently suspended players shall not remain within the playing facility or its surrounds.

16. Accidents/Injuries

a. if a goal is scored before the game is stopped it shall be allowed if it would have been scored had the accident not occurred.

b. if a player is incapacitated, the umpire may stop the game.

c. an injured or bleeding player should leave the field as soon as it is safe to do so and receive treatment off the field unless medical reasons prevent this.

d. players shall not return to the field until their wounds have been dressed and no player remain on, enter, or re-enter the field wearing blood stained clothing.

e. if an umpire is incapacitated, the game shall be stopped; if injured and cannot continue, should be replaced.

f. the game shall be restarted with a face-off, with the appropriate penalty or with a center pass if a goal was scored.

Reprinted by permission of the International Hockey Federation.

For a complete copy of the Rules of Hockey, including Appendices A–E, contact your national governing body.

Goal!
Top goalscorers are renowned for the ability to turn tight situations near the mouth of the goal into scoring opportunities.

Ice hockey
Essentials

With the puck constantly moving at speeds of up to 100 mph, this is reputed to be the fastest game in the world. Players sport an array of protective equipment to protect themselves against the puck as well as against crashes into other players, the boards, and the ice itself.

The rink (National Hockey League)

200 ft by 85 ft, with corners rounded in the arc of a circle of radius 28 ft. Surrounded by "boards," 40–48 in in height above the ice surface. Divided in half by a red line (center line) and into three zones by two blue lines. International rinks, such as those used in the Olympics, are a few feet shorter and almost 15 feet wider.

Goal crease Face-off area
Center face-off area
11 ft
60 ft
58 ft
11 ft
5 ft
20 ft
30 ft
200 ft
85 ft

Face-offs occur at the center of the circled areas or at the spots marked "A."

Safety glass
The puck in ice hockey is hard and travels at incredible speeds, so spectators at ice hockey games are protected by a high wall of shatterproof glass or Perspex on top of the boards.

The sticks

Wood or other approved material. Maximum length 63 in from the heel to the end of the shaft, 12 ½ in from the heel to the end of the blade. The blade must be 2–3 in in width. The goalkeeper's stick is larger. It has a maximum width of 3 ½–4 ½ in at the heel and maximum length of 15 ½ in from heel to blade end. A player chooses his stick carefully and treats it with care.

The puck

Vulcanized rubber or other approved material. 1 in thick, 3 in in diameter, and 5 ½–6 ounces in weight. It is kept frozen during a game.

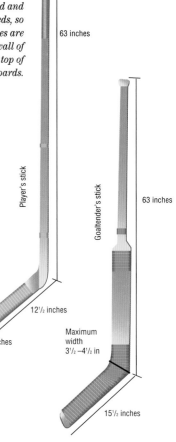

63 inches
Player's stick
Goaltender's stick
63 inches
12½ inches
2–3 inches
Maximum width 3½–4½ in
15½ inches

Ice zones
An ice hockey rink is divided into three zones: the defending zone in front of your goal; the attacking zone in front of your opponents' goal; and the neutral zone in the middle. The goal mouth is painted red so that it is clearly visible against the white ice.

48 in
72 in

The goals

Positioned 11 ft from each end of the rink and in the center of a red line 2 in wide, drawn across the width of the ice and continued up the sides of the boards (the "goal line"). Red goalposts are set 6 ft apart, extend 4 ft above the ice surface and are joined by a red crossbar. A white nylon net is attached to each goal frame. In international hockey, the goals are positioned 13 ft from each end of the rink.

Dress

Uniform throughout a team. Jerseys, short pants, socks, and skates. Jerseys feature individual identifying numbers and players' surnames. All players must wear a protective helmet. All other protective equipment, except gloves and goalkeepers' leg guards, must be worn under the uniform.

Keeping your head
With the puck moving faster than a car, head protection is absolutely vital. All players wear a helmet, and players born after 1974 must wear a visor.

Skates

Ice hockey skates have blades ⅛ in wide—thicker than those found on speed or figure skating skates. They are shorter, too.

Officials

In the NHL a referee, two linesmen, game timekeeper, penalty timekeeper, official scorer, and two goal judges.

First play

Play starts with a face-off when the referee drops the puck on the ice between the sticks of two opposing centers.

Side by side

Ice hockey is a heavy contact sport and players are free to shove an opponent off the puck. However, they are not allowed to "board check" an opponent, which means throwing them violently into the sideboards, or "charge" them, which means basically running, jumping, or charging into an opponent.

The players

Two teams of six players on the ice at a time. Not more than 18 players, excluding two goalkeepers, are permitted per team.

Playing line-up

1 goalkeeper	4 center
2 right defenseman	5 right wing
3 left defenseman	6 left wing

HOW TO PLAY

Each team attempts to score goals by hitting the puck into their opponents' goal. Players use their sticks to pass or dribble the puck across the ice. It may also be kicked, but not in order to score a goal. *See Rule 70 (page 76).*

Starting

The home team chooses an end to defend and the game then starts with a face-off in the center of the rink. Two players (one from each team) stand facing each other with the blades of their sticks on the ice, each player facing his opponent's goal. All other players must remain outside the center face-off area until the puck has been played. The referee or a linesman drops the puck on the ice between the two starting players, who each try to gain possession of it with their sticks.

Face-offs

Face-offs occur either at the center of the rink or in one of the end zone face-off spots—or at the point where an infringement occurred. A player in his attacking zone must place his blade on the ice first. Face-offs are a valuable opportunity to win control of the puck.

RULES OF ICE HOCKEY
•••••••••••••••••••

These rules are abridged and summarized. Changes from the official rules are indicated in italics.

SECTION ONE—
THE RINK
Rules 1–12
See page 70.

SECTION TWO—
TEAMS
Rules 13–18
See page 71.

SECTION THREE—
EQUIPMENT
Rules 19–24
See page 70.

SECTION FOUR—
PENALTIES
Rules 25–33B

Penalties shall be actual playing time and shall be divided into the following classes:

1. Minor penalty—the offending player (excluding the goalkeeper) is ruled off the ice for two minutes. No substitutes are allowed during this time.

2. Bench minor penalty— as above, but may be served by any player of the offending team, apart from the goalkeeper.

3. Major penalty—as above, but the player is sent off for five minutes. A third major penalty results in the player being sent off for the remainder of the game.

4. Misconduct penalty—the player (excluding the goalkeeper) is sent off for 10 minutes. A substitute is permitted.

5. Match penalty— suspension for the remainder of the game. A substitute is permitted after five minutes have elapsed.

6. Penalty shot—the Referee places the puck on the center face-off spot for the player taking the shot at goal. The player may skate with the puck toward the goal before shooting. Only the opposing goalkeeper may defend.

If a goalkeeper incurs a minor penalty, major penalty, or misconduct penalty, the penalty is served by another member of his team. However, if he incurs three major penalties in one game, a game misconduct penalty or a match penalty, he is removed

from the game and replaced by a substitute.

SECTION FIVE—
OFFICIALS
Rules 34–40A
See page 71.

SECTION SIX—PLAYING RULES

Rule 41 Abuse of Officials and Other Misconduct

a) A misconduct penalty shall be imposed on any player who uses obscene, profane, or abusive language to any person or who intentionally knocks or shoots the puck out of the reach of an Official who is retrieving it or who deliberately throws any equipment out of the playing area.

b) A minor penalty shall be assessed to any player who challenges or disputes the rulings of any Official during a game. If the player persists in such challenge or dispute, he shall be assessed a misconduct penalty and any further dispute will result in a game misconduct penalty being assessed to the offending player.

Rule 42 Adjustment to Clothing or Equipment

a) Play shall not be stopped nor the game delayed by reasons of adjustments to clothing, equipment, skates, or sticks.

For an infringement of this Rule, a minor penalty shall be given.

Rule 43 Attempt to Injure

a) A match penalty shall be imposed on any player who deliberately attempts to injure an opponent. A substitute for the penalized player shall be permitted at the end of the fifth minute.

b) A game misconduct penalty shall be imposed on any player who deliberately attempts to injure an Official, Manager, Coach, or Trainer in any manner.

Rule 44 Board Checking

a) A minor or major penalty, at the discretion of the Referee, based on the degree of violence of the impact with the boards, shall be imposed on any player who checks an opponent in such a manner that causes the

opponent to be thrown violently in the boards.

b) When a major penalty is imposed under this Rule for a foul resulting in an injury to the face or head of an opponent, a game misconduct shall be imposed.

Rule 45 Broken Stick

(a) A player without a stick may participate in the game. A player whose stick is broken may participate in the game provided he drops the broken stick. A minor penalty shall be imposed for an infraction of this Rule.

(b) A goalkeeper may continue to play with a broken stick until a stoppage of play or until he has been legally provided with a stick.

(c) A player who has lost or broken his stick may only receive a stick at his own players' bench or be handed one from a teammate on the ice, and may not receive a stick thrown on the ice from any part of the rink. A minor penalty shall be imposed for an infraction of this Rule.

Rule 46 Butt-Ending

(NOTE) Butt-ending shall mean using the end of the shaft of the stick in a jabbing motion.

(a) A double-minor penalty will be imposed on a player who attempts to butt-end an opponent.

(b) A major penalty and a game misconduct shall be imposed on a player who butt-ends an opponent.

(c) A match penalty shall be imposed on a player who injures an opponent as a result of a butt-end.

Rule 47 Charging

Charging shall mean the actions of a player who, as a

result of distance traveled, shall violently check an opponent in any manner. A charge may be the result of a check into the boards, into the goal from or in open ice.

(a) A minor or major penalty shall be imposed on a player who skates or jumps into, or charges an opponent in any manner.

Rule 48 Checking from Behind

A check from behind is a check delivered on a player who is not aware of the impending hit, therefore UNABLE TO DEFEND HIMSELF, and contact is made on the back part of the body. When a player intentionally turns his body to create contact with his back, no penalty shall be assessed.

(a) Any player who cross-checks, pushes, or charges from behind an opponent who is unable to defend himself shall be assessed a major and a game misconduct. This penalty applies anywhere on the playing surface.

Rule 49 Clipping

Clipping is the act of throwing the body, from any direction, across or below the knees of an opponent.

(a) A player may not deliver a check in a clipping manner, nor lower his own body position to deliver a check on or below an opponent's knees.

Rule 50 Cross-Checking

(NOTE) A cross-check shall

Official crash
Players hurtle around the rink so fast that even the referee sometimes gets involved in collisions.

mean a check rendered with both hands on the stick, and the extending of the arms, while the check is being delivered.

(a) A minor or major penalty, at the discretion of the Referee, shall be imposed on a player who cross-checks an opponent.

When a major penalty is assessed for cross-checking, an automatic game misconduct penalty shall be imposed on the offending player.

Rule 51 Delaying the Game

(a) A minor penalty shall be imposed on any player or goalkeeper who delays the game by deliberately shooting or batting the puck with his stick outside the playing area.

Rule 52 Deliberate Injury of Opponents

(a) A match penalty shall be imposed on a player who deliberately injures an opponent in any manner.

Rule 53 Elbowing

Elbowing shall mean the use of an extended elbow in a manner that may or may not cause injury.

(a) A minor or major penalty, at the discretion of the Referee, shall be imposed on any player who uses his elbow to foul an opponent.

(b) When a major penalty is imposed under this Rule for a foul resulting in an injury to the face or head of an opponent, a game misconduct shall be imposed.

Rule 54 Face-Offs
See page 71.

Rule 55 Falling on Puck

(a) A minor penalty shall be imposed on a player other than the goalkeeper who deliberately falls on or gathers the puck into his body.

Rule 56 Fisticuffs

An instigator of an altercation shall be a player who by his actions or demeanor demonstrates any/some of the following criteria: distance traveled; gloves off first; first punch thrown; menacing attitude or posture; verbal instigation or threats; conduct in retaliation to a prior game incident.

An altercation is a situation involving two players, with at least one to be penalized.

(a) A major penalty shall be imposed on any player who engages in fisticuffs. In addition, a minor, major, and a game misconduct, at the discretion of the Referee, shall be imposed on any player involved in fisticuffs.

Rule 57 Goals and Assists
See page 74.

Rule 58 Gross Misconduct

The Referee may impose a "GROSS MISCONDUCT" penalty on any player, Manager, Coach, or Trainer who is guilty of gross misconduct of any kind. Any person incurring a gross misconduct penalty shall be suspended for the balance of the game.

Rule 59 Handling Puck with Hands

(a) If a player, except a goalkeeper, closes his hand on the puck, the play shall be stopped and a minor penalty shall be imposed on him. A goalkeeper who holds the puck for longer than three seconds shall be given a minor penalty unless he is actually being checked by an opponent.

Rule 60 Head-Butting

(a) A double minor penalty

shall be imposed on a player who attempts to head-butt an opponent.

(b) A major and a game misconduct penalty shall be imposed on a player who head-butts an opponent.

Rule 61 High Sticks

A high stick is one which is carried above the height of the opponent's shoulders. A player is permitted accidental contact on an opponent if the act is committed as a normal follow through of a shooting action.

(a) Any contact made by a stick on an opponent above the shoulders is prohibited and a minor shall be imposed subject to section (b) of this Rule.

(b) When a player carries or holds any part of his stick above the shoulders of the opponent so that injury results, the Referee shall:

(i) Assess a double minor penalty for all contact that causes an injury, whether accidental or careless, in the opinion of the Referee.

(ii) Assess a match penalty to a player who, in the opinion of the Referee, attempted to injure an opponent.

➡ *page 76*

Elbowing, Rule 53

High sticks, Rule 61

Foul play
Many ice hockey rules specify different types of fouls including high sticks, hooking, head-butting, and slashing.

Hands off
Players are allowed to use an arm to block an opponent provided they do not grab them or otherwise hold on to them with hands, arms, or legs.

Shooting for goal
Although a goal can be scored from anywhere on the ice, most goals are scored from fairly close in. The best shooting position is from a small area directly in front of the goal called the "slot." Typically an attacker will pick up the puck in the slot and attempt a wrist shot: the stick is swept along the ice until the player makes contact with the puck with a quick snap of the wrist. Often players will aim at the top and bottom corners of the goal—the very places where the goalkeeper is at his most vulnerable.

How to win

Goals are scored when the puck is put into the goal in any way other than via an intentional kick (if the puck deflects off a player's foot, the goals is allowed). When a player scores a goal, an assist is credited to any teammate(s) who took part in the play immediately prior to the goal. The team with the most goals wins.

KEY RULES

• A game consists of three 20-minute periods with intervals of 15 minutes between each. Teams change ends after each period. If the score is tied at the end of the game an additional period of five minutes is played, with the first team to score winning the game. If neither team scores in the overtime, the game is declared a tie.

• Six players only are allowed on the rink at one time, but a coach may make as many substitutions as he likes during a game. Typically, players are substituted in groups (called "shifts"). This allows a front line, for example, to play as a well-oiled unit.

• The puck may be passed among teammates within any one of the three zones. A player must not pass it forward to a teammate in another zone while his team is in control of the puck or an offside penalty is incurred. However, players of a defending team may make and take forward passes within their half of the rink (i.e., up to the center line) without incurring the same penalty. (This is the Passing Rule.)

• A player is offsides when both his skates are beyond the line bounding a particular zone at the time when the puck crosses into that zone.

• Icing the puck means shooting it from behind the center line to beyond the opposition's goal line. If it enters the net a goal is scored, otherwise play is stopped as soon as a defender reaches it. Play is restarted with a face-off from the offending team's half. *See Rule 48 (page 72).*

• A penalty is incurred if a player commits an offense such as charging into an opponent *(Rule 47)*, carrying his stick above shoulder height *(Rule 61)*, falling on the puck *(Rule 55)*, engaging in fisticuffs *(Rule 56)* or butt-ending, cross-checking, hooking, or spearing an opponent with his stick *(Rules 46, 50, 64 and 86).*

Icing the puck

Penalties for conduct potentially harmful to an opponent generally involve the removal of a player from the game for a set period of time. During that time, his team must skate with fewer players (i.e., he cannot be replaced). Note that in most cases if the penalized player is the goalie, a teammate is allowed to serve the penalty for him.

SKILLS AND TACTICS

• A player must be adept at controlling the fast-moving puck with his stick (or feet), passing, receiving, and shooting it swiftly and accurately. Of course, the pace of the game also demands excellent skating skills. Top players have the ability to travel at high speeds as well as start, stop, or change direction in a matter of seconds.

• A *break-out play* involves setting up an attack once a team has gained possession of the puck in their defensive zone, with the defensemen passing it and moving it up toward the forwards, often rebounding it off the boards to evade checkers.

• Shots for goal are best made from the slot—the area directly in front of the goal.

Hogging the goal
The goal may be small, but so too is the puck, which can easily slip through small gaps. Goalies spread themselves out to block as much of the goal as possible, and the heavy padding needed to protect a goalie from frequent hits by fast-moving pucks means they occupy even more of the goal area. Nevertheless, pucks do get through.

Off the wall
An attacker under pressure from a defender will often play the puck off the boards at an angle, either to get around his opponent or to pass the puck to a teammate who may be able to set up an attack.

Splits
The goalkeeper frequently gets into all kinds of contortions in his attempt to protect the goal.

continued from page 73

(iii) Assess a match penalty to a player who, in the opinion of the Referee, deliberately injured an opponent.

Batting the puck above the normal height of the shoulders with a stick is also prohibited.

Rule 62 Holding an Opponent
A minor penalty shall be imposed on a player who holds an opponent by using his hands, arms, or legs.

(NOTE) A player is permitted to use his arm in a strength move, by blocking his opponent, provided he has body position and is not using his hands in a holding manner, when doing so.

Rule 63 Holding an Opponent's Stick
A player is not permitted to hold an opponent's stick. A minor penalty shall be assessed to a player who holds an opponent's stick.

Rule 64 Hooking
Hooking is the act of using the stick in a manner that enables a player to restrain an opponent.

(a) A minor penalty shall be imposed on a player who impedes the progress of an opponent by hooking with his stick.

(b) A major penalty and a game misconduct shall be imposed on any player who injures an opponent by hooking.

Rule 65 Icing the Puck
(a) For the purpose of this Rule, the center red line will divide the ice into halves. Should any player of a Team, equal or superior in numerical strength to the opposing Team, shoot, bat, or deflect the puck from his own half of the ice beyond the goal line of the opposing Team, play shall be stopped and the puck faced off at the end face-off spot of the offending Team, unless, on the play, the puck shall have entered the net of the opposing Team, in which case the goal shall be allowed.

For the purpose of this Rule, the point of last contact with the puck by the Team in possession shall be used to determine whether icing has occurred or not.

Rule 66 Illegal Puck
If at any time while play is in progress, a puck other than the one legally in play shall appear on the playing surface, the play shall not be stopped but shall continue with the legal puck until the play then in progress is completed by change of possession.

Rule 67 Interference
A minor penalty shall be imposed, for example, on a player who interferes with or impedes the progress of an opponent who is not in possession of the puck, restrains an opponent who is attempting to forecheck, causes an opponent who is not in possession to be forced off-side or deliberately knocks a stick out of an opponent's hand.

Rule 68 Interference by/with Spectators
The referee shall stop play if a spectator interferes with a player (unless he is in possession, in which case the play is completed first). A player who interferes with a spectator incurs a gross misconduct penalty.

Rule 69 Kicking a Player
A match penalty shall be imposed on any player who kicks or attempts to kick another player.

Whether or not an injury occurs, the Referee will impose a five-minute time penalty.

Rule 70 Kicking the Puck
(a) Kicking the puck shall be permitted in all zones. A goal cannot be scored by an attacking player who uses a distinct kicking motion to propel the puck into the net. A goal cannot be scored by an attacking player who kicks a puck that deflects into the net off any player, goalkeeper, or Official.

(b) A puck that deflects into the net off an attacking player who does not use a distinct kicking motion, is a legitimate goal.

Rule 71 Kneeing
Kneeing is the act of a player making a distinct movement of his knee.

A minor, major, or match penalty shall be imposed on any player who fouls an opponent by kneeing.

Close encounter
Ice hockey is a physical sport and body contact between players is commonplace. But players must use their sticks for the puck only—not for swinging at vulnerable opponents.

Lost puck
The puck must be kept on the move at all times. If during a scramble a player falls on it and the puck disappears from view, the referee immediately stops the game. The game is then restarted with a face-off from the point where the puck was lost.

Rule 72 Leaving Players' or Penalty Bench

A game misconduct penalty shall be imposed on the player who was the first or second player to leave the players' or penalty bench from either or both teams during an altercation or for the purpose of starting one.

Rule 73 Obscene or Profane Language or Gestures

A player incurs a game misconduct penalty for using obscene gestures and a misconduct penalty for using profane language anywhere on the rink.

Rule 74 Offsides

A player is off-side when both skates (but not his stick) are completely over the outer edge of the determining center line or blue line involved in the play when the puck crosses the outer edge of this line. For an intentional offside, the puck is faced off at the end face-off spot in the offending team's defending zone.

Rule 75 Passes

See page 75

Rule 76 Physical Abuse of Officials

Players are suspended for 20, 10, or three games, depending on the degree of the offense.

Rule 77 Preceding Puck into Attacking Zone

(a) Players of the attacking team must not precede the puck into the attacking zone.

(b) For violation of this Rule, the play is stopped and the puck shall be faced off in the neutral zone at the face-off spot nearest the attacking zone of the offending Team.

(NOTE) A player actually controlling the puck who shall cross the line ahead of the puck shall not be considered offside.

Rule 78 Protection of Goalkeeper

(a) A minor penalty for interference shall be imposed on a player who, by means of his stick or his body, interferes with or impedes the movements of the goalkeeper by actual physical contact.

Rule 79 Puck Must Be Kept in Motion

(a) The puck must be kept in motion at all times.

(b) A minor penalty shall be imposed on any player, including the goalkeeper, who holds, freezes, or plays the puck with his stick, skates, or body in such a manner as deliberately to cause a stoppage of play.

(NOTE) With regard to a goalkeeper, this Rule applies outside of his goal crease area.

Rule 80 Puck Out of Bounds or Unplayable

When a puck goes outside the playing area, strikes any obstacles apart from the boards or glass, becomes lodged in the netting of a goal or is "frozen" between opposing players, it shall be faced off from a suitable spot.

Rule 81 Puck Out of Sight

Should a scramble take place or a player accidentally fall on the puck and the puck be out of sight of the Referee, he shall immediately blow his whistle and stop the play. The puck shall then be faced off at the point where the play was stopped unless otherwise provided for in the Rules.

Rule 82 Puck Striking Official

(a) Play shall not be stopped if the puck touches an Official anywhere on the rink, regardless of whether a Team is shorthanded or not.

Rule 83 Refusing to Start Play

If a team refuses to start play when ordered to, the Referee shall impose a two-minute penalty on a player of the offending team. Continued refusal incurs a fine of $200 for the Manager or Coach of the team, followed by a forfeit to the non-offending team if refusal still persists.

Rule 84 Roughing

A minor altercation not worthy of a major penalty.

A minor penalty shall be imposed on a player who strikes an opponent.

Rule 85 Slashing

(a) A minor or major and a game misconduct penalty, at the discretion of the Referee, shall be imposed on any player who impedes the progress of an opponent by slashing

(swinging) with his stick.

(b) A major and a game misconduct penalty shall be imposed on any player who injures an opponent by slashing.

Rule 86 Spearing

(a) A double minor penalty will be imposed on a player who spears *(stabs an opponent with the point of the stick blade)* an opponent and does not make contact.

(b) A major and a game misconduct shall be imposed on a player who spears an opponent.

Rule 87 Start of Game and Periods

See page 71.

Rule 88 Throwing Stick

If a defending player deliberately throws his stick at the puck or puck carrier in his defending zone and no goal is scored, a penalty shot is awarded to the attacking team. If the opposing goalkeeper has been removed and this act prevents the puck carrier from scoring, a goal is awarded to the attacking team. Otherwise, a player who throws his stick anywhere on the ice incurs a minor penalty.

Rule 89 Tied Game

See page 74.

Rule 90 Time of Match

See page 74.

Rule 91 Tripping

(a) A minor penalty shall be imposed on any player who shall place his stick or any portion of his body in such a manner that it shall cause his opponent to trip and fall.

Rule 92 Time-Outs

Each Team shall be permitted to take one 30-second time-out during the course of any game. This time-out must be taken during a normal stoppage of play.

Rule 93 Video Goal Judge

Details the situations subject to review by the Video Goal Judge.

These rules are reprinted by permission of the National Hockey League. A complete copy of the rules is available from the League.

Men's lacrosse
Essentials

Tracing its roots to the Iroquois, who believed it to be a sacred game, men's lacrosse is a full-contact sport involving players armed with crosses and an array of protective gear, battling it out to gain possession of the ball. Today, its popularity is spreading westward from the eastern United States, where it has long been a popular collegiate sport. An indoor version of the game, played with fewer players on a smaller court, is also popular in Canada.

End lines
Goal
Goal crease
Goal area
110 yds
10 yds
Goal area line
20 yds
Center line
10 yds
10 yds
Special substitution area
Side lines
6 yds
60 yds

The ball
White or orange rubber, 7.75–8 in in circumference and 5–5.25 oz in weight.

The field
Rectangular, 110 yds long and 60 yds wide, with lines marked in white. Soft flexible cones are placed at each corner, at each end of the substitution gate and at the end of the halfway line, which is opposite the bench area.

Officials
One head referee, two additional referees, a chief bench official, a timekeeper, two penalty timekeepers for each team, and a scorer for each team.

Dress
All players must wear protective gloves and a helmet with a face mask and chinstrap. Jerseys are the same color for the whole team and feature players' individual numbers on both front and back.

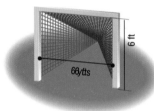

6 ft
6 yrds

The goals
Two vertical posts joined by a crossbar, painted orange and fitted with a pyramidal shaped cord netting. The posts are 6 ft apart and the crossbar is 6 ft from the ground. Each goal is 15 yds from each end line and inside a circle (the goal crease) of radius 9 ft.

The crosse
There are different lengths and head sizes. A short crosse is 40–42 in, a long crosse is 52–72 in. Apart from the goalkeeper's crosse, only four long crosses per team are allowed at a time. The head of the crosse must measure between 4 and 10 in at its widest point. The head of the goalkeeper's crosse may measure up to 15 in. This stick may be any length.

The teams
Ten players a side—a goalkeeper, three defenders, three midfielders, and three attackers—and up to 13 substitutes.

The crosse's net allows the ball to lodge.

Fast and free
Despite their heavily armored upper bodies, men's lacrosse players usually wear no protection whatsoever on their legs. Lacrosse is an extremely fast-moving game with the ball traveling at high speeds and players need to move without undue encumbrance.

Armed and ready
With the possible exception of ice hockey, men's lacrosse is the most physical of all stick sports. It is a tough game, in which protective gloves, helmet, and arm pads are absolutely essential.

Wrong move
Men's lacrosse is certainly a brutal sport but some things are not allowed. It is forbidden, for instance, to hit an opponent over the head with the crosse.

HOW TO PLAY

Each team attempts to score by getting the ball into the opposition's goal. The ball is carried, thrown, or batted with the crosse and only the goalkeeper, while within his own goal crease, can touch it with his hands.

Starting

A toss determines the choice of goals. Play is then started with a face-off. The referee places the ball on the ground at the center of the field, and one player from each team stands facing the other on his own side of the line. They then assume their face-off positions. Both crosses rest on the center line, parallel to each other, on either side of the ball. Once these positions have been assumed, the referee calls "set" and, on his whistle, either player may attempt to play the ball with his crosse.

How to win

Each goal scores one point. The team with the most points wins.

KEY RULES

A match is divided into four periods of 20 minutes, with a break at halftime. At the end of each quarter the teams change ends.

• In the event of a tie, two periods of four-minutes overtime are played, after which, if the scores are still even, the match is decided with the "sudden death" procedure: four-minute periods are played (with teams changing ends after each) until a goal is scored.

• Body-checking is permitted, but the opponent must be in possession of the ball or within 9 feet of either a loose ball or a ball in flight. Body-checks (take outs) must be made from the front or side, below the neck but not lower than the hip.

• Less serious offenses are penalized by possession of the ball being awarded to the opposition at the place where the foul occurred. If the opposition already has possession, the offending player is sent off the field for 30 seconds. Technical fouls include handling the ball, pushing or holding an opponent or his crosse, delaying the game, and being offside. More serious offenses are termed "personal

GRAY AREA

The avoidable body-check of an opponent after he has passed or shot the ball is an offense but, with the ball being propelled at speeds of up to 120 mph, it can be difficult for a referee to judge the status of the ball at the moment of impact.

Where was the ball?
This kind of body-check is legal if the player is within 6 ft of a ball in flight. But with the ball traveling as fast as an express train there is frequent dispute over just how close the ball was.

fouls" and incur a penalty of suspension from the game for one to three minutes and loss of possession if applicable. *See Section 10, Personal Fouls (pages 80 and 81).*

SKILLS AND TACTICS

All players need strength, perseverance, and courage to keep up with the demands of this intense game. *Attackers* need to excel in the art of shooting.

Midfielders must be versatile players, skilled at passing, catching, and running with the ball, as well as scooping it up from the ground.

The main task of the *defenders* is to "check" opponents. To counteract the fact that an advancing player can evade opponents effectively by running with the ball, defenders play with longer crosses. Top level players are expert at dislodging the ball with a blow to an opponent's gloved hand or crosse.

Men's lacrosse is quite a coach-led game, with a variety of offensive formations. Although it is a stick sport, lacrosse's tactics have a lot in common with those used in basketball, such as the fast break and zone defense. *See Basketball (page 138).*

Passing away
The best midfield players are fast on their feet, very good at running with the ball, and good at passing. This midfielder has managed to get the ball away just before being tackled—and all this while running at high speed.

Men's Lacrosse
• • • • • • • • • • • • • • •

The rules of men's lacrosse are extremely detailed. Here we give a basic outline of the major rules.

Italics indicate rules that have been edited.

Sections 1 to 8
See pages 78 and 79.

Section 9 Technical Fouls
Rule 50 The Penalty for Technical Fouls

50.1 The penalty for a technical foul shall be as follows:
i) If the offending team has possession of the ball, or if the ball is loose at the time a technical foul is committed, then possession shall be awarded to the opposing team at the point where the ball was when the foul occurred.
ii) If the opponents of the offending team have possession of the ball at the time a technical foul is committed, then the penalty shall be suspension from the field of play for 30 seconds for the player committing the foul.
50.2 If a technical foul occurs prior to the start of the game, or after the scoring of a goal or the end of a period, then the opponents are awarded the ball.

Rule 51 The Nature of a Technical Foul

51.1 Technical fouls are those of a less serious kind.
Any breach of the rules of play as set forth in this section shall be a technical foul unless that breach is specifically listed as a personal or expulsion foul in Sections 10 or 11.
Rules 52–67 are examples of technical fouls.

Rule 52 Interference

A player may not interfere in any manner with an opponent in an attempt to keep him from a loose ball, except when both are within 9 ft of a loose ball.

Rule 53 Pushing

53.1 A player may not push an opponent with his crosse.
53.2 A player may not push an opponent unless the opponent has possession of the ball or the opponent is within 3 yds of a loose ball.
53.3 A player may not push an opponent from the rear. Pushing from the rear is defined as exerting enough pressure to force an opponent to move in a

The face-off
To start the game the ball is placed on the ground in the center of the field between the backs of the crosses of two opponents. The crosses have to lie along the ground with the heads an inch apart. As soon as the referee blows his whistle the players can go for the ball with crosse or feet.

direction other than that in which he intends to go or, if in the direction he intends to go, then at a greater speed than he intends.

Rule 54 Illegal Pick

54.1 No offensive player shall move into and make contact with a defensive player with the purpose of blocking that defensive player from the man he is marking.
Before any contact is made the offensive player must be stationary and motionless, and he must be standing in his normal stance.
54.2 No offensive player shall hold his crosse rigid or extend his crosse rigid to impede the normal movement of a defender.

Rule 55 Holding

55.1 A player shall not *normally* hold an opponent or an opponent's crosse.

Rule 56 Kicking an Opponent's Crosse

56.1 A player may not deliberately step on or kick the crosse of an opponent.

Rule 57 Handling the Ball

57.1 A player shall not touch the ball with his hand(s) while it is in play, except the goalkeeper in his crease.

Rule 58 Withholding the Ball from Play

A player shall not withhold the ball from play in any manner.
A player shall not lie on a loose ball on the ground.
A player shall not trap a loose ball on the ground with his stick longer than is necessary for him to control the ball and pick it up in one continuous motion.

Rule 59 Illegal Actions with the Crosse

59.1 A player shall not throw his crosse under any circumstances.
59.2 A player shall not take part in the play of the game in any

manner unless he is grasping his crosse with at least one hand.
A broken crosse is considered no crosse.
59.3 During the play of the game, a player may not exchange his crosse for another except to replace a broken crosse, but players who are legally on the playing field may exchange crosses.

Rule 61 Illegal Procedure

61.1 Any action by a player or a substitute of a technical nature that is not in conformity with the rules and regulations governing the play of the game shall be termed illegal procedure.
Illegal procedures include: Leaving the penalty box before being authorized to do so by the penalty timekeeper (this constitutes a foul). Delaying the game. Failure to be at least 10 yds from a face-off at the time the whistle is blown. Failure to be at least 5 yds from an

opponent having a free play.

Rule 62 Stalling

62.1 Any deliberate action on the part of a team in possession of the ball to maintain possession of the ball outside the attack goal area by holding or passing the ball without reasonable effort to attack its opponents' goal is a technical foul known as "stalling." *There is a procedure for ensuring that the stalling team does not delay the game.*

Rule 65 Offside

65.1 A team is offside, provided that the ball is in play, when:
i) it has fewer than three men in its attack half of the field between the center line and the end line;
ii) it has fewer than four men in its defensive half of the field between the center line and the end line.

Section 10 Personal Fouls

Rule 68 The Penalty for a Personal Foul

68.1 The penalty for a personal foul shall be suspension from the game for a period of one to three minutes, depending on the referees' diagnosis of the severity and intention of the foul. The ball shall normally be given to the team that has been fouled. If the foul occurs prior to the start of the game, or after

Take-out
Tackling in men's lacrosse is a bruising business. It involves simply charging at your opponent with your shoulder and knocking him over. This is called the take-out.

the scoring of a goal or the end of a period, then the ball shall be awarded to the opponents of the offending team at the center of the field.

Rule 69 The Nature of a Personal Foul

Personal fouls include illegal body-checking (such as of an opponent who is not in possession of the ball), slashing (swinging the crosse recklessly), cross-checking (checking an opponent with the crosse handle), tripping, unnecessary roughness, and unsportsmanlike conduct.

Rule 76 Player Committing Five Personal Fouls

76.1 Any player committing five personal fouls shall be "fouled out" of the game, and shall not be allowed to take any further part in it.

76.2 A substitute for such a player shall be allowed to enter the game at such a time as the fouled-out player would have been permitted to reenter the game had he not committed five personal fouls.

Section 11 Expulsion Fouls

Rule 77 The Penalty for an Expulsion Foul

77.1 The penalty for an expulsion foul shall be suspension for the remainder of the game.

77.2 In the case of an expulsion foul against a player or a substitute, a substitution may be made after a lapse of three minutes.

77.3 In the case of an expulsion foul against a coach, non-playing member of a squad, or someone officially connected with a team, the in-home (a pre-nominated player) of the offending team shall be suspended from the game for three minutes, and he must remain in the penalty box for the entire three minutes.

Rule 78 The Nature of an Expulsion Foul

78.1 The act of deliberately striking or attempting to strike an opponent, a non-playing member of the opponents' squad, a coach, or anyone controlling the play of the game with the hand, crosse, ball, or otherwise by a player, a substitute, a non-playing member of a squad, a coach, or anyone officially connected with a team may be an expulsion foul.

78.2 Where a fight occurs on the field of play, and the officials have "frozen" the benches, by indicating to the team personnel who are on the benches that they should remain there, then any team personnel pushing past an official in order to join in a fight may be expelled from the game.

78.3 Where two players from competing teams are fighting and a third participant enters the altercation, then the third man into the altercation shall be expelled from the game.

78.4 Refusal to accept the authority of the officials, or the use of foul or abusive language may be an expulsion foul.

Section 12 Execution of Penalties

Rule 79 Player Committing Foul

79.1 A player who has been sent out of the game by a referee shall report immediately to the timer's table. He must remain in the penalty box, subject to the rules below, until released by the penalty timekeeper.

79.2 In the case of a time penalty, the time refers to the time for which the player will be off the field and out of the game. The timing of a penalty will begin when the penalized player sits down on one of the seats in the penalty box, or when the whistle blows to restart play, whichever is the later. If there are no empty seats left in the relevant penalty box, then the penalized player should kneel on one knee beside the seats.

Rule 80 Restarting Play After a Penalty

80.1 When a penalty occurs in the offended team's defensive half of the field and penalty time is to be served, the ball shall be awarded to any player of the offended team on the offensive side of the center line.

80.2 In *nearly* all other cases, the ball shall be awarded to any player of the offended team at the point where the ball was when play was suspended.

Rule 81 Simultaneous Fouls

81.1 When a member of a team commits a foul, and then a member of the opposing team commits a foul, then the fouls shall be considered simultaneous fouls, provided that the fouls are not separated by a whistle that has restarted play, or by the scoring of a goal.

81.2 When simultaneous fouls have been committed and they are all technical, the fouls cancel, *and the team in possession retains possession where the ball was when the whistle sounded. If no team is in possession, the ball is faced off where it was when the whistle sounded. But if at least one of the fouls was a personal, then all fouls are time served, and the team with less penalty time will be awarded the ball.*

Rule 82 The Slow Whistle Technique

82.1 If a defending player commits a foul, and the attacking team has possession of the ball at the time that the foul occurs, and, in the opinion of the referees, a scoring play is imminent, and the act of fouling does not cause the attacking player who is in possession to lose the ball, then the referee will throw a signal flag and withhold his whistle until such time as the scoring play has been completed.

Rule 83 The Play-On Technique

83.1 Where a player commits a loose-ball technical foul, and the offended team may be disadvantaged by the immediate suspension of play, then the referee shall visually and verbally signal "Play-on," and he shall withhold his whistle until such time as the situation involving the potential advantage has been completed.

These rules are reprinted by permission of the International Lacrosse Federation.

Shooting stars
Attackers who can catch the ball in the air and quickly make a shot—hurling the ball fast and accurately— into the tiny goal are invaluable.

Women's lacrosse
Essentials

Unlike the men's game, this is a noncontact version of lacrosse in which only the goalkeepers wear protective clothing. Another major difference is the size of the playing field, which for this game has no set boundaries.

The field

The playing area has no required boundaries, although an area of 110 m by 60 m (120 yds by 66 yds) is desirable. There is a goal circle (2.6 m/ 3 yds radius) at each end of the field and a center circle (9 m/ 10 yds radius) in the middle of the field. A 3 m (3½ yds) center line is marked in the middle, parallel to the goal lines.

The goals

Through the center of each goal circle is a goal line, marked parallel to the width of the field and 1.83 m (6 ft) in length. The posts of each goal are placed at either end of the goal lines and are joined by a crossbar, 1.83 m (6 ft) above the ground. The posts and crossbars are 5 cm (2 in) square or in diameter, constructed of wood or metal and painted white. A goal net is attached to the frame and also to the ground at a point 1.83 m (6 ft) behind the center of the goal line.

Dress

Shirt, kilt/shorts, and composition or rubber-soled shoes. Shirts are numbered front and back. All field players must wear mouthguards, but not head-gear or face masks. The goal-keeper must wear a helmet with face mask, a chest or body pad, a throat protector, padded gloves, arm pads, and leg pads. Captains wear a distinctive armband.

The keeper's pads
Only the goalkeeper may wear protective clothing. She can catch the ball with her hand, but must then put it in her stick and clear the ball within 10 seconds.

Officials

Up to three umpires, a scorer, and a timer.

The teams

Two teams of 12 players each.

The ball

Rubber, of any solid color, with a circumference of 20–20.3 cm (approx. 8 in) and a weight of 142–149 g (approx. 5 oz). It must bounce between 1.1 m and 1.3 m (approx. 3½ ft) when dropped from 1.8m onto concrete at a temperature of 65–75°F.

The crosse

Wood, plastic, fiberglass, nylon, leather, and/or gut. Only the handle may be constructed of aluminum or graphite.

Field player's crosse: a total length of .9–1.1 m (approx. 1 yd) and weight of no more than 567 g (20 oz). The crosse head must be 18–23 cm (approx. 10–12 in) in width and 25.4–30.5 cm (approx. 7–9 in) in length. The depth of the pocket, with the ball, must not exceed 6.3 cm (2½ in), the diameter of the ball.

Goalkeeper's crosse: a total length of .9–1.22 m (approx. 1 yd) and weight of no more than 773 g (27 oz). The crosse head must have a maximum inside measurement (width) of 30 cm (12 in) and a length of 40 cm (16 in). The depth of the pocket is unlimited.

Sticking with it
Women's lacrosse players can use their sticks to pass, throw, catch, or carry the ball.

HOW TO PLAY

Players attempt to propel the ball into goals at either end of the field in order to score. It may be carried, passed, thrown, or caught with the crosse. It must not be touched by any hands other than the goalkeeper's.

Starting

Teams toss for a choice of ends and play starts with a *draw*. Two players stand with their backs to the goal they are defending and with one foot toeing the center line. Their crosses are held back to back in the air, above hip level and parallel to and above the center line. The umpire places the ball between the crosses, says "Ready" and then blows the whistle, signaling the players to draw their crosses up and away. The ball must go higher than the heads of these players. All other players remain outside the center circle until the whistle blows.

How to win

A goal is scored when the ball passes completely over the goal lines. Goals scored by attacking players must be made with the crosse only—not the body—and *from outside the goal*

Goal line
Goal circle
15-m fan
Center line
18 m
3 m
82–92 m
Center circle
5.2 m
1.83 m

1.83 m
1.83 m
2.6 m

circle. The team with the most goals wins.

KEY RULES

• A game consists of two 25-minute periods with a 10-minute halftime break. Teams change ends at halftime.

• A player with the ball is required to hold her crosse away from her face and body. This gives opponents a chance to regain possession by tapping at the crosse with their own.

• If the game is stopped due to an irregular incident—if, for example, the ball goes out of bounds, becomes lodged in the umpire's clothing or two opponents foul simultaneously —then play starts again with a *throw.* Two opposing players stand 1 m (1 yd) apart, facing into play closest to the goal they are defending. The umpire then tosses the ball toward them and they both run in and try to catch it. Other players must remain at a distance of 4 m until the throw has been completed. *See Rule 15, (page 84).*

• Only the goalkeeper (or someone deputizing for her) may enter the goal circle. If the

ball enters the circle, only she may play it, although she must be inside the circle herself. The ball must also not be allowed to remain inside the goal circle for more than 10 seconds. *See Rules 17 and 18, (page 84).*

Crossed
Players carrying the ball must hold their crosse away from them, giving opponents an opportunity to dislodge the ball by tapping the stick in a controlled manner.

• All fouls are penalized with the award of a *free position.* The player who has been fouled places the ball in her crosse while all other players stand at least 4 meters (13 ft) away from her. When the whistle blows, she is free to run with the ball, pass it, or shoot it.

• Serious misconduct, such as unsportsmanlike behavior or dangerous play, can result not only in a free position but also in a warning (yellow card) or suspension (red card) of the offending player. *See Rule 19 (page 84) and Rule 22 (page 85).*

SKILLS AND TACTICS

A fast game with few interruptions, lacrosse requires great speed, stamina, and determination. A player in possession of the ball must minimize the opportunities for an opponent to attack her. In order to evade opponents, she combines secure, flexible handling of the crosse with the ability to maneuver out of tight situations, changing pace and direction and creating space for running or passing.

Defenders attempt to regain possession in a number of ways. They may intercept the ball as

GRAY AREA

Because women's lacrosse is so fast moving there are rules to prevent dangerous moves. One of these concerns the *pick.* A pick is an attacking player who deliberately blocks the path of a defender to prevent her from intercepting a teammate carrying the ball. A pick is only safe and legal if the player is within her opponent's field of vision so that the opponent can take evasive action. But this can be difficult for an umpire to judge.

it is passed between members of the opposing team; they may *steer* (i.e., follow an opponent closely, thereby forcing her to change her speed or direction or to pass the ball while in a weak position); or they may tackle by *crosse checking* (controlled tapping of an opponent's crosse in order to try and dislodge the ball).

Double crossed
When the ball is loose on the ground, players swoop in to catch it in their sticks, lift it into the air, and gain possession.

Rules of Women's Lacrosse

These rules are abridged and summarized. Changes to the official rules are indicated in italics.

Rules 1–13 *See pages 82–83.*

14. Ball outside field of play

When the ball crosses the boundary, it is deemed outside the field of play, and the umpire must blow the whistle.

A. If the ball is deliberately directed, carried, or propelled out-of-bounds it is a minor foul.

B. If the ball is accidentally carried or propelled out-of-bounds, the player nearest the ball places the ball in her crosse and stands 4 m (4½ yds) inside the boundary from the spot where the ball went out of play. Play resumes on the umpire's whistle and arm signal.

1) All players shall maintain their relative field position at the time the whistle was blown. No player may be closer to the boundary than the player awarded the ball.

2) The player with the ball must be given 1 m (1 yd) clear space by her opponent(s).

3) A Throw is taken when the two opposing players closest to the ball are equidistant.

C. Play is not to be resumed within 11 m (12 yds) of the center of the goal line.

15. The throw

Two opposing players stand with their feet and crosses at least 1 m apart. Each is nearer the goal she is defending and is facing in toward the game. The Throw must be taken at least 11 m from the center of the Goal Line. The umpire stands between 4 m and 8 m (9 yds) from the players, and as the whistle is blown, throws the balls with a short high arc toward the players so they catch it as they move in toward the game. No other player may be within 4 m of the players taking the Throw. If the Throw is inaccurate or is not touched by either player, it must be taken again. The Throw is taken when:

A. the ball goes into the goal off a non-player. The Throw should be taken to the side of the goal by two opponents nearest the goal.

B. the ball goes out-of-bounds and two opposing players are equally near the ball.

C. there is an incident unrelated

to the ball, and players are equidistant from the ball.

D. a ball lodges in the clothing of a field player or umpire.

E. two opponents foul simultaneously (major/major or minor/minor).

F. the game is restarted after an incident related to the ball when neither team had possession and two opposing players are equally near the ball, unless the accident has been caused by a foul.

G. the game is stopped for any reason not specified in the rules.

H. the attack fouls (major or minor) during a raised flag.

16. Conduct of play

A. A violation of any rule is a foul. The penalty for a foul is a Free Position.

B. All players must Stand when the whistle is blown. The umpire will indicate where the player taking the Free Position is to stand and where the offending player is to stand.

1) No player or her crosse is allowed within 4 m (4½ yds) of the player taking the Free Position.

2) A Free Position must not be taken within 11 m (12 yds) of the center of the Goal Line.

3) The player awarded the Free Position places the ball in her crosse, and on the umpire's whistle and visual arm signal she may run, pass, or shoot.

4) If two opposing players foul simultaneously and the fouls are equivalent (minor/minor or major/major), a Throw is taken. If the fouls are not equivalent, the team committing the major foul is penalized.

C. Advantage call

An umpire may refrain from enforcing any rule when it would penalize the non-offending team. If a player retains possession of the ball, even though she has been fouled, the umpire will indicate that she has seen the foul by extending her arm in the direction the player is attacking.

17. Goal circle rules

A. Only one player, either the goalkeeper or the person deputizing for her is allowed in the Goal Circle at any one time. No other player is allowed to enter or have any part of her body or crosse on or over the Goal Circle line at any time. A ball resting on the Goal Circle line is the goalkeeper's.

B. The goalkeeper, while within the Goal Circle:

1) must clear the ball within 10 seconds after it has entered

the Goal Circle.

2) may stop the ball with either hand and/or body as well as her crosse. If she catches the ball with her hand she must put it in her crosse and proceed with the game.

3) must remove a ball lodged in the goal netting or her clothing or pads, place it in her crosse and proceed with the game.

4) may reach out her crosse and bring the ball back into the Goal Circle provided no part of her body is grounded outside the Goal Circle.

C. When the goalkeeper or anyone deputizing for her is outside the Goal Circle: she loses all her goalkeeping privileges; she may only reenter the Goal Circle without the ball; she may propel the ball into the Goal Circle and then follow it in; and she must return to the Goal Circle to play the ball if it is inside the circle.

D. An unprotected field player: may only enter or remain in the Goal Circle when her team has possession of the ball; must immediately leave the Goal Circle when her team loses possession of the ball; may go into the Goal Circle to play a rolling ball; while within the Goal Circle, must clear the ball within 10 seconds after it has entered the Goal Circle and while within the Goal Circle, must remove a ball lodged in her clothing or crosse, place it in her crosse and proceed with the game.

18. Goal circle fouls and penalties

A. Goal Circle Fouls

1) A player must not follow through over the Goal Circle line with any part of her body or crosse at any time unless she is deputizing for the goalkeeper.

2) The goalkeeper or another player must not: allow the ball to remain within the Goal Circle for longer than 10 seconds; when inside the Goal Circle, reach beyond the Goal Circle to play the ball with any part of her body; draw the ball into her Goal Circle when any part of her is grounded outside the Goal Circle; when outside the Goal Circle, step into the Goal Circle with the ball; or throw any of her equipment to another player.

B. Penalties for Goal Circle Fouls

1) For all Goal Circle fouls, EXCEPT an unprotected field player illegally in the Goal Circle, the Free Position is taken

15 m (16½ yds) out from either side and level with the Goal Line.

2) An unprotected field player illegally in the Goal Circle is a major foul. The Free Position will be awarded at the center hash mark on the 11 m line to the attack player nearest this mark. The offending player is placed 4 m (4½ yds) behind and the Penalty Line cleared. The goalkeeper must not return to the Goal Circle until play has restarted.

19. Minor foul rules and penalties

A. Minor Foul Rules

A player commits a minor foul if she, for example: covers a ground ball with her crosse or body so denying an opponent an opportunity to play the ball; touches the ball with her hand; checks/tackles the crosse of an opponent who is trying to gain possession of the ball; throws her crosse; draws illegally after one caution; enters the center circle during the draw prior to the umpire's whistle; intentionally delays the game; adjusts the thongs of her crosse after an umpire's request to inspect it; deliberately directs, propels, or carries the ball out of bounds or fails to strike her crosse on the ground immediately if the ball becomes lodged in it. A goalkeeper must not be beyond 15 m (16½ yds) of her goal line during a draw or score a goal for her team or proceed beyond the center line at any time.

B. Minor Foul Penalties

1) For a minor foul, the offender is placed 4 m (4½ yds) from the player taking the Free Position, in the same direction from which she fouled. When the defense commits a minor foul within 15 m (16½ yds) of goal, the Free Position shall be taken on the 15-m Fan on a line which passes from the center of the Goal Line through the point where the foul occurred.

2) Repeated minor fouls shall be penalized as major fouls.

20. Major foul rules and penalties

A. Major Foul Rules

A player commits a major foul if she, for example: roughly or recklessly checks/tackles an opponent's crosse; strikes an opponent with her crosse; holds her crosse within a field crosse width of an opponent's head or neck; reaches across the opponent's body; makes a legal check impossible by holding her crosse near her own or a teammate's face or body while in possession; charges, blocks, barges, shoulders, or pushes into an opponent with the hand or back; propels the ball or shoots dangerously or without control; prevents the attacking team from shooting safely by blocking the goal with her body; detains an opponent by holding, tagging, pressing or pushing with an arm, leg, body, or crosse; trips or swipes at an opponent; violates the three-second rule (i.e., remains in the 11-m area at the front of the goal circle for longer than three seconds, unless marking an opponent within a stick's length).

B. Major Foul Penalties

1) For a major foul, the offender is placed 4 m (4½ yds) behind the player taking the Free Position. The Free Position is set up at the spot of the foul, but never closer than 11 m (12 yds) to the center of the Goal Line. If the foul occurs within the 11 m area, the Free Position is set up at the closest hash mark.

2) All players must clear the Penalty Lane of crosses and any part of their bodies when a Free Position is awarded for a major foul occurring within 11 m in front of the goal.

3) If the foul prevented an almost certain goal, the umpire may move any players positioned between the Free Position and the goal.

4) If any defender is in the Free Space to Goal when a Free Position is set, she should not be penalized for blocking the Free Space To Goal unless she does not immediately move out of this space after the umpire restarts play.

21. Advantage flag

A. Advantage Flag is raised instead of blowing a whistle for a major foul by defense when the attacking team is on a Scoring Play within 15 m (16½ yds) of goal. This includes the 15 m Fan and the playing area behind goal, which runs 9 m (10 yds) deep and 15 m to each side of the center of the goal Line.

B. A yellow flag is raised by the umpire when an attack player, with or without the ball, is fouled on a Scoring Play.

(A scoring play is a continuous effort by the attacking team to move the ball toward the goal and complete a shot on goal.)

C. The Scoring Play is over when:

Foul play
Women's lacrosse is a minimum contact sport. Holding a player down is a major foul—see Rule 20A

a shot is taken; the attacking team passes or carries the ball behind the level of the Goal Line and fails to continue the initial momentum to score a goal; the attacking team stops its continuous effort to complete a shot on goal; the attacking team fouls; the defense commits a subsequent foul that requires the game to be stopped; or the attacking team loses possession of the ball.

The Umpire must stop the Scoring Play immediately for a Free Space to Goal violation or for an unprotected player illegally in the Goal Circle.

D. Following the Advantage Flag:

1) If a shot on goal is successful, the goal counts.

2) If the attacking team chooses to shoot, the advantage indicated by the flag is complete and play continues.

3) If the Scoring Play ends without a further foul or shot on goal, a Free Position will be awarded to the attack player who was fouled and the penalized defender will be placed 4 m (4½ yds) behind.

For a foul:

a) between 11 m–15 m (12–16½ yds) in front of goal, the Free Position is awarded where the foul occurred.

b) within 11 m in front of goal, the Free Position is awarded on the closest hash mark and the Penalty Lane cleared.

c) behind goal, the Free Position is awarded on the 11 m mark on the Goal Line extension.

4) If any additional fouls by the defense end the Scoring Play, the Free Position is awarded to the attack player who was fouled at the 11 m hash mark nearest the most recent foul. The defender who fouled will be placed 4 m behind and the Penalty Lane cleared.

5) If the attacking team fouls (major or minor), a Throw will be taken beyond 15 m, level with the Goal Line extension.

6) Whenever the Penalty Lane is cleared and the goalkeeper is outside her Goal Circle and has not fouled, she may return to her Goal Circle.

22. Misconduct and suspensions

A. Misconduct and Suspensions
A player must not: conduct herself in a rough, dangerous, or unsportsmanlike manner; persistently cause infringement of the rules; deliberately endanger the safety of an opposing player; or exhibit any type of behavior that in the umpire's opinion amounts to misconduct.

B. Penalties

1) Misconduct and/or Suspension are treated as major fouls.

2) In addition to awarding the appropriate penalty, the Umpire may:

a) give a verbal caution.

b) warn the offending player with a Yellow Card.

c) suspend the offending player by showing a Red Card.

d) show a Red Card to suspend from further

participation in the game and/or send from the field without previous warning, a player, coach, or team/bench personnel guilty of dissent, misconduct, abusive language, or flagrant or repeated violations of the rules.

e) If a player, coach, or team/bench personnel is warned or suspended, the game is restarted within 30 seconds with a Free Position to the opponent nearest the ball when play was stopped.

23. Team fouls and penalties

A. Team Fouls

1) Delay of game.

2) Persistent fouling.

B. Team Foul Penalties

1) Delay of Game

a) On the first delay of game, the Umpire shall show the team's Captain a Green Card and award the appropriate penalty.

b) On the next delay of game, the umpire will show a Green and Yellow Card to the offending player and award the appropriate penalty. All subsequent offenders on that team shall receive a Green and Red Card suspension along with the appropriate penalty. The suspended player may return to the field on the next stoppage of play after a three-minute lapse of playing time.

2) Persistent Fouls

a) For persistent team fouls, the umpire shall show a Green Card to the team's captain and award the appropriate penalty (if applicable). On the next similar offense by that team, the umpire will show the offender a Green and Yellow Card. Regardless of the act, the offense will be penalized as a major foul.

b) The next player from the carded team who commits a subsequent Team Foul will receive a Green and Red Card suspension in addition to the penalty for a major foul. The suspended player may return to the field on the next stoppage of play after a three-minute lapse of playing time.

These rules are reprinted by permission of the International Federation of Women's Lacrosse Associations. For a complete copy of the rules, including Arm Signals for Umpires, Definitions and Tournament Rules, and Overtime Procedures, contact the IFWLA or your national association.

Cricket
Essentials

With rules dating to 1744, cricket is a traditional sport with a reputation for high standards of sportsmanship. Although the game is related to baseball, few North Americans play it or even understand its complex rules. But cricket is an immensely popular warm-weather sport in countries such as Britain, Australia, and even India, where it is a national obsession.

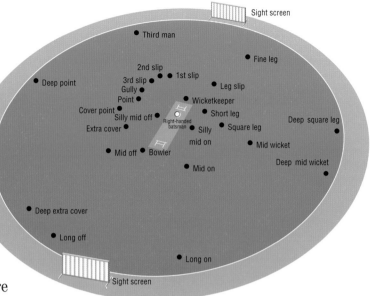

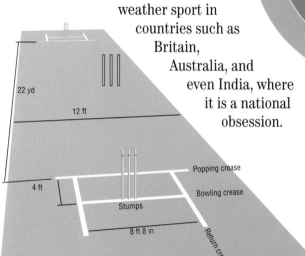

Above, all the possible fielding positions for a right-handed batsman. Only nine of these positions, in addition to the bowler and wicketkeeper, are occupied at any given time.

The playing field

Turf or non-turf. No specific size, although boundaries must be marked.

Officials

Two umpires.

The creases

The *bowling crease* is marked in line with the stumps. 8 ft 8 in in length, with the stumps at the center.

The *popping crease* is parallel to this. It is marked 4 ft from the center of the stumps and extends at least 6 ft on either side of the line of the wicket. (The batsman stands on this line as he awaits a delivery from the bowler).

The *return crease* is at right angles to the bowling crease. Marked to at least 4 ft behind the wicket it is considered to be of unlimited length.

The pitch

The pitch (playing field) is the area between the bowling creases. It is 12 feet wide with the (invisible) center line joining the two middle stumps of the wickets. The distance between the stumps is 22 yards. (For a non-turf pitch, the minimum width is 6 feet).

The players

Two sides of 11 players. Substitutes are allowed but they may not bat, bowl, or act as wicketkeeper.

Below, the crowd at a test match.

The bat

The overall length must be no more than 38 inches and the blade, which must be made of wood (willow), must not exceed 4 ¼ in at its widest part.

The ball

Spherical, cased in stitched red leather. Top grade balls weigh 5½–5 ¾ oz and have a circumference of 18¹³/₁₆–19 in.

The wickets

Two sets, each 9 in wide and consisting of three wooden stumps (28 in in height) with two wooden bails upon the top (4 ³/₈ in long). Placed opposite each other at a distance of 22 yds.

Willow and leather
Cricket relies on traditional materials for both equipment and clothing. Cricketers dress in cotton and wool whites and hit a leather ball with a bat made of willow.

Head gear
The only nontraditional item in the professional cricketer's dress is a helmet with face guard, often worn as protection from fast or dangerous balls.

Dress
All-white trousers, shirt, shoes, and sweater (with team colors as a trim) for test matches, colored outfits for one-day matches. The wicketkeeper wears leg pads and protective gloves and batsmen wear leg pads, gloves, and helmets.

Sight screens
Special screens to give batsmen a clear view of the bowler are positioned behind each wicket and outside the playing area, but close to the boundary line. Sizes vary.

HOW TO PLAY

Each team has one or two turns as the batting side. When batting, a team sends in two players at a time to "protect" the wickets from the opposition's bowlers. These batsmen score runs by running simultaneously between the wickets while successfully hit balls are being retrieved.

The fielding side attempts to get the batsmen out. Bowlers deliver balls toward each of the two wickets, attempting to get them past the batsmen. The two bowlers alternate by "overs"—6 (or 8) bowls at a time, not including wides or no-balls (*see Laws 24 and 25*). When 10 batsmen have been put out, this side starts its own batting innings.

Starting
The captains toss for the choice to bat or bowl/field first. When the umpire calls "play," the fielding team positions itself across the ground while the first two batsmen take their places in front of the wickets.

How to win
The team with the highest run total at the end of the match wins. Once the ball has been hit, the batsmen judge whether or not they each have time to run the length of the pitch once (one run), or more than once, while the ball is being retrieved. If the ball crosses the boundary line, four runs are automatically scored. If it is hit so that it crosses this line without first touching the ground, six runs are scored. In these cases the batsmen need not run.

Single runs may also be earned as a result of penalties. *See Laws 24, 25 and 26.* Each batsman's runs are totaled individually and the team's score is the sum of these.

KEY RULES

• Test matches run for five days, with a maximum of 30 hours play and two innings for each side. If the team batting second is all out more than 200 runs behind, they may be asked to bat again by the opposing team. If this team fails to score the runs necessary to catch up to the opposition, the match is then over.

• Shorter matches, such as the one-day matches for the World Cup, are "limited-over" competitions in which both teams have only one inning each. In these, a team attempts to score as many runs as it can before it runs out of overs or batsmen, whichever comes first.

• A batsman can be put out in a number of ways:
He is *bowled* if the bowler's ball knocks one of the bails off the stumps that he is guarding. *See Law 30 (page 89).*
He is *caught* if he hits the ball and it is caught by a member of the fielding side before it hits the ground. *See Law 32 (page 92).*
Leg before wicket (L.B.W.) occurs when his leg or any part of his body prevents the ball from hitting the stumps. *See Law 36 (page 93).*
If he is running toward a wicket but fails to make it in time to touch the ground between the popping and bowling creases with his bat before an opponent puts the wicket down, he is *run out*. *See Law 38 (page 93).*
If he is standing close to his wicket but is out of his ground, the wicketkeeper may take advantage of this lapse to knock the bails off the stumps with the ball, in which case he is *stumped*. *See Law 29 (page 89) and Law 39 (page 93).*

• In order for a defender to put a wicket down (an action that puts out a batsman), he must either 1) knock one or both bails off the stumps or 2) knock one of more of the stumps out of the ground *at the same time that he is holding the ball in one of his hands.*

THE LAWS OF CRICKET

Laws 1–4
Deal with players and substitutes. *See pages 86–87.*

Laws 5–11
Deal with equipment and the playing field. *See pages 86–87.*

Laws 12–17
Deal with match procedure. *See pages 86–87.*

Laws 18 and 19
Deal with scoring.

Law 20 Lost Ball

Law 21 The Result

Law 22 The Over

Law 23 Dead Ball

Law 24 No-Ball

1. Mode of Delivery
The umpire shall indicate to the striker whether the bowler intends to bowl over or round the wicket, overarm or underarm, or right- or left-handed. Failure on the part of the bowler to indicate in advance a change in his mode of delivery is unfair and the umpire shall call and signal "no-ball."

2. Fair Delivery—The Arm
For a delivery to be fair the ball must be bowled not thrown—see Note (a) below. If either umpire is not entirely satisfied with the absolute fairness of a delivery in this respect he shall call and signal "no-ball" instantly upon delivery.

Wide

No balls
The most common bowling faults are foot faults.

It is a "no-ball" if, during delivery, the bowler's front foot ends up beyond the popping crease.

It is a "no-ball" if, during delivery, the bowler's back foot is outside the return crease.

3. Fair Delivery—The Feet
The umpire at the bowler's wicket shall call and signal "no-ball" if he is not satisfied that in the delivery stride:
(a) the bowler's back foot has landed within and not touching the return crease or its forward extension or
(b) some part of the front foot whether grounded or raised was behind the popping crease.

4. Bowler Throwing at Striker's Wicket before Delivery.
If the bowler, before delivering the ball, throws it at the striker's wicket in an attempt to run him out, the umpire shall call and signal "no-ball." See Law 42 and Law 38.

5. Bowler Attempting to Run Out Non-Striker before Delivery
If the bowler, before delivering the ball, attempts to run out the non-striker, any runs that result shall be allowed and shall be scored as no-balls. Such an attempt shall not count as a ball in the over. The umpire shall not call "no-ball." See Law 42.12.

6. Infringement of the Laws by a Wicketkeeper or a Fieldsman
The umpire shall call and signal "no-ball" in the event of the wicketkeeper infringing Law 40.1 or a Fieldsman infringing Law 41.2 or Law 41.3.

7. Revoking a Call
An umpire shall revoke the call "no-ball" if the ball does not leave the bowler's hand for any reason. See Law 23.2.

8. Penalty
A penalty of one run for a no-ball shall be scored if no runs are made otherwise.

9. Runs from a No-Ball
The striker may hit a no-ball and whatever runs result shall be added to his score. Runs made otherwise from a no-ball shall be scored no-balls.

10. Out from a No-Ball
The striker shall be out from a no-ball if he breaks Law 34 and either batsman may be run out or shall be given out if either breaks Law 33 or Law 37.

11. Batsman Given Out Off a No-Ball
Should a batsman be given out off a no-ball the penalty for bowling it shall stand unless runs are otherwise scored.
Notes
(a) Definition of a Throw
A ball shall be deemed to have been thrown if, in the opinion of either umpire, the process of straightening the bowling arm, whether it be partial or complete, takes place during that part of the delivery swing that directly precedes the ball leaving the hand. This definition shall not debar a bowler from the use of the wrist in the delivery swing.
(b) No-Ball not Counting in Over
A no-ball shall not be reckoned as one of the over. See Law 22.3.

Law 25 Wide Ball

1. Judging a Wide
If the bowler bowls the ball so high over or so wide of the wicket that in the opinion of the umpire it passes out of reach of the striker, standing in a normal guard position, the umpire shall call and signal "wide ball" as soon as it has passed the line of the striker's wicket.

The umpire shall not adjudge a ball as being wide if:
(a) The striker, by moving from his guard position, causes the ball to pass out of his reach.
(b) The striker moves and thus brings the ball within his reach.

2. Penalty
A penalty of one run for a wide shall be scored if no runs are made otherwise.

3. Ball Coming to Rest in Front of the Striker
If a ball that the umpire considers to have been delivered comes to rest in front of the line of the striker's wicket, "wide"

Wides
Wides are called when a ball is too wide or too high for the batsman to reach.

The ball is a "wide" if it passes outside the return crease— provided the batsman does not move toward it.

A ball is a "wide" if it passes high over the batsman's head.

shall not be called. The striker has a right, without interference from the fielding side, to make one attempt to hit the ball. If the fielding side interfere, the umpire shall replace the ball where it came to rest and order the fieldsmen to resume the places they occupied in the field before the ball was delivered. The umpire shall call and signal "dead ball" as soon as it is clear that the striker does not intend to hit the ball, or after the striker has made one unsuccessful attempt to hit the ball.

4. Revoking a Call
The umpire shall revoke the call if the striker hits a ball that has been called "wide."

5. Ball Not Dead
The ball does not become dead on the call of "wide ball"—see Law 23.4.

6. Runs Resulting from a Wide
All runs that are run or result from a wide ball that is not a no-ball shall be scored wide balls, or if no runs are made one shall be scored.

7. Out from a Wide
The striker shall be out from a wide if he breaks Law 35 or Law 39. Either batsman may be run out and shall be out if he breaks Law 33 or Law 37.

8. Batsman Given Out Off a Wide
Should a batsman be given out off a wide, the penalty for bowling it

Byes
Byes are runs made without the batsman hitting the ball.

A "leg bye" is a run taken when the ball deflects off any part of the batsman's body but his hands.

shall stand unless runs are otherwise made.
Notes
(a) Wide Ball not Counting in Over *A wide ball shall not be reckoned as one of the over—see Law 22.3.*

Law 26 Bye and Leg-Bye

1. Byes
If the ball, not having been called "wide" or "no-ball" passes the striker without touching his bat or person, and any runs are obtained, the umpire shall signal "bye" and the run or runs shall be credited as such to the batting side.

2. Leg-Byes
If the ball, not having been called "wide" or "no-ball" is unintentionally deflected by the striker's dress or person, except a hand holding the bat, and any runs are obtained the umpire shall signal "leg-bye" and the run or runs scored shall be credited as such to the batting side.
Such leg-byes shall only be scored if, in the opinion of the umpire, the striker has:
(a) attempted to play the ball with his bat, or
(b) tried to avoid being hit by the ball.

3. Disallowance of Leg-Byes
In the case of a deflection by the striker's person, other than in 2(a) and (b) above the umpire shall call and signal "dead ball" as soon as one run has been completed or when it is clear that a run is not being attempted or the ball has reached the boundary. On the call and signal of "dead ball" the batsmen shall return to their original ends

and no runs shall be allowed.

Law 27 Appeals

1. Time of Appeals
The umpires shall not give a batsman out unless appealed to by the other side, which shall be done prior to the bowler beginning his run-up or bowling action to deliver the next ball. Under Law 23.1(g) the ball is dead on "over" being called; this does not, however, invalidate an appeal made prior to the first ball of the following over provided "time" has not been called. See Law 17.1.

2. An Appeal "How's That?"
An appeal "How's that?" shall cover all ways of being out.

3. Answering Appeals
The umpire at the bowler's wicket shall answer appeals before the other umpire in all cases except those arising out of Law 35 or Law 39 or Law 38 when this occurs at the striker's wicket.
When either umpire has given a batsman not out, the other umpire shall, within his jurisdiction, answer the appeal or a further appeal, provided it is made in time in accordance with 1. above.

4. Consultation by Umpires
An umpire may consult with the other umpire on a point of fact that the latter may have been in a better position to see and shall then give his decision. If, after consultation, there is still doubt remaining the decision shall be in favor of the batsman.

5. Batsman Leaving his Wicket under a Misapprehension
The umpires shall intervene if satisfied that a batsman, not having been given out, has left his wicket under a misapprehension that he has been dismissed.

6. Umpire's Decision
The umpire's decision is final. He may alter his decision, provided that such alteration is made promptly.

7. Withdrawal of an Appeal
In exceptional circumstances the captain of the fielding side may seek permission of the umpire to withdraw an appeal providing the outgoing batsman has not left the playing area. If this is allowed, the umpire shall cancel his decision.

Law 28 The Wicket Is Down

1. Wicket Down
The wicket is down if:
(a) Either the ball or the striker's bat or person completely removes either bail from the top of the stumps. A disturbance of a bail, whether temporary or not, shall not constitute a complete removal, but the wicket is down if a bail in falling lodges between two of the stumps.
(b) Any player completely removes with his hand or arm a bail from the top of the stumps, providing that the ball is held in that hand or in the hand of the arm so used.
(c) When both bails are off, a stump is struck out of the ground by the ball or a player strikes or pulls a stump out of the ground, providing that the ball is held in the hand(s) or in the hand of the arm so used.

Clean cut
A square cut is one of the most powerful strokes. It is made when an underpitched ball gives the batsman plenty of time to strike the ball with the bat almost horizontal to send it shooting towards the boundary.

2. One Bail Off
If one bail is off, it shall be sufficient for the purpose of putting the wicket down to remove the remaining bail, or to strike or pull any of the three stumps out of the ground in any way of the ways stated in 1. above.

3. All the Stumps Out of the Ground
If all the stumps are out of the ground, the fielding side shall be allowed to put back one or more stumps in order to have an opportunity of putting the wicket down.

4. Dispensing with Bails
If owing to the strength of the wind, it has been agreed to dispense with the bails in accordance with Law 8 Note
(a) the decision as to when the wicket is down is one for the umpires to decide on the facts before them. In such circumstances and if the umpires so decide the wicket shall be held to be down even though a stump has not been struck out of the ground.
Notes
(a) Remaking the Wicket
If the wicket is broken while the ball is in play, it is not the umpire's duty to remake the wicket until the ball has become dead—see Law 23. A member of the fielding side, however, may remake the wicket in such circumstances.

Law 29 Batsman Out of His Ground

1. When out of his Ground
A batsman shall be considered to be out of his ground unless some part of his bat in his hand or of his person is grounded behind the line of the popping crease.

Law 30 Bowled

1. Out Bowled
The striker shall be out bowled if:
(a) His wicket is bowled down, even if the ball first touches his bat or person.
(b) He breaks his wicket by hitting or kicking the ball on to it before the completion of a

➡ *page 92*

Twister
Instead of relying on pace and power to beat the batsman (which is what a "fast" bowler does), spin bowlers rely on fooling batters with the flight of the ball. A leg spin bowler holds the ball with his first three fingers well spaced apart, with the tips around the seam of the ball. The effect is to send the ball spinning toward the batsman's leg side.

SKILLS AND TACTICS

Batsmen will meet the ball with a combination of defensive and attacking shots so as to protect their wicket while also scoring as many runs as possible. Defensive strokes play the ball safely down to the ground, away from the wicket. Attacking strokes such as the drive are used to hit the ball some distance away from the pitch, to either side or straight ahead, to gain time for runs.

Bowlers have to develop their own pace and style. Most fall into two categories—fast and spin bowlers. The ball must bounce before it reaches the batsman. Most players will specialize as bowlers or batsmen. All players must be good *fieldsmen*, however—constantly on the alert, ready to retrieve and return the ball quickly, or catch a ball in the air to get a batsman out. They must be able to judge in an instant which wicket is the more vulnerable and, therefore, which teammate to throw to. In some instances, a quick-thinking fieldsman will run at the wicket himself to save time if he thinks he has a chance of putting it down.

Speed merchants
Fast bowlers hurl the ball toward a batsman at a ferocious pace. The sight of such a bowler building up his pace on his run-up is often enough to intimidate an insecure batsman standing at the wicket.

Above, standard field positions when an off-spin bowler is delivering the ball to a batsman.

Below, standard field positions when a right-handed outswing bowler is delivering the ball to a batsman.

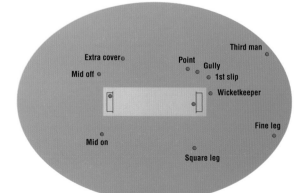

Umpire's hand signals

Boundary: six   *Dead ball*

Boundary: four   *Leg-bye*

Bye   *Wide*

No-ball   *Out*

Short run

Hand signals
Umpires use a variety of signals so that the scorers and everyone on the field can understand decisions instantly.

Howzat!
A batsman is not out unless a player on the opposing team appeals immediately. So games are often interrupted by loud cries of "howzat!" (i.e., "How's that?").

GRAY AREAS

Of all the ways a player can be out, L.B.W. is the one that causes the most dispute and discussion. The problems arise either over whether the ball was on target or whether the player was genuinely attempting a stroke. The fact is the umpire's decision is paramount in all cases.

Disputes also arise because cricket boards and authorities sometimes introduce special playing conditions, such as for the Wide law, for particular kinds of match (e.g., one-day matches). This often leads to misunderstanding among players who are familiar with the normal conditions.

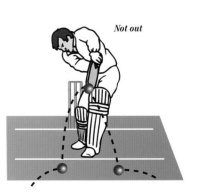

Out L.B.W.   *Not out*

Leg before wicket
L.B.W. decisions often cause disputes but a batsman whose leg blocks a ball heading for the wicket after pitching on the offside or straight before the wicket (left) is usually called out. A batsman whose leg obstructs a ball pitched outside the leg stump or hits the ball first with his bat (right) is usually not out.

continued from page 89

stroke, or as a result of attempting to guard his wicket. See Law 34.1.
Notes
(a) Out Bowled—Not L.B.W.
The striker is out bowled if the ball is deflected onto his wicket even though a decision against him would be justified under Law 36.

Law 31 Timed Out

1. Out Timed Out
An incoming batsman shall be out timed out if he willfully takes more than two minutes to come in—the two minutes being timed from the moment a wicket falls until the new batsman steps on to the field of play.

If this is not complied with and if the umpire is satisfied that the delay was willful and if an appeal is made, the new batsman shall be given out by the umpire at the bowler's end.

2. Time to Be Added
The time taken by the umpire to investigate the cause of the delay shall be added at the normal close of play.
Notes
Batsmen Crossing on Field of Play
It is an essential duty of the captains to ensure that the ingoing batsman passes the outgoing one before the latter leaves the field of play.

Law 32 Caught

1. Out Caught
The striker shall be out caught if the ball touches his bat or if it touches below the wrist his hand or glove, holding the bat, and is subsequently held by a fieldsman before it touches the ground.

2. A Fair Catch
A catch shall be considered to have been fairly made if:
(a) The fieldsman is within the field of play throughout the act of making the catch.
(i) The act of making the catch shall start from the time when the fieldsman first handles the ball and shall end when he both retains complete control over the further disposal of the ball and remains within the field of play.
(ii) In order to be within the field of play, the fieldsman may not touch or ground any part of

Cricketing colors
Although traditional cricket whites are still worn for most test matches, players taking part in the one-day matches usually dress more colorfully.

his person on or over a boundary line. When the boundary is marked by a fence or board the fieldsman may not ground any part of his person over the boundary fence or board, but may touch or lean over the boundary fence or board in completing the catch.
(b) The ball is hugged to the body of the catcher or accidentally lodges in his dress or, in the case of the wicketkeeper, in his pads.
However, a striker may not be caught if a ball lodges in a protective helmet worn by a fieldsman, in which case the umpire shall call and signal "dead ball." See Law 23.
(c) The ball does not touch the ground even though a hand holding it does so in effecting the catch.
(d) A fieldsman catches the ball, after it has been lawfully played a second time by the striker, but only if the ball has not touched the ground since being first struck.
(e) A fieldsman catches the ball after it has touched an umpire, another fieldsman, or the other batsman. However a striker may not be caught if a ball has touched a protective helmet worn by a fieldsman.
(f) The ball is caught off an obstruction within the boundary provided it has not previously been agreed to regard the obstruction as a boundary.

3. Scoring of Runs
If a striker is caught, no runs shall be scored.
Notes
(a) Scoring from an Attempted Catch
When a fieldsman carrying the ball touches or grounds any part of his person on or over a boundary marked by a line, six runs shall be scored.
(b) Ball Still in Play
When a fieldsman releases the

ball before he crosses the boundary, the ball will be considered to be still in play and it may be caught by another fieldsman. However, if the original fieldsman returns to the field of play and handles the ball, a catch may not be made.

Law 33 Handled the Ball

1. Out Handled the Ball
Either batsman on appeal shall be out "handled the ball" if he willfully touches the ball while in play with his hand not holding the bat unless he does so with the consent of the opposite side.

Law 34 Hit the Ball Twice

1. Out Hit the Ball Twice
The striker, on appeal, shall be out "hit the ball twice" if, after the ball is struck or is stopped by any part of his person, he willfully strikes it again with his bat or person except for the sole purpose of guarding his wicket: this he may do with his bat or any part of his person other than his hands, but see Law 37.2.
For the purpose of this law, a hand holding the bat shall be regarded as part of the bat.

2. Returning the Ball to a Fieldsman
The striker, on appeal, shall be out under this law, if, without the consent of the opposite side, he uses his bat or person to return the ball to any of the fielding side.

3. Runs from Ball Lawfully Struck Twice
No runs except those which result from an overthrow or penalty, see Law 41, shall be scored from a ball lawfully struck twice.

Law 35 Hit Wicket

1. Out Hit Wicket
The striker shall be out "hit wicket" if, while the ball is in play:
(a) His wicket is broken with any part of his person, dress, or equipment as a result of any action taken by him in preparing to receive or in receiving a delivery, or in setting off for his first run, immediately after playing, or playing at, the ball.
(b) He hits down his wicket whilst lawfully making a second stroke for the purpose of guarding his wicket within the provisions of Law 34.1.
Notes
(a) Not Out Hit Wicket
A batsman is not out under this law should his wicket be broken in any of the ways referred to in 1(a) above if:

(i) It occurs while he is in the act of running, other than in setting off for his first run immediately after playing at the ball, or while he is avoiding being run out or stumped.

(ii) The bowler after starting his run-up or bowling action does not deliver the ball; in which case the umpire shall immediately call and signal "dead ball."

(iii) It occurs whilst he is avoiding a throw-in at any time.

Law 36 Leg before Wicket

1. Out L.B.W.

The striker shall be out L.B.W. in the circumstances set out below:

(a) Striker Attempting to Play the Ball

The striker shall be out L.B.W. if he first intercepts with any part of his person, dress, or equipment a fair ball that would have hit the wicket and that has not previously touched his bat or a hand holding the bat, provided that:

(i) The ball pitched, in a straight line between wicket and wicket or on the off side of the striker's wicket, or was intercepted full pitch.
and

(ii) the point of impact is in a straight line between wicket and wicket, even if above the level of the bails.

(b) Striker Making No Attempt to Play the Ball

The striker shall be out L.B.W. even if the ball is intercepted outside the line of the off-stump, if, in the opinion of the umpire, he has made no genuine attempt to play the ball with his bat, but has intercepted the ball with some part of his person and if the other circumstances set out in (a) above apply.

Law 37 Obstructing the Field

1. Willful Obstruction

Either batsman, on appeal, shall be out obstructing the field if he willfully obstructs the opposite side by word or action.

2. Obstructing a Ball from Being Caught

The striker, on appeal, shall be out should willful obstruction by either batsman prevent a catch being made.

This shall apply even though the striker causes the obstruction in lawfully guarding his wicket under the provisions of Law 34. See Law 34.1.

Law 38 Run Out

1. Out Run Out

Either batsman shall be out run out if in running or at any time while the ball is in play—except in the circumstances described in Law 39—he is out of his ground and his wicket is put down by the opposite side. If, however, a batsman in running makes good his ground he shall not be out run out, if he subsequently leaves his ground, in order to avoid injury, and the wicket is put down.

2. "No-Ball" Called

If a no-ball is called, the striker shall not be given run out unless he attempts to run.

3. Which Batsman Is Out

If the batsmen have crossed in running, he who runs for the wicket that is put down shall be out; if they have not crossed, he who has left the wicket that is put down shall be out. If a batsman remains in his ground or returns to his ground and the other batsman joins him there, the latter shall be out if his wicket is put down.

4. Scoring of Runs

If a batsman is run out, only that run that is being attempted shall not be scored. If however an injured striker himself is run out, no runs shall be scored. See Law 2.7.

Notes

(a) Ball Played on to Opposite Wicket

If the ball is played on to the opposite wicket neither batsman is liable to be run out unless the ball has been touched by a fieldsman before the wicket is broken.

(c) Run Out off a Fieldsman's Helmet

If, having been played by a batsman, or having come off his person, the ball rebounds directly from a fieldsman's helmet on to the stumps, with either batsman out of his ground, the batsman shall be "Not out."

Law 39 Stumped

1. Out Stumped

The striker shall be out stumped if, in receiving the ball, not being a no-ball, he is out of his ground otherwise than in attempting a run and the wicket is put down by the wicketkeeper without the intervention of another fieldsman.

2. Action by the Wicketkeeper

The wicketkeeper may take the ball in front of the wicket in an attempt to stump the striker only if the ball has touched the bat or the person of the striker.

Law 40 The Wicketkeeper

1. Position of the Wicketkeeper

The Wicketkeeper shall remain wholly behind the wicket until a ball delivered by the bowler touches the bat or person of the striker, or passes the wicket, or until the striker attempts a run. In the event of the wicketkeeper contravening this law, the umpire at the striker's end shall call and signal "no-ball" at the instant of delivery or as soon as possible thereafter.

2. Restriction on Actions of the Wicketkeeper

If the wicketkeeper interferes with the striker's right to play the ball and to guard his wicket, the striker shall not be out, except under Laws 33, 34, 37, and 38.

3. Interference with the Wicketkeeper by the Striker

If in the legitimate defense of his wicket, the striker interferes with the wicketkeeper, he shall not be out, except as provided for in Law 37.2.

Law 41 The Fieldsman

1. Fielding the Ball

The fieldsman may stop the ball with any part of his person, but if he willfully stops it otherwise, five runs shall be added to the run or runs already scored; if no runs have been scored five penalty runs shall be awarded. The run in progress shall count provided that the batsmen have crossed at the instant of the act. If the ball has been struck, the penalty shall be added to the score of the striker, but otherwise to the score of byes, leg-byes, no-balls, or wides as the case may be.

2. Limitation of Onside Fieldsmen

The number of onside fieldsmen behind the popping crease at the instant of the bowler's delivery shall not exceed two. In the event of infringement by the fielding side the umpire at the striker's end shall call and signal "no-ball" at the instant of delivery or as soon as possible thereafter.

3. Position of Fieldsmen

While the ball is in play and until the ball has made contact with the bat or the striker's person or has passed his bat, no fieldsman, other than the bowler, may stand on or have any part of his person extended over the pitch (measuring 22 yds by 10 ft). In the event of a fieldsman contravening this law, the umpire at the bowler's end shall call and signal "no-ball" at the instant of delivery or as soon as possible thereafter. See Law 40.1.

4. Fieldsmen's Protective Helmets

Protective helmets, when not in use by members of the fielding side, shall only be placed, if above the surface, on the ground behind the wicketkeeper. In the event of the ball, when in play, striking a helmet while in this position, five penalty runs shall be awarded, as laid down in Law 41.1 and Note (a).

Law 42 Unfair Play

These laws are reprinted by permission of the Marylebone Cricket Club. Contact the MCC for a complete copy of the Laws of Cricket.

Bouncer
Bouncers are fast, short pitched balls that bounce up sharply toward the batsman's head. They are not actually illegal but they are sometimes considered unfair.

Baseball
Essentials

The national summer game of the United States, baseball has now achieved immense popularity in Latin America and Japan as well. Subtle and complex, it forces pitchers, batters, and team managers into sophisticated guessing games, trying to outwit the opposition and gain important advantages.

The field

Grass or artificial turf. Consists of an outfield (various sizes) and an infield—a square (or "diamond") with 90-foot sides. Each side marks the distance between two bases. Home base is marked by a five-sided slab of whitened rubber; first, second, and third bases are marked by 15-inch square white canvas bags, attached to the ground. The pitcher's mound is a raised area (a little hill) in the middle of the infield. It includes at its highest point a rectangular slab of whitened rubber, 24 inches by 6 inches. The distance between this slab (the "rubber") and home plate is 60 feet, 6 inches.

Coaches' box
3rd base
On deck circle
Pitcher's
2nd base
$60\frac{1}{2}$ ft
Home plate
1st base
90 ft
Grass line—95 ft from pitcher's plate
Foul line
Fence 60 ft from base or foul line

Players

Two teams of nine players each. When fielding, team members assume the following positions:

1. pitcher
2. catcher
3. first baseman
4. second baseman
5. third baseman
6. shortstop
7. left fielder
8. center fielder
9. right fielder

These numbers are used in a short-hand notation to keep track of what happened in a game.

HOW TO PLAY

The object of the game is to score runs by completing the circuit of all bases, beginning and ending at home plate. Only the batting team may score. Teams take turns at bat, and the fielding side must get three players on the batting side out. Doing so ends their opponent's turn at bat and forces the opposition to switch sides.

Starting

Once both teams have established their batting order, the home team takes the field and the visiting team prepares to bat first. The home plate umpire yells, "Play Ball!"

How to win

The team that scores the most runs wins. One run is scored for every player who completes the circuit of bases. A batter can reach base safely in a number of ways, but he generally succeeds by hitting the ball somewhere within the field of play where it can neither be caught before hitting the ground nor thrown to first base faster than the batter himself can get there. Depending on where the ball is hit, the batter may be able to make it past first base. If he does not make it back to home plate on his own, he must rely on hits from teammates (or other positive events) to advance him further. A ball hit in fair territory over a fence at the back of the outfield is a home run, and the batter and any other runners on base automatically complete the circuit.

Dress

Uniform throughout a team. All players' uniforms feature 6 in numbers on the back. Leagues may require teams to always wear one distinctive uniform or they may allow two sets—a white one for home games and a different color for away games. Uniforms must not feature glass buttons, polished metal, or any patterns that might suggest the shape of a baseball. The catcher may wear a leather mitt (not more than 38 in in circumference and $15\frac{1}{2}$ in in length), the first baseman also may wear a special leather glove or mitt (not more than 12 in in length). All other fielders wear a leather glove. The pitcher's glove must not be white or grey. The catcher must wear a catcher's protective helmet and all players, while at bat, must use some type of protective helmet.

This catcher is trying to throw out a runner who is attempting to steal a base.

Officials

One umpire for each base. Important games may feature two additional umpires, one positioned along each of the outfield foul lines.

The bat

A smooth, round stick; one piece of solid wood. Not more than 42 in in length and not more than $2\frac{3}{4}$ in in diameter at the thickest part.

The ball

Spherical, a core of cork, rubber, or similar material, wound with yarn and covered with white horsehide or cowhide. A weight of 5–5 $\frac{1}{4}$ oz and circumference of 9–9 $\frac{1}{4}$ in.

KEY RULES

• Unless extended to resolve a tie or shortened by foul weather, a game consists of nine innings. Visiting teams bat in the "top half" of an inning; home teams in the "bottom half." The game is ended if the home team enters the bottom half of the last inning with the lead. A visiting team only wins if the bottom half of the last inning is complete. If the home team scores the winning run in the bottom of the last inning, the game ends at that moment.

• The *strike zone* is an area directly above the home plate. In terms of height, this zone begins at a line level to the bottom of the batter's kneecap and ends level to his armpits as he assumes a batting stance. A pitch that does not keep to this zone is called a "ball" and after four balls, a batter is allowed to "walk" to first base. If a pitch is within the strike zone and a batter fails to swing at it, a strike is called. A strike is also called if a batter swings at any pitch and either misses it entirely or hits it into foul territory. After three strikes a batter is out, but the third strike can only be called if 1) the batter swings at the ball and misses it; 2) fails to swing at a pitch in the strike zone; or 3) hits the ball directly back into the catcher's glove and the catcher holds on to it. Otherwise, the "count" holds at strike two.

• A batter is also out if a ball he hits is caught before it touches the ground or if he or first base is *tagged* (touched by a fielder who has possession of the ball) before he makes it to first base. When the batter hits a fair ball into *fair territory* (anywhere on or between the foul lines) he

Strike zone
For a strike the ball must be within the strike zone, which depends on the batter's stance and lies between the midriff and the knees.

may start running to first base, or further if he has time. *See Rule 6, The Batter (page 96).*
• A player who has reached a base can be put out if he is tagged by a fielder in possession of the ball when he is not in contact with a base. This can occur because runners will often move off a base toward the next one in an effort to get a head start. If the fielders get the ball to a player who can tag him before he either returns to his base or advances to the next one, he is out.
• Runners must not deviate too far from the direct line between bases simply to avoid being tagged. If they do, they are out, unless they stray from this line so as not to interfere with a fielder's play. (Likewise, interference on the part of the fielding team is also penalized.)
• Only one runner can occupy a base at a time and runners must proceed around the circuit in the order that they batted. A *force play* occurs when a batter becomes a runner and runs toward first base, forcing a player already occupying this base to proceed to the next one (as well as any runners ahead of him in turn). *See Rule 7, The Runner (page 98).*
• If a runner is being forced to a new base as described above, he is out if a fielder in

possession of the ball touches the base he is advancing toward before he arrives there. If he is not being forced (i.e., if he has the option of returning to the base he has last touched

Big swing
A baseball is difficult to hit well so scoring is low. The key for the batter is keeping a low, even swing.

because there is no runner there), tagging the base with the ball is not sufficient to record an out. Rather, the runner himself must be tagged by the fielder before he arrives "safely" at the new base.
• A number of rules govern the

actions of the pitcher. For instance, the pitcher must keep one foot on the "rubber" on the mound) until he has released the ball. Failure to do so may result in a *balk,* which allows all runners to advance one base. Balks are also called for other illegal acts by the pitcher, including feinting (moving as if he is about to pitch the ball and then failing to do so), delivering the ball while not facing the batter, or dropping the ball while touching the rubber. *See Rule 8.01 (page 101) and Rule 8.05 (page 102).*
• The *designated hitter* rule used by some leagues involves using a substitute player for a pitcher when it is his turn to bat. The designated hitter does not participate when his team is fielding. *See Rule 7, The Runner (pages 98–101).*

SKILLS AND TACTICS

Excellent hand-eye coordination and a powerful swing are two basic skills a batter requires. However, judgment is also vital, since he must make snap decisions about whether a pitch (moving at speeds up to 100 mph) will arrive inside or outside his strike zone. Making contact with a pitch outside the strike zone is not only more difficult, but it will also often lead to a weakly hit ball even if successful. In addition, the first job of the batter is to reach base in any way possible. "Taking" four balls (pitches outside the strike zone), before making an out, results in a walk—a free pass to first base.

If a pitch is hit, a batter needs to run quickly in his attempt to get to first base or beyond. Sometimes a batter will *bunt* (tap the ball carefully somewhere within the infield). In such cases the pressure is on him to get to first base extremely quickly. Once on base, a speedy runner may attempt to *steal* the next base, which involves surprising the opposition by running to the next base without the benefit of another hit ball. All runners need enough speed to score from third base on a *sacrifice fly,* which involves a ball hit deep into the outfield in the air. Once the ball is caught, any runner *standing on his base* is allowed to run for the next one, attempting to get there before the outfielder's throw arrives. Infielders also need to catch throws from teammates cleanly.

RULES OF BASEBALL

This is an abridged version of the official rules of baseball.

1 Objectives of the Game
See How to win (page 94).

2 Definitions of Terms

3 Game Preliminaries

4 Starting and Ending a Game
See Starting (page 94) and Key rules (page 95).

5 Putting the Ball in Play. Live Ball

5.01 At the time set for beginning the game the umpire shall call "Play."

5.02 After the umpire calls "Play" the ball is alive and in play and remains alive and in play until for legal cause, or at the umpire's call of "Time" suspending play, the ball becomes dead. While the ball is dead no player may be put out, no bases may be run and no runs may be scored, except that runners may advance one or more bases as the result of acts that occurred while the ball was alive (such as, but not limited to a balk, an overthrow, interference, or a home run or other fair ball hit out of the playing field).

5.03 The pitcher shall deliver the pitch to the batter who may elect to strike the ball, or who may not offer at it, as he chooses.

5.04 The offensive team's objective is to have its batter become a runner, and its runners advance.

5.05 The defensive team's objective is to prevent offensive players from becoming runners, and to prevent their advance around the bases.

5.06 When a batter becomes a runner and touches all bases legally he shall score one run for his team.

5.07 When three offensive players are legally put out, that team takes the field and the opposing team becomes the offensive team.

5.08 If a thrown ball accidentally touches a base coach, or a pitched or thrown ball touches an umpire, the ball is alive and in play. However, if the coach interferes with a thrown ball, the runner is out.

5.09 The ball becomes dead and runners advance one base, or return to their bases, without liability to be put out, when:

(a) A pitched ball touches a batter, or his clothing, while in his legal batting position; runners, if forced, advance.

(b) The plate umpire interferes with the catcher's throw; runners may not advance. Note: The interference shall be disregarded if the catcher's throw retires the runner.

(c) A balk is committed; runners advance (See Penalty 8.05).

(d) A ball is illegally batted; runners return.

(e) A foul ball is not caught; runners return. The umpire shall not put the ball in play until all runners have retouched their bases.

(f) A fair ball touches a runner or an umpire on fair territory before it touches an infielder including the pitcher, or touches an umpire before it has passed an infielder other than the pitcher.

If a fair ball goes through, or by, an infielder, and touches a runner immediately back of him, or touches a runner after being deflected by an infielder, the ball is in play and the umpire shall not declare the runner out. In making such decision the umpire must be convinced that the ball passed through, or by, the infielder and that no other infielder had the chance to make a play on the ball; runners advance, if forced.

(g) A pitched ball lodges in the umpire's or catcher's mask or paraphernalia, and remains out of play, runners advance one base.

(h) Any legal pitch touches a runner trying to score; runners advance.

5.10 The ball becomes dead when an umpire calls "Time." The umpire-in-chief shall call "Time":

(a) When in his judgment weather, darkness, or similar conditions make immediate further play impossible.

(b) When light failure makes it difficult or impossible for the umpires to follow the play.

(c) When an accident incapacitates a player or an umpire.

(1) If an accident to a runner is such as to prevent him from proceeding to a base to which he is entitled, as on a home run hit out of the playing field, or an award of one or more bases, a substitute runner shall be permitted to complete the play.

(d) When a manager requests "Time" for a substitution, or for a conference with one of his players.

(e) When the umpire wishes to examine the ball, to consult with either manager, or for any similar cause.

(f) When a fielder, after catching a fly ball, falls into a bench or stand, or falls across ropes into a crowd when spectators are on the field. As pertains to runners, the provisions of 7.04 (c) shall prevail. If a fielder after making a catch steps into a bench, but does not fall, the ball is in play and runners may advance at their own peril.

(g) When an umpire orders a player or any other person removed from the playing field.

(h) Except in the cases stated in paragraphs (b) and (c) (1) of this rule, no umpire shall call "Time" while a play is in progress.

5.11 After the ball is dead, play shall be resumed when the pitcher takes his place on the pitcher's plate with a new ball or the same ball in his possession and the plate umpire calls "Play." The plate umpire shall call "Play" as soon as the pitcher takes his place on his plate with the ball in his possession.

6 The Batter

6.01 (a) Each player of the offensive team shall bat in the order that his name appears in his team's batting order.

(b) The first batter in each inning after the first inning shall be the player whose name follows that of the last player who legally completed his time at bat in the preceding inning.

6.02 (a) The batter shall take his position in the batter's box promptly when it is his time at bat.

(b) The batter shall not leave his position in the batter's box after the pitcher comes to set position, or starts his wind-up. Penalty: If the pitcher pitches, the umpire shall call "Ball" or "Strike," as the case may be.

(c) If the batter refuses to take his position in the batter's box during his time at bat, the umpire shall order the pitcher to pitch, and shall call "Strike" on each such pitch. The batter may take his proper position after any such pitch, and the regular ball and strike count shall continue, but if he does not take his proper position before three strikes are called, he shall be declared out.

6.03 The batter's legal position shall be with both feet within the batter's box.
Approved Ruling: The lines defining the box are within the batter's box.

6.04 A batter has legally completed his time at bat when he is put out or becomes a runner.

6.05 A batter is out when:

(a) His fair or foul fly ball (other than a foul tip) is legally caught by a fielder.

(b) A third strike is legally caught by the catcher.

(c) A third strike is not caught by the catcher when first base is occupied before two are out.

(d) He bunts foul on third strike.

(e) An infield fly is declared.

(f) He attempts to hit a third strike and the ball touches him.

(g) His fair ball touches him before touching a fielder.

(h) After hitting or bunting a fair ball, his bat hits the ball a second time in fair territory. The ball is dead and no runners may advance. If the batter-runner drops his bat and the ball rolls against the bat in fair territory and, in the umpire's judgement, there was no intention to interfere with the course of the ball, the ball is alive and in play.

(i) After hitting or bunting a foul ball, he intentionally deflects the course of the ball in any manner while running to first base. The ball is dead and no runners may advance.

(j) After a third strike or after he hits a fair ball, he or first base is tagged before he touches first base.

(k) In running the last half of the distance from home base to first base, while the ball is being fielded to first base, he runs outside (to the right of) the 3-ft line, or inside (to the left of) the foul line, and in the umpire's judgment in so doing interferes with the fielder taking the throw at first base; except that he may run outside (to the right of) the 3-ft line or inside (to the left of) the foul line to avoid a fielder attempting to field a batted ball.

(l) An infielder intentionally drops a fair fly ball or line drive, with first, first and second, first and third, or first, second and third base occupied before two are out. The ball is dead and runner or runners shall return to their original base or bases. Approved Ruling: In this situation, the batter is not out if the infielder permits the ball to drop untouched to the ground, except when the infield fly rule applies.

(m) A preceding runner shall, in the umpire's judgment, intentionally interfere with a fielder who is attempting to catch a thrown ball or to throw a ball in an attempt to complete any play.

(n) With two out, a runner on third base, and two strikes on the batter, the runner attempts to steal home base on a legal pitch and the ball touches the runner in the batter's strike zone. The umpire shall call "Strike three," the batter is out, and the run shall not count; before two are out, the umpire shall call "Strike three," the ball is dead, and the run counts.

6.06 A batter is out for illegal action when:

(a) He hits a ball with one or both feet on the ground entirely outside the batter's box.

(b) He steps from one batter's box to the other while the pitcher is in position ready to pitch.

(c) He interferes with the catcher's fielding or throwing by stepping out of the batter's box or making any other movement that hinders the catcher's play at home base. Exception:

Batter is not out if any runner attempting to advance is put out, or if runner trying to score is called out for batter's interference.

(d) He uses or attempts to use a bat that, in the umpire's judgment, has been altered or tampered with in such a way to improve the distance factor or cause an unusual reaction on the baseball. This includes bats that are filled, flat-surfaced, nailed, hollowed, grooved, or covered with a substance such as paraffin, wax, etc. No advancement on the bases will be allowed and any out or outs made during a play shall stand.

In addition to being called out, the player shall be ejected from the game and may be subject to additional penalties as determined by his league president.

6.07 Batting out of Turn

(a) A batter shall be called out, on appeal, when he fails to bat in his proper turn, and another batter completes a time at bat in his place.

(1) The proper batter may take his place in the batter's box at any time before the improper batter becomes a runner or is put out, and any balls and strikes shall be counted in the proper batter's time at bat.

(b) When an improper batter becomes a runner or is put out, and the defensive team appeals to the umpire before the first pitch to the next batter of either team, or before any play or attempted play, the umpire shall (1) declare the proper batter out;

and (2) nullify any advance or score made because of a ball batted by the improper batter or because of the improper batter's advance to first base on a hit, an error, a base on balls, a hit batter or otherwise.

Note: If a runner advances, while the improper batter is at bat, on a stolen base, balk, wild pitch, or passed ball, such advance is legal.

(c) When an improper batter becomes a runner or is put out, and a pitch is made to the next batter of either team before an appeal is made, the improper batter thereby becomes the proper batter, and the results of his time at bat become legal.

(d) (1) When the proper batter is called out because he has failed to bat in turn, the next batter shall be the batter whose name follows that of the proper batter thus called out; (2) When an improper batter becomes a proper batter because no appeal is made before the next pitch, the next batter shall be the batter whose name follows that of such legalized improper batter. The instant an improper batter's actions are legalized, the batting order picks up with the name following that of the legalized improper batter.

6.08 The batter becomes a runner and is entitled to first base without liability to be put out (provided he advances to and touches first base) when:

(a) Four "balls" have been called by the umpire.

(b) He is touched by a pitched ball that he is not attempting to hit unless (1) The ball is in the strike zone when it touches the batter, or (2) The batter makes no attempt to avoid being touched by the ball.

If the ball is in the strike zone when it touches the batter, it shall be called a strike, whether or not the batter tries to avoid the ball. If the ball is outside the strike

zone when it touches the batter, it shall be called a ball if he makes no attempt to avoid being touched.

Approved Ruling: When the batter is touched by a pitched ball that does not entitle him to first base, the ball is dead and no runner may advance.

(c) The catcher or any fielder interferes with him. If a play follows the interference, the manager of the offense may advise the plate umpire that he elects to decline the interference penalty and accept the play. Such election shall be made immediately at the end of the play. However, if the batter reaches first base on a hit, an error, a base on balls, a hit baseman, or otherwise, and all other runners advance at least one base, the play proceeds without reference to the interference.

(d) A fair ball touches an umpire or a runner on fair territory before touching a fielder. If a fair ball touches an umpire after having passed a fielder other than the pitcher, or having touched a fielder, including the pitcher, the ball is in play.

6.09 The batter becomes a runner when:

(a) He hits a fair ball.

(b) The third strike called by the umpire is not caught, providing (1) first base is unoccupied, or (2) first base is occupied with two out.

(c) A fair ball, after having passed a fielder other than the pitcher, or after having been touched by a fielder, including the pitcher, shall touch an umpire or runner on fair territory.

(d) A fair ball passes over a fence or into the stands at a distance from home base of 250 ft or more. Such hit entitles the batter to a home run when he shall have touched all bases legally. A fair fly ball that passes out of the playing field at a point less than 250 ft from home base shall entitle the batter to advance to second base only.

(e) A fair ball, after touching the ground, bounds into the stands, or passes through, over or under a fence, or through or under a scoreboard, or through or under shrubbery, or vines on the fence, in which case the batter and the runners shall be entitled to advance two bases.

(f) Any fair ball that, either before or after touching the ground, passes through or under a fence, or through or under a scoreboard, or through any opening in the fence or scoreboard, or through or under shrubbery, or vines on the fence, or that sticks in a fence or scoreboard, in which case the batter and the runners shall be entitled to two bases.

(g) Any bounding fair ball is deflected by the fielder into the stands, or over or under a

➡ *page 98*

Winning stroke
A straight swing and a strong follow-through are needed to propel the ball over the outfield fences for a home run.

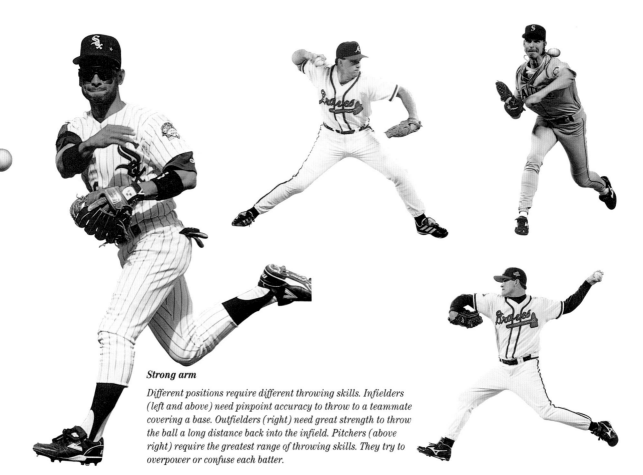

Strong arm

Different positions require different throwing skills. Infielders (left and above) need pinpoint accuracy to throw to a teammate covering a base. Outfielders (right) need great strength to throw the ball a long distance back into the infield. Pitchers (above right) require the greatest range of throwing skills. They try to overpower or confuse each batter.

continued from page 97

fence on fair or foul territory, in which case the batter and all runners shall be entitled to advance two bases.

(h) Any fair fly ball is deflected by the fielder into the stands, or over the fence into foul territory, in which case the batter shall be entitled to advance to second base; but if deflected into the stands or over the fence in fair territory, the batter shall be entitled to a home run. However, should such a fair fly be deflected at a point less than 250 ft (76 m) from home plate, the batter shall be entitled to two bases only.

6.10 Any league may elect to use the Designated Hitter Rule.

(a) In the event of interleague competition between clubs of leagues using the Designated Hitter Rule and clubs of the leagues not using the Designated Hitter Rule, the rule will be used as follows:

1. In World Series or exhibition games, the rule will be used or not used as is the practice of the home team.

2. In All-Star games, the rule will only be used if both teams and both Leagues so agree.

(b) The Rule provides as follows:

A hitter may be designated to bat for the starting pitcher and all subsequent pitchers in any game without otherwise affecting the status of the pitcher(s) in the game. A designated hitter for the pitcher must be selected prior to the game and must be included in the line-up cards presented to the umpire-in-chief. The designated hitter named in the starting line-up must come to bat at least one time, unless the opposing club changes pitchers. It is not mandatory that a club designate a hitter for the pitcher, but failure to do so prior to the game precludes the use of a designated hitter for that game. Pinch hitters for a designated hitter may be used. Any substitute hitter for a designated hitter becomes the designated hitter. A replaced designated hitter shall not reenter the game in any capacity. The designated hitter may be used defensively, continuing to bat in the same position in the batting order, but the pitcher must then bat in the place of the substituted defensive player, unless more than one substitution is made, and the manager then must designate their spots in the batting order. A runner may be substituted for the designated hitter and the runner

assumes the role of designated hitter. A designated hitter may not pinch run. A designated hitter is "locked" into the batting order. No multiple substitutions may be made that will alter the batting rotation of the designated hitter.

Once the game pitcher is switched from the mound to a defensive position this move shall terminate the designated hitter rule for the remainder of the game. Once a pinch hitter bats for any player in the batting order and then enters the game to pitch, this move shall terminate the designated hitter role for the remainder of the game. Once the game pitcher bats for the designated hitter this move shall terminate the designated hitter role for the remainder of the game. (The game pitcher may only pinch-hit for the designated hitter.) Once a designated hitter assumes a defensive position this move shall terminate the designated hitter role for the remainder of the game. A substitute for the designated hitter need not be announced until it is the designated hitter's turn to bat.

7 The Runner

7.01 A runner acquires the right

to an unoccupied base when he touches it before he is out. He is then entitled to it until he is put out, or forced to vacate it for another runner legally entitled to that base.

7.02 In advancing, a runner shall touch first, second, third, and home base in order. If forced to return, he shall retouch all bases in reverse order, unless the ball is dead under any provision of Rule 5.09. In such cases, the runner may go directly to his original base.

7.03 Two runners may not occupy a base, but if, while the ball is alive, two runners are touching a base, the following runner shall be out when tagged. The preceding runner is entitled to the base.

7.04 Each runner, other than the batter, may without liability to be put out, advance one base when:

(a) There is a balk.

(b) The batter's advance without liability to be put out forces the runner to vacate his base, or when the batter hits a fair ball that touches another runner or the umpire before such ball has been touched by, or has passed a fielder, if the runner is forced to advance.

(c) A fielder, after catching a fly ball, falls into a bench or

Forced out
When a fielder throws the ball to a baseman so quickly that a runner forced to run to that base is beaten, the runner is out.

Tagged out
Occasionally runners are put out when a fielder "tags" (touches) him with the ball when he is running between bases.

stand, or falls across ropes into a crowd when spectators are on the field.

(d) While he is attempting to steal a base, the batter is interfered with by the catcher or any other fielder.

Note: When a runner is entitled to a base without liability to be put out, while the ball is in play, or under any rule in which the ball is in play after the runner reaches the base to which he is entitled, and the runner fails to touch the base to which he is entitled before attempting to advance to the next base, the runner shall forfeit his exemption from liability to be put out, and he may be put out by tagging the base or by tagging the runner before he returns to the missed base.

7.05 Each runner including the batter-runner may, without liability to be put out, advance:

(a) To home base, scoring a run, if a fair ball goes out of the playing field in flight and he touched all bases legally; or if a fair ball that, in the umpire's judgment, would have gone out of the playing field in flight, is deflected by the act of a fielder in throwing his glove, cap, or any article of his apparel.

(b) Three bases, if a fielder deliberately touches a fair ball with his cap, mask, or any part of his uniform detached from its proper place on his person. The ball is in play and the batter may advance to home base at his peril.

(c) Three bases, if a fielder deliberately throws his glove at and touches a fair ball. The ball is in play and the batter may advance to home base at his peril.

(d) Two bases, if a fielder deliberately touches a thrown ball with his cap, mask, or any part of his uniform detached from its proper place on his person. The ball is in play.

(e) Two bases, if a fielder deliberately throw his glove at and touches a thrown ball. The ball is in play.

(f) Two bases, if a fair ball bounces or is deflected into the stands outside the first or third base foul lines; or if it goes through or under a field fence, or through or under a scoreboard, or through or under shrubbery or vines on the fence; or if it sticks in such fence, scoreboard, shrubbery, or vines.

(g) Two bases when, with no spectators on the playing field, a thrown ball goes into the stands, or into a bench (whether or not the ball rebounds into the field), or over or under or through a

field fence or on a slanting part of the screen above the backstop, or remains in the meshes of a wire screen protecting spectators. The ball is dead. When such wild throw is the first play by an infielder, the umpire, in awarding such bases, shall be governed by the position of the runners at the time the ball was pitched; in all other cases the umpire shall be governed by the position of the runners at the time the wild throw was made.

Approved Ruling: If all runners, including the batter-runner, have advanced at least one base when an infielder makes a wild throw on the first play after the pitch, the award shall be governed by the position of the runners when the wild throw was made.

(h) One base, if a ball, pitched to the batter, or thrown by the pitcher from his position on the pitcher's plate to a base to catch a runner, goes into a stand or a bench, or over or through a field fence or backstop. The ball is dead.

Approved Ruling: When a wild pitch or passed ball goes through or by the catcher, or deflects off the catcher, and goes directly into the dugout, stands, above the break, or any area where the ball

is dead, the awarding of bases shall be one base. One base shall also be awarded if the pitcher while in contact with the rubber, throws to a base, and the throw goes directly into the stands or into any area where the ball is dead.

If, however, the pitched or thrown ball goes through or by the catcher or through the fielder, and remains on the playing field, and is subsequently kicked or deflected into the dugout, stands, or other area where the ball is dead, the awarding of bases shall be two bases from position of runners at the time of the pitch or throw.

(i) One base, if the batter becomes a runner on Ball Four or Strike Three, when the pitch passes the catcher and lodges in the umpire's mask or paraphernalia. If the batter becomes a runner on a wild pitch that entitles the runners to advance one base, the batter-runner shall be entitled to first base only.

7.06 When obstruction occurs, the umpire shall call or signal "Obstruction."

(a) If a play is being made on the obstructed runner, or if the

➡ *page 100*

continued from page 99

batter-runner is obstructed before he touches first base, the ball is dead and all runners shall advance, without liability to be put out, to the bases they would have reached, in the umpire's judgment, if there had been no obstruction. The obstructed runner shall be awarded at least one base beyond the base he has last legally touched before the obstruction. Any preceding runners, forced to advance by the award of bases as the penalty for obstruction, shall advance without liability to be put out.

(b) If no play is being made on the obstructed runner, the play shall proceed until no further action is possible. The umpire shall then call "Time" and impose such penalties, if any, as in his judgment will nullify the act of obstruction.

7.07 If, with a runner on third base and trying to score by means of a squeeze play or a steal, the catcher or any other fielder steps on, or in front of home base without possession of the ball, or touches the batter or his bat, the pitcher shall be charged with a balk, the batter shall be awarded first base on the interference and the ball is dead.

7.08 Any runner is out when:

(a) (1) He runs more than 3 ft (0.9 m) away from a direct line between bases to avoid being tagged unless his action is to avoid interference with a fielder fielding a batted ball; or (2) after touching first base, he leaves the baseline, obviously abandoning his effort to touch the next base. Approved Ruling: When a batter becomes a runner on third strike not caught, and starts for his bench or position, he may advance to first base at any time before he enters the bench. To put him out, the defense must tag him or first base before he touches first base.

(b) He intentionally interferes with a thrown ball; or hinders a fielder attempting to make a play on a batted ball.

(c) He is tagged, when the ball is alive, while off his base. Exception: A batter-runner cannot be tagged out after overrunning or oversliding first base if he returns immediately to the base.

Approved Ruling: (1) If the impact of a runner breaks a base loose from its position, no play can be made on that runner at that base if he had reached the base safely.

Approved Ruling: (2) If a base is dislodged from its position during a play, any following runner on the same play shall be considered as touching or occupying the base if, in the umpire's judgment, he touches or occupies the point marked by the dislodged bag.

(d) He fails to retouch his base after a fair or foul ball is legally caught before he, or his base, is tagged by a fielder. He shall not be called out for failure to retouch his base after the first following pitch, or any play or attempted play. This is an appeal play.

(e) He fails to reach the next base before a fielder tags him or the base, after he has been forced to advance by reason of the batter becoming a runner. However, if a following runner is put out on a force play, the force is removed and the runner must be tagged to be put out. The force is removed as soon as the runner touches the base to which he is forced to advance, and if he overslides or overruns the base, the runner must be tagged to be put out. However, if the forced runner, after touching the next base, retreats for any reason toward the base he has just occupied, the force play is reinstated, and he can again be put out if the defense tags the base to which he is forced.

(f) He is touched by a fair ball in fair territory before the ball has touched or passed an infielder. The ball is dead and no runner may score, nor runners advance, except runners forced to advance. Exception: If a runner is touching his base when touched by an infield fly, he is not out although the batter is out. If runner is touched by an infield fly when he is not touching his base, both runner and batter are out.

(g) He attempts to score on a play in which the batter interferes with the play at home base before two are out. With two out, the interference puts the batter out and no score counts.

(h) He passes a preceding runner before such runner is out.

(i) After he has acquired legal possession of a base, he runs the bases in reverse order for the purpose of confusing the defense or making a travesty of the game. The umpire shall immediately call "Time" and declare the runner out.

(j) He fails to return at once to first base after overrunning or oversliding that base. If he attempts to run to second he is

out when tagged. If, after overrunning or oversliding first base he starts toward the dugout, or toward his position, and fails to return to first base at once, he is out, on appeal, when he or the base is tagged.

(k) In running or sliding for home base, he fails to touch home base and makes no attempt to return to the base, when a fielder holds the ball in his hand, while touching home base, and appeals to the umpire for the decision.

7.09 It is interference by a batter or a runner when:

(a) After a third strike he hinders the catcher in his attempt to field the ball.

(b) After hitting or bunting a fair ball, his bat hits the ball a second time in fair territory. The ball is dead and no runners may advance. If the batter-runner drops his bat and the ball rolls against the bat in fair territory and, in the umpire's judgment, there was no intention to interfere with the course of the ball, the ball is alive and in play.

(c) He intentionally deflects the course of a foul ball in any manner.

(d) Before two are out and a runner on third base, the batter hinders a fielder in making a play at home base; the runner is out.

(e) Any member or members of the offensive team stand or gather around any base to which a runner is advancing, to confuse, hinder, or add to the difficulty of the fielders. Such runner shall be declared out for the interference of his teammate or teammates;

(f) Any batter or runner who has just been put out hinders or impedes any following play being made on a runner. Such runner shall be declared out for the interference of his teammate.

(g) If, in the judgment of the umpire, a base runner willfully and deliberately interferes with a batted ball or a fielder in the act of fielding a batted ball with the obvious intent to break up a double play, the ball is dead. The umpire shall call the runner out for interference and also call out the batter-runner because of the action of his teammate. In no event may bases be run or runs scored because of such action by a runner.

(h) If, in the judgment of the umpire, a batter-runner willfully and deliberately interferes with a batted ball or a fielder in the act of fielding a batted ball, with the obvious intent to break up a double play, the ball is dead; the

umpire shall call the batter-runner out for interference and shall also call out the runner who had advanced closest to the home plate regardless where the double play might have been possible. In no event shall bases be run because of such interference.

(i) In the judgment of the umpire, the base coach at third base, or first base, by touching or holding the runner, physically assists him in returning to or leaving third base or first base.

(j) With a runner on third base, the base coach leaves his box and acts in any manner to draw a throw by a fielder.

(k) In running the last half of the distance from home base to first base while the ball is being fielded to first base, he runs outside (to the right of) the 3-ft line, or inside (to the left of) the foul line and, in the umpire's judgment, interferes with the fielder taking the throw at first base, or attempting to field a batted ball.

(l) He fails to avoid a fielder who is attempting to field a batted ball, or intentionally interferes with a thrown ball, provided that if two or more fielders attempt to field a batted ball, and the runner comes in contact with one or more of them, the umpire shall determine which fielder is entitled to the benefit of this rule, and shall not declare the runner out for coming in contact with a fielder other than the one the umpire determines to be entitled to field such a ball.

(m) A fair ball touches him on fair territory before touching a fielder. If a fair ball goes through, or by, an infielder, and touches a runner immediately back of him, or touches the runner after having been deflected by a fielder, the umpire shall not declare the runner out for being touched by a batted ball. In making such decision the umpire must be convinced that the ball passed through, or by, the fielder, and that no other infielder had the chance to make a play on the ball. If, in the judgment of the umpire, the runner deliberately and intentionally kicks such a batted ball on which the infielder has missed a play, then the runner shall be called out of interference.

Penalty for Interference: The runner is out and the ball is dead.

7.10 Any runner shall be called out, on appeal, when:

(a) After a fly ball is caught, he

fails to retouch his original base before he or his original base is tagged.

(b) With the ball in play, while advancing or returning to a base, he fails to touch each base in order before he, or a missed base, is tagged.

Approved Ruling: (1) No runner may return to touch a missed base after a following runner has scored. (2) When the ball is dead, no runner may return to touch a missed base or one he has left after he has advanced to and touched a base beyond the missed base.

(c) He overruns or overslides first base and fails to return to the base immediately, and he or the base is tagged.

(d) He fails to touch home base and makes no attempt to return to that base, and home base is tagged.

Any appeal under this rule must be made before the next pitch, or any play or attempted play. If the violation occurs during a play that ends a half-inning, the appeal must be made before the defensive team leaves the field. An appeal is not to be interpreted as a play or attempted play. Successive appeals may not be made on a runner at the same base. If the defensive team on its first appeal errs, a request for a second appeal on the same runner at the same base shall not be allowed by the umpire. (Intended meaning of the word "err" is that the defensive team in making an appeal threw the ball out of play. For example, if the pitcher threw to first base to appeal and threw the ball into the stands, no second appeal would be allowed.) Appeal plays may require an umpire to recognize an apparent "fourth out." If the third out is made during a play in which an appeal play is sustained on another runner, the appeal play decision takes precedence in determining the out. If there is more than one appeal during a play that ends a half-inning, the defense may elect to take the out that gives it the advantage. For the purpose of this rule, the defensive team has "left the

field" when the pitcher and all infielders have left fair territory on their way to the bench or clubhouse.

7.11 The players, coaches or any member of an offensive team shall vacate any space (including both dugouts) needed by a fielder who is attempting to field a batted or thrown ball.
Penalty: Interference shall be called and the batter or runner on whom the play is being made shall be declared out.

7.12 Unless two are out, the status of a following runner is not affected by a preceding runner's failure to touch or retouch a base. If, upon appeal, the preceding runner is third out, no runners following him shall score. If such third out is the result of a force play, neither preceding nor following runners shall score.

him to the pitch without interruption or alteration. He shall not raise either foot from the ground, except that in his actual delivery of the ball to the batter, he may take one step backward, and one step forward with his free foot. When a pitcher holds the ball with both hands in front of his body, with his entire pivot foot on, or in front of and touching but not off the end of the pitcher's plate, and his other foot free, he will be considered in the wind-up position.

(b) The Set Position. Set position shall be indicated by the pitcher when he stands facing the batter with his entire pivot foot on, or in front of, and in contact with, and not off the end of the pitcher's plate, and his

A throw from the outfield.

8 The Pitcher

8.01 Legal pitching delivery. There are two legal pitching positions, the wind-up position and the set position, and either position may be used at any time. Pitchers shall take signs from the catcher while standing on the rubber.

(a) The Wind-up Position. The pitcher shall stand facing the batter, his entire pivot foot on, or in front of and touching and not off the end of the pitcher's plate, and the other foot free. From this position any natural movement associated with his delivery of the ball to the batter commits

other foot in front of the pitcher's plate, holding the ball in both hands in front of his body and coming to a complete stop. From such set position he may deliver the ball to the batter, throw to a base or step backward off the pitcher's plate with his pivot foot. Before assuming set position, the pitcher may elect to make any natural preliminary motion such as that known as "the stretch." But if he so elects, he shall come to set position before delivering the ball to the batter. After assuming set position, any natural motion

associated with his delivery of the ball to the batter commits him to the pitch without alteration or interruption.

Preparatory to coming to a set position, the pitcher shall have one hand on his side; from this position he shall go to his set position as defined in Rule 8.01 (b) without interruption and in one continuous motion. The whole width of the foot in contact with the rubber must be on the rubber. A pitcher cannot pitch from off the end of the rubber with just the side of his foot touching the rubber. The pitcher, following his stretch, must (a) hold the ball in both hands in front of his body and (b) come to a complete stop. This must be enforced. Umpires should watch this closely. Pitchers are constantly attempting to "beat the rule" in their efforts to hold runners on bases and in cases where the pitcher fails to make a complete "stop" called for in the rules, the umpire should immediately call a "Balk."

(c) At any time during the pitcher's preliminary movements and until his natural pitching motion commits him to the pitch, he may throw to any base provided he steps directly toward such base before making the throw.

(d) If the pitcher makes an illegal pitch with the bases unoccupied, it shall be called a ball unless the batter reaches first base on a hit, an error, a base on balls, a hit batter, or otherwise.

(e) If the pitcher removes his pivot foot from contact with the pitcher's plate by stepping backward with that foot, he thereby becomes an infielder and if he makes a wild throw from that position, it shall be considered the same as a wild

throw by any other infielder.

8.02 The pitcher shall not:
(a) (1) Bring his pitching hand in contact with his mouth or lips while in the 18-ft circle surrounding the pitching rubber.

➡ *page 102*

continued from page 101

Exception: Provided it is agreed to by both managers, the umpire prior to the start of a game played in cold weather, may permit the pitcher to blow on his hand.

Penalty: For violation of this part of this rule the umpires shall immediately call a ball. However, if the pitch is made and a batter reaches first base on a hit, an error, a hit batsman, or otherwise, and no runner is put out before advancing at least one base, the play shall proceed without reference to the violation. Repeated offenders shall be subject to a fine by the league president.

(2) Apply a foreign substance of any kind to the ball;

(3) expectorate on the ball, either hand or his glove;

(4) rub the ball on his glove, person or clothing;

(5) deface the ball in any manner;

(6) deliver what is called the "shine" ball, "spit" ball, "mud" ball, or "emery" ball. The pitcher, of course, is allowed to rub the ball between his bare hands.

Penalty: For violation of any part of this rule 8.02(a) (2 to 6) the umpire shall:

(a) Call the pitch a ball, warn the pitcher and have announced on the public address system the reason for the action.

(b) In the case of a second offense by the same pitcher in the same game, the pitcher shall be disqualified from the game.

(c) If a play follows the violation called by the umpire, the manager of the offense may advise the plate umpire that he elects to accept the play. Such election shall be made immediately at the end of the play. However, if the batter reaches first base on a hit, an error, a base on balls, a hit batsman, or otherwise, and no other runner is put out before advancing at least one base, the play shall proceed without reference to the violation.

(d) Even though the offense elects to take the play, the violation shall be recognized and the penalties in (a) and (b) will still be in effect.

(e) The umpire shall be the sole judge on whether any portion of this rule has been violated.

(b) Have on his person, or in his possession, any foreign substance. For such infraction of this section (b) the penalty shall be immediate ejection from the game.

(c) Intentionally delay the game by throwing the ball to players other than the catcher, when the batter is in position, except in an attempt to retire a runner.

Penalty: If, after warning by the umpire, such delaying action is repeated, the pitcher shall be removed from the game.

(d) Intentionally pitch at the batter.

If, in the umpire's judgment, such a violation occurs, the umpire may elect either to:

1. Expel the pitcher, or the manager and the pitcher, from the game, or

2. may warn the pitcher and

Landslide
Base runners often finish their run to a base other than first with a slide that lands them on the base.

the manager of both teams that another such pitch will result in the immediate expulsion of that pitcher (or a replacement) and the manager.

If, in the umpire's judgment, circumstances warrant, both teams may be officially "warned" prior to the game or at any time during the game.

8.03 When a pitcher takes his position at the beginning of each inning, or when he relieves another pitcher, he shall be permitted to pitch not to exceed eight preparatory pitches to his catcher during which play shall be suspended. A league by its own action may limit the number of preparatory pitches to less than eight preparatory pitches. Such preparatory pitches shall not consume more than one minute of time. If a sudden emergency causes a pitcher to be summoned into the game without any opportunity to warm up, the umpire-in-chief shall allow him as many pitches as the umpire deems necessary.

8.04 When the bases are unoccupied, the pitcher shall deliver the ball to the batter within 20 seconds after he receives the ball. Each time the pitcher delays the game by violating this rule, the umpire

shall call "Ball." The intent of this rule is to avoid unnecessary delays. The umpire shall insist that the catcher return the ball promptly to the pitcher, and that the pitcher take his position on the rubber promptly. Obvious delay by the pitcher should instantly be penalized by the umpire.

8.05 If there is a runner, or runners, it is a balk when:

(a) The pitcher, while touching his plate, makes any motion naturally associated with his pitch and fails to make such delivery.

(b) The pitcher, while touching his plate, feints a throw to first base and fails to complete the throw.

(c) The pitcher, while touching his plate, fails to step directly toward a base before throwing to that base.

(d) The pitcher, while touching his plate, throws, or feints a throw to an unoccupied base, except for the purpose of making a play.

(e) The pitcher makes an illegal pitch.

(f) The pitcher delivers the ball to the batter while he is not facing the batter.

(g) The pitcher makes any motion naturally associated with his pitch while he is not touching the pitcher's plate.

(h) The pitcher unnecessarily delays the game.

(i) The pitcher, without having the ball, stands on or astride the pitcher's plate or while off the plate, he feints a pitch.

(j) The pitcher, after coming to a legal pitching position, removes one hand from the ball other than in an actual pitch, or in throwing to a base.

(k) The pitcher, while touching his plate, accidentally or intentionally drops the ball.

(l) The pitcher, while giving an intentional base on balls, pitches when the catcher is not in the

catcher's box.

(m) The pitcher delivers the pitch from set position without coming to a stop.

Penalty: The ball is dead, and each runner shall advance one base without liability to be put out, unless the batter reaches first on a hit, an error, a base on balls, a hit batter, or otherwise, and all other runners advance at least one base, in which case the play proceeds without reference to the balk.

Approved Ruling: In cases where a pitcher balks and throws wild, either to a base or to a home plate, a runner or runners may advance beyond the base to which he is entitled at his own risk.

Approved Ruling: A runner who misses the first base to which he is advancing and who is called out on appeal shall be considered as having advanced one base for the purpose of this rule.

8.06 A professional league shall adopt the following rule pertaining to the visit of the manager or coach to the pitcher:

(a) This rule limits the number of trips a manager of coach may make to any one pitcher in any one inning.

(b) A second trip to the same pitcher in the same inning will cause this pitcher's automatic removal.

(c) The manager or coach is prohibited from making a second visit to the mound while the same batter is at bat, but

(d) if a pinch-hitter is substituted for this batter, the manager or coach may make a second visit to the mound, but must remove the pitcher. A manager or coach is considered to have concluded his visit to the mound when he leaves the 18-ft circle surrounding the pitcher's rubber.

9 The Umpire

10 The Official Scorer

The Official Major League Baseball Rules are copyrighted works owned by the Office of the Commissioner of Baseball and are used with permission of Major League Baseball Properties, Inc.

A copy of the complete rules, including various explanations to the rules, as well as the rules of scoring, is available from the League.

Softball
Essentials

A close relative of baseball, this game differs mostly in terms of game length (fewer innings), equipment used (a bigger ball, aluminum bats), and field distances (shorter). The basic principles resemble those of baseball, but the differences make softball popular with amateurs at all skill levels. Nevertheless, some teams, such as the women's Olympic teams, perform at a very high skill level.

Softball team
Of the nine fielding positons in softball, only pitchers and catchers stand in precisely prescribed positions when fieldng. The other fielders will vary their position based on where they think a batter is most likely to hit the ball.

The field
For adults bases are 60 ft apart and the outfield fences (if any) are set at a radius of 225 ft (men) or 200 ft (women) from the home plate. The pitching distance from the pitching rubber to the home plate is 46 ft (men) or 40 ft (women). A pitching circle of radius 8 ft.

The bat
Generally made of aluminum alloy (although metal, bamboo, fiberglass, or other International Softball Federation approved materials may be used). No longer than 34 in and weighing no more than 38 oz. A safety grip is required on softball bats due to the short distances and the closeness of the infielders.

The ball
White, spherical, larger than a baseball. A circumference of 12 in and a weight of 6 1/4–7 oz. The ball is of flat seam style with no less than 88 stitches in each cover.

Foul line
Fence
3rd base
See distance table on pg104
Pitching rubber
2nd base
Batter's box
Home plate
same length as the diamond
16 ft
Home plate
Pitching distance See distance table on pg104
1st base
Foul line

Back to basics
Softball is sometimes played on a completely marked out field, but more often than not amateurs play on any open grass area with just four bases and the pitching rubber marked.

Players

Nine players per team.
The positions are:
pitcher (1)
catcher (2)
first baseman (3)
second baseman (4)
third baseman (5)
shortstop (6)
left fielder (7)
center fielder (8)
right fielder (9).
See baseball diagram on page 94.

Strong arm
Although softball pitchers pitch underhand, a skilled pitcher is capable of dominating batters every bit as effectively as a pitcher in baseball. For this reason, many top-level games are relatively low-scoring.

Base to base
A player on base may run for the next base as soon as the ball leaves the pitcher's hand. She will only do so, however, if she is confident that she can beat a throw from the catcher.

Dress

Uniform in color and style throughout a team. All catchers wear a mask, throat protector, helmet, body protector, and shin-guards. All offensive players wear helmets while batting and baserunning. Shoes may feature soft or hard rubber cleats. Spikes on the sole or heel must not exceed ³/₄ in.

Officials

A plate umpire (who stands behind the catcher to judge balls and strikes) and a base umpire (to judge base decisions).

HOW TO PLAY

The two teams take turns batting and fielding. The batting team sends players to home plate to face the pitcher. Each batter attempts to advance around the circuit of bases (beginning and ending at home plate) without making an *out*. If a player successfully completes the circuit, a run is scored. It is the goal of the fielding side to get players out before they can complete the circuit. Once three players have been made out, the two teams switch sides (the fielding team becomes the batting team and vice-versa).

Starting

If no team is designated the home team, a coin toss decides who will bat first.

How to win

One run is scored for every player who returns to home plate after touching first, second, and third bases *safely* (i.e., without making an out). The team with the most runs at the end of the game wins.

Distance table

Game	Division	Bases	Pitching	Fences
Adult				
Fast pitch	Female	60 ft (18.29 m)	40 ft (12.2m)	200 ft (60.96 m)
	Male	60 ft (18.29 m)	46 ft (14.0 m)	225 ft (68.58m)–250 ft (76.20 m)
Modified	Female	60 ft (18.29 m)	40 ft (12.2m)	200 ft (60.96 m)
	Male	60 ft (18.29 m)	46 ft (14.0 m)	265 ft (80.80 m)
Slow pitch	Female	65 ft (19.81 m)	46 ft (14.0 m)	250 ft (76.20 m)
	Male	65 ft (19.81 m)	46 ft (14.0 m)	275 ft (83.82 m)
	Co-ed	65 ft (19.81 m)	46 ft (14.0 m)	275 ft (83.82 m)
	Super	65 ft (19.81 m)	46 ft (14.0 m)	300 ft (91.44 m m)
Youth				
Fast pitch	Girls under 10	55 ft (16.76 m)	35 ft (10.67 m)	150 ft (45.72 m)–175 ft (53.34 m)
	Boys under 10	55 ft (16.76 m)	35 ft (10.67 m)	150 ft (45.72 m)–175 ft (53.34 m)
	Girls under 12	60 ft (18.29 m)	35 ft (10.67 m)	175 ft (53.34 m)–200 ft (60.96 m)
	Boys under 12	60 ft (18.29 m)	40 ft (12.2 m)	175 ft (53.34 m)–200 ft (60.96 m)
	Girls under 15	60 ft (18.29 m)	40 ft (12.2 m)	175 ft (53.34 m)–200 ft (60.96 m)
	Boys under 15	60 ft (18.29 m)	46 ft (14.0 m)	175 ft (53.34 m)–200 ft (60.96 m)
	Girls under 19	60 ft (18.29 m)	40 ft (12.2 m)	200 ft (60.96 m)–225 ft (68.58m)
	Boys under 19	60 ft (18.29 m)	46 ft (14.0 m)	200 ft (60.96 m)–225 ft (68.58m)
Fast pitch	Girls under 10	55 ft (16.76 m)	35 ft (10.67 m)	150 ft (45.72 m)–175 ft (53.34 m)
	Boys under 10	55 ft (16.76 m)	35 ft (10.67 m)	150 ft (45.72 m)–175 ft (53.34 m)
	Girls under 12	60 ft (18.29 m)	40 ft (12.2 m)	175 ft (53.34 m)–200 ft (60.96 m)
	Boys under 12	60 ft (18.29 m)	40 ft (12.2 m)	175 ft (53.34 m)–200 ft (60.96 m)
	Girls under 15	65 ft (19.81 m)	46 ft (14.0 m)	225 ft (68.58m)–250 ft (76.20 m)
	Boys under 15	60 ft (18.29 m)	46 ft (14.0 m)	250 ft (76.20 m)–275 ft (83.82 m)
	Girls under 19	65 ft (19.81 m)	46 ft (14.0 m)	225 ft (68.58m)–250 ft (76.20 m)
	Boys under 19	65 ft (19.81 m)	46 ft (14.0 m)	275 ft (83.82 m)–300 ft (91.44 m m)

KEY RULES

• A game consists of seven innings.

• The pitcher's delivery is made underarm and must begin with both feet in contact with the pitching rubber and the ball held with both hands in front of the body. The pitch itself begins when one hand is taken off the ball. A pivot foot is used to maintain contact with the rubber or to push off from it.

• A pitcher's delivery (i.e., *the pitch*) arrives at home plate either inside or outside the *strike zone,* which is the space over any part of the plate no higher than the batter's arm pit and no lower than his knee when he assumes his natural batting stance. If the batter does not swing at a pitch that arrives outside the strike zone, it is called a *ball.* If the pitcher throws four balls to a batter before the batter either puts the ball in play or *strikes out* (*see* below), the batter is issued a *walk*—he is allowed to occupy first base.

• If a pitch arrives inside the strike zone and the batter does not swing at it, it is called a strike. It is also a strike if a batter swings at and misses any pitch, whether inside or outside the strike zone. After three strikes, the batter is out. (A strike is also called if the batter hits a pitch into foul territory, which is anywhere not on or inside the foul lines. However, a *third* strike cannot be recorded in this manner. A batter with two strikes who fouls off a pitch still has two strikes, and another pitch must be made.)

• If a batter hits the ball in fair territory (anywhere on or between the two baselines), he becomes a runner, attempting to reach first base before the ball is retrieved and thrown to a fielder with at least one foot on first base. If the ball is hit where it is difficult to retrieve quickly, he may attempt to advance further than first base. In such cases, it is no longer sufficient for the ball to beat a runner to a base. In order to be made out, the runner must be tagged (touched) by someone holding the ball before making contact with the base.

• The batter is automatically out if a ball hit into the air is caught before it touches the ground.

• Runners must stand on the base they occupy until the pitcher releases the ball. As soon as the ball leaves the pitcher's hand, they may advance toward the next base, and they may continue to try to advance as long as the ball remains in play. However, runners must return to the base they legally occupied at the time of the pitch if the ball is hit into foul territory or if the ball is hit into the air and caught. In this latter case, the runner must return to his base before the fielder catching the ball manages to throw it to someone with at least one foot on the base. If the throw beats the runner, the runner is out.

Runners are also out if they are touched with the ball in the hand of a fielder while they are not in contact with a base, if they deviate too much from the direct line between bases in order to avoid being touched by a fielder in possession of the ball, if they overtake the runner in front of them, if they are hit by a fair ball, or if the ball reaches the fielder at the base before they do and they do not have the option of returning to the previous base because it is now occupied by a teammate.

SKILLS

The main skills in softball are throwing, catching, pitching, and batting.

Fielders have to be very good at catching a hard, fast-moving ball with their gloved hand and transferring it quickly to their throwing arm. They also have to be strong, accurate throwers so that they can get the ball to a baseman without making him step off the base.

Pitchers: the underhand throw typically used by the pitcher in softball looks easy but it is surprisingly difficult. Fast and accurate pitchers are highly valued. A good fast-pitch pitcher can throw a "rise ball," a "drop," a "curve ball," a "change-up," and a straight fast ball. The use of these various pitches makes it more difficult for the batter to hit the ball.

Batters: hitting a softball well requires both timing and strength. Good batting is not only about belting the ball as far as possible. A good hitter wants to reach base in any way possible and will also try to hit the ball solidly through gaps between the fielders. A disciplined hitter will also watch pitches carefully; if the pitcher throws four balls, he draws a walk—a free pass to first base.

Slow-pitch softball
This popular recreational game requires an underhand delivery with an arc of between 6 and 12 ft. There are four outfielders rather than the three for fast pitch, the bases are 65 ft apart, and pitching for men and women is at 50 ft. Scores are much higher in slow pitch as it is considered a hitter's game, whereas the fast-pitch game tends to be pitcher controlled.

Free hand
Despite its name, the ball in softball is very far from soft and a glove is essential equipment for anyone fielding. A right-handed fielder wears a glove on her left hand for catching so that her right hand is free to throw the ball.

Rounders
Essentials

Predating baseball, which it resembles, rounders is an English game simple to understand and organize. It is played by people of all ages and ability levels.

The field

Grass, gravel, asphalt, or any surface suitable for running on, although mixed surfaces are not permitted. Marked out with four vertical posts, 1.2 m (4 ft) high and supported by stands heavy enough to keep them upright in wind. Posts are placed 12 m (about 40 ft) apart.

1.2 m
3rd post
2nd post
12 m (about 40 ft)
Bowling square
2.5 m
1st post
4th post
2 m
Batting square

Easy to organize
Rounders can be played with just a bat and ball and as few as six players on either team.

Beaten to the post
Unlike baseball, in which bases are flat, rounders players run between posts with heavy rubber stands.

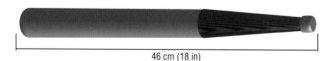

46 cm (18 in)

The bat

Round, made of wood, aluminum, or plastic. Ideally one for each member of the batting team since runners keep their bat with them at all times. No more than 46 cm (18 in) in length. It must not measure more than 17 cm (6½ in) round at its thickest part.

The ball

White. Leather, with a weight of 70–85 g (2½–3 oz) and a circumference of 18–20 cm (7–8 in).

The players

Two teams with a minimum of six and a maximum of 15 players each, although there may be no more than nine in the field at a time. No more than five male players are allowed on mixed teams.

Dress

All players must be clearly numbered. Spiked footwear is prohibited, although cleats 30 mm (1¼ in) in circumference at the base, 12 mm (½ in) maximum length) are allowed.

Officials

Two umpires.

HOW TO PLAY

The two teams take turns batting and fielding. Each player on the batting side gets one chance to hit the ball (per inning), attempting to run around the track to the fourth post—whether or not the ball has been successfully hit. A runner may complete the track in one go or in stages. The fielding side attempts to get as many batters out as possible.

Starting

The captain winning the toss chooses to bat or field first. The fielding team positions itself across the field, while the batting players wait in the back area for their turn to bat. The first batter takes up position in the batting square to meet the ball of the first bowler.

How to win

If a batter hits the ball successfully and manages to touch the fourth post, one *rounder* is scored. A *half-rounder* is scored by completing the track in the same way, but without hitting the ball. A *penalty half-rounder* is scored if the bowler delivers two consecutive no-balls to a batter, or if a fielder obstructs a batter. The team with the most rounders wins. *See Rule 7, scoring (page 109).*

KEY RULES

• A match consists of two innings. A team that is five or more rounders behind after the first innings bats again and, if it fails to exceed the other team's total after its second innings, the game is declared over.

• Each batter is entitled to one good ball only (three for the last remaining batter). Having hit the ball, attempted to hit it, or let it pass, the batter must run to at least the first post, carrying the bat. Only one batter can stay at a post at a time, so if one batter needs to run to the next post, the batter in front must also run forward. *See Rule 4, Batting (page 108).*

• A "*no-ball*" occurs when a ball is higher than the batter's head or lower than the batter's knee, is wide on the hitting side of the batter, is aimed at the batter's body, is aimed at the non-hitting side of the batter, is not delivered with a smooth and continuous action, or if the bowler does not have both feet within the bowling square until the ball is released. A penalty half-rounder is awarded if a bowler delivers two consecutive no-balls to a batter. *See Rule 5, Bowling (page 109).*

• Batters have right of way when running around the track. If obstruction does occur, a half rounder is awarded to the batting team. Likewise, a batter must not obstruct a fielder by deviating from the track. The penalty is a half-rounder to the fielding side. *See Rule 4b, Obstruction—Batting Side (page 108), and Rule 6c, Fielding Side Obstruction (page 109).*

• A batter is out if he fails to keep both feet within the batting square until the ball has been hit or passed, if a fielder touches the post ahead of him with the ball (or hand holding the ball), or if he runs to the inside of a post. *See Rule 4c, Batter Out (page 108).*

Out

A batter is out if a fielder touches a post, toward which the batter is running, with the ball or with the hand holding the ball, before the batter can touch it. A really quick post fielder may be able to put out the batter running toward her post, then throw the ball to another post fielder to put out a second batter.

SKILLS

Batters need a good sense of timing and coordination. They must be able to strike a ball with one fluid movement, sending it deep into the field, allowing time to complete the track. Good *bowlers* are adept at using speed and spin to make an otherwise straightforward, underarm delivery difficult to hit. *Fielders* must be quick, accurate, and constantly aware of the state of play.

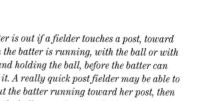

ROUNDERS
THE RULES
· · · · · · · · · ·

Rule 1 Equipment
See page 106.

Rule 2 The Field
See The field (page 106).

Rule 3 The Game
See How to play (page 107).

Rule 4 Batting
(A) A Batter
(a) while waiting for his/her turn to bat shall be in the backward area, well away from the fourth post and batting square.
(b) shall stand with both feet within the batting square and shall not cross the front or back line of the square during hitting, or in the course of attempting to hit a good ball or until the ball has passed him/her.

NB This does not prevent a batter from leaving the batting square while the fielding side adjust its fielding positions, or during a break in play.
(c) shall have only one good ball bowled to him/her and shall also be deemed to have hit the ball if s/he strikes the ball with the bat or the hand holding the bat.
(d) must run to first post after having hit, attempted to hit, or let pass the first good ball delivered by the bowler.
(e) who hits a ball so that it pitches in the backward area shall have made a "backward hit" (this does not refer to balls that drop in the forward area and afterwards go behind).
(f) may, at his/her own discretion, take a "No-Ball" and score in the usual way; s/he shall have been considered to have taken the ball if s/he has come within reach of, made contact with, or passed first post.
(g) shall be entitled, if s/he is the only batter left in on entering the square:
(i) to have the option of 3 good balls but shall forfeit the right to any remaining balls if s/he is caught or takes the ball. (S/he shall be considered to have taken the ball if s/he has come within reach of, made contact with, or passed the first post). S/he can then be put out in any of the usual ways or when the ball has been thrown full pitch or placed in the batting square.
(ii) to a rest of one minute after each rounder s/he may score.

(B) Obstruction–Batting Side
(a) While waiting to bat or after being given out, shall stand behind the marked line in the backward area out of the way of the backstop and fourth post fielders.
Penalty: The umpire shall award a half rounder to the fielding side in the event of obstruction.
(b) A batter shall be considered to have obstructed if s/he:
(i) impedes the player who is fielding the ball by deviating from the running track;
(ii) intentionally deflects the course of the ball;
(iii) verbally misleads the other team.
Penalty: The umpire shall declare the batter out and any rounder scored due to the obstruction shall be declared void.
(c) While running round the track within the rules, a batter shall have right of way.
(d) A non-striking batter causing an obstruction and a rounder being scored by the striking batter on his ball, the rounder would be declared void, but the striking batter would remain in. (The obstructing batter would be declared out.)

(C) Batter Out
A batter shall be declared out:
(i) if the ball be caught from bat or hand holding the bat except on a no-ball.
(ii) if his/her foot projects over the front or back line of the batting square before s/he has hit the ball or it has passed him/her, except on a no-ball.
(iii) if s/he runs to the inside of a post, unless prevented from reaching it by an obstructing fielder.
(iv) if a fielder touches the post immediately ahead with the ball or the hand holding the ball while the batter is running to the post and before the batter has touched the post, except for first post in the case of a no-ball.
NB If any post and/or base(s) should be moved either accidentally or deliberately from the correct position(s):
(a) if any part of the base is in contact with the base spot then contact should be made with the base.
(b) if both the post and the base are moved out of position then contact should be made with the ground marking indicating the correct position of the posts(s).

(v) if s/he obstructs a fielder or intentionally deflects the course of the ball.
(vi) if s/he overtakes another batter.
(vii) if s/he loses contact or runs at any time when the bowler has the ball and is in his/her square (except an overrun or unless ordered to do so by an umpire).
(viii) if s/he loses contact with the post during the bowler's action but before s/he releases the ball.
(ix) if after having been ordered to make contact with a post a batter has not done so.
(x) if s/he drops or throws his/her bat deliberately.

(D) Side Out
(a) Where there is no batter awaiting his/her turn to bat, all the batters on the running track can be put out simultaneously, by the ball being thrown full pitch or placed by any fielder into the batting square before any batter has reached and touched fourth post.
(b) Where there is no batter waiting his/her turn to bat and the bowler has possession of the ball in the bowling square so that no batter can leave a post the side shall be declared out.

(E) Procedure of Game
While waiting at a post a member of the batting team shall have the advantage of running on if a no-ball is bowled and not taken by the batter. S/he can, at his/her discretion, continue to run around the track in the normal way.

Similarly a batter need not run for every ball bowled unless the next batter immediately behind him/her is obliged to run. More than one batter may be put out between the delivery of consecutive balls.

(F) Running Around the Track
A batter:
(a) shall run around the track carrying his/her bat in an attempt to reach fourth post having passed outside each post or the correct position of the post(s) if any has been displaced. Posts must be passed in the order first, second, third, fourth and a batter is permitted to halt at one or more posts if s/he chooses. On reaching fourth post s/he shall rejoin the waiting batters. A batter who drops the bat accidentally will be allowed to continue to run round the track until the bowler has

possession of the ball in the bowling square. The bat shall then be returned to the batter.
Penalty: The umpire shall declare the player out if s/he runs deliberately inside a post or deliberately drops or throws his/her bat. (When trying to make contact with a post, a batter who goes inside the post owing to obstruction by the fielder is not out.)
(b) shall not run beyond the first post after a backward hit until the ball returns or has been returned to the forward area.
Penalty: The umpire shall order him/her back to the first post.
(c) shall not wait between posts.
Penalty: The umpire shall order him/her to continue and make contact with the next post.
(d) stopping (even temporarily) within reach of a post shall make and maintain contact with it using his/her hand or bat except that s/he may run on whenever the bowler is not in possession of the ball and in his/her square.
Penalty:
(1) If s/he does not make contact, the umpire shall order him/her to do so, and if s/he does not, the umpire shall declare him/her out.
(2) If s/he loses contact or runs at any time when the bowler has the ball and is in his/her square (except an overrun) or unless ordered to do so by an umpire or during the bowler's action but before s/he releases the ball, the umpire shall declare him/her out.
(e) shall continue his/her run to the next post if s/he is between posts when the bowler becomes in possession of the ball and is in his/her square but may not run past the post.
Penalty: The umpire shall order the player back to the post s/he passes.
(f) may not remain at the same post as another batter.
Penalty: The umpire shall order the player who batted first to run on and s/he may be put out in the usual ways.
(g) shall not return to a post unless s/he is ordered to do so by the umpire, or unless in the umpire's opinion s/he has overrun a post.
Penalty: The umpire shall order him/her on to the next post and s/he may be put out in the usual ways. A batter may return to fourth post to make contact before the next ball is bowled.
(h) when completing the track, shall not overtake any batter

who is running ahead.

Penalty: The umpire shall declare the batter who overtakes to be out.

(i) must touch fourth post with his/her hand or bat.

Penalty: The umpire shall declare him/her out if the fourth post is touched with the ball or with the hand holding the ball by the fielding side provided that another ball has not been bowled.

Rule 5 Bowling
(A) The Bowler
(a) The bowler shall deliver one good ball to each incoming batter, except the last remaining incoming batter who is entitled to have the option of three good balls.

(b) A bowler may leave the bowling square to field the ball.

(c) A bowler may not deliver two consecutive no-balls to the same batter.

Penalty: half-rounder to the batting team.

(d) A dummy throw or bowl is not allowed. The ball must be delivered in the direction of the batting square. A player losing contact through a dummy ball will be allowed to return to his/her original position.

(B) No-Ball
(a) Decisions on height are based on the actual height of the batter. Decisions on direction are based on the position of the batter when the bowler releases the ball.

(b) A no-ball is one that:
(i) is higher than the top of the head or lower than the knee when it reaches the batter.
(ii) hits the ground on the way to the batter.
(iii) would hit the batter.
(iv) is on the non–hitting side of the batter.
(v) is wide on the hitting side of the batter.
(vi) is not delivered with a continuous and smooth underarm pendulum action (this does not prevent spin).
(vii) is bowled when the bowler fails to keep both feet within the bowling square until the ball is released (the lines of the square are considered to be part of the square and the bowler should be penalized only when part of his/her foot projects over the line).

(C) Bowling Substitutes
See 3. The Game.

Rule 6 Fielding
(A) The Fielder
(a) If a fielder touches the post immediately ahead with the ball or the hand holding the ball, while the batter is running to that post and before the batter has touched the post the batter shall be declared out, excepting first post in the event of a no-ball.

(b) A fielder may put a batter out if s/he catches the ball directly from the bat or the hand holding the bat, except in the case of a no-ball.

(c) A fielder may prevent a "live" batter who is at or within reach of a post from scoring by touching the next post with the ball or the hand holding the ball. This does not prevent the batter continuing his/her run. The "live" batter is defined as the batter to whom the most recent ball was bowled irrespective of whether the ball was a no-ball or not.

(B) Side Out
(i) where there is no batter waiting his/her turn to bat, all the batters on the running track may be put out simultaneously, by the ball being thrown full pitch or placed by a fielder into the batting square before any batter has reached and touched fourth post.

(ii) Where there is no batter waiting his/her turn to bat and the bowler has possession of the ball in the bowling square so that no batter can leave a post, the side shall be declared out.

(C) Fielding Side Obstruction
Obstruction of the batter occurs if, in the opinion of the umpire, the batter was impeded while running round the track or during his/her batting action or was verbally misled.
Penalty: The umpire shall award half a rounder to the batting team and the batter shall be allowed to make contact with the post to which s/he is running.

Rule 7 Scoring
(A) One Rounder
(a) One rounder only may be scored from any one hit. In the case of a no-ball that is hit and caught, the batter may still score in the usual way.

(b) One rounder shall be scored if, after hitting the ball, the batter succeeds in running round the track and touches fourth post, or from first post when the ball returns or has

been returned by a fielder to the forward area after a backward hit, provided that:
(i) s/he has not overtaken any other batter.
(ii) the bowler has not delivered another ball.
(iii) while s/he was waiting at a post, the post immediately ahead was not touched by a fielder with the ball or the hand holding the ball.

(B) Half-Rounder
Half a rounder shall be scored by the batter if s/he completes the track fulfilling the same conditions as for scoring one rounder but without hitting the ball.

(C) Penalty Half-Rounder
A penalty half-rounder shall be awarded to the batting team when:
(a) the bowler delivers two consecutive no-balls to the same batter. After a penalty half-rounder has been awarded for two consecutive no-balls the previous no-balls are cancelled and the count starts again.
(b) a fielder obstructs a batter.

(D) One Rounder and Penalty Half-Rounders
It should be noted that the rounder may be scored with the addition of the award:
(a) One penalty half rounder if the ball that is hit is the second consecutive no-ball to that batter.
(b) One penalty half-rounder if the batter is obstructed.
(c) Two penalty half-rounders if both (a) and (b) apply.

These rules are reprinted by permission of the English National Rounders Association. A complete set of the Rules of Rounders, including Hints to umpires, can be obtained from the Association.

Big swing
The rounders bat is small and held in one hand. To hit the ball well, a batter has to give a strong flick of the wrist and turn the hand over at the same time as turning the shoulders to follow through.

Tennis
Essentials

Popular worldwide, tennis can be enjoyed by players of almost any skill level. Top players, however, enjoy the benefits of both international recognition and lucrative cash prizes.

Officials

For high-level matches, an umpire, referee and assistants. *See Rule 29, Role of Court Officials (page 120).*

The court

Rectangular, 78 ft long and 36 ft wide. Only doubles matches use the entire width; single matches use the center 27 ft, which are invariably marked off and divided into two courts by a net across the center and then into two service courts and a back court on either side of this by lines on the ground. Surfaces may be grass, clay, plastic, concrete, or—rarely—wood.

Server

Center mark

Service court

Central service line

Service line

Singles court sideline

Doubles court sideline

Net-cord judge

Umpire

Receiver

Baseline

The players

One a side for singles, two for doubles. Men or women or mixed.

Dress

A shirt and shorts or skirt. In organized tournaments, clothing is usually white, although colors are often permitted. Shoes should be fairly lightweight with a reasonable amount of grip.

The racket

Aluminum, graphite or composite, various weights, with a single layer of strings of uniform pattern. The frame must not exceed 29 in in overall length for professional play. Its overall width must be no more than 12 $\frac{1}{2}$ in.

Below, clay court.

The net

Mesh, suspended from a cord or metal cable attached to the tops of two posts that are positioned 3 feet outside each sideline at the center of the court. The top of the net must be 3 feet above the ground at its center, at which point the net is also held taut by a vertical white strap.

The ball

Yellow or white, with a fabric cover. Between 2 $\frac{1}{2}$ and 2 $\frac{5}{8}$ in in diameter and between 2 and 2 $\frac{1}{16}$ oz in weight. The ball must rebound to a height of 53–58 in when dropped from a height of 100 in.

White out

Traditionally, tennis was played strictly in white – a shirt and shorts for men, and shirt and skirts for women. In recent years, however, a much broader range of colors has started to be used. Of course, recreational players wear whatever they are comfortable in.

HOW TO PLAY

Two players (singles matches) or four players (doubles matches) hit the ball alternately with rackets so that it passes over the net and into the opponent's court. When a player fails to return the ball legally to his opponent, he loses a point.

Starting

The winner of a toss chooses an end or the right to serve or receive first. The player serving first stands with his feet behind the baseline on the right-hand side of his court. His feet must remain behind the baseline and within the imaginary extensions of the center mark and the sideline. The ball is then thrown into the air and struck with the racket before it hits the ground. It must land in the receiver's right-hand service court to be "in." If not "in," a *fault* is called. The server has two chances to make a good service; if he fails, the point is lost ("double fault").

How to win

Players must win points, games and, then, sets in order to win a match. When a player loses his first point, his score remains "love" (nil) while his opponent's becomes "15." The second point won by a player is called "30," the third "40," and the fourth point is the one needed to win the game. If the score is 40-all, a "deuce" is called. Either player must now score two additional points in succession to win. When the first one is scored, the umpire will call "Advantage server/receiver" (depending on which player scored), but if this player fails to win the second point, the score reverts back to deuce, and the process begins again.

The first player to win six games wins a set, unless the score reaches five all—in which case two additional games are played. If the score remains tied after those two games (six all), a tie-break game is generally played *(see Rule 27, page 120)* to determine a winner. However, a tournament may opt to have the players continue to play additional games until one achieves a two-game margin over his opponent.

A match has a maximum of five sets for men and three sets for women. Once a player has won three sets in a five-set match or two sets in a three-set match, the match is over.

KEY RULES

• The ball is allowed to bounce only once in a player's court before it must be returned. It must bounce once following a service, but during a rally it need not bounce at all. If a return does bounce, however, it must do so on or within the boundaries of the opponent's court in order to be "good."

High-speed service
New light, tough racket materials have made professional tennis a very fast, demanding game. Men's services frequently cross the net at speeds of over 130 mph. Today's top women players also serve at very high speeds—in excess of 110 mph.

• It is a "let" if a served ball hits the net before landing in the receiver's court. The point is replayed in this case.

• Play is continuous. Service alternates between players with each game and ends are changed at the end of the first, third, and every subsequent alternate game of a set. *See Rule 16 (page 117).* After the third set (men) or second set (women) in professional matches, players may be allowed a 10-minute break. *See Rule 30, Continuous Play and Rest Periods (page 120).*

• To prevent excessively long sets, a tie-break game is generally played to determine the winner of a set in the case of a six-all score. In tie-break games, the first player to reach at least seven points while maintaining a margin of at least two points over his opponent, wins the game (and the set). The player who is due to serve does so first. After this, the service alternates with every two points scored. In doubles, each player serves for two points in rotation, following the sequence already established for the set. *See Rule 27, (page 120).*

RULES OF TENNIS
• • • • • • • • • • • •

The Singles Game

1. The court

The court shall be a rectangle 78 ft (23.77 m) long and 27 ft (8.23 m) wide. It shall be divided across the middle by a net suspended from a cord or metal cable of a maximum diameter of one-third of an inch (0.8 cm), the ends of which shall be attached to, or pass over, the tops of the two posts, which shall not be more than 6 in (15 cm) square or 6 in (15 cm) in diameter. These posts shall not be higher than 1 in (2.5 cm) above the top of the net cord. The centers of the posts shall be 3 ft (.914 m) outside the court on each side and the height of the posts shall be such that the top of the cord or metal cable shall be 3 ft 6 in (1.07 m) above the ground.

When a combined doubles (*see Rule 34*) and singles court with a doubles net is used for singles, the net must be supported to a height of 3 ft 6 in (1.07 m) by means of two posts, called "singles sticks," which shall be not more than 3 inches (7.5 cm) square or 3 in (7.5 cm) in diameter. The centers of the singles sticks shall be 3 ft (.914 m) outside the singles court on each side.

The net shall be extended fully so that it fills completely the space between the two posts and shall be of sufficiently small mesh to prevent the ball passing through. The height of the net shall be 3 ft (.914 m) at the center, where it shall be held down taut by a strap not more than 2 in (5 cm) wide and completely white in color. There shall be a band covering the cord or metal cable and the top of the net of not less than 2 in (5 cm) nor more than 2 ½ in (6.35 cm) in depth on each side and completely white in color.

There shall be no advertisement on the net, strap band or singles sticks.

The lines bounding the ends and sides of the court shall respectively be called the baselines and the sidelines. On each side of the net, at a distance of 21 ft (6.40 m) from it and parallel with it, shall be drawn the service lines. The space on each side of the net between the service line and the sidelines shall be divided into two equal parts called the service courts by the center service line, which must be 2 in (5 cm) in width, drawn half-way between, and parallel with, the sideline. Each baseline shall be bisected by an imaginary continuation of the center service line to a line 4 in (10 cm) in length and 2 in (5 cm) in width called "the center mark" drawn inside the court, at right angles to and in contact with such baselines. All other lines shall be not less than 1 inch (2.5 cm) nor more than 2 in (5 cm) in width, except the baseline which may be not more than 4 in (10 cm) in width, and all measurements shall be made to the outside of the lines. All lines shall be of uniform color. If advertising or any other material is placed at the back of the court, it may not contain white, or yellow. A light color may only be used if this does not interfere with the vision of the players.

If advertisements are placed on the chairs of the linesmen sitting at the back of the court, they may not contain white or yellow. A light color may only be used if this does not interfere with the vision of the players.

Note 1: In the case of the Davis Cup or other Official Championships of the International Tennis Federation, there shall be a space behind each baseline of not less than 21 ft (6.4 m), and at the sides of not less than 12 ft (3.66 m). The chairs of linesmen may be placed at the back of a court within 21 ft (6.4m) or at the side of the court within the 12 ft (3.66 m), provided they do not protrude into that area more than 3 ft (.914 m).

Note 2: In the case of the stadium courts in the Davis Cup World Group and the Fed Cup Main Draw there should be space behind each baseline of not less than 27 ft (8.23 m) and at the sides of not less than 15 ft (4.57 m).

Note 3: At club or recreational level, the space behind each baseline should be not less than 18 ft (5.5 m) and at the sides not less than 10 ft (3.05 m).

Below, an indoor court.

2. Permanent fixtures

The permanent fixtures of the court shall include not only the net, posts, singles sticks, cord or metal cable, strap, and band but also, where there are any such, the back and side stops, the stands, fixed or movable seats and chairs around the court, and their occupants, all other fixtures around and above the court, and the Umpire, Net-cord Judge, Foot-fault Judge, Linesmen, and Ball Boys when in their respective places.

3. The ball

The ball shall have a uniform outer surface consisting of a fabric cover and shall be white or yellow in color. If there are any seams they shall be stitchless. The ball shall be more than 2 ½ in (6.350 cm) and less than 2 ⅝ in (6.668 cm) in diameter and more than 2 oz (56.7 g) and less than 2 1/16 oz (58.5 g) in weight. The ball shall have a bound of more than 53 in (134.62 cm) and less than 58 in (147.32 cm) when dropped 100 in (254.00 cm) upon a concrete base. The ball shall have a forward deformation of more than .220 in (.559 cm) and less than .290 in (.737 cm) and return deformation of more than .315 in (.800 cm) and less than .425 in (1.080 cm) at 18 lb (8.165 kg) load. The two deformation figures shall be the averages of three individual readings along three axes of the ball and no two individual readings shall differ by more than .030 in (.076 cm) in each case. For play above 4, 000 ft (1219 m) in altitude above sea level, two additional types of ball may be used. The first type is identical to those described above except that the bound shall be more than 48 in (121.92 cm) and less than 53 in (134.62 cm) and shall have an internal pressure that is greater than the external pressure. This type of tennis ball is commonly known as a pressurized ball. The second type is identical to those described above except that it shall have a bound of more than 53 in (134.62 cm) and less than 58 in (147.32 cm) and shall have an internal pressure that is approximately equal to the external pressure and have been acclimatized for 60 days or more at the altitude of the specific tournament. This type of tennis ball is commonly known as a zero-pressure or non-pressurised ball. All tests for bound, size, and deformation shall be made in accordance with the regulations in Appendix 1. The International Tennis Federation shall rule on the question of whether any ball or prototype complies with the above specifications or is otherwise approved for play. Such ruling may be taken on its own initiative, or upon application by any party with a bona fide interest therein, including any player, equipment manufacturer, or National Association or members thereof. Such rulings and applications shall be made in accordance with the applicable review and hearing procedures of the International Tennis Federation, copies of which may be obtained from the Federation.

4. The racket

Rackets failing to comply with the following specifications are not approved for play under the Rules of Tennis:
(a) The hitting surface of the racket shall be flat and consist of a pattern of crossed strings connected to a frame and alternately interlaced or bonded where they cross; the stringing pattern shall be generally uniform and in particular, not less dense in the center than in any other area. The strings shall be free of attached objects and protrusions other than those utilized solely and specifically to limit or prevent wear and tear or vibration, and which are reasonable in size and placement for such purposes.
(b) For professional play, the frame of the racket shall not exceed 29 in (73.66 cm) in overall length, including the handle, as from 1st January 1997. For non-professional play, the frame of the racket shall not exceed 29 in (73.66cm) in overall length, including the handle, as from 1st January 2000. The frame of the racket shall not exceed 12 ½ in (31.75 cm) in overall width. The strung surface shall not exceed 15 ½ in (39.37 cm) in overall length, and 11 ½ in (29.21 cm) in overall width.
(c) The frame, including the handle, shall be free of attached objects and devices other than those utilized solely and specifically to limit or prevent wear and tear or vibration, or to distribute weight. Any objects and devices must be reasonable in size and placement for such purposes.
(d) The frame, including the handle, and the strings shall be free of any device that makes it possible to change materially the shape of the racket, or to change the weight distribution in the direction of the longitudinal axis of the racket that would alter the swing moment of inertia during the playing of a point. The International Tennis Federation shall rule on the question of whether any racket or prototype complies with the above specifications or is otherwise approved or not approved, for play. Such ruling may be undertaken on its own initiative, or upon application by any party with a bona fide interest therein, including any player, equipment manufacturer, or National Association or

➡ *page 116*

In the line of fire
The player receiving a serve stands diagonally opposite the server. In top-level games the receiver usually stands well towards the back of the court or even outside. Only this far back allows time to get to a fast-moving first serve. This player has adopted the two-hand backstroke grip, now increasingly popular with women players for extra power both on service returns and other shots from the back of the court.

SKILLS
• • • • •

Tennis requires the same mobility, ball control, and strategic thinking as most racket sports. Players also need to be able to combine power, and finesse with a high degree of accuracy.

Serving is an essential skill to master. Because the server has complete control of the ball this is an opportunity to quickly gain the upper hand. A strong player serves the ball hard and fast, making sure that it lands in, yet, so deep into the corners of the receiver's court that it is near impossible to return. If the ball cannot be returned at all, this is called an "ace."

The forehand and backhand drive are basic *ground strokes.* They are strong shots, usually played from near the baseline that travel the length of the court. Players turn sideways to the net and follow through with the swing of the racket to give the ball power and momentum. For backhand drives, many players achieve greater control and force by gripping the racket with both hands.

The *volley* is an aggressive shot, played before the ball has bounced in a player's court. It involves punching the ball with a short, quick movement. A well-judged volley will allow an opponent very little time to respond, particularly if it is aimed at an unguarded area close to the net.

An overhead *smash* is generally used as an attempt to win the point. The action is similar to that used for the service.

The addition of spin—topspin or underspin (slice)—is a relatively complex skill. By tilting the face of the racket, the behavior of the ball in the air or as it rebounds in the receiver's court can be made unpredictable. Topspin will cause it to bounce to a much lower height than anticipated, while slice can be used to make it swerve through the air.

Forehand drive
Below, Britain's Tim Henman prepares for a forehand drive. He has a full backswing and will hit the ball with the face of the racket square to the ball, "following through" for maximum power.

Service power
The tennis serve is a dramatic overhead smash that involves the player's whole body in addition to the racket arm. Accelerating the ball from a standstill to cannonball speed requires the player to effectively throw the head of the racket at the ball. The movement begins at the ankles then moves rapidly up through the body as the server twists to strike the ball with maximum force.

Aerial combat
*Playing backhanded
and off the ground,
John McEnroe, a
tennis great of the
70s and 80s, is still
able to return his
opponent's shot.*

Backhand
*Below, Pete Sampras,
the dominant men's
player of the 1990s,
uses a backhand stroke.
the backhand stroke is
made with the racket
up across the body and
so is usually much
weaker than the
forehand. However, a
skilled player can more
than make up for the
lack of power with
highly accurate placing
and clever disguise of
their shot.*

Ground control
*Left, the forehand
volley is an attacking
stroke played from
the front of the court
with a short
"punching" action.*

continued from page 113

members thereof. Such rulings and applications shall be made in accordance with the applicable Review and Hearing Procedures of the International Tennis Federation, copies of which may be obtained from the Federation.

5. Server and receiver

The players shall stand on opposite sides of the net; the player who first delivers the ball shall be called the server, and the other the receiver.

6. Choice of ends and service

The choice of ends and the right to be server or receiver in the first game shall be decided by toss. The player winning the toss may choose or require his opponent to choose:

(a) The right to be Server or receiver, in which case the other player shall choose the end; or

(b) The end, in which case the other player shall choose the right to be server or receiver.

7. The service

The service shall be delivered in the following manner. Immediately before commencing to serve, the Server shall stand with both feet at rest behind (i.e., further from the net than) the baseline, and within the imaginary continuations of the center mark and sideline. The server shall then project the ball by hand into the air in any direction and before it hits the ground strike it with his racket, and the delivery shall be deemed to have been completed at the moment of the impact of the racket and the ball. A player with the use of only one arm may utilize his racket for the projection.

8. Foot fault

The server shall throughout the delivery of the Service:
a) Not change his position by walking or running. The Server shall not by slight movements of the feet which do not materially affect the location originally taken up by him be deemed "to change his position by walking or running."

Behind the line
Left, France's Mary Pierce arches backwards preparing for a powerful serve, always careful not to overstep the baseline, thereby, making a foot fault.

b) Not touch, with either foot, any area other than that behind the baseline within the imaginary extension of the center mark and sidelines.

9. Delivery of service

(a) In delivering the service, the Server shall stand alternately behind the right and left halves of the court beginning from the right in every game. If service from a wrong half of the court occurs and is undetected, all play resulting from such wrong service or services shall stand, but the inaccuracy of station shall be corrected immediately if it is discovered.

(b) The ball served shall pass over the net and hit the ground within the service court that is diagonally opposite, or upon any line bounding such court, before the receiver returns it.

10. Service fault

The service is a fault:
(a) If the Server commits any breach of Rules 7, 8, or 9(b);
(b) If he misses the ball in attempting to strike it;
(c) If the ball served touches a permanent fixture (other than the net, strap, or band) before it hits the ground.

11. Second service

After a fault (if it is the first fault) the Server shall serve again from behind the same half of the court from which he served that fault, unless the service was from the wrong half, when in accordance with Rule 9, the Server shall be entitled to one service only from behind the other half.

12. When to serve

The Server shall not serve until the receiver is ready. If the latter attempts to return the service, he shall be deemed ready. If, however, the receiver signifies that he is not ready, he may not claim a fault because the ball does not hit the ground within the limits fixed for the service.

13. The let

In all cases where a let has to be called under the rules, or to provide for an interruption to play, it shall have the following interpretations:
(a) When called solely in respect of a service that one service only shall be replayed.
(b) When called under any other circumstance, the point shall be replayed.

14. The "let" in service

The service is a let:
(a) If the ball served touches the net, strap or band, and is otherwise good, or, after touching the net, strap or band, touches the receiver or anything he wears or carries before hitting the ground.
(b) If a service or a fault is delivered when the receiver is not ready (see Rule 12).

In case of a let, that particular service shall not count, and the server shall serve again, but a service let does not annul a previous fault.

15. Order of service

At the end of the first game the receiver shall become server, and the server receiver; and so on alternately in all the subsequent games of a match. If a player serves out of turn, the player who ought to have served shall serve as soon as the mistake is discovered, but all points scored before such discovery shall stand. A fault served before such discovery shall not stand. If a game shall have been completed before such discovery, the order of service shall remain as altered.

16. When players change ends

The players shall change ends at the end of the first, third, and every subsequent alternate game of each set, and at the end of each set unless the total number of games in such set is even, in which case the change is not made until the end of the first game of the next set.

If a mistake is made and the correct sequence is not followed, the players must take up their correct station as soon as the discovery is made and follow their original sequence.

17. The ball in play

A ball is in play from the moment at which it is delivered in service. Unless a fault or a let is called it remains in play until the point is decided.

18. Server wins point

The Server wins the Point:
(a) If the ball served, not being a let under Rule 14, touches the receiver or anything he wears or carries, before it hits the ground;
(b) If the receiver otherwise loses the point as provided by Rule 20.

19. Receiver wins point

The receiver wins the point:
(a) If the Server serves two consecutive faults;
(b) If the Server otherwise loses the point as provided by Rule 20.

20. Player loses point

A player loses the point if:
(a) He fails, before the ball in play has hit the ground twice consecutively, to return it directly over the net (except as provided in Rule 24 (a) or (c)); or
(b) He returns the ball in play so that it hits the ground, a permanent fixture, or other object, outside any of the lines which bound his opponent's court; or
(c) He volleys the ball and fails to make a good return even when standing outside the court; or
(d) In playing the ball he deliberately carries or catches it on his racket or deliberately touches it with his racket more than once; or
(e) He or his racket (in his hand or otherwise) or anything which he wears or carries touches the net, posts, singles sticks, cord or metal cable, strap or band, or the ground within his opponent's court at any time while the ball is in play; or
(f) He volleys the ball before it has passed the net or
(g) The ball in play touches him or anything he wears or carries, except his racket in his hand or hands; or
(h) He throws his racket at and hits the ball; or
(i) He deliberately and materially

changes the shape of his racket during the playing of the point.

21. Player hinders opponent

If a player commits any act that hinders his opponent in making a stroke, then, if this is deliberate, he shall lose the point or if involuntary, the point shall be replayed.

22. Ball falls on line

A ball falling on a line is regarded as falling in the court bounded by that line.

23. Ball touches Permanent fixtures

If the ball in play touches a permanent fixture (other than the net, posts, singles sticks, cord or metal cable, strap or band) after it has hit the ground, the player who struck it wins the point; if before it hits the ground, his opponent wins the point.

24. A good return

It is a good return:
(a) If the ball touches the net, posts, singles sticks, cord or metal cable, strap or band, provided that it passes over any of them and hits the ground within the court; or

➡ *page 120*

Service follow-through.
On fast courts a strong server will quickly move to the net ready to volley—immediately putting pressure on his opponent.

TACTICS

Top players tend to be one of two types. The *serve-and-volley* player excels on a fast court (e.g., clay). He begins with a powerful serve and then quickly moves to the net to meet his opponent's weak return with a volley or a smash.

Baseline players do better on slow courts (e.g., grass). Their tactic is to play mostly from the back of their court, maintaining rallies until a winning shot can be made, or until their opponent makes a mistake.

Grand Slam
The four most prestigious events in the tennis world are the Australian Open (January), the French Open (May/June), Wimbledon (June/July), and the U.S. Open (August/September). These tournaments are played in Melbourne, Paris, London, and New York, respectively.

Forehand slice
A player can achieve tremendous power with the racket by hitting the ball square, but many winning shots involve slicing the racket against the ball to set it spinning. Above, the player has given his forehand return a little backspin by slicing under the ball. Backspin lofts the ball slightly higher in the air, so the shot has to be aimed slightly lower than for a straight drive.

Top spin
Jeremy Bates, right, prepares to return the ball with a topspin by slicing over the top of the ball with the racket. This causes the ball to spin forward so that it travels fast, staying low after the bounce.

Fast return
Left, Germany's Steffi Graf chases across court, preparing to hit the ball square for a fast forehand return.

continued from page 117

(b) If the ball, served or returned, hits the ground within the proper court and rebounds or is blown back over the net, and the player whose turn it is to strike reaches over the net and plays the ball, provided that he does not contravene Rule 20 (e); or

(c) If the ball is returned outside the posts, or singles sticks, either above or below the level of the top to the net, even though it touches the posts or singles sticks, provided that it hits the ground within the proper court; or

(d) If a player's racket passes over the net after he has returned the ball, provided the ball passes the net before being played and is properly returned; or

(e) If a player succeeds in returning the ball, served or in play, which strikes a ball lying in the court.

25. Hinderance of a player

In case a player is hindered in making a stroke by anything not within his control, except a permanent fixture of the court, or except as provided for in Rule 21, a let shall be called.

26. Score in a game

If a player wins his first point, the score is called 15 for that player; on winning his second point, the score is called 30 for that player; on winning his third point, the score is called 40 for that player; and the fourth point won by a player is scored game for that player except as below:-

If both players have won three points, the score is called deuce; and the next point won by a player is scored advantage for that player. If the same player wins the next point, he wins the game; if the other player wins the next point the score is again

called deuce; and so on, until a player wins the two points immediately following the score at deuce, when the game is scored for that player.

27. Score in a set

(a) A player (or players) who first wins six games wins a set; except that he must win by a margin of two games over his opponent and where necessary a set shall be extended until this margin is achieved.

(b) The tie-break system of scoring may be adopted as an alternative to the advantage set system in paragraph (a) of this Rule provided the decision is announced in advance of the match.

In this case, the following Rules shall be effective:

The tie-break shall operate when the score reaches six games all in any set except the third or fifth set of a three-set or five-set match, when an ordinary advantage set shall be played, unless otherwise decided and announced in advance of the match.

The following system shall be used in a tie-break game:

Singles

(i) A player who first wins seven points shall win the game and the set provided he leads by a margin of two points. If the score reaches six points all, the game shall be extended until this margin has been achieved. Numerical scoring shall be used throughout the tie-break game.

(ii) The player whose turn it is to serve shall be the server for the first point. His opponent shall be the server for the second and third points and thereafter each player shall serve alternately for two consecutive points until the winner of the game and set has been decided.

(iii) From the first point, each service shall be delivered alternately from the right and left courts, beginning from the right court. If service from a wrong half of the court occurs and is undetected, all play resulting from such wrong service or services shall stand, but the inaccuracy of the station shall be corrected immediately if it is discovered.

(iv) Players shall change ends after every six points and at the conclusion of the tie-break game.

(v) The tie-break game shall count as one game for the ball change, except that, if the balls are due to be changed at the beginning of the tie-break, the change shall be delayed until the second game of the following set.

Doubles

In doubles the procedure for singles shall apply. The player whose turn it is to serve shall be the server for the first point. Thereafter each player shall serve in rotation for two points, in the same order previously in that set, until the winners of the game and set have been decided.

Rotation of Service

The player (or pair in the case of doubles) whose turn it was to serve first in the tie-break game shall receive service in the first game of the following set.

28. Maximum number of sets

The maximum number of sets in a match shall be 5, or, where women take part, 3.

29. Role of court officials

In matches where an umpire is appointed, his decision shall be final; but where a referee is appointed, an appeal shall lie to him from the decision of an umpire on a question of law, and in all such cases the decision of the referee shall be final. In matches where assistants to the umpire are appointed (Linespersons, Net-cord Judges,

Foot-fault Judges) their decisions shall be final on questions of fact except that if in the opinion of an umpire a clear mistake has been made he shall have the right to change the decision of an assistant or order a let to be played. When such an assistant is unable to give a decision he shall indicate this immediately to the umpire who shall give a decision. When an umpire is unable to give a decision on a question of fact he shall order a let to be played. In Davis Cup matches or other team competitions where a referee is on court, any decision can be changed by the referee, who may also instruct an umpire to order a let to be played.

The referee, in his discretion, may at any time postpone a match on account of darkness or the condition of the ground or the weather. In any case of postponement the previous score and previous occupancy of courts shall hold good, unless the referee and the players unanimously agree otherwise.

30. Continuous play and rest periods

Play shall be continuous from the first service until the match is concluded, in accordance with the following provisions:

(a) If the first service is a fault, the second service must be struck by the server without delay.

The receiver must play to the reasonable pace of the server and must be ready to receive when the server is ready to serve. When changing ends a maximum of one minute thirty seconds shall elapse from the moment the ball goes out of play at the end of the game to the time the ball is struck for the first point of the next game.

The umpire shall use his discretion when there is interference that makes it impracticable for play to be continuous. The organizers of international circuits and team events recognized by the ITF may determine the time allowed between points, which shall not at any time exceed twenty (20) seconds from the moment the ball goes out of play at the end of one point to the time the ball is struck for the next point.

(b) Play shall never be suspended, delayed, or interfered with for the purpose of enabling a player to recover his strength, breath, or physical condition. However, in the case

Big smash
America's Andre Agassi has just jumped to produce maximum power for an overhead drive.

of accidental injury, the umpire may allow a one-time three-minute suspension for that injury.

(c) If, through circumstance outside the control of the player, his clothing, footwear, or equipment (excluding racket) become out of adjustment in such a way that it is impossible or undesirable for him to play on, the umpire may suspend play while the maladjustment is rectified.

(d) The umpire may suspend or delay play at any time as may be necessary and appropriate.

(e) After the third set, or when women take part, the second set, either player shall be entitled to a rest, which shall not exceed 10 minutes, or in countries situated between latitude 15 degrees north and latitude 15 degrees south, 45 minutes and furthermore, when necessitated by circumstances not within the control of the players, the umpire may suspend play for such a period as he may consider necessary. If play is suspended and is not resumed until a later day, the rest may be taken only after the third set (or when women take part, the second set) of play on such a later day, completion of an unfinished set being counted as one set. If play is suspended and is not resumed until 10 minutes have elapsed in the same day, the rest may be taken only after three consecutive sets have been played without interruption (or when women take part, two sets), completion of an unfinished set being counted as one set.

Any nation and/or committee organizing a tournament, match, or competition is at liberty to modify this provision or omit it from its regulations provided this is announced before the event commences. With respect to the Davis Cup and Fed Cup, only the International Tennis Federation may modify this provision or omit it from its Regulations.

(f) A tournament committee has the discretion to decide the time allowed for a warm-up period prior to a match but this may not exceed five minutes and must be announced before the event commences.

(g) When approved point penalty and non-accumulative point penalty systems are in operation, the umpire shall make his decisions within the terms of those systems.

(h) Upon violation of the principle that play shall be continuous, the umpire may, after giving due warning, disqualify the offender.

31. Coaching

During the playing of a match in a team competition, a player may receive coaching from a captain who is sitting on the court only when he changes ends at the end of a game, but not when he changes ends during a tie-break game.

A player may not receive coaching during the playing of any other match. The provisions of this rule must be strictly construed.

After due warning an offending player may be disqualified. When an approved point penalty system is in operation, the umpire shall impose penalties according to that system.

32. Ball change

In cases where balls are to be changed after a specified number of games, if the balls were not changed in the correct sequence, the mistake shall be corrected when the player, or pair, in the case of doubles, who should have served with new balls is next due to serve. Thereafter the balls shall be changed so that the number of games between changes shall be that originally agreed.

THE DOUBLES GAME

33. The Doubles game

The above Rules shall apply to the Doubles Game except as below.

34. The doubles court

For the doubles court, the court shall be 36 ft (10.97 m) in width, i.e., 4 ½ ft (1.37 m) wider on each side than the Court for the Singles Game, and those portions of the singles sidelines that lie between the two service lines shall be called the service sidelines. In other respects, the court shall be similar to that described in Rule 1, but the portions of the singles sidelines between the baseline and service line on each side of the net may be omitted if desired.

35. Order of service in doubles

The order of serving shall be decided at the beginning of each set as follows:

The pair who have to serve in the first game of each set shall

decide which partner shall do so, and the opposing pair shall decide similarly for the second game. The partner of the player who served in the first game shall serve in the third; the partner of the player who served in the second game shall serve in the fourth, and so on in the same order in all the subsequent games of a set.

36. Order of receiving in doubles

The order of receiving the service shall be decided at the beginning of each set as follows:-

The pair who have to receive the service in the first game shall decide which partner shall receive the first service, and that partner shall continue to receive the first service in every odd game throughout that set. The opposing pair shall likewise decide which partner shall receive the first service in the second game and that partner shall continue to receive the first service in every even game throughout that set. Partners shall receive the service alternately throughout each game.

37. Service out of turn in doubles

If a partner serves out of his turn, the partner who ought to have served shall serve as soon as the mistake is discovered, but all points scored, and any faults served before such discovery, shall be reckoned. If a game shall have been completed before such discovery, the order of service remains as altered.

38. Error in order of receiving in doubles

If during a game the order of receiving the service is changed by the receivers it shall remain as altered until the end of the game in which the mistake is discovered, but the partners shall resume their original order of receiving in the next game of that set in which they are receivers of the service.

39. Service fault in doubles

The service is a fault as provided for by Rule 10, or if the ball touches the server's partner or anything that he wears or carries, but if the ball served touches the partner of the receiver, or anything which he wears or carries, not being a let under Rule 14 (a) before it hits the ground, the server wins the point.

40. Playing the ball in doubles

The ball shall be struck alternately by one or other player of the opposing pairs, and if a player touches the ball in play with his racket in contravention of this Rule, his opponents win the point.

Note: Except where otherwise stated, every reference in these Rules to the masculine includes the feminine gender.

AMENDMENT TO THE RULES OF TENNIS
International Tennis Federation Rule 69
The official and decisive text to the Rules of Tennis shall be for ever in the English language and no alteration or interpretation of such Rules shall be made except at an Annual General Meeting of the Council, nor unless notice of the resolution embodying such alteration shall have been received by the Federation in accordance with Rule 21 (Notice of Resolutions) and such resolution or one having the like effect shall be carried by a majority of two-thirds of the votes recorded in respect of the same.

Any alteration so made shall take effect as from the first day of January following unless the Meeting shall by the like majority decide otherwise.

The Committee of Management shall have power, however, to settle all urgent questions of interpretation subject to confirmation at the General Meeting next following.

This Rule shall not be altered at any time without the unanimous consent of a General Meeting of the Council.

These Rules are reprinted by permission of the International Tennis Federation.

The complete Rules of Tennis, including Appendix I (Regulations for making tests), Appendix II (Rules of Wheelchair Tennis) and Suggestions on How to Mark out a court are available from the Federation or from many local governing organizations.

Badminton
Essentials

More than a simple recreational game, badminton can be an extremely competitive and skilled sport, as demonstrated in international competitions such as the Olympics. Formalized by British officers in 19th-century India, badminton remains a very popular game in much of Southeast Asia.

The players
One player on each side for singles, two on each side for doubles.

Officials
An umpire and, in some events, a referee.

Dress
There are no strict rules. For a man, shorts and a lightweight shirt are practical, while a woman may replace the shorts with a skirt. Clothing should allow ease of movement.

The net
Ideally hung from two posts, both 1.55 m (approx. 5 ft) in height from the court's surface and positioned on the doubles sidelines. The net itself should be 760 mm (30 in) in depth, of dark color, and with a mesh of

The court
Rectangular. As in tennis, lines generally mark out a court that can be used for either singles or doubles, although a singles-only court is possible.

between 15 and 20 mm (approx. 0.7 in). The top of the net must be edged with a 75 mm (3 in) white tape and must measure 1.524 m (5 ft) from the court's surface at the center and 1.55 m (approx. 5 ft) over the doubles sidelines.

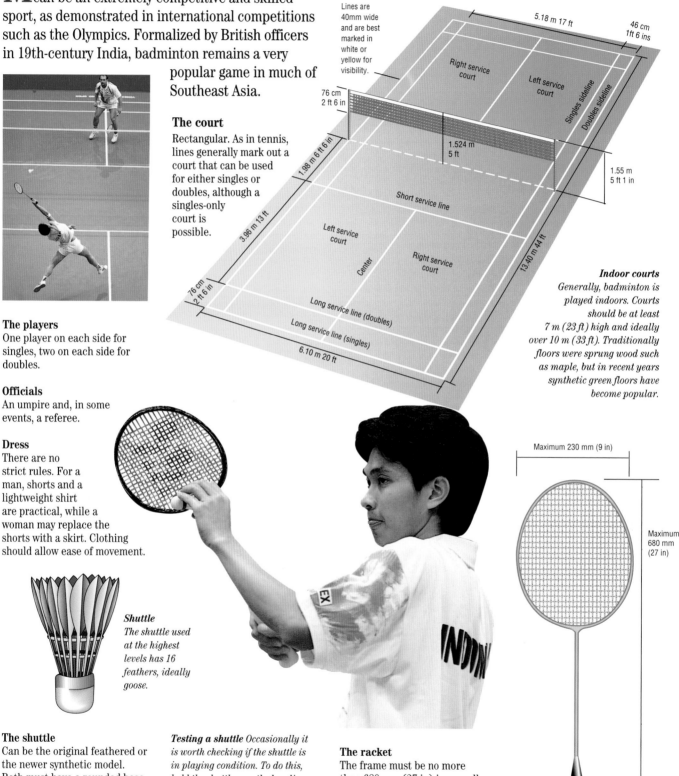

Lines are 40mm wide and are best marked in white or yellow for visibility.

5.18 m 17 ft

46 cm 1ft 6 ins

Right service court

Left service court

Singles sideline

Doubles sideline

76 cm 2 ft 6 in

1.524 m 5 ft

1.98 m 6 ft 6 in

1.55 m 5 ft 1 in

Short service line

3.96 m 13 ft

Left service court

Center

Right service court

13.40 m 44 ft

76 cm 2 ft 6 in

Long service line (doubles)

Long service line (singles)

6.10 m 20 ft

Indoor courts
Generally, badminton is played indoors. Courts should be at least 7 m (23 ft) high and ideally over 10 m (33 ft). Traditionally floors were sprung wood such as maple, but in recent years synthetic green floors have become popular.

Maximum 230 mm (9 in)

Maximum 680 mm (27 in)

Shuttle
The shuttle used at the highest levels has 16 feathers, ideally goose.

The shuttle
Can be the original feathered or the newer synthetic model. Both must have a rounded base of 25.8 mm (approx 1 in) diameter and a total weight between 4.74 and 5.50 g (approx 0.2 oz). The speed of the shuttle depends on its weight. (Manufacturers produce a variety of different speeds.)

Testing a shuttle Occasionally it is worth checking if the shuttle is in playing condition. To do this, hold the shuttle over the baseline and use an underarm stroke to hit it at an upwards angle, straight to the other back boundary line. If the speed is correct it will land no less than 530 mm (21 in) and no more than 990 mm (39 in) short of the opposite line.

The racket
The frame must be no more than 680 mm (27 in) in overall length and 230 mm (9 in) in overall width. The stringed area is flat and of a uniform pattern. Frames are generally made of graphite or aluminum, while natural gut gives the best performance for the strings.

HOW TO PLAY

Singles

Players compete for the opportunity to serve, since only the player serving can score points. Following a good serve, the receiver seeks to return the shuttle to his opponent, who then attempts to return it to him, and so on. If a server wins a rally, he wins a point. If the server loses a rally *(see Law 15, Faults, page 125)*, the right to serve (and score points) reverts to his opponent.

Doubles

As above, except the serve is passed from one player to his partner before it is "lost" to the receiving side.

Starting

The winner of a toss decides whether to pick an end or to serve or receive first. The first serve is an underarm shot from the right service court to a receiver in the court diagonally opposite.

How to win

Points may only be scored when serving. Generally a match consists of three games, each won by the first side to score 15 points, except for women's singles games, which are won by the first to score 11 points. HOWEVER, if the score reaches 13-all (or 9-all for women), the player who first reached 13 (or 9) can choose to "set" the game, in which case the score reverts to "Love-all" and the game goes to the first player to win 5 points (3 points for women). Similarly, if a game has not been "set" and the score reaches 14-all (or 10-all for women), the first player to score 14 can choose to set the game at that point. Now, the first to 3 points (or 2 points for women) wins the game. If the choice is made not to set, the first to score 15 (or 11) wins as usual. The first player or team to win two games wins the match. *See Law 9, Scoring (page 124).*

KEY RULES

• Players change ends after each game and midway through the third game (based on the leader's points). *See Law 10, Change of Ends (page 124).*

• Any one of a number of *faults* will mean either the loss of the right to serve or a point to the opposition. It is a fault if the

Shot in the arm
One of the first strokes that beginners learn is the high shot. This loops the shuttle high over the net to force opponents far back in the court, weakening their attack.

Drop shot
Because a shuttle, unlike a tennis ball, decelerates very rapidly, the drop shot that delicately places the shuttle just over the net is a common attacking shot in badminton.

shuttle touches the ground on or within the boundaries of a player's court or if a player hits the shuttle so that it lands outside the boundaries of his opponent's court. Faults are also called for many other reasons, including if the shuttle hits the clothing or body of a player. *See Law 15, Faults (page 125).*

• Strict rules govern how to serve. Both server and receiver must have part of both feet on the ground within the boundaries of the appropriate service court. The shuttle must be hit while it is below the waist of the server and the head of the racket must be below the hand holding the racket. *See Law 11, Service (page 124).*

• Circumstances, such as a shuttle stuck atop the net,

Back breaker
The backhand drive is an attacking shot often used in doubles to hit the shuttle hard and fast down the sidelines.

sometimes require a "let" to be called. The rally is canceled and the server serves again. *See Law 16, Lets (page 125).*

SKILLS

A successful player needs to be fit and alert to keep up with the quick-fire rallies that

characterize badminton. Although control of the racket with the arm and wrist is all-important, balance, speed, and footwork are also vital if a player is to use stroke skills anywhere inside the court at a moment's notice.

The grip

Because the racket is so light, it is held firmly but not tightly. The basic forehand grip, assumed by "shaking hands" with the racket with the stringed area at right angles to the ground, allows flexibility, enabling both power strokes and delicate shots. Two other variations for specific shots are the backhand and the flat grip.

Strokes

Forehand and backhand drives are made by hitting the shuttle flat and low over the net, generally from the middle or back of the court. They are fast, attacking shots requiring control and power. The player places both feet firmly and pivots the body to follow through on the stroke.

The smash is an aggressive overhead stroke, which, if used at the right moment, instantly weakens an opponent's game. It is often used to score points. Ideally the shuttle travels steeply and quickly downwards, catching an opponent off guard and causing a weak return or a missed shot altogether.

Net shots are neat, effective shots played close to the net. The aim is to gently tap the shuttle just over the net with a flick of the wrist so that the opposition is unable to reach it in time.

TACTICS

In any game, the aim is to make any combination of these and other strokes as unpredictable as possible in order to wear down opponents and weaken their defense.

GRAY AREA

Q. Since the lines form part of the court, would it be a fault if a player stood on a line?

A. Yes it could be. Although a shuttle hitting a line is always "in," a player, when **serving** or **receiving**, is outside the court if either foot so much as touches the line.

Ready to serve

BADMINTON
● ● ● ● ● ● ● ● ●

The Laws

1. The Court
See The court (page 122).

2. Posts

3. Net
See The net (page 122).

4. Shuttle
See The shuttle (page 122).

5. Racket
See The racket (page 122).

6. Approved Equipment
For specifications and rulings contact the International Badminton Federation.

7. Players
See (page 123).

8. Toss
See Starting (page 123).

9. Scoring
9.1 The opposing sides shall play the best of three games unless otherwise arranged.
9.2 Only the serving side can add a point to its score.
9.3 In doubles and men's singles a game is won by the first side to score 15 points, except as provided in Law 9.6.
9.4 In ladies' singles a game is won by the first side to score 11 points, except as provided in Law 9.6.
9.5.1 If the score becomes 13-all or 14-all (9-all or 10-all in ladies' singles), the side which first scored 13 or 14 (9 or 10) shall have the choice of "setting" or "not setting" the game (Law 9.6).
9.5.2 This choice can only be made when the score is first reached and must be made before the next service is delivered.
9.5.3 The relevant side (Law 9.5.1) is given the opportunity to set at 14-all (10-all in ladies' singles) despite any previous

decision not to set by that side or the opposing side at 13-all (9-all in ladies' singles).
9.6 If the game has been set, the score is called "Love-all" and the side first scoring the set number of points (Law 9.6.1 to 9.6.4) wins the game.
  9.6.1 13-all setting to 5 points.
  9.6.2 14-all setting to 3 points.
  9.6.3 9-all setting to 3 points.
    9.6.4 10-all setting to 2 points.
    9.7 The side winning a game serves first in the next game.

10. Change of Ends
10.1 Players shall change ends:
  10.1.1 At the end of the first game;
  10.1.2 Prior to the beginning of the third game (if any); and
  10.1.3 In the third game, or in a one-game match, when the leading score reaches:
-6 in a game of 11 points
-8 in a game of 15 points
10.2 When players omit to change ends as indicated by Law 10.1, they shall do so immediately when the mistake is discovered and the existing score shall stand.

11. Service
11.1 In a correct service:
  11.1.1 Neither side shall cause undue delay to the delivery of the service;
  11.1.2 The server and receiver shall stand within diagonally opposite service courts without touching the boundary lines of these service courts; some part of both feet of the server and receiver must remain in contact with the surface of the court in a stationary position until the service is delivered (Law 11.4);
  11.1.3 The server's racket shall initially hit the base of the shuttle while the whole of the shuttle is below the server's waist;
  11.1.4 The shaft of the server's racket at the instant of hitting the shuttle shall be pointing in a downward direction to such an extent that the whole of the head of the racket is discernibly below the whole of the server's hand holding the racket;
  11.1.5 The movement of the server's racket must continue forwards after the start of the service (Law 11.2) until the service is delivered; and
  11.1.6 The flight of the shuttle shall be upwards from the server's racket to pass over the net, so that, if not intercepted, it falls in the receiver's service

court.
11.2 Once the players have taken their positions, the first forward movement of the server's racket head is the start of the service.
11.3 The server shall not serve before the receiver is ready, but the receiver shall be considered to have been ready if a return of service is attempted.
11.4 The service is delivered when, once started (Law 11.2), the shuttle is hit by the server's racket or the shuttle lands on the floor.
11.5 In doubles, the partners may take up any positions that do not unsight the opposing server or receiver.

12. Singles
12.1 The players shall serve from, and receive in, their respective right service courts when the server has not scored or has scored an even number of points in that game.
12.2 The players shall serve from, and receive in, their respective left service courts when the server has scored an odd number of points in that game.
12.3 If a game is set, the total points scored by the server in that game shall be used to apply Laws 12.1 and 12.2.
12.4 The shuttle is hit alternately by the server and the receiver until a "fault" is made or the shuttle ceases to be in play.
  12.5.1 If the receiver makes a "fault" or the shuttle ceases to be in play because it touches the surface of the court inside the receiver's court, the server scores a point. The server then serves again from the alternate service court.
  12.5.2 If the server makes a "fault" or the shuttle ceases to be in play because it touches the surface of the court inside the server's court, the server loses the right to continue serving, and the receiver then becomes the server, with no point scored by either player.

13. Doubles
13.1 At the start of a game, and each time a side gains the right to serve, the service shall be delivered from the right service court.
13.2 Only the receiver shall return the service: should the shuttle touch or be hit by the receiver's partner, the serving side scores a point.
13.3.1 After the service is returned, the shuttle is hit by either player of the serving side and then by either player of the

receiving side, and so on, until the shuttle ceases to be in play.
  13.3.2 After the service is returned, a player may hit the shuttle from any position on that player's side of the net.
  13.4.1 If the receiving side makes a "fault" or the shuttle ceases to be in play because it touches the surface of the court inside the receiving side's court, the serving side scores a point, and the server serves again.
  13.4.2 If the serving side makes a "fault" or the shuttle ceases to be in play because it touches the surface of the court inside the serving side's court, the server loses the right to continue serving, with no point scored by either side.
  13.5.1 The player who serves at the start of any game shall serve from, or receive in, the right service court when that player's side has not scored or has scored an even number of points in that game, and the left service court otherwise.
  13.5.2 The player who receives at the start of any game shall receive in, or serve from, the right service court when that player's side has not scored or has scored an even number of points in that game, and the left service court otherwise.
  13.5.3 The reverse pattern applies to the partners.
  13.5.4 If a game is set, the total points scored by a side in that game shall be used to apply Laws 13.5.1 to 13.5.3.
13.6 Service in any turn of serving shall be delivered from the alternate service courts, except as provided in Laws 14 and 16.
13.7 The right to serve passes consecutively from the initial server in any game to the initial receiver in that game, and then consecutively from that player to that player's partner and then to one of the opponents and then the opponent's partner, and so on.
13.8 No player shall serve out of turn, receive out of turn, or receive two consecutive services in the same game, except as provided in Laws 14 and 16.
13.9 Either player of the winning side may serve first in the next game and either player of the losing side may receive.

14. Service-Court Errors
14.1 A service-court error has been made when a player:
  14.1.1 Has served out of turn;
  14.1.2 Has served from the wrong service court; or
  14.1.3 Standing in the wrong

service court, was prepared to receive the service and it has been delivered.

14.2 When a service-court error has been made, then:

14.2.1 If the error is discovered before the next service is delivered, it is a "let" unless only one side was at fault and lost the rally, in which case the error shall not be corrected.

14.2.2 If the error is not discovered before the next service is delivered, the error shall not be corrected.

14.3 If there is a "let" because of a service-court error, the rally is replayed and the error corrected.

14.4 If a service-court error is not to be corrected, play in that game shall proceed without changing the player's new service courts (nor, when relevant, the new order of serving).

15. Faults

It is a "fault":

15.1 If a service is not correct (Law 11.1).

15.2 If the server, in attempting to serve, misses the shuttle.

15.3 If, on service, the shuttle is caught on the net and remains suspended on top or, on service, after passing over the net is caught in the net.

15.4 If in play, the shuttle:

15.4.1 Lands outside the boundaries of the court;

15.4.2 Passes through or under the net;

15.4.3 Fails to pass the net;

15.4.4 Touches the roof, ceiling, or side walls;

15.4.5 Touches the person or dress of a player; or

15.4.6 Touches any other object or person outside the immediate surroundings of the court;

(Where necessary, on account of the structure of the building, the local badminton authority may, subject to the right of veto of its National Organization, make by-laws dealing with cases in which a shuttle touches an obstruction.)

15.5 If, when in play, the initial point of contact with the shuttle is not on the striker's side of the net. (The striker may, however, follow the shuttle over the net with the racket in the course of a stroke.)

15.6 If, when the shuttle is in play, a player:

15.6.1 Touches the net or its supports with racket, person, or dress;

15.6.2 Invades an opponent's court with racket or person in

any degree except as permitted in Law 15.5; or

15.6.3 Invades an opponent's court under the net with racket or person such that an opponent is obstructed or distracted;

15.6.4 Obstructs an opponent, i.e., prevents an opponent from making a legal stroke where the shuttle is followed over the net.

15.7 If, in play, a player deliberately distracts an opponent by any action such as shouting or making gestures.

15.8 If, in play, the shuttle:

15.8.1 Be caught and held on the racket and then slung during the execution of a stroke;

15.8.2 Be hit twice in succession by the same player with two strokes;

15.8.3 Be hit by a player and player's partner successively; or

15.8.4 Touches a player's racket and continues towards the back of that player's court.

15.9 If a player is guilty of flagrant, repeated, or persistent offenses under Law 18.

16. Lets

"Let" is called by the umpire, or by a player (if there is no umpire) to halt play.

16.1 A "let" may be given for any unforeseen or accidental occurrence.

16.2 If a shuttle is caught on the net and remains suspended on top, or after passing over the net is caught in the net, it is a "let" except during service.

16.3 If during service, the receiver and server are both faulted at the same time, it shall be a "let."

16.4 If the server serves before the receiver is ready. it shall be a "let."

16.5 If during play, the shuttle disintegrates and the base completely separates from the rest of the shuttle, it shall be a "let."

16.6 If a line judge is unsighted and the umpire is unable to make a decision, it shall be a "let."

16.7 When a "let" occurs, the play since the last service shall not count, and the player who served shall serve again, except when Law 14 is applicable.

17. Shuttle not in Play

A shuttle is not in play when:

17.1 It strikes the net and remains attached there or suspended on top;

17.2 It strikes the net or post and starts to fall towards the surface of the court on the striker's side of the net;

17.3 It hits the surface of the court; or

17.4 A "fault" or "let" has occurred.

18. Continuous Play, Misconduct, Penalties

18.1 Play shall be continuous from the first service until the match is concluded, except as allowed in Laws 18.2 and 18.3.

18.2 An interval not exceeding five minutes is allowed between the second and third games of all matches in all of the following situations:

18.2.1 In international competitive events;

18.2.2 In International Badminton Federation (IBF) sanctioned events; and

18.2.3 In all other matches (unless the National Organization has previously published a decision not to allow such an interval).

18.3 When necessitated by circumstances not within the control of the players, the umpire may suspend play for such a period as the umpire may consider necessary. If play be suspended, the existing score shall stand and play be resumed from that point.

18.4 Under no circumstances shall play be suspended to enable a player to recover his strength or wind, or to receive instruction or advice.

18.5.1 Except in the intervals provided in Laws 18.2 and 18.3,

no player shall be permitted to receive advice during a match.

18.5.2 Except during the interval described in Law 18.2, no player shall leave the court during a match without the umpire's consent.

18.6 The umpire shall be sole judge of any suspension of play.

18.7 A player shall not:

18.7.1 Deliberately cause suspension of play;

18.7.2 Deliberately interfere with the speed of the shuttle;

18.7.3 Behave in an offensive manner; or

18.7.4 Be guilty of misconduct not otherwise covered by the Laws of Badminton.

18.8 The umpire shall administer any breach of Law 18.4, 18.5, or 18.7 by:

18.8.1 Issuing a warning to the offending side;

18.8.2 Faulting the offending side, if previously warned; or

18.8.3 In cases of flagrant offense or persistent offences, faulting the offending side and reporting the offending side immediately to the referee, who shall have the power to disqualify.

18.9 Where a referee has not been appointed, the responsible official shall have the power to disqualify.

19. Officials and Appeals

For details contact the International Badminton Federation.

Space does not permit the inclusion of Appendixes 1 to 5 or the Recommendations to Court Officials, which can be obtained, together with the complete Laws of Badminton, from the IBF or contact your local governing authority.

Lunge time
Badminton involves rapid movements across the court to reach the shuttle, and running forward to the net usually ends in a long lunge.

Squash
Essentials

A test of endurance and hand-eye coordination, squash is an intense and physically demanding game. Racquetball, a similar game played with a smaller racket and a lighter ball (for greater bounce), is also popular in North America.

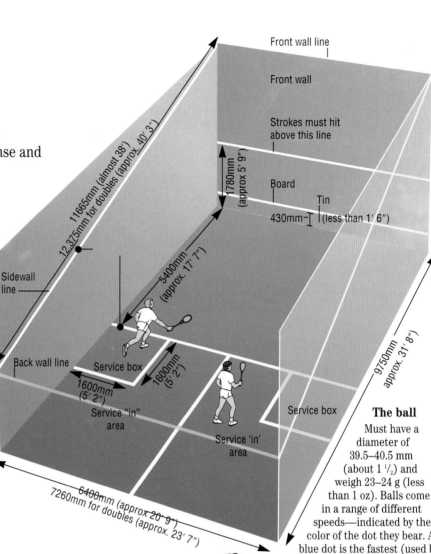

Front wall line

Front wall

Strokes must hit above this line

1780mm (approx 5' 9")

Board

Tin

430mm — (less than 1' 6")

11665mm (almost 38") 12.375mm for doubles (approx. 40' 3")

5400mm (approx. 17' 7")

4570mm (almost 15' 6")

Sidewall line

2130mm — (approx 7')

Back wall line

Service box

1600mm (5' 2")

1600mm (5' 2")

Service "in" area

Service 'in' area

Service box

9750mm approx. 31' 8")

6400mm (approx 20' 9") 7260mm for doubles (approx. 23' 7")

The court

A rectangular box with a level floor and four vertical walls of varying height. Below the "board" is an area at the base of the front wall, usually surfaced with metal and known as the "tin." Although the dimensions and floor markings for the two games are technically different, squash and racquetball are sometimes played on the same courts in North America. When this happens, a removable board is attached to the front wall for a squash match.

Rackets

Preferably made of graphite with two layers of strings woven into a uniform pattern. Strings may be gut, nylon, or a suitable substitute.

Players

Two players. (A game of doubles is also possible, but this has an entirely different set of rules and court dimensions.)

Dress

A light shirt with shorts or a skirt. Proper squash shoes feature a heel and rubber sole designed for the game. They must not mark the floor.

Officials

A marker and a referee.

The ball

Must have a diameter of 39.5–40.5 mm (about 1 $\frac{1}{2}$) and weigh 23–24 g (less than 1 oz). Balls come in a range of different speeds—indicated by the color of the dot they bear. A blue dot is the fastest (used by beginners). A yellow dot is the super-slow ball used for matches.

The racket

Squash rackets have a smaller, rounder head than tennis rackets and a long shaft that is sometimes hollowed out to reduce vibration. Maximum weight 255 gm (about 9 oz.).

Hard and fast

Squash is demanding because the ball travels very fast, not just off the front wall, but off all the other walls as well. Sometimes a player has to hit the ball off the back wall so hard that it reaches the front wall above the board, as this player is doing here. Such shots demand substantial power.

HOW TO PLAY

Two players attempt to outlast each other in rallies, taking turns striking the ball down the court and back again, making sure the ball hits the front wall on the way, without first touching the floor or either of the players.

Starting

Before play begins, the players are given five minutes to warm up the ball. This allows the air inside the ball to expand and provide extra bounce. The right to serve first is then decided by spinning a racket using a distinctive mark on the racket. (For each game after this, the winner of the previous game serves first.) The server then elects a box to serve from, alternating boxes with each point until the service is lost.

How to win

A match is the best of three or five games. The first player to score nine points wins the game, but at eight-all the receiver may choose to play on to nine points ("set one") or ten points ("set two"). Points may only be scored by the server. If the server loses a stroke, the service passes to the opponent. The new server must now win a stroke to score a point.

KEY RULES

• Play is continuous, as far as possible, with intervals of only 90 seconds between the warm up and the first game, and then between all following games. *See Rule 7, Continuity of Play (page 128).*

• The ball must always strike the front wall above the board. It may do this via another wall or walls, but always before the ball bounces on the floor or touches any part of a player. *See Rule 6, Good Return (page 128).*

• A player may allow the ball to bounce only once before being returned, otherwise a "down" or "not up" is called and the rally is lost.

• Many of the rules of squash arise from the fact that the game is played in such a confined space. If a striker's return is heading *straight for the front wall* but is blocked by the opponent, the striker wins the stroke. Wherever possible, players must allow their opponent direct access to the ball and the freedom to hit it to any part of the front wall. *For details see Rule 9, Hitting an Opponent with the Ball (page 129)*

• If a striker faces interference or is afraid of injuring an opponent, a let must be requested with the words "Let please"—before the shot is played. If a let is awarded, the rally starts again. *See Rule 12 (page 132).*

The serve
The serve in squash is relatively tame compared with a tennis service, but it is the best chance a player gets to select where the ball will land in relation to his or her opponent. Points can only be won off service, so a skillful serve is important.

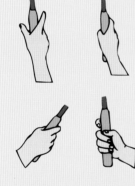

The grip
The most popular grip in squash is called the 'shake hands' grip. The idea is to "shake hands" with the racket so that the top edge of the shaft goes into the V between the thumb and forefinger with the forefinger slightly separated from the other three.

Jansher Khan, *World Champion in the late 1980s.*

Shoes for squash are well padded to protect feet and ankles from shock. They must also have rubber soles that provide a good grip but will not mark the floor.

RULES OF THE WORLD SINGLES GAME

1. The Game

See page 126.

2. The Score

See How to Win (page 127)

3. Points

See page 127.

4. The Service

4.1 Play commences with a service and the right to serve first is decided by the spin of a racket. Thereafter, the server continues to serve until losing a stroke, whereupon the opponent becomes the server, and this procedure continues throughout the match. At the commencement of the second and each subsequent game the winner of the previous game serves first.

4.2 At the beginning of each game and each hand the server has the choice of serving from either box and thereafter shall serve from alternate boxes while remaining the server. However, if a rally ends in a let, the server shall serve again from the same box.

4.3 When serving, a player shall drop or throw the ball from either a hand or the racket before striking it. Should the player, having dropped or thrown the ball, make no attempt to strike it, the ball shall be dropped or thrown again for that service.

4.4 A service is good when it does not result in the server serving the handout. The server

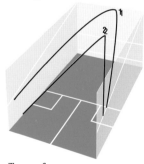

Types of serve
The ball is often served with a hammer drive or a lob. A lob (1) from the right service box sends the ball high into the middle of the front wall so that it loops back into the far court, hitting the side wall just below the out line; a drive (2) powers the ball staight back into the angle between the wall and the floor, making a return awkward.

serves the handout and loses the stroke if:

4.4.1 The ball, after being dropped or thrown for service, touches a wall, the floor, ceiling, or any object(s) suspended from the walls or ceiling before being served. —Called "Fault."

4.4.2 At the time of striking the ball the server fails to have part of one foot in contact with the floor within the service box without any part of that foot touching the service-box line (part of that foot may project over this line provided that it does not touch the line). —Called "Foot fault."

4.4.3 The server makes one or more attempts to strike the ball, but fails to do so.—Called "Not up."

4.4.4 The ball is not struck correctly. —Called "Not up."

4.4.5 The ball is served out. — Called "Out."

4.4.6 The ball is served against any wall of the court before the front wall. —Called "Fault."

4.4.7 The ball is served onto the floor or onto or below the service line. —Called "Fault" if above the board and "Down" if on the floor or on or below the board.

4.4.8 The first bounce of the ball, unless volleyed by the receiver, is on the floor on or outside 10 short or half court lines of the quarter court opposite to the server's box.— Called "Fault."

4.5 The server must not serve until the Marker has completed calling the score.

5. The Play

See page 127.

6. Good Return

6.1 A return is good if the ball, before it has bounced more than once upon the floor, is returned correctly by the striker onto the front wall above the board, either directly or via sidewall(s) and/or back wall, without first touching the floor or any part of the striker's body or clothing, or the opponent's racket, body or clothing, provided the ball is not hit out.

6.2 It shall not be considered a good return if the ball touches the board before or after it hits the front wall and before it bounces on the floor, or if the

racket is not in the player's hand at the time the ball is struck.

7 Continuity of Play

After the first service is delivered play shall be continuous so far as is practical provided that:

7.1 At any time play may be

Sheer volley
In squash the ball is usually hit on the volley or half volley. It is very rarely allowed to bounce completely. The aim is typically to strike the ball just over the top of the board so that your opponent has very little time to get to the ball for the volley.

suspended, owing to bad light or other circumstances beyond the control of the players, for such period as the Referee shall decide. The score shall stand. If another court is available when the court originally in use remains unsuitable, the match may be transferred to it if both players agree or as directed by the Referee.

In the event of play being suspended for the day the score shall stand unless both players agree to start the match again.

7.2 An interval of 90 seconds shall be permitted between the end of the warm-up and the commencement of the first game and also between all games. Players may leave the court during such intervals but must

be ready to play prior to the expiry of the 90-second time interval.

By mutual consent of the payers play may commence or resume prior to the expiry of the 90-second time interval.

7.3 Provided a player satisfies the Referee that a change of equipment, clothing, or footwear is necessary, the player may leave the court, but is required to effect the change as quickly as possible, and shall be allowed a period not exceeding 90 seconds for this purpose.

7.4 When 15 seconds of a permitted 90-second time interval remain the Referee shall call "15 seconds" to advise the players to be ready to resume play. At the end of this interval the Referee shall call "Time." The calls should be made in a loud voice. It is the responsibility of the players to be in a position to hear the calls of "15 seconds" and "Time."

7.5 A player suffering illness or disability has the choice of continuing or resuming play without delay, conceding the game in progress, or conceding the match. If conceding the game, the player shall retain any points already scored and at the conclusion of the 90-second interval between games shall either resume play or concede the match.

However, if the illness or disability involves visible blood flow, a continuation or resumption of play is not permitted. The player shall leave the court but is not required at that time to concede the game in progress. If the player wishes to resume play, the illness or disability shall be dealt with by the Referee as a self-inflicted injury and the provisions of Rule 16.2 shall apply.

7.6 In the event of an injury to a player the Referee shall refer to the provisions of Rule 16.

7.7 The Referee shall apply the provisions of Rule 17 to a player who in the opinion of the Referee, delays play unreasonably. Such delay may be caused by:

7.7.1 Unduly slow preparation

to serve or to receive service.

7.7.2 Prolonged discussion with the Referee.

7.7.3 Delay in returning to the court, having left under the terms of Rule 7.2, 7.3 or 15.1.

7.8 If an object, other than a player's racket, falls to the floor of the court while a rally is in progress the requirements are:

7.8.1 The Referee, on becoming aware of a fallen object, shall stop play immediately.

7.8.2 A player becoming aware of a fallen object may stop play and appeal for a let.

7.8.3 If the object falls from a player, then that player shall lose the stroke unless Rule 7.8.5 applies or unless the cause is a collision with the opponent. In the latter case a let shall be allowed except that if an appeal for interference is made the Referee shall apply the provisions of Rule 12.

7.8.4 If the object falls from a source other than a player a let shall be allowed unless Rule 7.8.5 applies.

7.8.5 If a player has already made a clear winning return when the object falls to the floor of the court, then that player shall win the stroke.

7.9 If a player drops a racket, the Referee shall allow the rally to continue unless Rule 12, 13.1.1, 13.1.3, or 17 applies.

8. Strokes

A player wins a stroke:

8.1 Under Rule 4.4 when the player is the receiver.

8.2 If the opponent fails to make a good return of the ball when the opponent is the striker, unless a let is allowed or a stroke is awarded to the opponent.

8.3 If the ball touches the opponent (including anything worn or carried), without interference, when the opponent is the non-striker, except as is otherwise provided for in Rules 9 and 10. If interference occurs, then the provisions of Rule 12 apply. In all cases the Referee shall rule accordingly.

8.4 If a stroke is awarded to the player by the Referee as provided for in the rules.

9. Hitting an Opponent with the Ball

If the ball, before reaching the front wall, hits the striker's

opponent (including anything worn or carried), the ball shall cease to be in play and:

9.1 Unless Rule 9.2 applies, the striker shall win the stroke if the return would have been good and the ball would have struck the front wall without first touching any other wall.

9.2 If the return would have been good, but the striker has either followed the ball around and turned or the ball has passed around the striker who, in either case, strikes the ball to the right of the body after the ball has passed to the left (or vice versa), then a let shall be allowed in all cases.

9.3 If the ball either had struck or would have struck any other wall and the return would have been good, a let shall be allowed unless, in the opinion of the Referee, a winning return has been prevented, in which case the striker shall win the stroke.

10. Further Attempts to Hit the Ball

If the striker strikes at and misses the ball, further attempts to strike it may be made. If, after being missed, the ball touches the opponent (including anything worn or carried), then, in the opinion of the Referee:

10.1 If the striker could otherwise have made a good return, a let shall be allowed, or

10.2 If the striker could not have made a good return, the striker shall lose the stroke.
If any such further attempt is successful but results in a good return being prevented from reaching the front wall by hitting the striker's opponent (including anything worn or carried), a let shall be allowed in all circumstances. If any such further attempt would not have resulted in a good return, the striker shall lose the stroke.

11. Appeals

The loser of a rally may appeal against any decision of the marker affecting that rally.
An appeal to the Referee under Rule 11 should be prefaced with the words "Appeal please." Play shall then cease until the Referee has given the decision.

If an appeal under Rule 11 is

➡ *page 132*

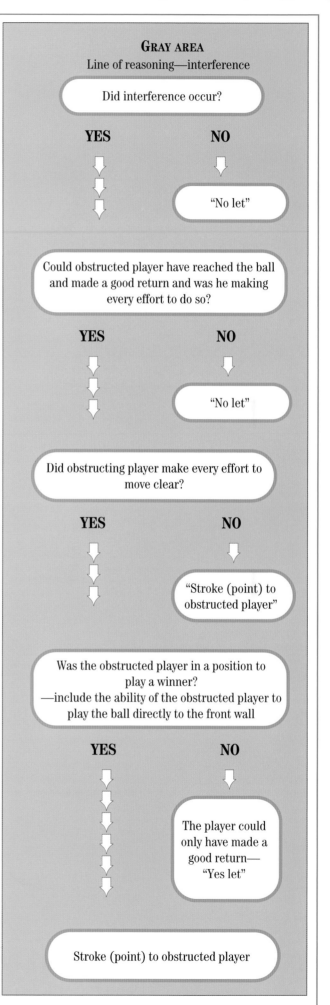

GRAY AREA
Line of reasoning—interference

Did interference occur?

YES   **NO**

"No let"

Could obstructed player have reached the ball and made a good return and was he making every effort to do so?

YES   **NO**

"No let"

Did obstructing player make every effort to move clear?

YES   **NO**

"Stroke (point) to obstructed player"

Was the obstructed player in a position to play a winner?
—include the ability of the obstructed player to play the ball directly to the front wall

YES   **NO**

The player could only have made a good return—
"Yes let"

Stroke (point) to obstructed player

Forehand

The basic stroke in squash is the forehand ground stroke, which gives good control and can be quite powerful. It is usually used when running back to play an overlength ball into the back corner. The aim is to drive the ball down the wall the length of the court into the back corner. It is important to watch the head of the racket and not swing too wildly.

Backhand

The backhand ground stroke is also a powerful drive but typically it is used to drive the ball across court. It requires great control so that the follow through does not endanger an opponent. The backhand shot is also essential for lifting the ball out of tight corners on the backhand side of the court.

SKILLS

Racket skills are all-important in the game of squash, but these must be combined with a high level of fitness. Although the court is relatively small, a player covers this ground many times over in a game, often at great speed. A skilled player will also be able to vary the pace in order to wear down an opponent.

Strokes

A good, secure grip is necessary for precision and control, but it must also allow flexibility of the wrist. The basic *forehand ground stroke* can be used from anywhere along the length of the court. It is a controlled driving shot that can be quite powerful. The *backhand ground stroke* takes care of shots from the other side of the court. In between strokes it is best to wait with the racket poised in front of the body, ready for backhand or forehand strokes. The *volley* is a quick-response stroke, meeting the ball before it bounces on the floor. This is an effective attacking shot, often making it very difficult for an opponent to manage a return. The *drop* is another potential winning stroke, particularly if the opponent is fooled into anticipating a driving shot and remains on the "T" (the intersection of the short line and the half-court line). The ball is played near the tin or along the sidewall, making it nearly impossible to reach and return in time. *Boast* shots are clever angle shots made by playing the ball on to a sidewall so that it rebounds directly on to the front wall and on to the floor, or on to the opposite sidewall and then to the floor. A well-judged boast shot will often surprise an opponent.

Blocked volley

In squash there is often no time to make a full swing at the ball. As a result, squash players often have to play a blocked volley.

Overhead volley or smash

The overhead volley is often used to cut off high cross-court lobs. The aim is to play the ball at a point in front of and above the racket shoulder.

1 *The shot begins with the racket dropped down the back, the back arched and the racket arm held high with the wrist cocked.*

TACTICS

Because a rally can be exhausting, both players try to conserve energy by dominating the court from the T (the intersection of the short line and the half-court line). This position guarantees the shortest possible distance to any area of the court and also enables a player to place shots that are difficult to reach, thus tiring opponents out.

Boasting

A boast shot bounces off the sidewall before hitting the front. One of the most effective is the "tickle boast." This is a delicate shot played near the front wall and designed to drop low into the front of the court. The player often disguises this stroke by pretending to play a drive then checking the downswing to cock his wrist, "tickling" the ball into the corner.

2 *The racket arm then swings over in a throwing action, with the arm at full length to give maximum leverage and a fast-moving racket head, striking the ball downwards at the top of the swing.*

3 *As with all squash strokes, it is important to follow through. The player should hit the ball with the back of the non-racket shoulder at the beginning of the stroke and only turn full-face towards the end.*

Continued from page 129

disallowed, the Marker's decision shall stand. If the Referee is uncertain, a let shall be allowed except where provided for in the Notes to Referees (see complete rules).

Appeals upheld or Referee intervention under Rule 20.4 are dealt with in each specific situation below.

11.1 Appeals on Service

11.1. If the Marker calls "Fault," "Foot fault," "Not up," "Down," or "Out" to the service, the receiver may appeal, either immediately or at the end of the rally if the receiver has played or attempted to play the ball. If, in the opinion of the Referee, the service was not good, the Referee shall stop play immediately and award the stroke to the receiver.

11.2 Appeals on Play other than Service

11.2.1 If the Marker calls "Not up" or "Out" following a player's return, the player may appeal. If the appeal is upheld, the Referee shall allow a let except that if, in the opinion of the Referee:

The Marker's call has interrupted that player's winning return, the Referee shall award the stroke to the player.

The Marker's call has interrupted or prevented a winning return by the opponent, the Referee shall award the stroke to the opponent.

11.2.2 If the Marker fails to call "Not up," "Down," or "Out" following a player's return, the opponent may appeal either immediately or at the end of the rally if the opponent has played or attempted to play the ball. If, in the opinion of the Referee, the return was not good, the Referee shall stop play immediately and award the stroke to the opponent.

12. Interference

12.1 The player whose turn it is to play the ball is entitled to freedom from interference by the opponent.

12.2 To avoid interference the opponent must make every effort to provide the player with:

12.2.1 Unobstructed direct access to the ball.

12.2.2 A fair view of the ball.

12.2.3 Freedom to hit the ball.

12.2.4 Freedom to play the ball directly to any part of the front wall.

12.3 Interference occurs if the opponent fails to fulfill any of the requirements of Rule 12.2, irrespective of whether the opponent makes every effort to fulfill those requirements.

12.4 A player encountering possible interference has the choice of continuing with play or of stopping and appealing to the Referee.

12.4.1 The correct method of appeal, whether a let or a stroke is sought by a player, is with the words "Let please."

12.4.2 An appeal may be made only by the player (the person whose turn it is to play the ball). The appeal must be made either immediately after the interference occurs or, where the player clearly does not continue with play beyond the point of interference, without undue delay.

12.5 The Referee shall decide on the appeal and shall announce the decision with the words "No let," "Yes let" or "Stroke to [name of appropriate player]." In assessing the situation the only relevant opinion is that of the Referee, and the decision of the Referee shall be final.

12.6 The Referee shall not allow a let and the player shall lose the rally if:

12.6.1 There has been no interference.

12.6.2 Interference has occurred but either player would not have made a good return or

the player has not made every effort to get to the ball.

12.6.3 The player has clearly accepted the interference and played on.

12.6.4 The player has created the interference in moving to the ball.

12.7 The Referee shall allow a let if there has been interference which the opponent has made every effort to avoid and the player would have made a good return.

12.8 The Referee shall award a stroke to the player if:

12.8.1 There has been interference that the opponent has not made every effort to avoid and the player would have made a good return.

12.8.2 There has been interference that the opponent has made every effort to avoid and the player would have made a winning return.

12.8.3 The player has refrained from hitting the ball, which, if hit, would clearly have struck the opponent going directly to the front wall, or to a sidewall, but in the latter case would have been a winning return (unless in either case turning, ball passing around player, or further attempt applies).

12.9 The Referee is also empowered to allow a let under Rule 12.7 or to award a stroke under Rule 12.8 without an appeal having been made, if necessary stopping play to do so.

12.10 The provisions of Rule 17, Conduct On Court, may be applied in interference situations. The Referee shall, stopping play if it has not already stopped, apply an appropriate penalty if:

12.10.1 The player has made unnecessary physical contact with the opponent or vice versa.

12.10.2 The player has endangered the opponent with

an excessive racket swing.

13. Lets

In addition to lets allowed under other rules, lets may or shall be allowed in certain other cases. Any request for a let should be prefaced by the words "Let please."

13.1 A let may be allowed:

13.1.1 If the ball in play touches any article lying on the floor.

13.1.2 If the striker refrains from hitting the ball owing to a reasonable fear of injuring the opponent.

13.1.3 If, in the opinion of the Referee, either player is distracted by an occurrence on or off the court.

13.1.4 If, in the opinion of the Referee, a change in court conditions has affected the result of the rally.

13.2 A let shall be allowed:

13.2.1 If the receiver is not ready and does not attempt to return the service.

13.2.2 If the ball breaks during play.

13.2.3 If the Referee is asked to decide an appeal and is unable to do so.

13.2.4 If an otherwise good return has been made but the ball either lodges in any part of the playing surface of the court, preventing it from bouncing more than once upon the floor, or the ball goes out on its first bounce.

13.3 If the striker appeals for a let under Rules 13.1 (1 to 4); in order for a let to be allowed the striker must have been able to make a good return. For a non-striker appeal under Rules 13.1.1, 13.1.3 and 13.1.4 this is not a requirement.

13.4 No let shall be allowed under Rules 13.1.2 and 13.2.1 if the player attempts to play the ball but may be allowed under Rules 13.1.1, 13.1.3, 13.1.4, 13.2.2, 13.2.3, and 13.2.4.

13.5 The appeals requirements of Rule 13 are:

13.5.1 An appeal by the player is necessary for a let to be allowed under Rules 13.1.2 (striker only), 13.1.3, 13.2.1 (striker only), and 13.2.3.

13.5.2 An appeal by the player or Referee intervention without appeal is applicable to Rules 13.1.1, 13.1.4, 13.2.2, and 13.2.4.

Situations in which a let is played

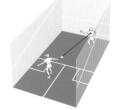

1. Sometimes when the ball hits an opponent when it would have hit the front wall (see Rule 9)..

2. When the player is unable to hit the ball without being in danger of hitting his opponent.

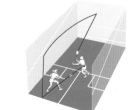

3. If the striker's shot hits his opponent unwittingly after a follow through.

14. The Ball

14.1 At any time, when the ball is not in actual play, another ball may be substituted by mutual consent of the players, or on appeal by either player at the discretion of the Referee.

14.2 If a ball breaks during play, it shall be replaced promptly by another ball.

14.3 If a ball has broken during play but this has not been established, a let for the rally in which the ball broke shall be allowed if the server appeals prior to the next service or if the receiver appeals prior to attempting to return that service.

14.4 The provisions of Rule 14.3 do not apply to the final rally of a game. An appeal in this case must be immediately after the rally.

14.5 If a player stops during a rally to appeal that the ball is broken only to find subsequently that the ball is not broken, then that player shall lose the stroke.

14.6 Between games the ball shall remain within the court unless removal is permitted by the Referee.

15. Warm-Up

15.1 Immediately preceding the start of play the two players together shall be allowed on the court of play a period of five minutes for the purpose of warming up the ball to be used for the match.

After two and a half minutes of the warm-up, the Referee shall call "Halftime" and ensure that the players change sides unless they mutually agree otherwise. The Referee shall also advise when the warm-up period is complete with the call of "Time."

15.2 Where a ball has been substituted under Rule 14 or when the match is being resumed after considerable delay, the Referee shall allow the ball to be warmed up to playing condition. Play shall then resume on the direction of the Referee, or upon mutual consent of the players, which- ever is the earlier.

15.3 The ball may be warmed up by either player between the end of the five-minute warm-up and start of play, between games and when the opponent is changing equipment.

16. Injury

16.1 In the event of an injury to a player the Referee shall decide whether the injury category is:

16.1.1 Self-inflicted (where the injury to the player was not contributed to by the opponent).

16.1.2 Contributed (where the injury was accidentally contributed to, or accidentally caused by, the opponent).

16.1.3 Opponent-inflicted (where the injury was caused by the opponent's dangerous play, or by a deliberate or dangerous action).

16.2 For a self-inflicted injury the Referee shall allow the injured player three minutes to recover from the injury. This time interval may be extended at the discretion of the Referee only if the injury involves visible blood flow. The Referee shall call "Time" at the end of the three-minute period and at the end of any additional period permitted. If the injured player has not returned to court when "Time" is called the Referee shall award the match to the opponent.

If additional recovery time is needed by the player beyond the total time permitted by the Referee, the Referee shall require the injured player to resume play; or concede one game, accept the time interval available, and then either resume play or concede the match.

16.3 For a contributed injury (Rule 16.1.2) the Referee shall allow one hour for the injured player to recover, or such additional time as is provided for in the time schedule of the competition. The injured player must, by the end of this period of time, resume play or concede the match. If play is resumed the score at the conclusion of the rally in which the injury occurred shall stand, except that if play is resumed on another day the match may start again if both players agree.

16.4 For an opponent-inflicted injury (Rule 16.1.3) the Referee shall apply an appropriate Rule 17 penalty, except that if the injured player requires time to recover the Referee shall award the match to the injured player.

16.5 Irrespective of the category of injury, or of illness, or disability, a player shall not resume play while a wound that is bleeding remains uncovered, or blood flow is visible from a covered wound or on any part of the player's body, or with blood-stained clothing.

16.6 An injured player, having been granted a period of recovery time, may resume play prior to the expiry of that period of time provided that the opponent is also ready to resume play.

16.7 If a player resumes play, having treated bleeding that resulted from a contributed injury, and that wound again begins to bleed, the Referee shall then consider this under the category of a self-inflicted injury, and the provisions of Rule 16.2 shall apply.

16.8 If a player resumes play, having treated bleeding that resulted from a self-inflicted injury, and that wound again begins to bleed, the Referee shall require the player to concede the match; or concede one game, accept the time interval available, and then either resume play or concede the match.

16.9 If a player claims injury and the Referee is not satisfied that an injury has occurred, the Referee shall require the player to resume play; or concede one game, accept the time interval available and then either resume play or concede the match.

17. Conduct on Court

If the Referee considers that the behavior of a player on court could be intimidating or offensive to an opponent, official or spectator, or could in any way bring the game into disrepute, the player shall be penalized.

Offenses that should be dealt with under this rule include audible and visible obscenities; verbal and physical abuse; dissent to Marker or Referee; abuse of racket, ball, or court; and coaching, other than during the interval between games. Other offenses include unnecessary physical contact and excessive racket swing, unfair warm-up, late back on court, dangerous play or action, and wasting time.

For these and any other offenses which, in the opinion of the Referee, justify the application of this rule, one of the following penalty provisions shall be applied.

Warning by the Referee (called a Conduct Warning).

Stroke awarded to opponent (called a Conduct Stroke).

Game awarded to opponent (called a Conduct Game).

Match awarded to opponent (called a Conduct Match).

18. Control of a Match
19. Duties of a Marker
20. Duties of a Referee

These rules are reprinted by permission of the World Squash Federation. For a complete copy of the Rules, including notes to Referees and Appendices 1–11, contact the WSF or your local governing organization.

High ball
High balls are generally a gift to an opponent, allowing the ball to be smashed low and hard towards the board, in any direction.

Table tennis
Essentials

The simplicity and accessibilty of table tennis, commonly known as ping pong, make it one of the most widely played sports in the world. Yet its reputation as a fun pastime for all ages and abilities belies the fact that competition level players have amazing skills and reflexes.

1.525m (approx. 5 ft)

2.74m (8 ft 11 in)

76cm (approx. 2 ft 6 in)

The table
Rectangular, with a dark colored, matte playing surface that yields a uniform bounce of about 23 cm (9 in) when a standard ball is dropped on to it from a height of 30 cm (11.8 in). Divided into two equal courts by a net.

Officials
An umpire and an assistant umpire.

Players
Two for singles, four for doubles.

Serving
To start a rally in table tennis one player serves by throwing the ball at least 6 inches from the palm of the hand and then striking the ball with the paddle as it falls.

The net
A net suspended from a cord attached to two posts, each 6 in high and joined to the table with clamps. The bottom of the net must be as close to the playing surface as possible. The top of the net must measure 6 in above the playing surface.

HOW TO PLAY

In singles, two players take turns striking the ball after it has bounced once in their court so that it passes over (or around) the net and into their opponent's court. Failure to return (or serve) the ball legally to an opponent results in a lost point. In doubles there is a set striking order to follow. The serve is received by one opponent who must return it to the server's partner. That player then returns it to the receiver's partner, who returns it to the server. And so on. This sequence is maintained throughout a rally.

Starting

Players may practice for up to two minutes on the table before a match. The winner of a toss has the choice of ends or the option of serving or receiving first. Whoever serves first must strike the ball so that it bounces once on their side of the net before it enters the opponent's court. After every five serves the service passes to the opposing side. *See Rule 2.6, A Good Service (page 136).*

How to win

The first player or pair to score 21 points wins the game. If there is a score of 20-all, the first to score two points *more than the opponent* wins. (Service alternates in this situation.) A match is the best of three or five games.

Stance
A table tennis player needs a good stance for quick movement around the table. A good stance starts with feet about as wide apart as the shoulders, and the knees slightly bent in a crouching position so that the chin is directly above the knees. The playing arm is held out in front with the elbow bent.

KEY RULES

• When serving, the ball must be thrown into the air to a height of at least 6 in, with the palm—not the fingers—of the server's free hand. It may be struck only after it has begun to fall. It must be struck while it is behind the server's end line, but no further back from the table than the part of the server's body other than the arm, head, or leg, which is farthest from his end line. *See Rule 2.6 , A Good Service (page 136).*
• A white line down the center of the table divides each court into two for doubles games. Services must be made from the right-hand court and land in the opposite right-hand court. As with the striking sequence, the service passes from the first server to the first receiver, then to the first server's partner and then to the first receiver's partner.
• Players or pairs swap ends after each game. In the last game, ends are changed as soon as either side reaches 10 points. *See Rule 2.13, The Choice of Serving, Receiving and Ends (page 136).*
• If, after 15 minutes, a game is still unfinished and both sides have not scored at least 19 points, the Expedite System comes into play. For the remainder of the game, service alternates after each point scored. If the receiver makes 13 successive good returns, he wins the point.
See Rule 2.15, The Expedite System (page 137).

LAWS OF TABLE TENNIS

(The masculine gender is used throughout but may refer to men or women.)

2.1 The Table
See The Table (page 134).

2.2 The Net Assembly
See The Net (page 1340).

2.3 The Ball
See The Ball (page 134).

2.4 The Paddle
See The Paddle (page 134).

2.5 Definitions

2.5.1 A *rally* is the period during which the ball is in play.

2.5.2 The *ball* is in play from the last moment at which it is stationary on the palm of the free hand before being intentionally projected in service until the rally is decided as a let or a point.

2.5.3 A *let* is a rally of which the result is not scored.

2.5.4 A *point* is a rally of which the result is scored.

2.5.5 The *racket hand* is the hand carrying the racket.

2.5.6 The *free hand* is the hand not carrying the racket.

2.5.7 A player *strikes* the ball if he touches it in play with his racket, held in the hand, or with his racket hand below the wrist.

2.5.8 A player *obstructs* the ball if he, or anything he wears or carries, touches it in play when it has not passed over the playing surface or his end line, not having touched his court since last being struck by his opponent.

2.5.9 The *server* is the player due to strike the ball first in a rally.

2.5.10 The *receiver* is the player due to strike the ball second in a rally.

2.5.11 The *umpire* is the person appointed to control a match.

2.5.12 The *assistant umpire* is the person appointed to assist the umpire with certain decisions.

2.5.13 Anything that a player *wears or carries* includes anything that he was wearing or carrying at the start of the rally.

2.5.14 The ball shall be regarded as passing *over or around* the net assembly if it passes over, under, or outside the projection of the net assembly outside the table or if, in a return, it is struck after it has bounced back over or around the net.

2.5.15 The *end line* shall be regarded as extending indefinitely in both directions.

2.6 A Good Service

2.6.1 At the start of service the ball shall be stationary, resting freely on the flat, open palm of the server's free hand, behind the end line, and above the level of the playing surface.

2.6.2 The server shall then project the ball near vertically upwards, without imparting spin, so that it rises at least 6 in (16cm) after leaving the palm of the free hand and then falls without touching anything before being struck.

2.6.3 As the ball is falling the server shall strike it so that it touches first his court and then, after passing over or around the net assembly, touches directly the receiver's court; in doubles, the ball shall touch successively the right half-court of server and receiver.

2.6.4 The ball and the racket shall be above the level of the playing surface from the last moment at which the ball is stationary before being projected until it is struck.

2.6.5 When the ball is struck it shall be behind the server's end line but not farther back than the part of the server's body, other than his arm, head, or leg, which is farthest from his end line.

2.6.6 It is the responsibility of the player to serve so that the umpire or assistant umpire can see that he complies with the requirements for a good service.

2.6.6.1 If the umpire is doubtful of the legality of a service but neither he nor the assistant umpire is sure that it is illegal, he may, on the first occasion in a match, warn the server without awarding a point.

2.6.6.2 If subsequently in the match the same player's service is of dubious legality, for the same or for any other reason, he shall not be given the benefit of the doubt and the receiver shall score a point.

2.6.6.3 Whenever there is a clear failure to comply with the requirements for a good service, no warning shall be given, and the receiver shall score a point, on the first as on any other occasion.

2.6.7 Exceptionally, the umpire may relax the requirements for a good service where he is notified, before play begins, that compliance is prevented by physical disability.

2.7 A Good Return
See (page 135)

2.8 The Order of Play
See How to Play (page 135)

2.9 A Let

2.9.1 The rally shall be a let:

2.9.1.1 if in service the ball, in passing over or around the net assembly, touches it, provided the service is otherwise good or the ball is obstructed by the receiver or his partner;

2.9.1.2 if the service is delivered when the receiving player or pair is not ready, provided that neither the receiver nor his partner attempts to strike the ball;

2.9.1.3 if failure to make a good service or a good return or otherwise to comply with the Laws is due to a disturbance outside the control of the player;

2.9.1.4 if play is interrupted by the umpire or the assistant umpire;

2.9.1.5 if, in doubles, the wrong player serves or receives.

2.9.2 Play may be interrupted

2.9.2.1 to correct an error in the order of serving, receiving, or ends;

2.9.2.2 to introduce the expedite system;

2.9.2.3 to warn or penalize a player;

2.9.2.4 because the conditions of play are disturbed in a way that could affect the outcome of the rally.

2.10 A Point

2.10.1 Unless the rally is a let, a player shall score a point:

2.10.1.1 if his opponent fails to make a good service;

2.10.1.2 if his opponent fails to make a good return;

2.10.1.3 if the ball, after he has made a good service or a good return, touches anything other than the net assembly before being struck by his opponent;

2.10.1.4 if the ball, after his opponent has struck it, passes over his end line without having touched his court;

2.10.1.5 if his opponent obstructs the ball;

2.10.1.6 if his opponent strikes the ball twice successively;

2.10.1.7 if his opponent strikes the ball with a side of the racket blade whose surface does not comply with the requirements of 2.4.3;

2.10.1.8 if his opponent, or anything his opponent wears or carries, moves the playing surface;

2.10.1.9 if his opponent, or anything his opponent wears or carries, touches the net assembly;

2.10.1.10 if his opponent's free hand touches the playing surface;

2.10.11 if a doubles opponent strikes the ball out of proper sequence;

2.10.1.12 if, under the expedite system, he makes, or he and his doubles partner make, 13 successive good returns, including the return of service.

2.11 A Game

2.12 A Match
See How to Win (page 135)

2.13 The Choice of Serving, Receiving, and Ends

2.13.1 The right to choose the initial order of serving, receiving, and ends shall be decided by lot and the winner may choose to serve or to receive first or to start at a particular end.

2.13.2 When one player or pair has chosen to serve or to receive first or to start at a particular end, the other player or pair shall have the other choice.

2.13.3 After each five points have been scored, the receiving player or pair shall become the serving player or pair and so on until the end of the game, unless both players or pairs have scored 20 points or the expedite system is in operation, when the sequences of serving and receiving shall be the same but each player shall serve for only one point in turn.

2.13.4 In each game of a doubles match, the pair having the right to serve first shall choose which of them will do so and in the first game of a match the receiving pair shall decide which of them will receive first; in subsequent games of the match, the first server having been chosen, the first receiver shall be the player who served to him in the preceding game.

2.13.5 In doubles, at each change of service the previous receiver shall become the server and the partner of the previous server shall become the receiver.

2.13.6 The player or pair serving first in a game shall receive first in the next game of the match and in the last possible game of a doubles match the pair due to receive next shall change their order of receiving when first either pair scores 10 points.

2.13.7 The player or pair starting at one end in a game shall start at the other end in the next game of the match and in the last possible game of a match the players or pairs shall change ends when first either player or pair scores 10 points.

2.14 Out of Order of Serving, Receiving, or Ends

2.14.1 If a player serves or receives out of turn, play shall be interrupted by the umpire as soon as the error is discovered and shall resume with those players serving and receiving who should be server and receiver respectively at the score that has been reached, according to the sequence established at the beginning of the match and, in doubles, to the order of serving chosen by the pair having the right to serve first in the game during which the error is discovered.

2.14.2 If the players have not changed ends when they should have done so, play shall be interrupted by the umpire as soon as the error is discovered and shall resume with the players at the ends at which they should be at the score that has been reached, according to the sequence established at the beginning of the match.

2.14.3 In any circumstances, all points scored before the discovery of an error shall be reckoned.

2.15 The Expedite System

2.15.1 The expedite system shall come into operation if a game is unfinished after 15 minutes' play, unless both players or pairs have scored at least 19 points, or at any earlier time at the request of both players or pairs.

2.15.1.1 If the ball is in play when the time limit is reached, play shall be interrupted by the umpire and shall resume with service by the player who served in the rally that was interrupted.

2.15.1.2 If the ball is not in play when the time limit is reached, play shall resume with service by the player who received in the immediately preceding rally of the game.

2.15.2 Thereafter, each player shall serve for one point in turn until the end of the game and if the receiving player or pair makes 13 good returns the receiver shall score a point.

2.15.3 Once introduced, the expedite system shall remain in operation until the match's end.

Reprinted by permission of the International Table Tennis Federation.

To give a ball backspin the player slices down sharply under the ball as he strikes it.

To give a ball topspin a player slices the bat over the top of the ball as he hits it.

SKILLS AND TACTICS

Excellent anticipation and reaction skills, stamina, and coordination improve any player's game.

Two basic *grips* are used. The first is similar to the "shaking hands" grip used in many other racket games *(see Squash p. 127)*. The other is the "penholder" grip—the handle is held close to the base of the blade, as if it were a pen. Although this grip allows a much faster recovery time (since only one side of the paddle is ever used) it can make it difficult to return tricky backhand or angle shots.

Imparting spin to the ball is an essential skill. Attacking players use *topspin* to force a weak return from an opponent. This causes the ball to dart forwards suddenly as it hits the playing surface. *Backspin* has the effect of "holding back" the ball as it travels down the table. Both spins are acheived by angling the paddle as it makes contact with the ball, brushing it (rather than driving through it) to set it spinning.

Players will often try to confuse opponents by turning the paddle in their hands while waiting for a return—"twiddling." If the paddle has two different surface materials, the ball will rebound differently according to which one is used. The opponent will therefore not know what sort of return to expect.

Is this server going to slice under the ball to give it topspin?

GRAY AREA

Because players continually seek new ways to deceive their opponents, the service law is frequently changed to maintain a fair balance between server and receiver. A common (legal) technique is to hide the ball as it is struck, so that the receiver cannot judge the spin. Some conceal it with their arms or even their legs. In the past, some players struck the ball behind their backs—but this is now illegal.

Basketball
Essentials

Invented in Massachusetts in 1891 by James Naismith, who hung peach baskets for players to throw a ball into, basketball is now the most widely played and watched indoor sport in the world.

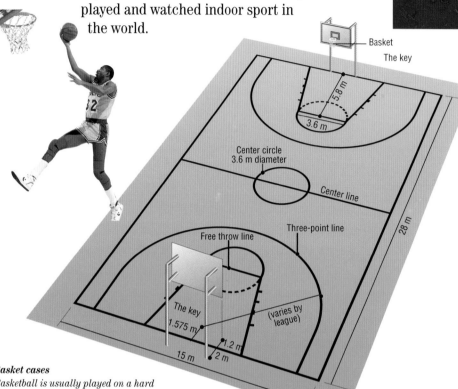

Basket
The key

5.8 m
3.6 m

Center circle
3.6 m diameter

Center line

Three-point line

Free throw line

28 m

The key
1.575 m

(varies by league)

1.2 m
2 m
15 m

Basket cases
Basketball is usually played on a hard court indoors. But it can be played anywhere a basket can be mounted, from a backyard to an office.

The court

Usually indoors, rectangular 28 m x 15 m (31 x 16 yds) for official competitions, with a flat, hard surface. The height of the ceiling or the lowest obstruction must be at least 7 m (23 ft), although most courts allow much more than that. Lines marking out the boundaries, center line and center circle, are all 5 cm (approx. 2 in) wide and drawn in the same color.

Technical equipment

A game clock to time periods of play, a stop-watch to time time-outs, a "shot clock" device (automatic, digital, indicating time in seconds) for the administration of the shooting rule. *See Rule 5, Art 18 (page 140).* And clearly audible signals for the timekeeper/scorer and shot clock operator.

Game for all
Basketball is a relatively easy game to organize, making it a popular pastime for people of various ages and skill levels.

Equipment

Two baskets, centered at opposite ends of the court, are 10 ft above the ground. Each is suspended from a rectangular backboard (either hardwood painted white or of a transparent material) approx. 1-inch think. The backboards are 6 ft wide and 3 ½ ft high, with the basket placed near the bottom. Each basket's ring is made of iron, painted orange, with an inside diameter of 1 ½ ft. The net is made of white cord. It is approx. 17 ½ inches long and constructed so that it checks the ball momentarily as it passes through.

Officials

A referee and an umpire, assisted by a timekeeper, a scorer, assistant scorer, and a shot clock operator.

Players

Although some leagues limit teams to a maximum of 10 players, the NBA allows 12. Five players per team are involved in play at any given time: generally, a center, two forwards, and two guards.

The ball

Spherical, of an approved shade of orange. An outer surface of leather, rubber, or synthetic material and a circumference of approx. 30 in. It must weigh between 567g and 650 g (20–23 oz) and when dropped on to the playing surface from a height of 1.80 m (2 yds), must rebound to a height of 1.20–1.40 m (4 ft) approximately.

HOW TO PLAY

Each team attempts to score points by shooting the ball into their opponents' basket, while preventing them from doing the same. The ball is passed, thrown, tapped, rolled, or dribbled in any direction on the court as provided in the rules.

Starting

The referee starts the game by stepping into the center circle with the ball. The opposing centers take their places in the circle. The referee tosses the ball up into the air between them and, once it begins to descend, both players attempt to tap it to their team members. This is called a "jump ball." *See Rule 6, Art. 26 (page 140).* The game clock is started when the ball is tapped the first time, and until such time, all other players must remain outside the center circle.

How to win

Points are scored by successfully shooting the ball through the oponent's basket. If this is done from a free throw, one point is awarded. Two points are scored for most shots made from the field during the course of play. If, however, the successful shot originates from beyond the "three-point line," three points are scored. The three-point line is a relatively recent innovation (it entered the NBA in 1980); the distance of the line varies from league to league.

Dress

Sleaveless shirts and shorts of the same dominant color contrasting with the uniforms of the opponents. The shirts have a number on the front and the back. Socks and shoes.

KEY RULES

• NBA games consist of four 12-minute periods with a halftime break. Most college and international games, however, consist of two 20-minute halves. If the score is tied at the end of regulation time, five-minute overtimes are added until a winner is determined.

• The ball is played with the hands only. When a player receives the ball when standing, he or she must not take more than one step, using the other foot as a pivot foot. If moving when the ball is received, two steps are allowed. *See Rule 7, Art. 39, Travel Rule (page 145).*

• Once a player has gained control of the ball, he or she may dribble it by throwing, tapping or rolling it on the floor, but the dribble ends as soon as the ball is touched simultaneously with both hands. Once the dribble has ended, the same player cannot begin to dribble again until after another player has handled the ball. *See Rule 7, Art. 38, Dribbling Rule (page 144).*

• Teams must shoot the ball within a set time period. In the NBA it is 24 seconds, but most other leagues allow a little more time. The ball must leave a shooter's hands before the time limit expires, and the shot must hit the rim, in order for the requirement to be met. *See Rule 5, Art. 18 (page 140).*

• *The ten-second rule* (Art. 42) states that a team must get the ball into its front court within 10 seconds of gaining control of it. *The three-second rule* restricts a player to only three consecutive seconds in the opponents' key while his team is in control of the ball. *See Rule 7, Art. (40 page 145).*

• Basketball is theoretically a no-contact sport, and unwarranted contact with an opponent will result in a player being charged with a foul. In most leagues, a player's fifth foul will result in his or her disqualification for the remainder of the game. However, in the NBA disqualification results from the sixth foul. A player who is fouled while shooting—or who is fouled after the opposition has exceeded a number of team fouls (the number varies by league)—is awarded with the opportunity to take one, two, or three free throws depending on circumstances.

• Free throws are an opportunity to score one point, uncontested, from a position behind the free-throw line and inside the semicircle. No other player is allowed into the key while the shot is being taken.

The Chicago Bulls have been the dominant team of the 1990s in the NBA. Talented players such as Scottie Pippen have helped make the Bulls famous worldwide.

Basketball can be played in sneakers but most serious players wear special basketball shoes that provide good grip and ankle support.

BASKETBALL THE RULES

These rules are abridged and summarized. Where the official rules have been edited, this is shown in italics.

Rule 1

The Game
Art. 1 The Definition
See How to play (page 139).

Rule 2

Dimensions and Equipment
Arts 2–4
See The court and equipment (page 138).

Rule 3

Officials and Their Duties
Arts 5–11

Rule 4

Players, Substitutes, and Coaches
Arts 12–15
See Players (page 138).

Rule 5

Timing Regulations
Art. 16 Playing Time
See Key rules (page 139).

Art. 17 Game Clock Operations
1. The game clock shall be started when:
   a. During a jump ball, the ball is legally tapped by a player(s) after having reached its highest point on a toss.
   b. After an unsuccessful free throw and the ball is to continue in play, the ball touches a player on the court.
   c. After a throw-in from out of bounds, the ball touches a player on the court.
2. The game clock shall be stopped when:
   a. Time expires at the end of a half or a period.
   b. An official blows his whistle.
   c. The 30-second signal is sounded.
   d. A field goal is scored against a team that has requested a charged time-out.

Art. 18 Thirty-second Rule
1. When a player gains control of a live ball on the court, a shot for goal must be attempted by his team within 30

Stopping the clock after a foul.

seconds.
2. Failure of the team in control of the ball to shoot for goal within 30 seconds will be indicated by the sounding of the 30-second signal.
3. The 30-second device shall be operated as follows:
   a. The 30-second device shall be started as soon as a player gains control of a live ball on the court.
   b. The device shall be stopped as soon as team control is ended (see Art. 28).
   c. The device shall be reset to 30 seconds and restarted only when a new 30-second period begins as player control is next established on the court.
   1. If the game is stopped because of an action(s) by an opponent(s) of the team in control of the ball, a new 30-second period shall be awarded to the team in control of the ball.
   2. The mere touching of the ball by an opponent does not start a new 30-second period if the same team remains in control of the ball.
   d. The 30-second

device shall be stopped but not reset when:
   1. The ball has gone out of bounds and the throw-in is to be taken by a player from the same team that was previously in control of the ball.
   2. The officials have suspended play to protect an injured player of the team in control of the ball.
   3. The game is stopped because of an action(s) by the team in control of the ball.
   The 30-second operator shall restart the device from the time it was stopped as soon as a player of the same team gains control of the ball on the court after the throw-in.
   e. For any other reason(s), a new 30-second period shall be awarded to the team in control of the ball, unless, in the judgment of the officials, the opponents have been placed at a disadvantage, in which case the officials shall not award a new 30-second period to the team in control of the ball.

Art. 19 Charged Time-out
A. Description
A time-out of one minute's duration shall be charged to a team under the following provisions:
1. For games played in 2x20 minutes, two charged time-outs may be granted to each team during each half of playing time and one charged time-out for each extra period.
2. For games played in 4x12 minutes, three charged time-outs may be granted to each team during each half (two periods) of playing time and one charged time-out for each extra period.
3. If the team responsible for the time-out is ready to play before the end of the charged time-out, the referee shall resume the game as soon as possible.
4. During the time-out, the players are permitted to leave the playing court and sit on the team bench.
B. Procedure
1. A coach or assistant coach has the right to request a charged time-out. He shall do so by going in person to the scorer and asking clearly for a "time-out," making the proper conventional sign with his hands.
Art. 20 Injury to Players or Officials
Art. 21 Tied Score and Extra Periods
See Key rules (page 139).

Rule 6

Playing Regulations
Art. 22 Decision of a Game
Art. 23 Beginning of the Game
See Starting (page 139).
Art. 24 Status of the Ball
1. The ball is in play (goes into play) when:
   a. An official with the ball enters the circle to administer a jump ball.
   b. An official enters the free-throw lane with or without the ball to administer a free throw.
   c. The ball is at the disposal of a player for a throw-in from out of bounds.
2. The ball becomes alive when:
   a. During a jump ball, it is legally tapped by a jumper(s) after having reached its highest point.
   b. An official places it at the disposal of a free-throw shooter.
   c. After a throw-in from out of bounds, it touches a player on the court.
3. The ball becomes dead when:
   a. Any goal is legally made.
   b. An official's whistle sounds while the ball is alive or in play.
   c. It is apparent that the ball will not go into the basket on a free throw for:
   1. A free throw which is to be followed by another free throw(s).
   2. A free throw which is to be followed by a further penalty.
   d. The 30-second operator's signal is sounded while the ball is alive.
   e. Time expires for a half or a period.
   f. The ball that is already in flight on a shot for goal is legally touched by a player of either team after time has expired for a half or a period, or after a foul has been called.
Art. 25 Location of a Player and of an Official
1. The location of a player is determined by where he is touching the floor. While he is in the air from a leap, he retains the same status as where he last touched the floor. This includes the boundary lines, the center line, the three-point line, the free-throw line, and the lines delimiting the free-throw lanes.
2. The location of an official is determined in the same manner as that of a player. When the ball touches an official, it is the same as touching the floor at the official's location.
Art. 26 Jump Ball
1. A jump ball takes place when an official tosses the ball between two opposing players.
2. For a jump ball to be legal, the

ball must be tapped with the hand(s) by one or both jumpers.

3. A jump ball shall take place at the nearest circle:

a. *When held ball* is called, that is, when one or more players of opposing teams have one or both hands firmly on the ball so that neither player could gain possession without undue roughness. If there are more than two players involved, the jump ball shall be between two opposing players of approximately the same height as designated by the official.

b. If the ball goes out-of-bounds and:

1. It was last touched simultaneously by two opponents, or

2. The official is in doubt as to who last touched the ball; or

3. If the officials disagree, the jump ball shall be between the two players involved.

c. Whenever a live ball lodges on the basket support: the jump ball shall be between any two opponents.

d. Whenever penalties of the same gravity are canceled according to Art. 59 and the result is a jump ball: the jump ball shall be between any two opponents.

e. Whenever the ball accidentally enters the basket from below: the jump ball shall be between any two opponents.

4. The following conditions shall apply:

a. During a jump ball the two jumpers shall stand with their feet inside that half of the circle that is nearer to their own baskets, with one foot near the center of the line that is between them.

b. The official shall then toss the ball upward (vertically) between the jumpers to a height greater than either of them can reach by jumping and such that it will drop between them.

c. The ball must be legally tapped by one or both of the jumpers after it reaches its highest point.

d. Neither jumper shall leave his position until the ball has been legally tapped.

e. Neither jumper may catch the ball or touch it more than twice until it has touched one of the eight non-jumpers, the floor, the basket, or the backboard. Under this provision four taps are possible, two by each jumper.

f. The other players shall remain outside the circle until the ball has been tapped.

Ball practice

Ball handling is a central skill in basketball. Players spend years developing their abilities.

g. If the ball is not tapped by one or both of the jumpers or if it touches the floor without being tapped by at least one of the jumpers, the jump ball shall be retaken.

h. Teammates may not occupy adjacent positions around the circle if an opponent desires one of the positions.

An infraction of conditions a., c., d., e., and f is a violation.

Art. 27 How the Ball Is Played

1. In basketball, the ball is played with the hands. It is a violation to run with the ball, kick it, or strike it with the fist.

2. Kicking the ball means striking it or blocking it with the knee, any part of the leg below the knee, or the foot. Such action is a violation only when it is done deliberately.

3. To accidentally contact or touch the ball with the foot or leg is not a violation.

Art. 28 Control of the Ball

1. A player is in control when:

a. He is holding or dribbling a live ball.

b. The ball is at his disposal for a throw-in during an out-of-bounds situation.

2. A team is in control when:

a. A player of that team is in control.

b. The ball is being passed between teammates.

3. Team control continues until:

a. An opponent secures control.

b. The ball becomes dead.

c. The ball is no longer in contact with the hand(s) of the shooter on a shot for goal.

Art. 29 Player in the Act of Shooting

Definitions:

Throw: to hold the ball in one or both hands and then project it through the air towards the basket.

Dunk: to force or attempt to force the ball downwards into the basket with one or both hands.

Tap: to strike the ball with the hand or hands towards the basket.

1. A player is in the act of shooting when, in the judgment of an official, he has started an attempt to score by throwing, dunking, or tapping the ball towards the opponents' basket and the attempt

continues until the ball has left the player's hand(s).

2. In the case of an airborne shooter, the act of shooting continues until the attempt is completed (the ball has left the hand(s) of the shooter) and both the player's feet return to the floor. Team control, however, ends when the ball is released.

3. For a foul to be considered to have been committed on a player in the act of shooting, the foul must occur, in the judgment of the official, after a player has started the continuous movement of his arm(s) in his attempt to shoot for goal. Continuous movement:

a. Begins when the ball comes to rest in the hand(s) of the player and the shooting motion, usually upward, has started.

b. May include arm(s) and/or body movement used by the player in his attempt to shoot for goal.

If the criteria regarding continuous movement are as stated above, then the player is considered to be in the act of shooting.

Note: There is no relationship between the number of steps taken and the act of shooting.

4. The goal shall count if made, even if the ball has left the player's hand after the whistle has blown.

This provision (number 4.) does not apply:

a. At the end of a period (see Art. 33).

b. When the 30-second signal sounds (see Art. 18).

5. The goal does not count if an entirely new effort (movement) is made after the whistle has blown.

6. A player who taps the ball towards the basket directly from a jump ball is not considered to be in the act of shooting.

Penalty

See Art. 47, Penalty 2.

Art. 30 Goal—When Made and its Value

1. A goal is made when a live ball enters the basket from above and remains within or passes through.

2. A goal from the field is credited to the team attacking the basket into which the ball is

➡ *page 144*

Some players make an art form of dribbling.

SKILLS AND POSITIONS

The basic skills in basketball are shooting, passing, dribbling, *rebounding* (gaining possession of the ball after a missed shot), and defending. Although some players specialize in one or more of these areas, all players need to be proficient with all of them. Teams generally play one center, two forwards, and two guards. *Centers* are usually the tallest players on the court. They tend to play close to the basket on both offense and defense, using their size to take shots close to the basket (on offense) or preventing opponents from *driving* to the basket for their own close shots (on defense). *Power forwards* are usually tall, strong players. Often gifted rebounders, they are sometimes high scorers, using their size and strength to power past defenders to the basket. *Small forwards* are usually quicker than power forwards and possess a better developed jump shot (a shot taken from somewhere away from the basket). Guards are usually the shortest players on a team (although in professional men's leagues, their height may be well over six feet). The *point guard* is

responsible for leading the attack, bringing the ball into the forecourt and setting up a play. This player is usually an expert passer and ball handler. The *shooting guard* is a pure shooter, who usually shoots from the outside (perhaps attempting many three-point goals) but is quick enough to drive past defenders to the basket.

Keep in mind that these positions and skills are generalizations. These are centers who shoot very well from the outside, power forwards who handle the ball well, and point guards who are as likely to shoot as to pass the ball to an open teammate.

Hold-up
The net in basketball is designed to slow the ball down momentarily after it passes through the hoop— so it is absolutely clear that a basket has been made.

High jump
Basketball centers are generally very tall. It is not uncommon to find players over 7 ft tall. Height like this gives them an edge in reaching for the basket, which is only 10 feet off the floor. An NBA player named Manute Bol was over 7 ft 7 in tall.

Shooting skills

Most basketball players shoot with one hand but they begin the shot with the other one on the ball to keep it steady as the ball is released. The ball should be kept close in front of the body, with the wrist and elbow of the shooting arm almost underneath.

As the shot is made the player straightens his arm upwards towards the basket. He then releases the ball with a powerful snap of the wrist, following through to ensure the ball's momentum.

Eyes not on the ball
When dribbling, it is important not to look at the ball all the time, but to look ahead to see where teammates and opponents are. Players begin to develop their dribbling skills when quite young.

High-speed dribble
Some players are so fast on their feet that they can use pure speed to beat a defender when dribbling. In a full-speed dribble the player pushes the ball out in front of him rather than protecting it with his body because he is moving into an empty space.

Off the chest
The most common pass in basketball is the chest pass, which is used when a player has a clear path to a teammate. To make the pass he holds the ball very close in front of the chest. He grips the ball with his fingers and thumbs only—that is, not his palms— with the tips of the thumbs pointing upwards. The pass is made by cocking the wrists and then stepping forward while sharply extending the arms.

TACTICS

On offense, teams tend to adopt one of two philosophies. Either they operate from a *half-court* set, in which the ball is brought methodically out of the backcourt and set plays are run, or they try to push the ball quickly into the forecourt on the run, hoping to create scoring opportunities before their opponents can take up positions on defense. The first approach generally slows down a game, using most of the shot clock before a shot is attempted, while the latter approach favors shots taken quickly, with much time still remaining on the shot clock. (In actual practice, a team will employ both approaches in any given game, but they tend to favor one approach or the other).

On defense, teams will either play a zone, in which defenders guard a portion of the court, or they will play *man-to-man*, in which a defender guards a particular opponent. In the NBA, zone defenses are illegal (a team spotted playing one will be warned once; after that, a free throw is awarded to the opposition every time the referee considers the team to be utilizing a zone defense).

Coaches can—and often do— make many substitutions throughout a game. Some coaches will experiment, utilizing "small" lineups (perhaps with three guards) in an attempt to out run and wear out the opposition, or "big" lineups, in an attempt to dominate a game with lots of size and muscle.

Protected dribble
When dribbling close to an opponent, it is important to shield the ball so that he cannot "steal" it. The technique is to keep the ball on the side away from the opponent, bouncing it close to the foot on that side with the knees bent. Always keep the body between the ball and the opponent, and let the free shoulder hang loose to bar the opponent's way if he goes for the steal.

Free throw
For a free throw the shooter stands just below the free-throw line while opponents and teammates stand outside the lane opposite the basket.

continued from page 141

thrown as follows:
    a. A goal from a free throw counts one point.
    b. A goal from the field counts two points.
    c. A goal from the three-point field goal area counts three points.

Art. 31 Throw-in
A. Following a field goal or a successful last free throw:
1. Any opponent of the team credited with the score shall be entitled to throw the ball in from any point out of bounds on or behind the endline at the end of the court where the goal was made.
2. He may pass it to a teammate on or behind the endline, but the five-second count starts the instant the ball is at the disposal of the first player out of bounds.
3. The official should not handle the ball unless by doing so the game can be resumed more quickly.
4. Opponents of the player making the throw-in shall not touch the ball after it passes through the basket. Allowances may be made for touching the ball accidentally or instinctively, but if the game is delayed by interfering with the ball, it is a technical foul.

B. Following an infraction or for any stoppage of play and the game is to be resumed by a throw-in (except after a valid free throw or field goal):
1. The player who is to throw the ball in, shall stand out of bounds as designated by the official, at the place nearest the point of the infraction or where the play was stopped, except directly

behind the backboard.
2. An official must hand the ball directly to, or place it at the disposal of, the player making the throw-in.
3. The player who is to make the throw-in shall not take and complete more than one normal step laterally (approximately 1 m (3 ft) and in more than one direction from the place designated by the official before releasing the ball.
    a. Several small steps in one direction are permitted provided the distance covered is not more than one normal step.
    b. To move backwards and perpendicular to the line as far as the circumstances will allow is permitted.

C. A player making a throw-in shall not violate the following provisions:
1. Touch the ball in the court before it has touched another player.
2. Step on the court while releasing the ball.
3. Consume more than five seconds before releasing the ball.
4. Throw the ball over the backboard to another player on the court.
5. Cause the ball to touch out of bounds, or to lodge on the basket support or to enter the basket before contacting a player on the court following the release of the ball for the throw-in.

D. Any other player may not have any part of his body over the boundary line before the ball has

been thrown across the line. An infraction of B.3., C, and D is a violation.
Penalty
The ball is awarded to the opponents for a throw-in at the point of the original throw-in.
Art. 32 Substitutions
Art. 33 When a Period or a Game is Terminated
1. A period, a half, or a game shall terminate at the sounding of the timekeeper's signal indicating the end of playing time.
2. When a foul is committed simultaneously with or just prior to the timekeeper's signal ending any half or any period, any eventual free throw(s) as a result of the foul shall be taken.
Art. 34 Game Lost by Forfeit
A team shall lose the game by forfeit if:
1. It refuses to play after

Personal foul
A player who makes contact with an opponent in the act of shooting commits a "personal foul." The penalty is one free throw if the shot was made, two if it was missed.

being instructed to do so by the referee.
2. By its actions it prevents the game from being played.
3. Fifteen minutes after the starting time, the team is not present or is not able to field five players.
Penalty
The game is awarded to the opponents and the score shall be 20 to zero. Further, the forfeiting team shall receive zero points in the classification.
Art. 35 Game Lost by Default
A team shall lose a game by default if, during the game, the number of players of that team on the court is less than two.
Penalty
If the team to which the game is awarded is ahead, the score at the time of the stoppage shall stand. If the team to which the game is awarded is not ahead, the score shall be recorded as two to zero in its favor.
Further, the defaulting team shall receive one point in the classification.

Rule 7
Violations
Art. 36 Violations
    1. A violation is an infraction of the rules.
    2. The penalty is the loss of the ball by the team that committed the violation.
    3. The ball is awarded to the opponents for a throw-in from out of bounds at the closest point to the infraction, except directly behind the backboard.
Article 37 Player Out of Bounds and Ball Out of Bounds
1. A player is out of bounds when any part of his body is in contact with the floor or any object other than a player on, above or outside the boundary lines.
2. The ball is out of bounds when it touches:
    a. A player or any other person who is out of bounds.
    b. The floor or any object on, above or outside a boundary line.
    c. The supports or the back of the backboards.
3. The ball is caused to go out of bounds by the last player to touch it or be touched by it before it goes out of bounds, even if the ball goes out of bounds by touching something other than a player.
Art. 38 Dribbling Rule
1. A dribble starts when a player, having gained control of the ball throws, taps or rolls it on the floor and touches it again before it touches another player.
2. The dribble is completed the

instant the player touches the ball simultaneously with both hands or permits the ball to come to rest in one or both hands.

3. There is no limit to the number of steps a player may take when the ball is not in contact with his hand.

4. The following are not dribbles:

a. Successive shots for goal.

b. Accidentally losing and then regaining player control (fumble) at the beginning or at the end of a dribble.

c. Attempts to gain control of the ball by tapping it from the vicinity of other players striving for it.

d. Tapping the ball from the control of another player.

e. Blocking a pass and recovering the ball.

f. Tossing the ball from hand(s) to hand(s) and permitting it to come to rest before touching the floor, provided he does not commit a traveling violation (See Art. 39).

5. A player shall not dribble a second time after his first dribble has ended, unless it is after he has lost control because of:

a. A shot for goal;

b. A tap by an opponent; or

c. A pass or fumble that has then touched or been touched by another player.

6. A player shall not throw the ball against a backboard and touch it again before it touches another player unless, in the opinion of the official, it was a shot.

Article 39 Travel Rule
A. Definitions

1. A pivot takes place when a player who is holding a live ball steps once or more than once in any direction with the same foot, while the other foot, called the "pivot" foot, is kept at its point of contact with the floor.

2. Traveling, or progressing with the ball (inside the playing court), is the moving of one or both feet in any direction while holding the ball in excess of the limits outlined in this article.

B. Establishing a Pivot Foot

1. A player who catches the ball with both feet on the floor may use either foot as the pivot foot. The moment one foot is lifted, the other becomes the pivot foot.

2. A player who catches the ball while moving or dribbling may stop and establish a pivot foot as follows:

a. If one foot is touching the floor:

1. That foot becomes the pivot foot as soon as the other foot touches the floor.

2. The player may jump off that foot and simultaneously land on both feet, then neither foot can be the pivot foot.

b. If both feet are off the floor and the player:

1. Lands simultaneously on both feet, then either foot may be the pivot foot. The moment one foot is lifted, the other becomes the pivot foot.

2. Lands on one foot followed by the other foot, then the first foot to touch

Triple threat

Pivoting is one of the most important skills in basketball. A player who receives the ball should pivot at once to face the basket, holding the ball to the chest with the knees bent and elbows spread out. This is called the triple threat position because a player can shoot, pass, or move into a dribble.

the floor is the pivot foot.

3. Lands on one foot, the player may jump off that foot and simultaneously land on **both** feet, then neither foot can be the pivot foot.

C. Progressing with the Ball

1. After having established a pivot foot:

a. On a pass or a try for a field goal, the pivot foot may be lifted but may not be returned to the floor before the ball is released from the hand(s),

b. To start a dribble, the pivot foot may not be lifted before **the** ball is released from the hand(s);

2. After coming to a stop when neither foot is the pivot foot:

a. On a pass or a try for a field goal, one or both feet may be lifted but may not be returned to the floor before the ball is released from the hand(s).

b. To start a dribble, neither foot may be lifted before the ball is released from the hand(s).

Art. 40 Three-second Rule

1. While his team is in control of the ball, a player shall not remain for more than three consecutive seconds in the opponents' restricted area.

2. The lines bounding the restricted area are part of the restricted area and a player touching one of these lines is in the area.

3. The three-second restriction is in force in all out-of-bounds situations. The count shall start at the moment the player making the throw-in is out of bounds and the ball is at

his disposal (is in play).

4. The three-second restriction does not apply:

a. While the ball is in the air during a shot for goal.

b. During a rebound.

c. When the ball is dead.

5. Allowance must be made for a player who, having been in the restricted area for less than three seconds, dribbles in to shoot for goal.

Art. 41 Closely Guarded Player

A closely guarded player (within one normal step) who is holding the ball shall pass, shoot, roll, or dribble the ball within five seconds.

Art. 42 Ten-second Rule

1. A team's frontcourt consists of the opponents' basket, the inbounds part of the backboard, and that part of the court limited by the end line behind the opponents' basket, the sidelines and the edge of the center line nearer to the opponents' basket. The other part of the court, including the center line and that team's basket, including the inbounds part of the backboard, is the team's backcourt.

2. When a player gains control of a live ball in his back court, his team must, within 10 seconds, cause the ball to go back into its frontcourt.

3. The ball goes into a team's frontcourt when it touches the frontcourt or touches a player who has part of

➡ *page 146*

Behind hand

A sleight of dribble "behind the back" is a great way of changing hands and throwing off a defender—although it is very difficult to master.

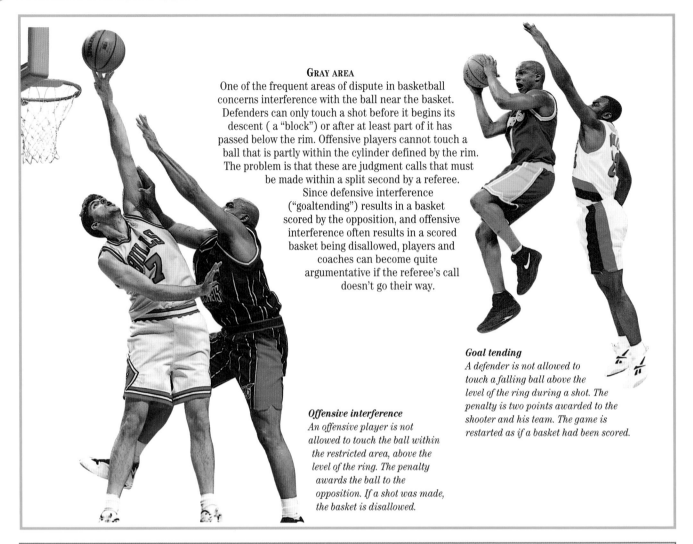

GRAY AREA

One of the frequent areas of dispute in basketball concerns interference with the ball near the basket. Defenders can only touch a shot before it begins its descent (a "block") or after at least part of it has passed below the rim. Offensive players cannot touch a ball that is partly within the cylinder defined by the rim. The problem is that these are judgment calls that must be made within a split second by a referee. Since defensive interference ("goaltending") results in a basket scored by the opposition, and offensive interference often results in a scored basket being disallowed, players and coaches can become quite argumentative if the referee's call doesn't go their way.

Goal tending
A defender is not allowed to touch a falling ball above the level of the ring during a shot. The penalty is two points awarded to the shooter and his team. The game is restarted as if a basket had been scored.

Offensive interference
An offensive player is not allowed to touch the ball within the restricted area, above the level of the ring. The penalty awards the ball to the opposition. If a shot was made, the basket is disallowed.

continued from page 145

his body in contact with the frontcourt.

Art. 43 Ball Returned to the backcourt

1. A player whose team is in control of the ball that is in the frontcourt may not cause the ball to go into his backcourt.
2. The ball is considered to have gone into the backcourt when a player of the team in control of the ball is:
   a. The last to touch the ball before it goes into the backcourt, and
   b. A player of that same team is the first to touch the ball after
      1. It has touched the backcourt; or
      2. If this player is in contact with the backcourt.
3. This restriction applies to all situations in a team's frontcourt, including throw-ins from out of bounds.
4. It does not apply to throw-ins from the midpoint of a sideline.

Art. 44 Interference with the Ball on Offense and Defense

During playing time:
1. An offensive or a defensive

player may not touch the ball when it is in its downward flight and completely above the level of the ring during a shot for a field goal.

This restriction applies only until:
   a. The ball touches the ring.
   b. It is evident that it shall not touch the ring.
2. A defensive player shall not touch the ball or the basket while the ball is within the basket.
3. An offensive or a defensive player shall not touch the basket or the backboard while the ball is in contact with the ring during a shot for a field goal.

Penalty

A. The ball becomes dead when the violation is called by the official(s).
1. If the violation is by the offense:
No point can be scored and the ball is awarded to the opponents for a throw-in from out of bounds at the free-throw line extended.
2. If the violation is by the defense:
The shooter is awarded two points, or three points if the field

goal was attempted from the three-point field goal area. The game is restarted from out of bounds behind the end line as though the shot for goal has been successful.

B. When a shot is taken near the end of playing time (for a period or a half) and the ball has left the player's hand and is in the air before time expired:
1. If the ball enters the basket directly, the goal shall count.
2. If the ball strikes the ring, rebounds and then enters the basket, the goals shall count.
3. If, after the ball has touched the ring, a player of either team touches the ball, the basket or the backboard, it is a violation.
   a. If a defensive player commits the violation, the goal shall count and either two or three points shall be awarded.
   b. If an offensive player commits the violation, the ball becomes dead and the goal, if scored, shall not count.
4. These provisions apply until it is evident that the shot will not be successful.

Rule 8

Personal Fouls

Art. 45 Fouls

1. A foul is an infraction of the rules when personal contact with an opponent or unsportsmanlike behavior is involved.
2. It is charged against the offender and consequently penalized according to the provisions of the relevant article of the rules.

Art. 46 Contact

1. Basketball is, theoretically, a no-contact game. Nevertheless, it is obvious that personal contact cannot be avoided entirely when 10 players are moving with great speed over a limited space.
2. If the personal contact is incidental and such contact does not place the opponent who has been contacted at a disadvantage, the contact should not be penalized.

Art. 47 Personal Foul

1. A personal foul is a player foul that involves contact with an opposing player, whether the ball is alive, in play, or dead.
2. A player shall not block, hold, push, charge, trip, impede the

progress of an opponent by extending his arm, shoulder, hip, knee, or foot, nor by bending his body into other than a normal position, nor shall he use any rough

tactics.

Definitions:

1. **Blocking:** is personal contact that impedes the progress of an opponent.

2. **Charging:** is personal contact, with or without the ball, by pushing or moving into an opponent's torso.

3. **Guarding from the Rear:** is personal contact with an opponent by a defensive player from behind the opponent. The mere fact that the defensive player is attempting to play the ball does not justify his making contact with an opponent.

4. **Handchecking:** is the action by a defensive player in a guarding situation where the hand(s) are used to contact an opponent to either impede his progress or to assist the defensive player in guarding his opponent.

5. **Holding:** is personal contact with an opponent that interferes with his freedom of movement. This contact (holding) can occur with any part of the body.

6. **Illegal Use of Hands:** occurs when a player contacts an opponent with his hand(s) in an attempt to play the ball. If such contact is only with the opponent's hand while it is on the ball, it shall be considered incidental.

7. **Pushing:** is personal contact with any part of the body that takes place when a player forcibly moves or attempts to move an opponent who has or does not have control of the ball.

8. **Illegal Screening:** is an attempt to illegally delay or prevent an opponent who does not control the ball from reaching a desired position on the playing court.

Penalty

A personal foul shall be charged to the offender in all cases. In addition:

1. If the foul is committed on a player who is not in the act of shooting:

   a. The game shall be resumed by a throw-in by the non-

offending team from out of bounds nearest the place of the infraction.

   b. If the offending team was in

the penalty, then Art. 58 will come into effect.

[This stipulates that for games of 2x20 minutes, when a team has committed seven (personal or

technical) player fouls in a half, all subsequent player personal fouls shall be penalized by the awarding of two free throws to the player offended against. The same penalty applies when a team has committed four (personal or technical) player fouls in one period of a game of 4x12 minutes.)

2. If the foul is committed on a player who is in the act of shooting:

   a. If the goal is made, it shall count and one free throw shall be awarded.

   b. If the shot for goal for two points is unsuccessful, two free throws shall be awarded.

   c. If the shot for goal for three points is unsuccessful, three free throws shall be awarded.

3. If a foul is committed by a player while his team is in control of the ball:

   a. The game shall be resumed by a throw-in by the non-offending team from out of bounds nearest the place of the infraction.

Comments

   A. **Principle of Verticality**

      1. On the basktball court, each

Laying up

A common shot when a player breaks free to the basket is a moving shot called a "lay up." A player takes two steps then jumps from one leg (with the opposite knee raised shooting with the right hand from the right-hand side of the basket (or vice-versa).

player has the right to a position on the floor and the space (cylinder) above him.

2. This principle protects the space on the floor which he occupies and the space above him.

3. As soon as the player leaves his vertical position (cylinder) and body contact occurs with an

opponent who had already established his own vertical position (cylinder), the player who left his vertical position (cylinder) is responsible for the contact.

   a. The defender must not be penalized for leaving the floor vertically (within his cylinder) or having his hands and arms extended above him and within the cylinder,

   b. The offensive player, whether on the floor or airborne, shall not cause contact with the defensive player or use his arms to create additional space for himself (clear out).

   B. **Legal Guarding Position**

1. A defensive player has established a legal guarding position when:

   a. He is facing his opponent, and

   b. He has both feet on the floor in a normal straddle position. The distance between his feet in a normal straddle position is generally proportional to his height.

2. The legal guarding position extends vertically above him (cylinder). He may raise his arms above his head but he must maintain them in a vertical postion inside the imaginary cylinder.

   C. **Guarding a Player Who Controls the Ball**

1. In guarding a player who controls (he is holding or dribbling) the ball, the elements of time and distance do not apply.

2. The player with the ball must expect to be guarded and must be prepared to stop or change his direction whenever an opponent takes a legal guarding position in front of him, even if this is done within a fraction of a second.

3. The guarding (defensive) player must establish a legal guarding position without causing body contact prior to taking his position.

4. Once the defensive player has established a legal guarding position, he must maintain this position (see number 5. below), that is, he may not extend his arms, shoulders, hips, or legs to prevent the dribbler from passing by him.

5. When judging a Block/Charge – player with the ball situation, an official shall use the following principles:

   a. The defensive player must establish an initial legal guarding position by facing the player with

➡ *page 148*

continued from page 147

the ball and having both feet on the floor.

b. The defensive player may remain stationary or move laterally or backwards in order to maintain the guarding position. In moving to maintain the guarding position, one or both feet may be off the floor for an instant, as long as the lateral or backwards movement is considered normal defensive movement.

c. The defensive player must be on the spot first and contact must occur on the torso. If the contact is on the torso, then the defensive player would be considered to have been on the spot first.

If the three items above are present, then the foul is caused by the player with the ball.

D. The Player Who Is in the Air

1. A player who has jumped in the air from a spot on the court has the right to land again on the same spot.

2. He has the right to land on another spot on the court, provided that:

a. The landing spot is not already occupied by an opponent(s) at the time of the takeoff.

b. The direct path between the takeoff and landing spot is not already occupied by an opponent(s).

3. If a player has taken off and landed but his momentum causes him to contact an opponent who has taken a legal guarding position near the landing spot, then the jumper is responsible for the contact.

4. A player may not move into the path of an opponent after the latter has jumped into the air.

5. Moving under a player who is in the air and contact occurs is always an unsportsmanlike foul and in certain cases, it may be a disqualifying foul.

E. Guarding a Player Who Does NOT Control the Ball

1. A player who does not control the ball is entitled to move freely on the court and take any position not already occupied by another player.

2. The elements of time and distance shall apply. This means that a defensive player cannot take a position:

a. So near to an opponent in motion that the latter does not have sufficient distance to either stop or change his direction.

b. So quickly in the path of a moving opponent that the latter does not have sufficient time or distance to either stop or change his direction. The distance is directly proportional to the speed of the opponent, never less than one and never more than two steps. If a player disregards the elements of time and distance in taking his position and body contact with an opponent occurs, he is responsible for the contact.

3. Once a defensive player has taken a legal guarding position, he may not prevent his opponent from passing him by extending his arms, shoulders, hips, or legs in his path. He may, however, turn or place his arm(s) in front of and close to his body to avoid injury.

4. Once a defensive player has taken a legal guarding position:

a. He may shift or move laterally or backwards in order to remain in the path of his opponent.

b. He may move forward toward his opponent; however, if body contact occurs, he is responsible for it.

c. He must respect the element of space, that is, the distance between himself and his opponent as per 2.b. above.

F. Screening – Legal and Illegal

1. Screening occurs when a player attempts to delay or prevent an opponent who does not control the ball from reaching a desired position on the court.

2. Legal screening takes pace when the player who is screening an opponent is:

a. Stationary (inside his cylinder) when contact occurs.

b. Has both feet on the floor when contact occurs.

3. Illegal screening takes place when the player who is screening an opponent:

a. Was moving when contact occurred.

b. Did not give the appropriate distance in setting a screen outside the field of vision of a stationary opponent when contact occurred.

c. Did not respect the elements of time and distance on an opponent in motion when contact occurred.

4. If the screen is set within the field of vision of a stationary opponent (frontal or lateral), a player may establish the screen as close to him, short of contact, as he desires.

5. If the screen is set outside the field of vision of a stationary opponent, the screener must permit the opponent to take one normal step toward the screen without making contact.

6. If the opponent is in motion, the elements of time and distance shall apply. The screener must leave enough space so that the player who is being screened is able to avoid the screen by stopping or changing direction. The distance required is never less than one normal step but never more than two steps.

7. A player who is legally screened is responsible for any contact with the player who has set up the screen.

G. Blocking

1. A player who is attempting to screen is committing a blocking foul if contact occurs when he is moving and his opponent is stationary or retreating from him.

2. If a player disregards the ball, faces an opponent, and shifts his position as the opponent shifts, he is primarily responsible for any contact that ensues, unless other factors are involved. The expression "unless other factors are involved" refers to deliberate pushing, charging, or holding of the player who is being screened.

3. It is legal for a player to extend his arm(s) or elbow(s) in taking position on the floor, but they must be lowered (inside the cylinder) when an opponent attempts to go by. If a player

Using the elbow
A player is allowed to screen the ball from a defender by spreading his elbows but he is not allowed to actually push the defender away.

fails to lower the arm(s) or elbow(s) and contact occurs, it is blocking or holding.

H. Touching Opponents with the Hands

1. The touching of an opponent with a hand or hands, in itself, is not necessarily an infraction. However, when the opponent is in the field of vision of a player, there is no justification in touching with the hands, and such action could be considered illegal personal contact. The Officials must decide whether an advantage has been gained.

2. If the contact restricts in any way the freedom of movement of an opponent, such contact is a foul.

3. A dribbler may not use an extended forearm or hand to prevent an opponent from securing the ball. Situations of this nature can result in an advantage not intended by the rules and could lead to increased contact between opponents.

I. Post Play

1. The principle of verticality also applies to post play. The offensive player in the post position and the opponent guarding him must respect each other's vertical rights (cylinder).

2. The post player must not be allowed to shoulder or hip his opponent out of position, nor interfere with the latter's freedom of movement by the use of extended elbows or arms.

3. The defensive player must not be allowed to interfere with the post player's freedom of movement by the illegal use of arms, knees, or other parts of the body.

Art. 48 Double Foul

A. A double foul is a situation in which two opposing players commit fouls against each other at approximately the same time.

Art. 49 Unsportsmanlike Foul

1. An unsportsmanlike foul is a personal foul on a player with or without the ball, which, in the opinion of the official, was deliberately committed by a player against an opposing player.

2. The unsportsmanlike foul must be interpreted the same way at the beginning as well as near the end of the game, that is, throughout the whole game.

3. The official must judge only the action.

4. To judge whether a foul is unsportsmanlike, the officials must apply the following principles:

 a. If a player commits a foul while making a legitimate effort to play the ball (normal basket ball play), it is not an unsportsmanlike foul.

 b. If, in the effort to play the ball, the player causes excessive contact (hard foul), then the contact shall be considered to be unsportsmanlike.

 c. Holding, hitting, or pushing a player who is away from the ball is usually an unsportsmanlike foul.

5. A player who repeatedly commits unsportsmanlike fouls may be disqualified.

Penalty

1. An unsportsmanlike foul shall be charged to the offender.

2. Free throw(s) shall be awarded to the non-offending team, followed by possession of the ball.

3. The number of free throws to be awarded shall be as follows:

 a. If the foul is committed on a player not in the act of shooting, two free throws.

 b. If the foul is committed on a player who is in the act of shooting, the goal, if made, shall count and in addition one free throw.

 c. If the foul is committed on a player in the act of shooting who fails to score, two or three free throws, according to the place from where the shot for goal was attempted.

4. During the free throw(s) all other players shall remain behind the free-throw line extended and behind the three-point field goal line until the free throw(s) have been completed.

5. After the free throw(s), whether or not the last free throw is successful, the ball shall be thrown in by any player of the free-throw shooter's team from out of bounds at mid-court on the sideline opposite

the scorer's table.

6. The player taking the throw-in shall have one foot on either side of the extended center line, and shall be entitled to pass the ball to a player at any point on the playing court.

Art. 50 Disqualifying Foul

Any flagrantly unsportsmanlike infraction of Art. 47, 49, 52 (technical foul by a player) or 53 (technical foul by coaches, substitutes or team followers) is a disqualifying foul.

Penalty

1. A disqualifying foul shall be charged to the offender.

2. He shall be disqualified and shall go to and remain in his team's dressing room for the duration of the game or, if he so chooses, he shall leave the building.

3. Free throw(s) shall be awarded to the non-offending team, followed by possession of the ball.

4. The number of free throws to be awarded shall be as follows:

 a. If the foul is committed on a player not in the act of shooting, two free throws.

 b. If the foul is committed on a player who is in the act of shooting, the goal, if made, shall count and in addition one free throw.

 c. If the foul is committed on a player in the act of shooting who fails to score, two or three free throws, according to the place from where the shot for goal was attempted.

5. During the free throw, all other players shall remain behind the free-throw line extended and behind the three-point field goal line until the free throw(s) have been completed.

6. After the free throw(s), whether or not the last free throw is successful, the ball shall be thrown in by any player of the free throw shooter's team from out of bounds at mid-court on the sideline opposite the scorer's table.

7. The player taking the throw-in shall have one foot on either side of the extended centre line, and shall be entitled to pass the ball to a player at any point on the playing court.

Magic Johnson, former player, during a short stint as coach of the Los Angeles Lakers in 1993.

Rule 9
Technical Fouls
Art. 51-55

These cover fouls that do not involve contact with an opponent, such as using offensive language, disrespectfully addressing an official, baiting an opponent, or obstructing his vision by waving his hands near his eyes or grasping the ring in such a way that the weight of the player is supported by the ring. The penalty is two free throws to the opponents.

Rule 10
General Provisions

Covers the awarding of fouls.

These rules are reprinted by permission of the International Basketball Federation (FIBA). A complete copy of the rules, including Official Game Procedures, is available from FIBA.

Handball
Essentials

This fast-moving team game traces its roots to ancient times. Today, it is an Olympic sport popular in many European countries. It is not related to "court" handball, a game played by two or four players against walls.

The court
Rectangular, 40 by 20 m (44 by 22 yds), divided into two halves by a center line.

40 m (44 yds)
Side line
Center line
4.5 m 4.5 m
Substitution lines
Free throw line
Penalty or 7-metre line
Goal area line
Goalkeeper refraining line
4 m
20 m (22 yds)
Goal line

The goals
One at either end, at the center of each goal line. Each consists of two posts, 2 m (6½ ft) high and 3 m (10 ft) apart, joined by a crossbar. Both are made of wood, light metal, or synthetic material and painted in two colors in alternate stripes. A net is attached to the goal.

The players
12 players per team, with a maximum of seven on the court at any one time, including one goalkeeper.

The ball
Spherical, with an outer casing of leather or synthetic material. The outer case must not be too shiny or slippery.

A weight of 425–475 g (15–16¾ oz) or 325–400 g (11½–14 oz) for women and juniors. A circumference of 54–56 cm (21¼–22 in). Two balls must be available at the start of a game, although the one chosen is then used throughout.

A ball in the hand
Unlike a basketball, which requires large hands to be gripped, a handball is small enough for almost anyone to hold in one hand. Its matte surface also keeps it from slipping too easily from the grip.
Because it is easy to hold, shots for goal are usually made by hurling the ball at the net with a single hand.

Dress
All players on a team dress identically, wearing sports shoes. Their colors must be clearly distinguishable from the other team. Both goalkeepers should wear colors that distinguish them from all other players and each other. Each captain wears a 4-cm (1.6-in) wide armlet around the upper arm.

Officials
Two referees, a scorer, and a timekeeper.

HOW TO PLAY

Teams score goals by getting the ball into their opponents' goal via shots taken from beyond the goal area line. Players may use their hands, arms, head, torso, thighs, and knees. The ball can be passed, dribbled, or rolled down the court.

Starting

The team winning the toss has the choice of ends or the option of beginning the game with a throw-off. The player taking it does so from the center of the court. Once the referee blows the whistle, the player has 3 seconds to execute the throw-off in any direction. All other players must be in their own half of the court and the players of the non-starting team must be at least 3 m (10 ft) from the player taking the throw.

How to win

A goal results when the ball completely crosses the goal line and passes into a goal. If it is prevented from doing so by, for example, a spectator on the court, a goal is awarded if it would have been scored otherwise. The team with the most goals wins.

KEY RULES

• A game consists of two 30 minute halves, with a 10-minute halftime. Teams change ends at the half. If there must be a winning team and the game is tied, two extra periods of four minutes are played.
• Players must not hold the ball for longer than three seconds, nor may they take more than three steps while in possession. They must also not intentionally touch the ball with any part of the leg below the knee.

Interception
Since players have to pass the ball frequently, defenders try to recapture the ball by intercepting passes.

• "Passive play" occurs when possession of the ball is maintained without an attempt to move into attack or to score a goal. This is penalized by a free throw to the opposing team. *See Law 7 (page 152).*
• Infringements are generally penalized in one of two ways. Most violations result in a free throw—taken by a player of the non-offending team from the place where the infringement occurred (none of his teammates may be on or within the free-throw line). Violations near the goal result in a penalty throw—taken by one player as a shot at goal from the 7-meter line (all other players remain behind the free-throw line). *See Laws 13 and 14 (page 152).*
• Serious violations (for rough play and the like) can also result in a two-minute suspension, during which the offending players team must play short-handed. *See Law 17 (page 153).*

SKILLS AND TACTICS

This is a rapid game of continuous action, requiring fitness and endurance as well as flexibility and balance. Good passing and catching skills enable a team to keep possession of the ball and attempt to score. The most common pass is the *overhand pass*, made with an arm bent at the elbow and stretched up and back to give the ball momentum.

An alternative is the *wrist pass*—made with a quick flick of the wrist in situations where a quick response and direction, rather than force or distance, are needed.

Opportunities for shooting at goal occur frequently and players must be ready to shoot on the move, from various angles, or from a jump.

When not on the attack, all the players of a team must play a rigorously defensive game, checking individual opponents and blocking the path of the ball wherever possible.

Ready to pass
Players are not allowed to hold the ball for longer than three seconds, nor may they take more than three steps while holding it— although they may run while bouncing the ball repeatedly. The game, therefore, generally depends on rapid passing from player to player.

Going for the ball
Players can try to capture the ball from an opponent with their arms, palms, and body. But they are not allowed to push, hold, run, jump into, trip, or hit an opponent. Is the play at right legal?

GRAY AREA

Rule 7.7 forbids players touching the ball twice— but there is an exception that can lead to dispute. A player is allowed to touch the ball twice if he first fumbles his catch. But he is not allowed to touch it again once he has caught it cleanly. It is the referee who must decide whether the ball was caught cleanly or not.

LAWS OF HANDBALL

These laws are abridged and summarized. Changes from the official laws are indicated in *italics*.

1. The Playing Court
2. Duration of Play
3. The Ball
4. The Players

See page 150.

5. The Goalkeeper

The goalkeeper may touch the ball with any part of his body in the act of defense but he may not use any part of his legs below the knee when the ball is stationary in the goal area or heading towards the playing area. He may leave the area while not in possession of the ball, but if he is in possession, this must only be in an attempt to control the ball in the act of defense. He may move without restriction inside the goal area, but the same restrictions as exist for all the other players apply as soon as he is outside.

6. The Goal Area

Court players (all apart from the goalkeeper) must not enter this area and if they do so they are penalized with a free throw (if they gain an advantage by doing so) or a penalty throw (if they gain an advantage over an attacking opponent in possession). If not in possession or no advantage is gained, a player does not incur a penalty. When the ball enters this area it belongs to the goalkeeper only.

7. Playing the Ball

It is permitted:

7.1 to throw, catch, push, or hit the ball using the hands (the hands may be open or closed), arms, head, torso, thighs, and knees.

7.2 to hold the ball for a maximum of three seconds, even when it is lying on the floor.

7.3 to take a maximum of three steps, whilst in possession of the ball. One step is considered taken when:

a) A player who is standing with both feet in contact with the floor lifts one foot and puts it down again, or moves one foot from one position to another.

b) A player who is in contact with the floor with one foot only, catches the ball and then makes contact with the ground with the other foot.

c) A player, after a jump, touches the floor with one foot only and then hops on the same foot or touches the ground with the other foot.

d) A player, after a jump, touches the floor with both feet simultaneously and then lifts one and puts it down again, or, moves one foot from one place to another.

7.4 While standing or running

a) To bounce the ball once and catch it with both hands.

b) To bounce the ball or to roll the ball on the ground repeatedly, with one hand and thereafter catch or pick up the ball in one or both hands.

7.5 To place the ball from one hand to the other. (It is not allowed to throw the ball from one hand to the other).

7.6 To play the ball while kneeling, sitting, or lying on the ground.

It is not permitted:

7.7 To touch the ball more than once unless it has first touched the ground or another player or any part of the goal. Where in the act of catching or stopping the ball, the player does not control the ball cleanly at the first attempt, and thereby fumbles in his/her efforts, such action shall not be penalized. However, where control of the ball has been established, the player must not touch it more than once after tapping or bouncing it.

7.8 To touch the ball with any part of the leg below the knee, except when the ball has been thrown against the legs of a player, by an opponent, and where the striking of the leg by the ball does not cause advantage to be gained by the player or his team.

7.9 To dive for the ball while it is lying or rolling on the ground.

7.10 To play the ball intentionally over the sideline or the teams own outer goal line.

7.11 To keep the ball in the team's possession without making any recognizable attempt to attack or to score a goal.

Such action is considered to be **"passive play"** and is penalized by a free throw against the offending team. The throw is executed from that place where the ball was when the play was interrupted.

7.12 Where the ball makes contact with one of the referees, on the court, the play shall continue as the referee is, in this instance, considered to be part of the field of play.

8. Approach to an Opponent

A player may try to gain possession of the ball using hands, arms, an open hand, or the torso. However it is forbidden to: obstruct an opponent by means of arms, hands, or legs; force an opponent into the goal area; hit or pull the ball from an opponent's hands; use a fist to dispossess him; throw the ball or feint with it in a dangerous manner towards an opponent; push, hold, run, or jump into, trip, or hit an opponent. The penalty incurred ranges from a free throw to the opposition to disqualification, depending on the degree of the offense.

9. Scoring

10. Throw-off

See Starting page 151.

11. Throw-in

A throw-in is awarded against the team to last touch the ball if it completely crosses the sideline, on the ground or in the air. It is taken from the place where the ball crossed. A throw-in may also be awarded if a defender deflects the ball over the outer goal line, in which case it is taken from the intersection of this line and the sideline.

12. Goalkeepers-Throw (Goal Throw)

12.1 A goal throw is awarded when the ball crosses the outer goal line, having last been touched by a member of the team attacking the goal or by the goalkeeper in the act of defending the goal.

12.2 The goal throw is executed by means of the goalkeeper throwing the ball into the playing area, from a position inside the goal area. The throw is made without any whistle signal from the referee. The throw is considered taken when the ball has crossed the goal area line.

12.3 If the ball shall, on occasion, come to rest in the goal area, the goalkeeper shall bring the ball back into play by throwing the ball into the playing court.

12.4 Following the execution of a goal throw, the goalkeeper is not allowed to make contact with the ball again until it has first touched another player.

13. Free Throw

13.1 A free throw is awarded for incorrect substitution or for infringements: by the goalkeeper, by court players in the goal area, when playing the ball, passive play, approaching an opponent, a throw-off, a throw-in, a goalkeeper's throw, a free throw, a penalty throw, a referee's throw, and a formal throw, unsporting conduct, and assault. 13.2–13.7 A free throw is taken without any whistle signal from the referee and from the place where the offense took place. Players of the attacking team must not cross or touch their opponents free-throw line until the throw has been taken. The referee will not award a free throw, if by so doing an advantage would be gained by the team causing the infringement and a disadvantage experienced by the team in possession of the ball. Where an infringement causes an attacking team to be placed at a disadvantage a free throw, at least, must be awarded. A free throw, at least, must be awarded if an infringement causes an attacking team to lose possession of the ball. A free throw must NOT be awarded if a player remains in full control of the ball in spite of the infringement.

If the game is interrupted, it shall be started by means of a free throw executed by the team having possession and from the place where the ball was at the time of the interruption. The free throw must be preceded by a whistle signal.

13.8 The ball **must** be put down **immediately** by a player in possession of the ball when a decision is made against him/her or his/her team.

14. Penalty Throw (7-Meter Throw)

14.1 **A 7-meter throw shall be awarded:**

a) When a clear chance of scoring a goal is prevented by an infringement, in any part of the court, and even where the offender is a team official

b) When the goalkeeper enters the goal area in possession of the ball or when standing inside the goal area, takes it into the goal area.

c) When a court player enters his/her own goal area to gain an advantage over an attacking opponent who is in possession of the ball.

d) When a court player deliberately plays the ball to his/her own goalkeeper inside the goal area and the goalkeeper touches the ball

e) When there is an unwarranted whistle signal that destroys a clear goal-scoring opportunity

f) When a clear goal-scoring opportunity is destroyed by interference of someone not authorized to be on the court

14.2 The penalty throw must be taken as a shot propelled towards the goal and within three seconds of the whistle signal given by the court referee.

14.3 The player taking the penalty throw must not touch or cross the 7-meter line before the ball has left the hand.

14.4 Once the penalty throw has been executed, the ball may not be played again until it has touched the goalkeeper or the goal.

14.5 While the penalty throw is being taken **all** players with the exception of the thrower must be positioned outside the free-throw line (9-meter line).

14.6 Players of the defending team must be at least 3 m (10 ft) from the 7-meter line, while a penalty throw is being taken. Where a defending player touches or crosses the 9-meter line or encroaches nearer than 3 m (10 ft) from the 7-meter line before the ball has left the thrower's hand, the referee shall decide as follows:

a) Goal if the ball goes into the goal

b) The retaking of the throw in all other cases

14.8 The referees shall not award a 7-meter throw for an infringement of the Rules by a defending team, if by doing so he/she causes a disadvantage to the attacking team.

A 7-meter throw, at least, must be awarded, if a clear goal scoring opportunity is destroyed and a goal does not result, due to an infringement of the Rules or an act of unsporting conduct, an unwarranted whistle signal, or by interference on the part of someone not authorized to be a part of the game. Where, in spite of an infringement, an attacking player retains full ball and body control, a penalty throw shall not be awarded.

15. Referee's Throw

15.1 **A game shall be restarted by means of a Referee's Throw when:**
a) The Rules have been infringed simultaneously, on the court, by players of both teams
b) The ball has touched the roof or fixed equipment above the playing court
c) An interruption of the game is

caused through no infringement of the Rules and while neither side was in possession of the ball.

15.2 There shall always be a "time out" when a referee's throw is awarded.

15.3 The execution of the referee's throw shall be from the center of the court by the court referee throwing the ball vertically into the air, following a whistle signal.

15.4 With the exception of one player from each team all other players must be positioned at least 3 m (10 ft) from the referee whilst the referee's throw is being executed. The two competing players shall stand either side of the referee, each on that side that is nearer to their own goal. The referee shall throw the ball into the air and the two players shall jump to try and gain possession. However, the ball may only be played after it has reached its highest point.

16. Execution of Formal Throws

16.1 All players must adopt the positions prescribed for the throw in question.

16.2 During the execution of the throw-off, throw-in, free throw and penalty throw, the thrower must keep at least a part of one foot in constant contact with the floor. It is permitted, however, for the player to repeatedly lift and put down the other foot.

16.4 A throw is considered to have been executed once the ball has left the hand of the thrower.

16.5 Once the player taking the throw has released the ball he/she is not allowed to play the ball again until it has first touched another player or the goal.

16.6 A goal may be scored directly from any throw.

16.7 When a throw-in or free throw is being taken, players of the team not in possession shall be at least 3 m (10 ft) from the thrower.

Free throw
During a free throw attackers must stay behind their opponents' free-throw line until the ball is thrown. The throw must be made within three seconds of the referee blowing his whistle.

17. Punishments

17.1 **A caution can be given for:**
a) Infringements concerning approach to an opponent.
A caution shall be given for:
b) infringements concerning the approach to an opponent and which are to be punished progressively.
c) Infringements of the Rules when an opponent is attempting to execute a throw.
d) Unsporting conduct by a player or official.

17.2 The referee shall indicate the decision to issue a caution to an offending player by holding up a yellow card.

17.3 **A suspension (2 minutes) shall be given**:
a) For an incorrect (faulty) substitution or for entering the court contrary to the Rules.
b) For repeated infringements of the Rules governing the approach to an opponent and which are to be punished progressively.
c) For repeated unsporting conduct by a player on the court.
d) When a player fails to place the ball down on to the floor, immediately, when a decision for an infringement has been made against an attacking team.
e) For repeatedly infringing the Rules when the opposing team are executing a formal throw.
f) In consequence of a disqualification of a player or team official.
In exceptional circumstances a suspension can be awarded without recourse to an initial caution.

17.4 The decision to suspend a player must be clearly indicated to the player concerned by the referee raising one arm in the air with two fingers extended.

17.5 **A disqualification shall be awarded:**
if a player who is not entitled to participate enters the court; for serious infringements relating to the approach to an opponent; for repeated unsporting conduct

by a team official or a player outside the court; for serious unsporting conduct by a player or team official; for a third period of suspension; or for an assault by a team official.

The disqualification of a player or a team official during the playing time shall always result in a period of suspension and the team's strength on the court being reduced by one.

17.6 When awarding a disqualification the referee shall indicate the punishment by the holding up of a red card. The disqualification of a player or official applies for the remainder of the playing time. The player or official must leave the court and the substitution area immediately. A disqualification reduces the number of players and/or officials available to the team. The team may, however, continue to play at full strength on the court following the expiry of the suspension time awarded against the disqualified player or official.

17.7 **An exclusion shall be given:** In the event of an assault, during the playing time both on and outside the court.

17.9 Any player having been given a period of suspension and who is guilty of another infringement, before the game is restarted shall be further punished by means of the most severe of the applicable punishments allowed for in the Rules.

17.10 In the event of a goalkeeper being suspended, disqualified, or excluded, another player must take up the position of goalkeeper.

17.11 The referees must caution any player they deem guilty of unsporting conduct, irrespective of whether such takes place on or outside the court.

18. The Referee
(Refers to referees).

These laws are reprinted by permission of the International Handball Federation. For a complete copy of the Laws of the Game, including various notes, Clarifications of the Rules and Regulations Governing the Substitution Area, contact the Federation or the United States Handball Federation.

Netball
Essentials

Although this game resembles basketball, two aspects set it apart from most other sports: the player with the ball may not move (though she may pivot) and only two members of a team are allowed to score.

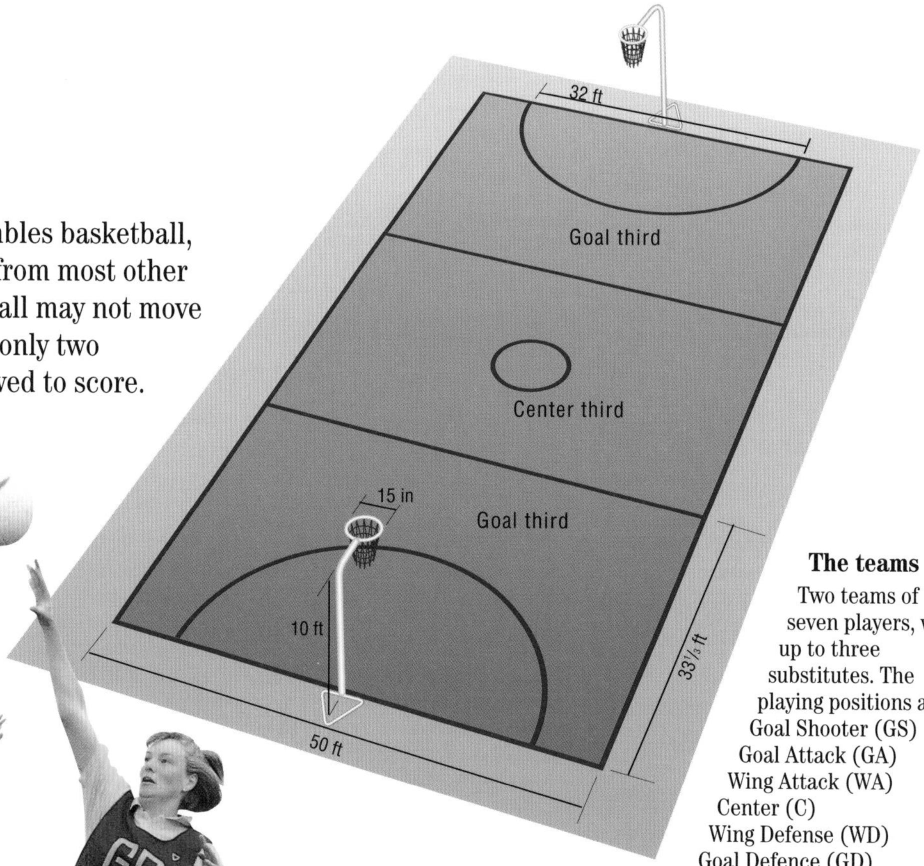

The court

Must have a firm surface. Lines divide the court into three equal parts, with a semicircle of radius 16 ft in in each of the far ends. Lines must not exceed 2 in in width.

32 ft

Goal third

Center third

15 in

Goal third

10 ft

50 ft

33⅓ ft

The teams

Two teams of seven players, with up to three substitutes. The playing positions are:
Goal Shooter (GS)
Goal Attack (GA)
Wing Attack (WA)
Center (C)
Wing Defense (WD)
Goal Defence (GD)
Goalkeeper (GK)
See bottom of page 155, for their positions on court.

Marking

Since players can't move with the ball, the offense depends on accurate passing. The defense depends on staying as close as allowed to an opponent ("marking").

Officials

Two umpires, two scorers, and a timekeeper.

Dress

A shirt with shorts or a skirt. Initials of playing positions (6 in high) must be worn both front and back above the waist. Shoes must not have spiked soles and no jewelry may be worn—even a wedding ring must be taped.

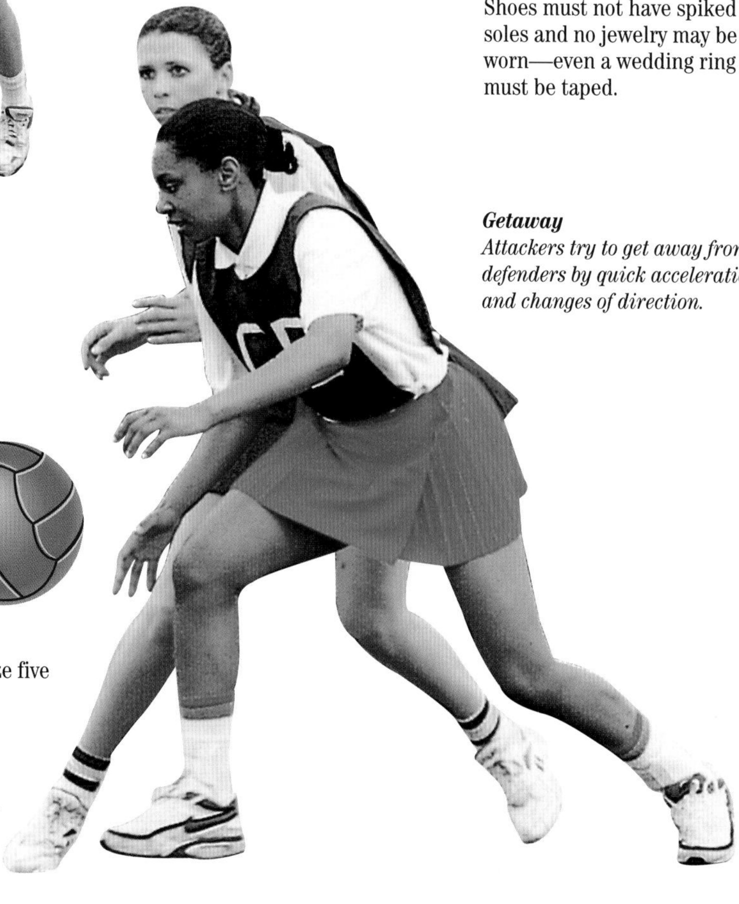

Getaway

Attackers try to get away from defenders by quick acceleration and changes of direction.

The goalposts

Two goalposts, 10 ft high, at the midpoint of each goal line, preferably inserted into the ground. Each has a metal ring (internal diameter 15 in) 6 in from the top. The attachment joining the ring and post must allow 6 in between the post and the near side of the ring.

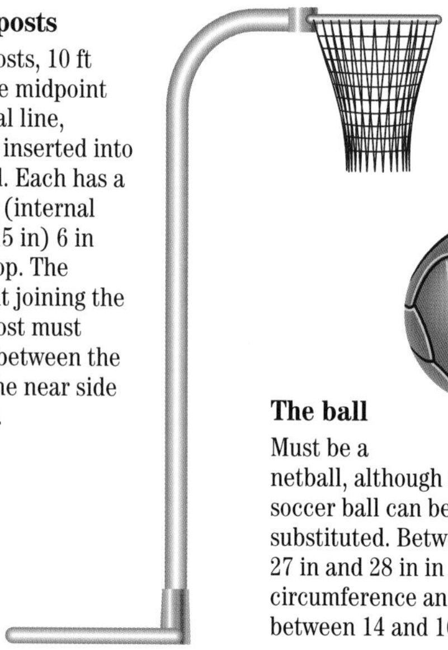

The ball

Must be a netball, although a size five soccer ball can be substituted. Between 27 in and 28 in in circumference and between 14 and 16 oz.

HOW TO PLAY

A team scores by passing the ball down the court and through the ring of their opponents' goal. Players can only move within the designated playing area for their position, and the ball must be passed, since a player holding it cannot run with it or dribble it.

Starting

The team winning a toss chooses either an end or the right to make the first pass. The center of the team making the pass then stands inside the center circle and is required to pass within three seconds of the umpire's whistle. Apart from the opposing center, all players remain outside the center third until the whistle blows. The two teams take turns making similar passes after each goal is scored.

How to win

Goals can only be scored by the goal shooter or the goal attack, both of whom attempt shots through their opponent's ring from anywhere within the goal circle. If a defending player deflects a shot and the ball goes through the ring, a goal is also scored. The team with the most goals wins. *See Rule 15, Scoring a Goal (page 156).*

KEY RULES

• A game consists of four quarters of 15 minutes each.

• A player may catch the ball with one or both hands or tip, bat, or bounce it to another player, but once caught, the ball must be passed or shot within 3 seconds. A player cannot bounce or throw the ball and then replay it, or roll the ball to another player. It is also against the rules to deliberately kick the ball, grab it from an opponent, or to play it while lying, sitting, or kneeling on the ground. *See Rule 13, Playing the Ball (page 156).*

• A player may not run with the ball. If the player lands on one foot when receiving the ball, the other foot may be used to regain balance or to change direction with any number of steps, pivoting on the landing foot. If the landing foot is lifted, the ball must be passed before the foot can be grounded again. If the player lands on both feet when receiving, either foot can be moved, but once it is, it becomes the stepping foot and the other becomes the landing foot and the rule applies as before. *See Rule 14, Footwork (page 156).*

• A pass is only allowed if there is room between the thrower and receiver for a third player.

See Rule 13.5, Passing Distances (page 156).

• Defenders are generally not allowed to come within three feet of their opponent. *See Rule 16, Obstruction (page 157).*

SKILLS

Catching

The ball should be caught with two hands whenever possible. Fingers and thumbs should be spread out to secure the catch. Balance is essential if a player is to intercept, secure, and then pass the ball accurately within the few seconds allowed, while also obeying the footwork rule.

Throwing

Players must be able to throw firmly and swiftly, anticipating the speed and direction of the receiver. A *shoulder pass,* made with one or both hands above the shoulder and slightly behind the body, is for long distances. A *chest pass* is made from the chest with both hands and is mostly used for short, direct passes. A *low pass* can be achieved with the underarm pass, swinging the ball forward from below the waist with one hand, while the *bounce pass* allows the ball to neatly dodge an opponent, bouncing too low for them to intercept before rebounding at an easy-to-catch height beyond them.

Shooting

An essential skill. Although the defending player must remain at least 3 ft from the shooter, their presence can make it difficult to shoot at the goal. An advanced player copes with interference and still shoots accurately, even in an off-balance position.

TACTICS

When a team is in attack, individual players try to break free from their opponents and reach a clear point to receive the ball and form a link down the court. Deceptive "trick" moves by the thrower and/or receiver are often used to confuse opponents.

Defense takes the form of zone defense (keeping guard over a particular area of the court and intercepting passes) or one-to-one marking (closely following individuals to hamper their play).

GRAY AREA

The rule that causes most dispute in netball is the "no contact" rule. The problem is that umpires interpret the phrase "which interferes" in different ways. The umpire must decide whether the contact interferes, and decisions vary according to whether the umpire thinks the player could cope successfully with the contact, the umpire's position at the time of the incident, his or her speed of judgement and so on.

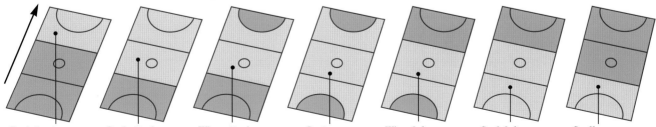

| Goal shooter zone | Goal attack zone | Wing attack zone | Center zone | Wing defense zone | Goal defense zone | Goalkeeper zone |

NETBALL THE RULES

I. Organization of the Game
Rules 1 to 7

See How to play (page 155).

II. Areas of Play
Rules 8 to 10

See diagram (page 155).

III. Conduct of the Game
11. Positioning of Players for Start of Play

12. Start of Play

See Starting (page 155).

13. Playing the Ball

13.1 A player may:
(i) Catch the ball with one or both hands.
(ii) Gain or regain control of the ball if it rebounds from the goalpost.
(iii) Bat or bounce the ball to another player without first having possession of it.
(iv) Tip the ball in an uncontrolled manner once or more than once and then:
    a) Catch the ball; or
    b) Direct the ball to another player.
(v) Having batted the ball once, either catch the ball or direct the ball to another player.
(vi) Roll the ball to oneself to gain possession.
(viii) Fall while holding the ball but must regain footing and throw within three seconds of receiving the ball.
(ix) Lean on the ball to prevent going offside.
(x) Lean on the ball on court to gain balance.
(xi) Jump from a position in contact with the court and play the ball outside the court, provided that neither the player nor the ball makes contact with the ground, or any object or person outside the court while the ball is being played.
13.2 A player may not:
(i) Strike the ball with a fist.
(ii) Deliberately fall on the ball to get it.
(iii) Attempt to gain possession of the ball while lying, sitting, or kneeling on the ground.
(iv) Throw the ball while lying, sitting, or kneeling on the ground.
(v) Use the goalpost as a support in recovering the ball going out of the court.
(vi) Use the goalpost as a

means of regaining balance, or in any other way for any other purpose.
(vii) Deliberately kick the ball (if a ball is thrown and accidentally hits the leg of a player it is not a kick).
Penalty: Free pass to the opposing team where the infringement occurred.
13.3 A player who has caught or held the ball shall play it or shoot for goal within three seconds. To play the ball a player may:
(i) Throw it in any manner and in any direction to another player;
(ii) Bounce it with one or both hands in any direction to another player.
13.4 A player who has caught or held the ball may not:
(i) Roll the ball to another player.
(ii) Throw the ball and play it before it has been touched by another player.
(iii) Toss the ball into the air and replay it.
(iv) Drop the ball and replay it.
(v) Bounce the ball and replay it.
(vi) Replay the ball after an unsuccessful shot at goal unless it has touched some part of the goalpost.
Penalty: Free pass to the opposing team where the

infringement occurred.
13.5 Passing Distances
13.5.1 Short Pass
(i) On the court: at the moment the ball is passed there must be room for a third player to move between the hands of the thrower and those of the receiver.
(ii) At the throw-in: at the moment the ball is passed there must be room on the court between the hands of the thrower and those of the receiver for a third player to attempt an interception.
Penalty: Free pass to the opposing team where the ball is caught.
13.5.2 Over a third
(i) The ball may not be thrown over a complete third without being touched or caught by a player who, at the time of touching or catching the ball, is wholly within that third or who lands in that third.
(ii) The player who lands with the first foot wholly within the correct third is judged to have received the ball in that third. The subsequent throw shall be considered to have been made from the third in which the player first landed.
(iii) The player who lands on both feet simultaneously with one foot wholly within the correct third and the other in the incorrect third shall be penalized.
Penalty: Free pass to the opposing team taken just beyond the second line that the ball has crossed, except where the ball thrown from the center third passes out of the court over the goal line, when a throw-in shall be taken.

Shooting circle
For a shot at goal to count a player must be inside the shooting circle.

14. Footwork

14.1 A player may receive the ball with one foot grounded or jump to catch and land on one foot and then:
(i) Step with the other foot in any

direction, lift the landing foot, and throw or shoot before this foot is regrounded.
(ii) Step with the other foot in any direction any number of times, pivoting on the landing foot. The pivoting foot may be lifted but the player must throw or shoot before regrounding it.
(iii) Jump from the landing foot on to the other foot and jump again, but must throw the ball or shoot before regrounding either foot.
(iv) Step with the other foot and jump, but must throw the ball or shoot before regrounding either foot.
14.2 A player may receive the ball while both feet are grounded, or jump to catch and land on both feet simultaneously and then:
(i) Step with either foot in any direction, lift the other foot and throw or shoot before this foot is regrounded.
(ii) Step with either foot in any direction any number of times pivoting on the other. The pivoting foot may be lifted but the player must throw or shoot before regrounding it.
(iii) Jump from both feet on to either foot, but must throw or shoot before regrounding the other foot.
(iv) Step with either foot and jump but must throw the ball or shoot before regrounding either foot.
14.3 A player in possession of the ball may not:
(i) Drag or slide the landing foot.
(ii) Hop on either foot.
(iii) Jump from both feet and land on both feet unless the ball has been released before landing.
Penalty: A free pass to the opposing team where the infringement occurred.

15. Scoring a Goal

15.1 A goal is scored when the ball is thrown or batted over and completely through the ring by Goal Shooter or Goal Attack from any point within the goal circle, including the lines bounding the goal circle:
(i) If another player throws the ball through the ring no goal is scored and play continues.
(ii) If a defending player deflects a shot for goal and the ball then passes over and completely through the ring, a goal is scored.
(iii) Goal Shooter or Goal Attack may shoot for goal or pass if the

ball is won at a toss-up in the goal circle.

(iv) If the whistle for an interval or "time" is blown before the ball has passed completely through the ring, no goal is scored.

(v) If the whistle for an interval or "time" is blown after a penalty pass or shot has been awarded in the goal circle, the penalty pass or shot shall be taken.

15.2 In taking a shot for goal a player shall:

(i) Have no contact with the ground outside the goal circle either during the catching of the ball or while holding it. It is not contact with the ground to lean on the ball, but if this happens behind the goal line the ball is considered to be out of court.

(ii) Shoot within three seconds of catching or holding the ball.

(iii) Obey the Footwork Rule.

Penalty: A free pass to the opposing team in the goal circle where the infringement occurred.

15.3 A defending player may not cause the goalpost to move so as to interfere with the shot at goal.

Penalty: Penalty pass or shot to the opposing team to be taken:

(i) From where the infringer was standing unless this places the non-offending team at a disadvantage.

(ii) If the infringer was out of court, on court near where the infringer was standing.

16. Obstruction

16.1 An attempt to intercept or defend the ball may be made by a defending player if the distance on the ground is not less than 0.9 m (3 ft) from a player in possession of the ball. When the ball is received, this distance is measured as follows:

(i) If the player's landing, grounded, or pivoting foot remains on the ground, the distance is measured from that foot to the nearest foot of the defending player.

(ii) If the player's landing, grounded, or pivoting foot is lifted, the distance is measured from the spot on the ground from which the foot was lifted to the nearer foot of the defending player.

(iii) If the player is standing or lands on both feet simultaneously and remains grounded on both feet, the distance is measured from whichever is the nearer foot of that player to the nearer foot of the defending player.

(iv) If the player is standing or lands on both feet

simultaneously and either foot is lifted, the other foot is considered to be the grounded foot from which the 0.9 m (3 ft) distance is measured.

16.2 From the correct distance, a defending player may attempt to intercept or defend the ball:

(i) By jumping towards the player with the ball, but if the landing is within 0.9 m (3 ft) of that player and interferes with the throwing or shooting motion, obstruction occurs.

(ii) If the player with the ball steps forward to lessen the distance of 0.9 m (3 ft) between them.

16.3 A player may be within 0.9 m (3 ft) of an opponent in possession of the ball, providing no effort is made to defend and there is no interference with that opponent's throwing or shooting action.

16.4 From the correct distance, a defending player may not attempt to intercept or defend the ball by stepping towards an opponent with the ball.

16.5 Obstruction of a player not in possession of the ball

16.5.1 A player is obstructing if within a distance of 0.9 m (3 ft) (measured on the ground) from an opponent without the ball, any movements are employed by that player (whether attacking or defending) that take the arms away from the body, other than those involved in natural body balance. Within this distance a player is not obstructing if the arms are outstretched:

(i) To catch, deflect, or intercept a pass or feint pass.

(ii) To obtain a rebound from an unsuccessful shot at goal.

(iii) Momentarily to signal for a pass, or to indicate the intended direction of movement.

16.6 Obstruction by intimidation

When a player with or without the ball intimidates an opponent it is obstruction.

Penalty for 16.1 to 16.6: Penalty pass or shot where the infringer is standing except where this places the non-offending team at a disadvantage, when the penalty shall be taken where the obstructed player was standing.

16.7 Defending a player who is out of court

16.7.1 A player may defend an opponent who has chosen to go out of court provided that the defending player does not leave the court or own playing area in order to defend.

Penalty: A penalty pass or penalty pass or shot from the point where the infringer leaves the court.

16.7.2 A player who goes out of court to collect a ball, to take a throw-in, or for any other valid reason, must be allowed back into the area of play near to the point at which the player left the

Physical contact is not allowed.

court or took the throw-in. Any opponent attempting to prevent the player from re-entering the court is penalized.

Penalty: A penalty pass or penalty pass or shot on court immediately opposite the point where the infringer was standing.

16.8 Obstruction by a player from out of court

16.8.1 A player who is standing out of court may not attempt to defend a player who is on the court.

Penalty: A penalty pass or penalty pass or shot on the court opposite the point where the infringer was standing.

17. Contact

17.1 Personal Contact

17.1.1 No player shall come into personal contact with an opponent in such a manner as to interfere with the opponent's play either accidentally or deliberately.

17.1.2 In an effort to attack or defend or to play the ball a player shall not:

(i) push an opponent in any way;

(ii) bump or rush into an opponent;

(iii) trip or knock an opponent in any way;

(iv) use any part of the body to interfere with an opponent's play;

(v) hold an opponent; this includes feeling to keep near an opponent;

(vi) charge an opponent, i.e., when jumping, bump against an opponent.

17.1.3 Whether attempting to attack or to defend, a player is responsible for any personal contact:

(i) If taking up a position so near an opponent that contact cannot be avoided.

(ii) If moving so quickly into the path of a moving player that contact cannot be avoided.

17.1.4 A player shall not contact another on any occasion or in any other way in such a manner as to interfere with the opponent's play.

17.2 Contact with the ball

17.2.1 A player, while holding the ball, shall not touch or push an opposing player with it in such a manner as to interfere with that opponent's play.

17.2.2 A player shall not, either accidentally or deliberately, place a hand or hands on, or remove from an opponent's possession, a ball held by an opposing player.

17.2.3 Where 17.2.1 and 17.2.2 occur simultaneously a toss-up is taken between those two players.

Penalty for 17.1 to 17.2.2:

Penalty pass or penalty pass or shot where the infringer is standing, except where this places the non-offending team at a disadvantage, when the penalty shall be taken where the contacted player was standing.

IV. CONDUCTING PENALTIES

The penalties awarded for the breaking of the rules are:

Free Pass

Penalty Pass or Shot

Throw-in

Toss-up

V. DISCIPLINE

These rules are reprinted by permission of the All-England Netball Association. A complete copy of the rules, including Rules IV and V, plus two Appendices, is available from the AENA.

Volleyball
Essentials

Originally designed as a game for those not fit enough to play basketball, volleyball enjoys wide popularity today both as a recreational game and as a competitive sport. The game is often played indoors on a hard-surface court, but a version of the game played on beaches is also increasingly popular.

The ball

Spherical, made of a flexible leather or synthetic leather case containing a bladder made of rubber or similar material. A circumference of 65–67 cm (approx. 26 in), weight of 260–280 g (approx. 9.5 oz) and an inside pressure of 0.30–0.325 kg/sq cm.

The net

9.5 m (31 ft) long and 1 m (3 ft) wide when hung taut. A height of 2.43 m (approx. 8 ft) (men) or 2.24 m (approx. 7 ft 4in) (women). Made of 10 cm (approx. 4 in) square black mesh, with a 5-cm (2-in) wide band of white canvas across the top and two 5-cm (2-in) wide/ 1-m (3-ft) long white side bands. Two flexible vertical antennae, 1.8 m (6 ft) long, are fastened at the outer edge of each side band to mark the boundaries that the ball must keep to when crossing the net.

Posts

Two rounded posts with a height of 2.55 m (8 ft). Fixed to the ground at a distance of 0.50–1 m (1½–3 ft) from each sideline.

Officials

A first referee, second referee, scorer, and four (FIVB World Competitions) or two line judges.

The court

Various surfaces, although world competitions always use wooden or synthetic surfaces only. (Beach volleyball is now a separate Olympic sport using a sand court of the same dimensions.) A playing court measuring 18 m x 9 m (approx. 59 x 30 ft), surrounded by a symmetrical rectangular free zone, minimum 3 m (10 ft) wide (wider for top level competitions). A minimum height of 7 m (23 ft) above the playing surface must be free from all obstructions. Indoor courts are generally light in color. The playing court is divided in two by a center line. Each half is then divided into a front and back zone by the attack line.

Lines of the service zone

End line — 3 m

Sideline — 0.8 m

2.55 m

Attack line

2.43 m Men
2.24 m Women — 1 m

Center line

3 m

Free zone

Front zone

Substitution zone

Back zone — 18 m

Free zone

Service zone — 9 m

Indoors or outdoors

Volleyball can be played indoors or outdoors, but most major tournaments are played indoors. The rules stipulate that indoor courts must be one color.

Dress

Shirt, shorts, and shoes, the same color throughout a team. Players' shirts are generally numbered (from 1 to 18) on the front and back.

Warm and bright

For competition volleyball, warmth and adequate lighting are essential. The temperature must never drop below 61°F (50°F for non-international games) nor rise higher than 77°F. Lighting should be between 1,000 and 1,500 lux.

Footwear

Most players wear light, pliable shoes without heels. However players may obtain permission from the officials to play barefoot.

The players

Two teams of six players each, with up to six substitutes. (Beach volleyball is usually two per side.)

HOW TO PLAY

Each team attempts to send the ball over the net to the opposite side by hitting it (mainly) with their hands or arms. They are allowed to hit the ball three times before sending it back, but must not catch it, hold it, or let it touch the ground in their own court.

Starting

The winner of the toss chooses the right to serve or receive, or a side of the court. All players except the server must be in their own court at the moment the ball is served, with each team arranged in two rows of three players—three front-row players (along the net) and three back-row players behind them. The ball is served by a player of the serving team standing behind the end line. The server hits the ball with one hand or arm, after which players are free to move about within their own court.

How to win

A point is scored for every rally played. If the receiving side fails to return the ball or commits a fault, one point is scored by the serving team. If the receiving team wins the rally they gain the right to serve, rotate one position clockwise and also win a point.

A set is won by the first team to score 25 points, with a lead of two points. If the score reaches 24-24, play continues until a two point lead is reached—for example 26-24, 27-25, 26-28 etc.

A match is won by the team that wins three sets—the best of five. If the set score reaches 2-2, a deciding (fifth) set is played as a tie-break, up to 15 points only, and again with a clear two-point lead required .

KEY RULES

• Service and court ends alternate between teams after each set and after one team has reached eight points in the fifth set. Within a team players rotate in a clockwise direction from their initial starting positions so that each has a turn in each of the six court positions. However, the same

player continues to serve from the baseline until the team loses a rally. When this occurs, each player of the opposing team moves around one place. A team's starting line-up is drawn up before a set to establish the order. Up to six substitutions may take place within a team in one set, in addition to any Libero substitutes.

• The ball may be played with any part of a player's body and it must be clearly hit, not held. Unintentional contact with the ball counts as a hit and the same player must not hit the ball twice consecutively, except when blocking at the net, or when making the first of the team's 3 hits. If two or three members of the same team touch the ball simultaneously this counts as two or three hits. *See Rule 14, Playing the Ball (page 160).*

• Faults, such as hitting the ball out-of-bounds,

Service jump
To serve, a player tosses the ball into the air with one or both hands and then knocks it over the net with one hand or part of the arm. Services include: the "hook," made with the body sideways to the net; the "tennis" serve, facing the net; and the "underhand" serve. Some competition players jump high in the air when serving for extra power.

Serving around
Every member of a volleyball team serves in rotation. The ball is always served by the back right-hand player and the players move clockwise around the court one position at a time.

lose a rally. If both teams commit faults simultaneously, the rally is replayed.

• A player must not touch the net while trying to play the ball. He also must not penetrate onto his opponents' court with any part of his body (unless with his hands or feet, provided part of his hand or foot remains in contact with, or above, the center line). *See Rule 16, Player at the Net (page 161).*

• Front-row players may attack (i.e., send over the net) the ball at any height, as well as block the ball (jump up to intercept or divert a ball arriving from the opposition). Back-row players may only attack hit at any height while they are in the back zone. If they move to the front zone, all attacking hits must be made when at least part of the ball is below the level of the net. They may not block the ball. *See Rule 18, Attack-Hit (page 164).*

SKILLS

The *serve* is a potentially dynamic start to a rally. The most basic is an underarm serve, although experienced players use a serve similar to that performed with a racket in tennis or the "jump" serve—in which a server throws the ball both up and forward and then runs to meet it, hitting it as he jumps into the air.

The *volley* is a basic two-handed overhead shot, used to keep the ball in play or pass it to another player.

The *dig* is made with both arms extended out to the front of the body and both hands clasped. The ball is met with the forearms. This is used to take the speed out of a forceful delivery or to make contact with a ball traveling low. Hardly any movement is used on impact.

The downward *smash* (or "spike") is made at the net by striking the ball rapidly downward into the opponents' court.

THE RULES OF VOLLEYBALL
❋ ❋ ❋ ❋ ❋ ❋ ❋ ❋ ❋

SECTION I: THE GAME

Chapter One: Facilities and Equipment
Rules 1–3
See page 158.

Chapter Two: Participants
Rules 4–5
See The Players (page 158).

Chapter Three: Playing Format
Rule 6-8
See Starting, How to win and Key Rules (page 159).

Set for a smash
The best volleyball teams take advantage of the "three touch" rule to set up a player for a smash. One player may pass the ball at the back of the court to a player near the net who sets it up at the right height for a spike.

7 Players' Positions
At the moment the ball is hit by the server, each team must be positioned within its own court in the rotational order (except the server).
7.4.1 The positions of the players are numbered as follows:
   a) the three players along the net are front-row players and occupy positions 4 (left), 3 (center), and 2 (right).
   b) the other three are back-row players and occupy positions 5 (left), 6 (center), and 1(right).
7.4.2 Relative positions between players
   a) each back-row player must be positioned further back from the center line than the corresponding front-row player.
   b) the front-row players and back-row players, respectively, must be positioned laterally in the order indicated in Rule 7.4.1.
7.4.3 The positions of players are determined and controlled according to the positions of their feet contacting the ground as follows:
   a) each front-row player must have at least part of one foot closer to the center line than the feet of the corresponding back-row player.
   b) each right (left) side player must have at least part of one foot closer to the right (left) sideline than the feet of the center player in the same row.
7.4.4 Once the ball has been served, the players may move and occupy any position on their own court and in the free zone.

7.5 Positional Fault
7.5.1 The team commits a positional fault if any player is not in the correct position at the moment the ball is hit by the server (Rule 7.4).
7.5.2 If the server commits a serving fault at the moment of the service hit, the server's fault is counted before a positional fault.
7.5.3 If the service becomes faulty after the service hit, it is the positional fault that will be counted.
7.5.4 A positional fault leads to the following consequences:
• the team is sanctioned with loss of rally.
• players positions are rectified.

7.6 Rotation
7.6.1 Rotational order is determined by the team's starting line-up and controlled with the service order and players' positions throughout the set.
7.6.2 When the receiving team has gained the right to serve, its players must rotate one position clockwise (player in position 2 rotates to position 1 to serve, player in 1 rotates to 6, etc.).

7.7 Rotational Faults
7.7.1 A rotational fault is committed when the service is not made according to the rotation order. It leads to the following consequences:
   a) the team is santioned with a loss of rally.
   b) the players' rotational order is rectified.
7.7.2 Additionally, the scorer should determine the exact moment the fault was committed. All points scored subsequently by the team at fault must be cancelled. The opponents' points remain valid. If that moment cannot be determined, no point(s) cancellation takes place, and loss of rally is the only sanction.

8 Substitution of Players
A substitution is the act by which the referee authorizes a player to leave the court and another player to occupy his position.

8.1 Limitations of Substitutions
8.1.1 Six substitutions is the maximum permitted per team per set. One or more players may be substituted at the same time.
8.1.2 A player of the starting line-up may leave the game and re-enter, but only once in a set, and only to the player's previous position in the line-up.
8.1.3 A substitute player may enter the game only once per set, in place of a player of the starting line-up, and can be replaced only by the same player.

8.2 Exceptional Substitution
An injured player who cannot continue playing should be legally substituted. If this is not possible, the team is entitled to make an exceptional substitution, beyond the limits of Rule 11.2.

8.3 Substitution for Expulsion
An expelled or disqualified player must be replaced through a legal substitution. If that is not possible, the team is declared incomplete.

8.4 Illegal Substitution
8.4.1 A substitution is illegal if it exceeds the limitations indicated in Rule 11.2.
8.4.2 When a team makes an illegal substitution and the play is resumed, the following procedure shall apply:
• the fault is penalized with the loss of a rally.
• the substitution is rectified.
• the points scored by the team at fault, after the fault was committed, are cancelled. The opponents' points remain valid.

8.5 The Libero Player
8.5.1 The Libero must be recorded on the score sheet before the match.
8.5.2 The Libero must wear a different colour uniform, shirt or jacket in contrast to the other members of the team (or with a different design).
The playing actions:
   a) the Libero is allowed to replace any player in a back row position.
   b) the Libero is restricted to perform as a back row player and is not allowed to complete an attack hit from anywhere if at the moment of the contact the ball is entirely higher than the top of the net.
   c) the Libero may not serve, block or attempt to block.
   d) a player may not complete an attack hit from higher than the top of the net, if the ball is coming from an overhead finger pass by a Libero in the front zone. The ball may be freely attacked if the Libero makes the same action from behind the front zone.
Replacement of players
   a) replacements involving the Libero are not counted as regular substitutions. They are unlimited, but there must be a rally between two Libero replacements. The Libero can only be replaced by the former player.
   b) Replacements can only take place:
      i) at the start of each set after the second referee has checked the starting line-up;
      ii) while the ball is out of play;
      iii) before the whistle for service.
   c) a Libero may only enter or leave the court by the sideline in front of the team bench between the attack line and the end line.
Replacement of an injured Libero:
   a) an injured Libero may be replaced during the match by any player who is not on court at the moment of the injury. The injured Libero may not re-enter to play for the remainder of the match.
   b) The player designated to replace an injured Libero must remain as a Libero for the remainder of the match.

Chapter Four: Playing Actions
9 States of Play
9.1 Ball "In Play"
The first referee's whistle authorizes the service.
9.2 Ball "Out of Play"
The rally ends with the referee's whistle.
9.3 Ball "In"
The ball is "in" when it touches the floor of the playing court including the boundary lines.
9.4 Ball "Out"
The ball is "out" when:
   a) the part of the ball that contacts the floor is completely outside the boundary lines,
   b) it touches an object outside the court, the ceiling or a person out of play,
   c) it touches the antennae, ropes, posts, or the net itself

outside the antennae/side bands,

d) it crosses completely underneath the vertical plane of the net.

10 Playing the Ball
Each team must play within its own playing area and space. The ball may, however, be retrieved from beyond the free zone.

10.1 Team Hits
The team is entitled to a maximum of three hits (in addition to blocking, Rule 15.4.1) for returning the ball. If more are used, the team commits the fault of "four hits."

10.1.1 Consecutive Contact
A player may not hit the ball twice consecutively (except Rule 10.2.3 and 15.2 & 15.4.2).

10.1.2 Simultaneous Contact
Two or three players may touch the ball at the same moment.

a) When two (3) teammates touch the ball simultaneously, it is counted as two (three) hits (except at blocking).

b) If simultaneous contacts by opponents lead to a "held ball," it is a double fault and the rally is replayed.

10.1.3 Assisted Hit
Within the playing area, a player is not permitted to take support from a team mate or any structure or object in order to reach the ball. However, the player who is about to commit a fault (touch the net or cross the center line etc.) may be stopped or held back by a teammate.

10.2 Characteristics of the Hit
10.2.1 The ball may touch any part of the body.

10.2..2 The ball must be hit, not caught or thrown. It can rebound in any direction.

10.2..3 The ball may touch various parts of the body, provided that the contacts take place simultaneously.

Exceptions:

a) At blocking, consecutive contacts may occur with one or more blockers provided that the contacts occur during one action.

b) At the first hit of a team (19.2) the ball may touch various parts of the body consecutively, provided that this occurs during one action.

10.3 Faults Playing the Ball
a) Four Hits: a team hits the ball four times before returning it

b) Assisted Hit: a player takes support from a teammate or any structure or object in order to reach the ball within the playing area.

c) Held Ball: a player does not hit the ball cleanly, but catches or holds it.

d) Double Contact: a player hits the ball twice in succession or the ball contacts various parts of the body successively.

11 Ball at the Net
11.1 Ball Crossing the Net
11.1.1. The ball sent to the opponents' court must go over the net within the crossing space. The crossing space is the part of the vertical plane of the net limited as follows:

• below, by the top of the net
• at the sides, by the antennae and their imaginary extension
• above, by the ceiling.

11.1.2 The ball that has crossed the net plane to the opponent's free zone (Rule 12) totally or partly outside of the crossing space, may be played back within the team hits provided that:

• the opponents' court is not touched by the player;
• the ball when played back crosses the net plane again through the external space on the same side of the court. The opposing team may not prevent such action.

11.2 Ball Touching the Net
When crossing the net (Rule 11.1.1) the ball may touch it, except during the service.

11.3 Ball in the Net (other than the service ball).
11.3.1 A ball driven into the net may be recovered within the limits of the three team hits.

11.2 If the ball rips the mesh of the net or tears it down, the rally is cancelled and replayed.

12 Player at the Net
12.1 Reaching Beyond the Net
12.1.1 In blocking, a blocker may touch the ball beyond the net, provided that there is no interference with the opponents' play before or during the latter's attack hit (Rule 15.3).

12..1.2 A player is permitted to pass a hand beyond the net after an attack hit, provided that the contact has been made within the player's own playing space.

12.2 Penetration Under the Net
12.2.1 It is permitted to penetrate into the opponents' space under the net, provided that this does not interfere with the opponents' play.

12.2.2 Penetration into the opponents' court:

a) to touch the opponents' court with a foot (feet) or hand(s) is permitted, provided that some part of the penetrating foot (feet) or hand(s) remains either in contact with or directly above the center line.

b) to contact the opponents'

court with any other part of the body is forbidden.

12.2.4 A player may enter the opponents' court after the ball is out of play (Rule 9.2). A player may penetrate into the opponents' free zone provided that there is no interference with the opponents' play.

12.3 Contact With the Net
12.3.1 Contact with the net is a fault, except when a player not attempting to play the ball accidentally touches the net.

12.3.2 Once a player has hit the ball, the player may touch the posts, ropes, or any other object outside the total length of the net provided that it does not interfere with play.

12.3.3 When the ball is driven into the net and causes it to touch an opponent, no fault is committed.

12.4 Player's Faults at the Net
It is a fault if:

a) a player touches the ball in the opponents' space before or during the opponents' attack hit (Rule 12.1.1).

b) a player penetrates into the opponents' space under the net interfering with the latter's play (Rule 12.2.1).

c) a player penetrates into the opponents' court (Rule 12.2.2).

d) a player touches the net (Rule 12.3.1).

13 Service
The service is the act of putting the ball into play by the right back-row player, placed in the service zone (Rule 13.4.1).

13.1 First Service in a Set
13.1.1 The first service of sets one and five is executed by the team determined by the toss (Rule 7.1).

13.1.2 The other sets will be started with the service of the team that did not serve first in the previous set.

13.2 Service Order
13.3.1 The players must follow the service order recorded on the line-up sheet.

13.2.2 After the first service in a set, the player to serve is determined as follows:

a) when the serving team wins the rally, the player who served before, serves again.

b) when the receiving team wins the rally, it gains the right to serve and rotates. The player who moves from the right front-row position to the right back-row position will serve.

13.3 Authorization of the Service
The first referee authorizes the service after having checked that

the two teams are ready to play and that the server is in possession of the ball.

13.4 Execution of the Service
13.4.1 The ball shall be hit with one hand or any part of the arm after being tossed or released and before it touches any other part of the body or the playing surface.

13.4.2 At the moment of the service hit or take-off for a jump service, the server must not touch the court (the end line included) nor the ground outside the service zone. After the service hit, the player may step or land outside the zone, or inside the court.

13.4.3 The server must hit the ball within eight seconds after the first referee whistles for service.

13.4.4 A service executed before the referee's whistle is cancelled and repeated.

13.5 Screening
13.5.1 The players of the serving team must not prevent their opponent, through individual or collective screening, from seeing the server and the path of the ball.

13.5.2 A player or group of players make a screen by waving arms, jumping or moving sideways during the execution of the service, or by standing grouped to cover the flight path of the ball.

13.6 Faults made During the Service
13.6.1 Serving Faults
The following faults lead to a change of service even if the opponents are out of position when the server:

a) violates the service order,

b) does not execute the service properly,

13.6.2 Faults After the Service Hit
After the ball has been correctly hit, the service becomes a fault (unless a player is out of position) if the ball:

a) touches a player of the serving team or fails to cross the vertical plane of the net,

b) touches the net,

c) goes "out,"

d) passes over a screen.

13.7 Faults After the Service and Positional Faults
13.7.1 If the server makes a fault at the moment of the service hit and the opponent is out of position, it is the serving fault which is penalized.

13.7.2 Instead, if the execution of the service has been correct,

➡ *page 164*

Beach game?
Beach volleyball is not just a game for sunbathers, but a major spectator sport. This is the arena at Clearwater, Florida.

Hand tennis
Unlike indoor volleyball, beach volleyball involves just two players.

Tennis serve
The tennis serve, facing the net, can be made either from a standstill or by stepping into the serve for extra power. The ball is hit with the open hand and the arm completely straight. The serve is followed through to carry the player forward into play.

Hand to hand
Above, two beach volleyball players clash at the net in a quick interchange. This is one of the only occasions on which part of a player's body may cross the net.

Service stations
The underarm and tennis services tend to be the most popular. Players often try to give the ball a spin to fool opponents.

The dig
With the dig, the two hands are kept close together and the ball is lifted with the forearms facing upward.

Just before receiving the ball the player bends his knees, then straightens them as he hits it.

Digging out
The dig is used by players receiving the ball from a serve or to play a ball that is too low to volley.

TACTICS

The standard procedure for receiving and returning the ball is the dig-set-spike approach. The three hits permitted to a team are used to absorb the speed of a serve, pass it (setting it up for the smash), and then spike (i.e., smash) it over the net, hopefully to win the rally.

Up for the spike
The spike involves smashing the ball down into the opposition's court to complete a classic three touch move.

Plan B
The best volleyball teams exploit the three touch rule in a number of carefully planned dig, set and spike movements. This player is indicating a maneuver.

Smashing run
While teammates set up the ball, the spiker runs in to gain maximum height, smashing the ball right at the net.

GRAY AREA
Traditionally volleyball was very strict about which parts of the body could be used to strike the ball, but in recent years the rules have been changed to allow other parts of the body to be used in order to make the game faster, better flowing, and more exciting for spectators. Rule changes have also allowed players more leniency when playing the ball, a move that has split players and coaches into those teaching the new skills and those who prefer a more traditional approach with a strict technical interpretation on the handling rules.

continued from page 161

but the service subsequently becomes faulty (touches the net, goes out, screened, etc.), the positional fault has taken place first and is penalized.

14 Attack-Hit
14.1 Definition
14.1.1 All actions to direct the ball toward the opponent, except service and block, are considered attack-hits.

18.1.2 During an attack-hit tipping is permitted if the contact is clean, and the ball is not caught or thrown.

14.1.3 An attack-hit is completed the moment the ball completely crosses the vertical plane of the net, or is touched by an opponent.

14.2 Restrictions of the Attack-Hit
A front-row player may complete an attack-hit at any height provided that the contact with the ball has been made within the player's own playing space.

14.2.2 A back-row player may complete an attack-hit at any height from behind the front zone:

   a) at take-off the player's foot (feet) must have neither touched nor crossed over the attack line.

   b) after the hit the player may land within the front zone.

14.2.3 A back-row player may also complete an attack-hit from the front zone, if at the moment of contact the ball is not entirely higher than the top of the net.

14.3 Attack-Hit Faults
An attack-hit fault is committed when:

   a) a player hits the ball within the playing space of the opposing team;

   b) a player hits the ball "out";

   c) a back-row player completes an attack-hit from the front zone, if at the moment of the hit the ball is entirely above the top of the net;

   d) a player completes an attack-hit on the opponents' service, when the ball is in the front zone and entirely higher than the top of the net.

15 Block
15.1 Blocking
15.1.1 Blocking is the action of players close to the net to intercept the ball coming from the opponents by reaching higher than the top of the net. Only front-row players are permitted to complete a block.

15.1.2 Block Attempt
A block attempt is the action of blocking without touching the ball.

15.1.3 Completed Block
A block is completed whenever the ball is touched by a blocker.

19.1.3 Collective Block
A collective block is executed by two or three players close to each other and is completed when one of them touches the ball.

15.2 Block Contact
Consecutive (quick and continuous) contacts may occur by one or more blockers, provided that the contacts are made during one action.

19.4.2 These contacts may occur with any part of the body.

15.3 Blocking Within the Opponent's Space
In blocking, the player may place his/her hands and arms beyond the net provided that this action does not interfere with the opponents' play. Thus, it is not permitted to touch the ball beyond the net until an opponent has executed an attack hit.

15.4 Block and Team Hits
15.4.1 A block contact is not counted as a team hit. Consequently, after a block contact, a team is entitled to three hits to return the ball.

15.4.2 The first hit after the block may be executed by any player, including the one who has touched the ball during the block.

15.5 Blocking the Service
To block an opponent's service is forbidden.

15.6 Blocking Faults
   a) The blocker touches the ball in the opponents' space either before or simultaneously with the opponents' action.

   b) A back-row player completes a block or participates in a completed one.

   c) A player blocks the opponents' service.

   d) The ball is sent "out" off the block.

   e) A player blocks the ball in the opponents' space from outside the antenna.

   f) A Libero completes or attempts a block, or participates in a completed block.

Chapter Five: Interruptions and Delays

16 Regular Game Interruptions
Regular game interruptions are time-outs and player substitutions.

16.1 Number of Regular Interruptions
Each team is entitled to a maximum of two time-outs and six player substitutions per set.

16.2 Request for Regular Interruptions
16.2.1 Interruptions may be requested only by the coach or

the game captain. The request is made by showing the corresponding hand signal when the ball is out of play and before the whistle for service.

16.2.2 A request for substitution before the start of a set is permitted and should be recorded as a regular substitution in that set.

16.3 Sequence of Interruptions
16.3.1 A request for one or two time-outs and one request for player substitution by either team may follow one another, with no need to resume the game.

16.3.2 However, a team is not authorized to make consecutive requests for player substitutions during the same interruption of play. Two or more players may be substituted during the same interruption (Rule 8.1.1).

16.4 Time-Outs
16.4.1 A time-out lasts for 30 seconds.

16.4.2 During all time-outs, the players in play must go to the free zone near their bench.

16.5 Player Substitution
16.5.1 Substitution must be carried out within the substitution zone (Rule 1.4.3).

16.5.2 A substitution shall last only the time needed for recording the substitution on the scoresheet, and allowing the entry and exit of the players.

16.5.3 At the moment of the request, the player(s) must be ready to enter, standing close to the substitution zone (Rule 1.4.3). If that is not the case, the substitution is not granted and the team is sanctioned for a delay (Rule 17.2).

16.5.4 If the coach intends to make more than one substitution, the number must be signaled at the time of the request. In this case, substitutions must be made in succession, one pair of players after another.

16.6 Improper Requests
It is improper to request an interruption:

   a) during a rally or at the moment of, or after, the whistle to serve;

   b) by a non-authorized team member;

   c) for player substitution before the game has been resumed from a previous substitution by the same team;

   d) after having exhausted the authorized number of time-outs and player substitutions;

16.6.2 Any improper request that does not affect or delay the game shall be rejected without any sanction unless repeated in the same set.

17 Game Delays
17.1 Types of Delay
Any action of a team that defers resumption of the game is a delay and includes:

   a) delaying a substitution;

   b) prolonging other interruptions, after having been instructed to resume the game;

   c) requesting an illegal substitution;

   d) repeating an improper request in the same match;

   e) delaying the game by a player in play.

17.2 Sanctions for Delays
17.2.1 "Delay warning" or "delay penalty" are team sanctions.

   a) delay sanctions remain in force for the entire match.

   b) all delay sanctions are recorded on the scoresheet.

17.2.2 The first delay by a team in a set is sanctioned with a "delay warning."

The sanction of delay warning is a team sanction.

17.2.3 The second and subsequent delays of any type by any player or other member of the same team in the same match constitute a fault and are sanctioned with a "delay penalty;" loss of rally (Rule 6.1.2).

17.2.4 Delay sanctions imposed before or between sets are applied in the following set.

18 Exceptional Game Interruptions
18.1 Injury
18.1.1 Should a serious accident occur while the ball is in play, the referee must stop the game immediately. The rally is then replayed.

18.1.2 If an injured player cannot be substituted, legally or exceptionally, the player is given a three-minute recovery time, but not more than once for the same player in the match. If the player does not recover, the team is declared incomplete.

18.2 External Interference
If there is any external interference during the game, play has to be stopped and the rally is replayed.

18.3 Prolonged Interruptions
18.3.1 If unforeseen circumstances interrupt the match, the first referee shall decide the measures to be taken to reestablish normal conditions.

18.3.2 Should one or several interruptions occur, not exceeding four hours in total, then:

   a) if the match is resumed on the same playing court, the interrupted set shall continue normally with the same score, players and positions. The sets already played will keep their scores.

b) if the match is resumed on another court, the interrupted set is cancelled and replayed with the same starting line-ups. The sets already played keep their scores.

18.3.3 Should one or several interruptions occur, exceeding four hours in total, the whole match shall be replayed.

19 Intervals and Change of Courts
19.1 Intervals
All intervals between sets last three minutes. During this period of time, the change of courts and line-up registration of the teams on the score sheets are made.
19.2 Change of Courts
19.2.1 After each set, the teams change courts, with the exception of the deciding set . Other team members change benches.
19.2.2 In the deciding set, once a team reaches eight points, the teams change courts without delay and the player positions remain the same.
If the change is not made at the proper time, it will take place as soon as the error is noticed. The score at the time that the change is made remains the same.

Chapter Six: Participants' Conduct
20.1 Sportsmanlike Conduct
20 1.1 Participants must know the Rules and abide by them.
20.1.2 Participants must accept referees' decisions with sportsmanlike conduct, without disputing them. In case of doubt,

clarification may be requested only through the game captain.
20.1.3 Participants must refrain from actions or attitudes aimed at influencing the decisions of the referees or covering up faults committed by their team.
20.2 Fair Play
20.2.1 Participants must behave respectfully and courteously in the spirit of Fair Play, not only towards the referees, but also towards officials, the opponents, team-mates and spectators.

21 Misconduct and its Sanctions
21.1 Minor Misconduct
It is the first referee's duty to prevent the teams from approaching the sanctioning level by issuing a verbal or hand signal warning to the team through the game captain. This warning is not a penalty and has no immediate consequences. It should not be recorded on the score sheet.
21.2 Misconduct Leading to Sanctions
Incorrect conduct by a team member towards officials, opponents, team mates or spectators is classified in three categories according to the seriousness of the offense.
21.2.1 Rude conduct: action contrary to good manners or moral principles or expressing contempt.
21.2.2 Offensive conduct: defamatory or insulting words or gestures.

21.2.3 Aggression: physical attack or intended aggression.
21.3 Sanction Scale
According to the judgement of the first referee, the sanctions to be applied are as set out in the chart below.

21.4 Application of Misconduct Sanctions
21.4.1 All misconduct sanctions are individual sanctions, remain in force for the entire match and are recorded on the score sheet.
21.4.2 The repetition of misconduct by the same team member in the same match is sanctioned progressively (the team member receives a heavier sanction for each successive offense).
21.4.3 Expulsion or disqualification due to offensive conduct or aggression does not require a previous

sanction.
21.5 Misconduct Before and Between Sets
Any misconduct occurring before or between sets is sanctioned according to Rules 21.3 (see chart) and sanctions apply in the following set.

SECTION II
Refers to Match Officials.

These rules are reprinted by permission of the International Volleyball Association. A complete copy of the Volleyball International Rules can be obtained from United States of America Volleyball.

Misconduct sanction scale

Categories	Occurrence (for a team) - Offender	Sanction	Cards	Consequence
Rude conduct	1st - any member	Penalty	Yellow	Loss of rally
	2nd - same member	Expulsion	Red	Shall leave the playing area and stay behind the bench in the Penalty Area for the remainder of the set
	3rd - same member	Disqualification	Red + Yellow jointly	Shall leave the Competition Control Area for the rest of the match
Offensive conduct	1st - any member	Expulsion	Red	Shall leave the playing area and stay behind the bench in the Penalty Area for the remainder of the set
	2nd - same member	Disqualification	Red + Yellow jointly	Shall leave the Competition Control Area for the rest of the match
Agression conduct	1st - any member	Disqualification	Red + Yellow jointly	Shall leave the Competition Control Area for the rest of the match

Delay sanction style

Delay	1st - any member	Delay Warning	Hand Signal No. 25	Prevention – No penalty
	2nd - (and subsequents) any member	Delay Penalty	Hand Signal No. 25 with yellow card	Loss of rally

Korfball
Essentials

A relative of Netball (*see* last chapter), this flexible no-contact game is played by men and women together either outdoors or indoors. It involves shooting the ball through baskets placed at either end of the court. The game owes its name to its origin in the Netherlands (*korfball* is Dutch for basketball).

Out line

Out line

2.5m
2.5m
2.5m
2.5m

Inner dividing line

40 m Indoor (44 yds)
60 m Outdoor (66 yds)

During a penalty all players, other than the taker, must observe a distance of 2.5 m from any point on an imaginary line between the spot and the post.

Penalty spot

Basket

6.67 m   2.5 m

20 m indoor (22 yds)
30 m outdoor (33 yds)

The court

Indoor courts are 40 m by 20 m (44 yds by 22 yds), outdoor (generally grass or artificial grass) are 60 m by 30 m (66 yds by 33 yds). Divided into two equal zones. The field of play is marked out by clearly visible lines or tape, 3–5 cm wide (approx 1½ in). The height of the ceiling for an indoor court must be no less than 7 m (23 ft).

Baskets

Cane, one color, fitted to round posts which are placed in each half, 6.66 m (22 ft) from each end. The basket is 25 cm (10 in) high, with an inner diameter of 39–41 cm (approx 16 in) and its top edge is 3.5 m (11 ft) above the ground.

Officials

A referee, a timekeeper, and two linesmen.

Grass court

Unlike basketball, which it in some ways resembles, korfball is often played outdoors on grass. The field of play is usually marked out by white tape. Indoors it is played on a smaller court on an artificial surface.

Mixed match

Korfball is a rare game explicitly designed for men and women to play together. A special rule (see Rule 16k, page 168) prevents anyone from interfering with a throw made by a member of the opposite sex.

The players

Two teams of four male and four female players each. Two men and two women are positioned in each zone. (Up to two substitutions are permitted, possibly more at the discretion of the referee in the case of injury.) Of course, single sex games are possible.

The ball

A number 5 soccer ball, round, with a leather (or approved material) outer casing. Two-colored for indoor games. It may, however, be only one color for outdoor games. A circumference of 68–71 cm (approx. 27 in) and a weight of 425–475 g (approx. 16 oz) at the start of a match.

Dress

Uniform throughout a team and different than that of the opposing team. Shoes must be worn. Players are not allowed to wear objects that may cause injuries during the game. The captain of each team must also wear a band on the upper part of the left arm.

On the run
Players are not normally allowed to run with the ball. However, they may continue running if they catch the ball on the run and combine it with a single throwing movement. It is up to the referee to decide whether the run was within the rules.

The rules of korfball actively encourage tactical awareness and cooperation within a team. For example, Rule 16e prevents a player from indulging in solo play and 16n (outlawing shooting from a defended position) makes it necessary for players to work together to establish free positions on the court from which shots may be taken.

HOW TO PLAY

Teams score goals by shooting the ball into their opponents' basket. The ball must be handled only with the hands—not with a fist or with the legs or feet. Players are not allowed to run with the ball; they must pass or shoot it quickly.

Starting

The home team chooses a basket for the first half and both teams arrange their players as attackers or defenders in the two zones. Play begins with a throw by an attacker from a point inside his zone, near the center of the field. Each time two goals have been scored, players' roles change, i.e., attackers become defenders and vice versa. At halftime there is a change of ends, but players' roles do not change.

How to win

The winner is the team with the most goals.

KEY RULES

• A game consists of two halves of 30 minutes each (35 minutes for outdoor games), with a 10-minute rest. Teams also have the right to two 60-second time-outs.

• Players must not run with the ball, but they are allowed to pivot on one foot while in possession and in a stationary position. If the ball is caught while running, the player must either stop completely or pass it to another player before he takes three steps.

• It is against the rules to knock the ball out of an opponent's hand or to impede her progress with an arm or leg extended across her path. Intentional contact is not permitted and

defense must not involve actual physical obstruction. Defenders attempt to intercept the ball to gain possession.

• Shots at goal must not be made from a defended position, i.e., when a defender is within arm's length of the shooter, facing him and nearer to the post than he is. *See Infringement of the Rules, Rule 16 (page 168).*

• Players must play the ball while in their own zones. The ball itself is out of bounds if it touches a boundary line or anything beyond it. An out-ball is penalized by a free pass against the offending team. *See Rule 17, Out-Ball (page 168).*

• A violation of the rules incurs a free pass taken from the spot where the infringement occurred. *See Rule 19, Free Pass (page 169).*

• An infringement that causes a team to lose a scoring opportunity awards a penalty shot to the non-offending team. This is taken from the penalty spot 2.5 m (8 ft) in front of the opposition's post. The attacking player taking the penalty must be allowed an unimpeded shot, all other players remaining at least 2.5 m (8 ft) from him until the ball is shot (or passed). *See Rule 20, penalty (page 169).*

SKILLS AND TACTICS

Agility and deft handling of the ball are important skills. However, good defensive play is also a vital element of the game. Players must master the art of "fair hindering"—marking (following) an opponent so that their moves and options with the ball are restricted as much as possible while respecting the ban on intentional physical contact.

High scoring
Since the basket in korfball is higher than in basketball, there is little possibility of even the tallest player jumping up and dunking the ball.

KORFBALL
THE RULES
INDOOR

Chapter 1 Hall, Ground, and Material: Rules 1–5

Chapter 2 Persons: Rules 6–10

See The players (page 166).

Chapter 3 The Game: Rules 11–15

See How to play (page 167).

16 Infringement of the Rules

During the game it is prohibited:
a) to touch the ball with leg or foot.
If the touching is unintentional and exerts no important influence upon the game it will not be punished.
b) to hit the ball with the fist
c) to take hold of the ball in a fallen position
d) to run with the ball
Running with the ball is contrary to the requirement of cooperation. Change of position with possession of the ball is therefore only permitted when otherwise it would be impossible to pass the ball fluently or to shoot or to stop with the ball.
In applying these principles three cases are to be distinguished.

1. When seizing the ball the player stands at rest.
In this case he may move one leg at will, provided the other one remains in its place. Turning on the latter is permitted.

2. When seizing the ball the player is running or jumping, first stops and afterwards throws the ball or shoots. The requirement is that, after seizing the ball, he has immediately and fully tried to come to a stop.
After coming to a stop, the same rules apply as mentioned under 1.

3. After seizing the ball while running or jumping the player throws the ball or shoots before he has come to a stop completely. In this case the player is not allowed to be still in possession of the ball at the moment that he places his foot on the ground for the third time after receiving the ball.
e) to avoid cooperation (solo-play)
Solo-play is not punishable:
1. when the player does not change his position appreciably.
2. when the avoidance of cooperation was not intentional.
f) to hand the ball to another of one's own team
g) to delay the game

The right place
In korfball you are not allowed to move with the ball at all, so position is everything. Each player must not only be well positioned to receive passes from teammates, but also well positioned to pass the ball on to someone else.

h) to knock, take, or run the ball out of an opponent's hand
i) to push, to cling to, or to hold off an opponent
This unlawful hindering of an opponent has to be punished no matter whether this opponent does or does not possess the ball even if the ball is in another zone. Every impediment of the free movement of an opponent is forbidden whether this is done deliberately or not.
This rule does not force a player to give way for another player, i.e., each player allowed to position himself just as he pleases. He will only be punished when he jumps so suddenly in the path of a moving opponent that a collision becomes inevitable.
j) to hinder an opponent excessively
This rule applies when the opponent has the ball in his possession.
The hindering player is allowed to hinder the throwing of the ball in the desired direction by actions that result in the ball being thrown against his hand or arm.
He is allowed to block the ball by bringing his arm in the path of the ball, but he must not:
1. hinder his opponent in the free use of his body by blocking the arm instead of the ball;
2. beat the ball or hit the throwing arm, i.e., the hindering arm or hand must not move toward the ball at the instant of contact.
Unexpected movements by an opponent will often cause a restriction in a player's freedom of movement. Such cases will not be punished, provided immediate action is taken by the opponent to restore the player's freedom of movement.
k) to hinder an opponent of the opposite sex in throwing the ball
l) to hinder an opponent who is already being hindered by another player
m) to play outside one's zone
n) to shoot from a defended position
The shot must be considered defended when the hindering defender satisfies each of the following three conditions:

1. he must be within arm's length of the attacker and must have his face turned toward him;
2. he must actually try to block the ball;
3. he must be nearer the post than the attacker, except when he and the attacker are near and on opposite sides of the post. In the latter case conditions 1 and 2 alone are sufficient.
o) to shoot after cutting past another attacker
Cutting occurs when a defender, who is within arm's length of his attacker, cannot follow this attacker because the attacker runs so close past another attacker that the defender collides with, or is likely to collide with, this attacker and is therefore forced to give up his position within arm's length.
p) to shoot from the defense zone, from a free pass or from a referee throw (throw-up).
q) to shoot when one plays without a personal opponent
This occurs when the defense has only three players against an attack of four players. In that case the captain of the attacking side must inform the referee and the other captain which of his attackers will not shoot.
The captain is entitled to change his decision during the match, but only after informing the referee and the other captain at a time when the ball is dead (i.e., the referee has blown for an infringement, a goal, etc). This

change of an attacker is only allowed twice between a change of zones. A goal can be made from a penalty by an attacker without a personal opponent.
r) to influence a shot by moving the post
s) to take hold of the post when jumping, running, or in order to move away quickly
t) to violate the conditions laid down for a free pass or a penalty
u) to play in a dangerous manner
For an attacker to force his defender, who is within arm's distance of the attacker, to collide at speed with another attacker.

17 Out-Ball

The ball is out as soon as it touches a boundary line of the field of play, the ground, a person, or an object outside the field of play. The ball is also out when it touches the ceiling or an object above the field of play.
In the case of an out-ball a free pass is awarded against the side who touched the ball last.

18 Referee Throw (Throw-Up)

When two opponents seize the ball simultaneously, the referee will stop play and will throw the ball up. The same applies when play must be restarted without one side being entitled to the ball. For this purpose the referee chooses two players from the zone concerned, who must be of the same sex and if possible of about the same height. These two players may touch the ball after the ball has reached its highest point during the throw-up. The other players must observe a distance of 2.5 m (8 ft) and may only touch the ball after one of the two selected players has touched the ball or after the ball has been in contact with the ground. The attacker selected by the referee for the throw-up is not allowed to shoot directly from the throw-up.

19 Free Pass

a) when to award a free pass

A free pass is awarded to the opposing side after the referee has indicated that one of the rules (16 or 17) has been violated.

b) place of the free pass

The free pass is taken from the spot where the infringement was committed. If the infringement was committed against a certain person (16h, i, j, k, l, and sometimes m), then the free pass is taken from the spot where this person was standing.

In the case of an out-ball or when 16 m (17.5 yds) has been violated on or outside the boundaries of the field of play, then the free pass is taken from outside the field near the boundary line where the ball or the offending player crossed the line.

When the ball is out because it touches the ceiling or an object above the field of play, the free pass is taken near one of the long boundaries and nearest to the spot where the ball touched the ceiling or the object.

c) how to take a free pass

At the moment that the player taking the free pass has, or can take, the ball in his hands the referee lifts one of his arms vertically and gives the signal with four fingers on his raised hand that he is going to whistle for the commencement of play within four seconds. Following the raising of the arm there are two possibilities (see A and B below).

A. 1. All the players are at a distance of at least 2.5 m (8 ft) from the taker of the free pass.

2. When the free pass is taken in the attack zone the players of the same team as the taker of the free pass are also at a distance of at least 2.5 m (8 ft) from each other.

As soon as the above situation exists within the four seconds preparation time the referee

shall blow his whistle to restart play. The player taking the free pass must bring the ball into play within no more than four seconds after the whistle has blown for the commencement of play (8c). If the taker of the free pass has not brought the ball into play within this period, then the referee shall blow his whistle and award a free pass to the other side. The players of the opposing team must remain meeting condition 1 until the taker of the free pass moves the ball or makes a clearly visible movement of an arm or leg.

The players of the same team as the taker of the free pass must remain meeting conditions 1 and 2 until the ball has been brought into play. The ball is brought into play when either 1. a player of the opposing team touches the ball or 2. a player of the same team as the player taking the free pass touches the ball while standing at least 2.5 m (8 ft) from the spot at which the pass has been taken or 3. the ball has traveled at least 2.5m (8 ft) from the place of the free pass (measured along the ground).

The player taking the free pass is not allowed to shoot directly from the free pass. He can only shoot when the ball has moved freely through the air and has been touched by another player. When the person taking the free pass touches a boundary line, or the playing area on the other side of the boundary line, after the referee has blown his whistle to indicate that the free pass can be taken and the ball has left his hands, then the referee awards a free pass to the opposing side on the other side of the boundary line.
B. When the players do not meet conditions 1 and 2 above

in A within four seconds of the referee raising his arm, he will whistle twice quickly in succession, the first time to re-start the game and the second time to stop play, and punish the infringing team with a free pass. If players from both teams are within 2.5 m (8 ft) then the referee will punish the player who is nearest to the taker of the free pass. If the referee considers players from both teams are at the same incorrect distance then the attacking team shall be penalized. When the defending team in the attacking zone makes this infringement for the second time at the same free pass the referee will give a penalty.

20 Penalty

a) when to award a penalty

Infringements that result in the loss of a scoring chance are punished by the award of a penalty to

the other side. A penalty can also be awarded for other infringements that repeatedly hinder the attack unfairly.

b) place of a penalty

The penalty must be taken from the penalty spot (see 2) that is 2.5 m (8ft) from the post as seen from the center of the field.

c) how to take a penalty

It is permitted to score directly from a penalty. The person taking the penalty must not touch the ground between the post and the penalty spot with any part of his body before the ball has left his hands. The penalty must be retaken if it is taken before the referee has blown his whistle to indicate that the penalty may be taken.

All other players must observe a distance of 2.5 m (8 ft) (in all directions) from any point on the imaginary line between the spot and the post. They must refrain from any actions or comments that may disturb the person taking the penalty.

If necessary the first, as well as the second, half of the match will be prolonged for the taking of a penalty.

These rules are reprinted by permission of the International Korfball Federation. A complete copy of the rules, including explanations to the rules and outdoor variations, is available from the Federation.

On the defense
Players can stand in the path of an attacker but they may not use their arms to prevent them from running past.

Lawn bowling
Essentials

Sometimes called simply "bowls" or "flat green bowls," this game for indoors or outdoors predates American bowling.

37–40 m (120–130 ft)

37–40 m (120–130 ft)

Bank
230 mm (9 in)
above green

5.5–5.8m

Rink

Ditch
200-380 mm
(8–15 in) wide,
50–200 mm
(2–8 in) deep

The green

Square with a grass or artificial surface. Sides measure 37–40 meters (120–132 ft) outdoors, although indoor greens may have sides as short as 34 meters (about 110 ft). The green is surrounded by a *ditch*, 8–15 inches wide, 2–8 inches deep. (Indoors, only the end of each rink must have a ditch). The green is boarded by a short wall, or *bank*, no less than 9 inches above the level of the green.

The green is divided into several rinks (lanes), numbered consecutively, 5.5–5.8 m (18–19 ft) wide for outdoor greens and 4.6–5.8 m (15–19 ft) indoors. White wooden pegs with green thread drawn tightly between them define the boundaries of each rink.

The mat

Black rubber, usually with a border of white, 600 mm (24 in) long and 360 mm (14 in) wide.

The jack

Spherical, white or yellow in color. A diameter of 63–64 mm (approx. 2.5 in) and weight of 225–285 g (8–10 oz) for outdoor games. For indoor games, the jack may be slightly larger and up to 6 ounces heavier.

Bowls

Wood, rubber, or mixed, with a diameter of 4.5–5.3 inches (non-wood bowls must be no larger than 5.2 inches in diameter). Maximum weight 3.5 lb. Black, brown, or other approved color. Each bowl must have an approved bias (the degree to which it deviates from a straight line as it travels down the green) and an individual distinguishing mark on both sides for international matches.

Smooth as a bowling green
Lawn bowling is frequently played outdoors on grass. Such natural lawns need a huge amount of work to maintain their perfectly smooth manicured surfaces.

Crown green bowls

Crown green bowls is played mostly in the north of England, where it originated. Generally a game between two players, it uses a green that has a raised "crown" at its center.

Officials

An umpire and a marker.

Dress

Traditionally all white for both men and women. Footwear is smooth and without heels to protect the surface of the green.

Players

Two players in a singles game; two teams of two players in a pairs game; two teams of three players in a triples game; two teams of four players in a fours game; two teams of equal size in a side game. Positions in order of playing are lead, second, third, etc. The last bowler is called the *skip*.

White or not?
Traditionally bowlers wore all white with brown shoes. There is an increasing tendency among younger players and those playing the sport at high levels to opt for colored tops and white shoes.

Hard choice
Bowls come in different sizes, weights, and colors and differences can be substantial. Experienced bowlers select a bowl to suit individual greens.

How to play

The object is for players to get their bowls closer to the jack than their opponents' bowls. Players (or teams) deliver bowls alternately. After all bowls are thrown, an "end" is over. The next end is played from the opposite end of the rink (lane).

Starting

Players or teams toss to decide who bowls first. The first bowler then centers the mat on the center line of the rink with its front edge 2 m (6.5 ft) from the ditch. (It is picked up after each end and moved to the other end of the rink). With one foot within or above the confines of the mat, the player delivers the jack, making sure that it remains inside the rink, at least 2 m from the front ditch and at least 21 m (69 ft) from the front of the mat (23 m from the mat when indoors). At this point, the player may throw his first bowl.

Foot faults

A delivery is legal if the player keeps one foot on the mat throughout.

A delivery is also legal if one of the player's feet is above the mat, but entirely within its confines.

A delivery is illegal if a player ends up with both feet entirely off and outside the confines of the mat.

Bowling
The best way to clasp a bowl is with a natural grip. The fingers spread around the ball and the thumb gives it extra security on the far side. The fingers should be roughly parallel and the bowl should lie straight in the palm ready to roll in any intended direction.

GRAY AREA
Because bowls are played in parallel rinks there is always a danger of bowls straying in from neighboring lanes. This is frequently a source of conflict. Traditionally players had lifted a bowl or jack to prevent it being knocked out of place by a stray bowl. In 1994 this practice was made legal (Law 37f), but there is still concern about how to use this law. The point is that the bowl may only be lifted when doing so will not affect play. It must be replaced in exactly the same place and at the same angle—which often leads to controversy.

Stand and deliver
A delivery begins with the player standing with both feet firmly on the mat pointing in the right direction. He then swings back his bowling arm at the same time as stepping rapidly forward on the opposite leg. Then with his free hand on his bent knee to steady himself he swings his arm forward and releases the bowl.

- If a bowl fails to travel at least 14 m from the front of the mat, ends up in a ditch (unless it is a toucher), or goes out of the rink, it is called a "dead bowl" and is removed from the rink. *See Law 35, Ball Accounted "Dead" (page 172).*

How to win
The player or team with the bowl closest to the jack wins the end. However, shots are scored for each bowl that is closer to the jack than any of the opposition's bowls. The winner is the player or team with the highest number of shots at the end of the match.

Note these variations for top level matches:

Singles—Each player throws four bowls per end, delivered alternately. The winner is the first to score 25 shots.

Pairs—Four bowls per player, played alternately. The game lasts for 21 ends.

Triples—Three bowls per player, played alternately. The game lasts for 18 ends.

Fours—Two bowls per player, played alternately. The game lasts for 21 ends.

KEY RULES

- A bowl must be "live" in order to score, i.e., it must come to rest within the boundaries of the rink, no less than 14 m from the front edge of the mat. A bowl becomes a *toucher* if it touches the jack on its original course on the green. A toucher remains live even if it ends up in the ditch. (Touchers are marked with chalk that is removed after each end). *See Laws 31–33 (page 172).*

- The jack becomes dead if it is driven away by a bowl so that it passes beyond the face of the bank, comes to rest beyond the side boundary, or rebounds to within 18 m (35 yds) (20 m for indoor games) of the front edge of the mat. A dead jack means that the end is dead and must be replayed from the start. *See Laws 40 and 41 (page 172).*

SKILLS AND TACTICS

The *draw* is a basic shot, played both forehand and backhand and used to guide the bowl toward the jack. Players must judge both length and line accurately—i.e., both the distance the bowl must travel and the curving path it must take. The *trail* uses a slightly overweighted delivery to not only hit the jack but also to shift its position on the green. The *drive*, or firing shot, is a bowl that is delivered with extra force in order to knock an opponent's bowls out of the way or to edge the jack out of position in order to break down an opponent's advantage.

The *skip* is in charge of the team and directs play. The *lead* establishes play with the first two bowls, trying to get them as close to the jack as possible and is followed by the *second*. The *third* acts generally as deputy to the skip. The third and skip in particular must be skilled at all aspects of the game. They are usually the most experienced members of the team.

Young or old
One of the attractions of lawn bowling is that people of all ages and fitness levels have a chance to develop expertise. Recently an Australian man celebrated his 100th birthday with a marathon game of bowls.

THE LAWS OF LAWN BOWLING
* * * * * * * * * *

Laws 1–30

See pages 170–171.

Movement of Bowls

31. "Live" Bowl

A bowl that, in its original course on the green, comes to rest within the boundaries of the rink, and not less than 14m (15.3 ft) from the front edge of the mat, shall be accounted as a "Live" Bowl and shall be in play.

32. "Touchers"

A bowl that, in its original course on the green touches the jack, even though such a bowl passes into the ditch within the boundaries of the rink, shall be counted as a "live" bowl and shall be called a "toucher." If after having come to rest a bowl falls over and touches the jack before the next succeeding bowl is delivered, or if in the case of the last bowl of an end it falls and touches the jack within the period of 30 seconds invoked under Law 52, such a bowl shall also be a "toucher."

No bowl shall be accounted a "toucher" by playing on to, or by coming into contact with, the jack while the jack is in the ditch. If a "toucher" in the ditch cannot be seen from the mat its position shall be marked by a white or colored indicator about 50 mm (2 in) broad placed upright on the top of the bank and immediately in line with the place where the "toucher" rests.

33. Marking a "Toucher"

A "toucher" shall be clearly marked with a chalk mark by a member of the player's team. If, in the opinion of either skip, or opponent in singles, a "toucher" or a wrongly chalked bowl comes to rest in such a position that the act of making a chalk mark, or of erasing it, is likely to move the bowl or to alter the head, the bowl shall not be marked or have its mark erased but shall be "indicated" as a "toucher" or "non-toucher" as the case may be. If a bowl is not so marked or not so "indicated" before the succeeding bowl comes to rest it ceases to be a "toucher." If both skips or opponents agree that any subsequent movement of the bowl eliminates the necessity for continuation of the "indicated" provision the bowl shall thereupon be marked or have a chalk mark erased as the case

may be. Care shall be taken to remove the "toucher" marks from all bowls before they are played, but should a player fail to do so, and should the bowl not become a "toucher" in the end in play, the marks shall be removed by the opposing skip or his deputy or marker immediately the bowl comes to rest unless the bowl is "indicated" as a "non-toucher" in circumstances governed by earlier provisions of this law.

34. Movement of "Touchers"

A "toucher" in play in the ditch may be moved by the impact of a jack in play or of another "toucher" in play, and also by the impact of a "non-toucher" that remains in play after the impact, and any movement of the "toucher" by such incidents shall be valid. However, should the "non-toucher" enter the ditch before the next succeeding bowl is delivered, it shall be dead, and the "toucher" shall be deemed to have been displaced by a dead bowl and the provisions of Law 37(e) shall apply.

35. Bowl Accounted "Dead"

(a) Without limiting the application of any other of these laws, a bowl shall be accounted dead if:
(i) not being a "toucher" it comes to rest in the ditch or rebounds onto the playing surface of the rink after contact with the bank or with the jack or a "toucher" in the ditch, or
(ii) after completing its original course, or after being moved as a result of play, it comes to rest wholly outside the boundaries of the playing surface of the rink, or within 14m (15.3 ft) of the front of the mat, or
(iii) in its original course, passes beyond a side boundary of the rink on a bias which would prevent its reentering the rink. (A bowl is not rendered "dead" by a player carrying it while inspecting the head.)
(b) Skips, or the opponents in singles, shall agree on the question as to whether or not a bowl is "dead." Any member of either team may request a decision from the skips, but no member shall remove any bowl prior to agreement by the skips. Once their attention has been drawn to the matter, the skips by agreement must make a decision. If they cannot reach agreement, the umpire must make an immediate decision.

36. Bowl Rebounding

Only "touchers" rebounding from the face of the bank to the ditch or the rink shall remain in play.

37. Bowl Displacement

(a) Displacement by rebounding "non-toucher"—bowl displaced by a "non-toucher" rebounding from the bank shall be restored as near as possible to its original position, by a member of the opposing team or by the marker.
(b) Displacement by a participating player—if a bowl, while in motion or at rest on the green, or a "toucher" in the ditch, be interfered with or displaced by one of the players, the opposing skip shall have the option of:
(i) restoring the bowl as near as possible to its original position;
(ii) letting it remain where it rests;
(iii) declaring the bowl "dead";
(iv) or declaring the end "dead."
(c) Displacement by a neutral object or neutral person (other than as provided in Clause (d) hereof):
(i) of the bowl in its original course—if such a bowl be displaced within the boundaries of the rink of play without having disturbed the head, it shall be replayed. If it be displaced and has disturbed the head, the skips, or the opponents in singles, shall reach agreement on the final position of the displaced bowl and on the replacement of the head, otherwise the end shall be "dead."

These provisions shall also apply to a bowl in its original course displaced outside the boundaries of the rink of play provided such bowl was running on a bias which would have enabled it to reenter the rink.
(ii) of a bowl at rest, or in motion as a result of play after being at rest—if such a bowl be displaced, the skips or opponents in singles, shall come to an agreement as to the position of the bowl and the replacement of any part of the head disturbed by the displaced bowl, otherwise the end shall be "dead."
(d) Displacement inadvertently produced—if a bowl be moved at the time of it being marked or measured it shall be restored to its former position by an opponent. If such displacement is caused by a marker or an umpire, the marker or umpire shall replace the bowl.
(e) Displacement by "dead" bowl—if a "touchers" in the ditch be displaced by a "dead" bowl from the rink of play, it shall be

restored to its original position by a player of the opposite team or by the marker.
(f) Displacement by a bowl from an adjoining rink—A bowl or jack at rest on the rink, if in danger of being moved by a bowl from an adjoining rink, may be lifted by the marker or any player at the head to allow the neutral bowl to pass, and then be replaced, provided such action would not influence the outcome of the head so moved.

38. "Line Bowls"

A bowl shall not be accounted as outside the line unless it be entirely clear of it. This shall be ascertained by looking perpendicularly down upon the bowl or by placing a square on the green or by use of a string, mirror, or other approved optical device.

39. Movement of Jack
A "Live" Jack in the Ditch

A jack moved by a bowl in play into the front ditch within the boundaries of the rink shall be deemed to be "live." It may be moved by the impact of a "toucher" in play and also by the impact of a "non-toucher" that remains in play after the impact, any movement of the jack by such incidents shall be valid. However, should the "non-toucher" enter the ditch at any time after impact it shall be "dead" and the jack shall be deemed to be "displaced" by a "dead" bowl and the provisions of Law 47 shall apply.

If the jack in the ditch cannot be seen from the mat its position shall be marked by a "white" indicator about 5 cm (2 in) broad and not more than 10 cm (4 in) in height, placed upright on the top of the bank and immediately in line with the place where the jack rests.

40. A Jack Accounted "Dead"— Outdoor Version

Should the jack be driven by a bowl in play so that it passes beyond the face of the bank or comes to rest wholly beyond the side boundary of the rink, i.e., over the bank, or over the side boundary, or into any opening or inequality of any kind in the bank, or rebound to a distance of less than 18 m (19.7 yds) in direct line from the center of the front edge of the mat to the jack in its rebounded position, it shall be accounted "dead."

41. "Dead" End

When the jack is "dead" the end

shall be regarded as a "dead" end and shall not be accounted as a played end even though all the bowls in that end have been played. All "dead" ends shall be played anew in the same direction unless both skips or opponents in singles agree to play in the opposite direction. After a "dead" end situation the right to deliver the jack shall always return to the player who delivered the original jack.

42. Playing to a Boundary Jack

The jack, if driven to the side boundary of the rink and not wholly beyond its limits, may be played to on either hand and, if necessary a bowl may pass outside the limits of the rink. A bowl so played, which comes to rest within the boundaries of the rink, shall not be accounted "dead."

If the jack be driven to the side boundary line and come to rest partly within the limits of the rink, a bowl played outside the limits of the rink and coming to rest entirely outside the boundary line, even though it has made contact with the jack, shall be accounted "dead" and shall be removed to the bank by a member of the player"s team.

43. A Damaged Jack

In the event of a jack being damaged, the umpire shall decide if another jack is necessary and, if so, the end shall be regarded as a "dead" end and another jack shall be substituted and the end shall be played anew.

44. A Rebounding Jack

If the jack is driven against the face of the bank and rebounds on to the rink, or after being played into the ditch, it be operated on by a "toucher," so as to find its way on to the rink, it shall be played to in the same manner as if it had never left the rink.

45. Jack Displacement

(a) **By a player**
If the jack be diverted from its course while in motion on the green, or displaced while at rest on the green, or in the ditch, by any one of the players, the opposing skip shall have the option of:
(i) restoring the jack to its former position;
(ii) allowing it to remain where it rests and playing the end to a finish;
(iii) or declaring the end "dead."
(b) **Inadvertently produced**

If the jack be moved at the time of measuring by a player it shall be restored to its former position by an opponent.

46. Jack Displaced by a Non-player

(a) If the jack, whether in motion or at rest on the rink, or in the ditch, be displaced by a bowl from another rink, or by any object or individual not a member of the team, the two skips or the opponents in a singles game shall decide as to its original position, and if they are unable to agree, the end shall be declared "dead."
(b) If the jack is displaced by a marker or umpire, in the process of measuring or in any other circumstances, the displaced jack shall be restored as near as possible by the marker or umpire to its original position of which he shall be the sole judge.

47. Jack Displaced by "Non-toucher"

A jack displaced in the rink of play by a "non-toucher" rebounding from the bank shall be restored, as near as possible, to its original position by a player of the opposing team or by the marker in the singles game. Should a jack, however, after having been played into the ditch, be displaced by a "dead" bowl it shall be restored to its marked position by a player of the opposing team or by the marker.

Laws 48–51 Fours Play

The basis of the game of bowls is fours play. *(See Players, page 170.)*

Result of End

52. "The Shot"

A shot or shots shall be adjudged by the bowl or bowls nearer to the jack than any other bowl played by the opposing player or players.

When the last bowl has come to rest, 30 seconds shall elapse, if either team desires, before the shots are counted.

Neither jack nor bowls shall be moved until each skip has agreed to the number of shots, except in circumstances where a bowl has to be moved to allow the measuring of another bowl.

53. Measuring Conditions to Be Observed

No measuring shall be allowed until the end has been

completed. All measurements shall be made to the nearest point of each object. If a bowl requiring to be measured is resting on another bowl that prevents its measurement, the best available means shall be taken to secure its position, whereupon the other bowl shall be removed. The same course shall be followed where more than two bowls are involved, or where, in the course of measuring, a single bowl is in danger of falling or otherwise changing its position. When it is necessary to measure to a bowl or jack in the ditch, and another bowl or jack on the green, whenever possible, the measurement shall be made with a flexible measure.

54. "Tie"—No Shot

When at the conclusion of play in any end the nearest bowl of each team is touching the jack, or is deemed to be equidistant from the jack, there shall be no score recorded. The end shall be declared "drawn" and shall be counted a played end.

55. Nothing in these laws shall be deemed to make it mandatory for the last player to play his last bowl in any end, but he shall declare to his opponent or opposing skip his intention to refrain from playing it before the commencement of determining the result of the end and this declaration shall be irrevocable.

These laws are reprinted by permission of the World Bowls Board, World Indoor Bowls Council, International Women's Bowling Board and the World Indoor Bowls Council Ladies Section. A complete copy of the Laws of the Game, including laws 56–73, can be obtained from the World Bowls Board.

Bowled over
The aim of bowls is simply to deliver the bowl as close to the jack as possible, but this simple goal presents a huge range of alternative plays and tactical skills that make it a complex and satisfying game.

Pétanque

Essentials

Pronounced "pay-TAWNK," this game was invented by a Frenchman who sought a sport to play on an equal footing with a recently disabled friend. Today, pétanque is frequently seen in public areas across France. A more flexible cousin of lawn bowling (it can be played on any open terrain), it is also similar to the Italian game of boccie.

The balls in pétanque are called boules.

The "track" (the piste)

The game may be played on any terrain, although if a marked-out area is used, its dimensions must be: 15 x 4 m (49 x 13 ft) for international competitions. Tracks as small as 12 x 3 m (39 x 10 ft) may be allowed for other competitions.

Players

Three players against three (triples), two against two (doubles), or one against one (singles). In triples, each player uses two boules and in doubles and singles, each player uses three.

Accessories

A tape measure is required to verify which of two boules is closer to the cochonnet. For greater precision in measuring distance, callipers are used. A notepad or hand-held score-keeper. People who have difficulty bending down can retrieve their boules with a strong magnet attached to a string.

The boule (pronounced "bool")

Metal, with a diameter of approx. 3 in and a weight of 650–800 g (23–28 oz). The boule must not be weighted, sanded down, or altered in any way.

The cochonnet (pro-nounced "ko-show-NAY")(or jack)

Made entirely of wood and painted any color. A diameter of approx. 1 in. Boules or cochonnet must not be changed during a game except when lost or broken.

Officials

An umpire (for competitions).

HOW TO PLAY

The cochonnet is thrown to a spot within the playing area and then both teams try to place their boules as close to it as possible. After the first boule has been thrown, the second team plays until at least one of its boules is closer to the cochonnet than their opponents' boule. If they manage to do this before they run out of boules, the first team then resumes play until it is successful or has run out of boules. The sequence continues until all boules on either side have been played (an "end"). The winner of the end starts the next end.

Starting

A toss decides which team will throw the *cochonnet* (French for "little pig") first. A member of that team chooses the starting point by tracing a circle 14–20 inches in diameter. The circle must be at least 3 feet from the playing boundaries and all obstacles. The player then throws the cochonnet while standing inside the circle. A player throwing from a wheelchair must place his chair so that the circle is in the middle of the wheels.

How to win

Points are determined at the conclusion of each end. The winning team receives one point for each boule closer than any boule of the opposing team (the maximum score in any one end is six). If one team has thrown all its boules and the other team manages to knock the cochonnet out of play, that team scores one point for each boule left unplayed. The game ends when one team has gained 13 points.

On a roll
Pétanque can be played on virtually any surface but it is usually played on a soft, dusty field so that lines can be marked with a measuring device known as callipers or "baguette."

The thrower can either throw the boule up in the air or roll it along the ground.

KEY RULES

• Boules must not be modified or tampered with in any way. In organized play, the penalties for violations are severe, sometimes resulting in lengthy bans from the sport.

• If the cochonnet is moved the game continues, provided that it does not roll beyond an agreed boundary and that it remains visible from the circle. Beyond the boundary, or out of sight, the cochonnet is deemed "dead" and the end is cancelled and replayed. However, if the cochonnet is knocked out of play when one team has thrown all its boules and the other team still has boules to play, the team with the boules gets one point for each one left unplayed. *See How to play, (page 174).*

• After each boule (or the cochonnet) is thrown, the next player to throw has a maximum of one minute to play their boule. Both feet must be inside the circle when it is thrown and must

remain so until the boule has hit the ground. No other part of the body may touch the ground outside the circle and all throws must be made from the same circle for the whole of an end. While a player is preparing and executing his throw, the spectators and fellow players must observe total silence. *See Boules (page 176).*

SKILLS AND TACTICS

Team members often specialize in shooting (*tireurs*—said, "tee-RURS") or in placing the boule (*pointeurs*—said, "pwan-TURS"), but singles players

must be good at both areas. The tireur's goal is knock an opponent's boule out of the game. The most successful shot is a *carreau* (kare-OH), in which the thrown boule replaces a boule on the ground. The pointeur's role is to get his boule as close to the cochonnet as possible.

A player's choice of boule may also affect his play. A pointeur may select a boule with striations, or grooves, which give the boule more grip on the ground. A tireur may play with a softer boule as there will be less recoil following impact. A softer boule soaks up the impact with another boule, and does not therefore rebound so easily.

Shooting boule
There are three main shots in pétanque. A "point" (PWANT) is a boule thrown to roll along the ground. A "boule portée" (bool por-TAY) is thrown through the air in an arc. These two shots attempt to place the boule near the cochonnet. Finally, a "tir" (TEAR) is a boule thrown on the run intended to knock a specified target. With a tir the opposing team traces out an acceptable arc around the target with a baguette. This player is going for a boule portée.

PÉTANQUE: THE RULES

General

Rules 1–4
See pages 174–175.

Play

Rules 5 and 6
See pages 174–175.

Rule 7

For the thrown cochonnet to be legal, the following conditions apply:

1) The distance from it to the nearest edge of the circle must be between:
• 4 m (13 ft) minimum and 8 m (26 ft) maximum for Minimes
• 5 m (16 ft) min. and 9 m (30 ft) max. for Cadets
• 6 m (20 ft) min. and 10 m (32 ft) max. for Juniors and Seniors.

2) The nearest edge of the circle must be 1 m from all obstacles and at least 1 m inside the boundary of the playing area.

3) The cochonnet must be at least 1 m minimum from all obstacles and from the boundary of the playing area.

4) The cochonnet must be visible to the player whose feet are entirely inside the circle and who is standing upright. In cases of dispute, the umpire will decide if the cochonnet is visible and there can be no appeal.

At the following end, the cochonnet is thrown from a circle drawn around the point where it finished at the previous end, except in the following cases:

(a) The circle would be less than 1 m from an obstacle or from the boundary of the playing area. In this case, the player will trace a circle in the nearest valid position from the obstacle and the boundary.

(b) The cochonnet could not be thrown out to all valid distances. In this case, the player may step back, in line with the previous end's line of play, until he or she is able to throw the cochonnet any valid distance up to the maximum distance allowed, and not beyond. This may only be done if the cochonnet cannot be thrown in any other direction to the maximum distance. If after three consecutive throws by the same team, the cochonnet has not been thrown correctly, it is then passed to the opposing team who also has three tries and who may move the circle back as described above. After this, the circle cannot be moved again even if this team has not succeeded with its three throws. In any case, the team who lost

the cochonnet after the first three tries plays the first boule.

Rule 8

If the cochonnet thrown is stopped by the umpire, a player, a spectator, an animal, or any moving object, it is not valid and must be rethrown without being included in the three throws to which the player or the team is entitled. After the throwing of the cochonnet and the first boule, an opponent still has the right to contest the validity of the cochonnet's position. If the objection is valid, both the cochonnet and the boule are re-thrown. If the opponent has also played a boule, the cochonnet is deemed valid and no objection can be accepted. For the cochonnet to be thrown anew, both teams must have accepted the throw as being illegal or the umpire must have declared it so. In either case the cochonnet must be rethrown. Any team continuing otherwise would lose the throw of the cochonnet.

Rule 9

The cochonnet is deemed dead in the following six cases:

(1) When, after having been thrown, it is not within the limits as defined in Rule 7.

(2) When during an end, it is moved outside the boundary of the playing area (normally the dead boule line) even if it comes back on to the playing area. A cochonnet on the line of the boundary is still in play. It only becomes dead after having completely crossed the boundary. Where a cochonnet floats freely in water the area of the puddle is out of play.

(3) When still on the terrain, the moved cochonnet is not visible from the circle, as defined in Rule 7. The umpire may temporarily move a boule to ascertain whether the cochonnet is visible or not.

(4) When the cochonnet is displaced to more than 20 m (22 yds) or less than 3 m (10 ft) from the throwing circle.

(5) When the moved cochonnet cannot be found after a five-minute maximum search time.

(6) When there is dead ground between the cochonnet and the throwing circle.

Rule 10

It is strictly forbidden for any player to remove, move, or flatten any obstacle on the terrain within the boundaries of the playing area. However, the player

about to throw the cochonnet is allowed to test the ground by tapping it no more than three times with one of his or her boules. Furthermore, the player who is about to play or one of his partners may fill in the hole that was made by the last boule thrown.

For not observing the above rules, the players will incur the following penalties:

(1) Warning.

(2) Disqualification of the ball thrown or about to be thrown.

(3) Disqualification of the guilty team.

(4) Disqualification of both teams in case of complicity.

Rule 11

If, during an end, the cochonnet is completely obscured by a leaf, piece of paper, etc., these objects are removed. If the stationary cochonnet is moved by the wind or slope of the terrain, it is put back in its place providing its position had been marked. The same applies if the cochonnet is moved accidentally by the umpire, a player, a spectator, a boule or cochonnet from another game, an animal, or any moving object. To avoid any argument, the players should mark the cochonnet's position. No claim can be accepted regarding a boule or cochonnet whose position has not been marked.

Rule 12

If, during an end, the cochonnet is moved onto an area where another game is in progress, either on marked or unmarked terrain, the cochonnet is valid subject to Rule 9. The players using this cochonnet will wait for the players in the other game to finish their end before completing their own. The players concerned are asked to show patience and courtesy.

Rule 13

If, during an end, the cochonnet becomes dead, one of three cases can apply:

a) If both teams have boules to play, the end is void.

(b) If only one team has boules left to play, then this team scores as many points as it has boules to play.

(c) If neither team has boules to play, the end is void.

Rule 14

1) If the cochonnet, having been hit, is stopped by a spectator or by the umpire, it remains where it stops.

2) If the cochonnet, having been hit, is stopped by a player, his opponent has the choice of:

(a) leaving the cochonnet in its new position.

(b) putting it back in its original position.

(c) placing it anywhere on the extension of a line from its original position to the point where it is found, but only on the playing area, and so that the end can be continued.

Paragraphs (b) and (c) can only be applied if the position of the cochonnet was previously marked. If it was not marked, the cochonnet will remain where it lies. If the cochonnet, having been knocked on, crosses a boundary of the playing area (the dead boule line) but comes to rest on a permitted area, it is deemed dead and the rules defined in Rule 13 apply.

Rule 15

If, during an end, the cochonnet is moved outside the boundary of the playing area, the next end is started at the point from which it was displaced providing (see Rule 7):

(a) the circle can be traced at 1m (3 ft) from any obstacle and from the boundary of the playing area.

b) The cochonnet can be thrown at all valid distances.

Boules

Rule 16

The first boule of an end is thrown by a player belonging to the team that has won the toss or the last scoring end. The player must not use any object to give aid in playing a boule or draw a line on the ground to indicate or mark the point of landing. Whilst playing his or her last boule, he or she must not carry another boule in the other hand. It is forbidden to wet the boules or the cochonnet. If the first boule played goes out of play, the opponent plays and so on alternately while there are no boules in play. If after shooting or pointing no boules are left in play, the rules defined in Rule 29 apply.

Rule 17

During the time allowed for a player to throw a boule the spectators and the other players must observe total silence. The opponents must not walk, gesticulate, or do anything that could disturb the player about to play. Only his or her teammate/s may stand between the circle and the cochonnet. The opponents must remain beyond the cochonnet or behind the player and, in both cases, to the side of the end's line of play and at a distance of at least 2 m (6.5 ft) from the one or the other. The players who do not observe these rules will be banned from the competition if, after a warning from the umpire, they persist in their conduct.

Rule 18
Once thrown, a boule may not be replayed; except that it must be replayed if it has been stopped or deviated accidentally from its course between the circle and the cochonnet by a boule or cochonnet coming from another game, or by an animal or by any other moving object (football, etc.), and also in the case defined in Rule 8, second paragraph. No one is allowed a practice throw during a game. If the terrains have been marked out by organizers (into separate pistes), the cochonnet must be thrown within the terrain (piste) allotted to each team. During an end, boules and cochonnets going outside the marked terrain are valid (except as in Rule 9 and 19). The following end is nevertheless played on the original marked terrain. If the terrains are surrounded by solid barriers, these must be a minimum of 30 cm (12 in) outside the dead-ball line, which will surround the terrain at a maximum distance of 4 m (13 ft). These rules apply also to the "Carré d'Honneur" (terrains used for finals, etc).

Rule 19
Any boule that goes entirely outside the boundary of the playing area (normally the dead boule line) is out of play. A boule straddling the boundary is valid. It only becomes dead after having completely crossed the boundary. If the boule subsequently comes back into the playing area, either because of the slope of the ground or by having rebounded from any object, moving or stationary, it is immediately taken out of the game. Anything that it has moved after re-entering the playing area is put back in place (if it has been previously marked). Any boule out of play must immediately be removed from the playing area, if it is not it will be deemed live as soon as the next boule has been played.

Rule 20
Any boule played that is stopped by a spectator or the umpire will

remain where it comes to rest. Any boule played that is stopped by a player to whose team it belongs is deemed out of play. Any boule pointed that is stopped by an opponent can, on the decision of the player, be replayed or left where it comes to rest. If a boule shot or hit is stopped by a player, the opponent has a choice to:
(a) leave it where it stopped, or
(b) place it on the extension line from the original position where it (boule or cochonnet) was hit from where it is found, but only within the boundary of the playing area and if its position was previously marked. Any player purposely stopping a moving boule is immediately disqualified, along with his or her team, for the game in progress.

Rule 21
Once the cochonnet is thrown, each player has one minute at most to play his or her boule. This time starts from the moment when the preceding boule or cochonnet has stopped or, if a point has to be measured, from the moment the outcome has been decided. This rule also applies to the throwing of the cochonnet after each end. Players not respecting this rule will incur penalties as stated in Rule 10.

Rule 22
If a stationary boule is moved by the wind or slope of the ground, etc., it is put back in its place. The same applies to any boule accidentally moved by a player, the umpire, a spectator, an animal, or any other moving object. To avoid any disagreement, the players should mark the positions of the boules and the cochonnet. No claim will be accepted for a boule or cochonnet that has not had its position marked, and the umpire will only give a decision according to the position of the boules and the cochonnet on the terrain.

Rule 23
A player who plays a boule other than his own receives a warning. The boule played is nevertheless valid but it must be immediately replaced, after measuring, if necessary. In the event of it occurring again during the game, the player's boule is disqualified, and everything that it has moved is put back in place. Before throwing a boule, the player should remove from it all traces of mud or any other substance.

Penalties for this rule are as stated in Rule 10. Players must not pick up the played boules before the completion of the end.

Rule 24
All boules thrown contrary to the rules are dead and everything they have moved is put back in place. The same applies to a boule played from a circle other than that from which the cochonnet was thrown. However, the opponent may play the advantage rule and count the erroneously played boule as valid. In this case, the boule pointed or shot and everything it may have displaced, is left in its new position. The team about to throw the cochonnet must erase any previous throwing circles located near the new one.

Points and measurements

Rule 25
To measure a point, it is permitted to move temporarily, after having marked their positions, the boules and any object situated between the cochonnet and the boule to be measured. After measuring, the boules and the objects moved are put back in place. If the objects cannot be moved, the measuring is done with the aid of callipers.

Rule 26
The measuring of a point is done by the player who played the last boule or by one of his or her teammates. The opponents still have the right to remeasure the point. Whatever positions the boules may hold, and at whatever stage the end may be, the umpire may be called to adjudicate and his or her decision is final. Measuring must be done with appropriate equipment, which each team must possess. It is for instance forbidden to measure with one's feet. Players who do not observe these rules will be banned from the competition if, after a warning from the umpire, they persist in their conduct.

Rule 27
At the finish of an end, all boules picked up before the agreement of points are void if their positions were not marked. No claims can be made on this subject.

Rule 28
If, while measuring, one of the players moves the cochonnet or a boule being measured, his or her team loses the point. If, during a measure, the umpire disturbs or

moves the cochonnet or one of the boules and if, after re-measuring, the point is held by the boule that (the umpire) had originally judged to be on, then, in all fairness, he or she may declare it so. Even if the point is no longer held by that boule, the umpire may, in all fairness, still declare that it wins the point.

Rule 29
If two boules belonging to opposing teams are equidistant from, or touching the cochonnet, the end is declared void if there are no more boules to be played, and the cochonnet is thrown by the team winning the previous end or toss. If only one team has boules left to play, it plays them and scores as many points as it has boules closer to the cochonnet than the nearest opponent's boule. If both teams have boules to play, the team that played the last boule plays again, then the other team, and so on alternately until a boule is holding the point. When only one team has boules left, they play them as in the above paragraph. If, after completion of the end, no boules remain within the boundary of the playing area (normally the dead-ball line), the end is declared void.

Rule 30
Any foreign bodies adhering to the boule or the cochonnet must be removed before measuring a point.

Rule 31
To be accepted, all claims must be made to the umpire. Claims made after the result of the game has been agreed cannot be considered. Each team is responsible for checking their opposing team (licenses, classification, terrain, boules, etc.).

DISCIPLINE
Rules 32–39
Deal with players' absence; late arrivals; replacement of players; the umpire's role and jurisdiction; penalties incurred for violation of the rules, violent behavior, or a lack of sporting spirit or respect; the role of the jury.

These abbreviated rules are reprinted by permission of the British Pétanque Association. A complete copy of the rules of pétanque is available from the B.P.A.

Track and field

T rack-and-field events are the oldest forms of organized sport, popular worldwide for testing the limits of human speed and strength. Track events involve speed, while field events generally

Olympic stadium, Atlanta, Georgia, 1996.

All races are run counterclockwise

1,500-m start

3,000-m start

The athletic field
The diagram shows the correct track markings and staggered starts for an eight-lane track.

Starting positions for 400 m
400-m hurdles
880m

10,000-m start
Finsh line

200-m start

110-m hurdles start

A mile is about 1,625 meters—about four times around the track.

involve strength or distance. Although most events are contested by individuals, a few pit teams against each other.

Track and lane measurements

The length of a standard outdoor track is 400 m (440 yds). The track should be at least 7.32 m (24 ft) wide, with at least six lanes (each lane is 1.22–1.25 m in width). Eight lanes or more are normal for big events. There should be adequate marking of the inner edge of the track. For cinder and other permanent (non-grass) tracks, a raised curb at least 5 cm (2 in) high and wide should mark the edge. Alternatively, the inner border can be marked with a 5-cm-wide white line, flagged or coned at intervals of 5 m to prevent competitors treading on the line itself. Lanes should be marked similarly by white lines, measured for width from the outside edge of one marking line, itself 5 cm wide, to the outside edge of the next line (working outward from the inner border of the track). For distance purposes, lanes should be measured 20 cm (8 in) outward from their respective inner borders, or 30 cm (12 in), in the case of the inner edge of the track if there is a raised curb.

A running track should be level, not exceeding a maximum lateral inclination of 1:100, or an overall inclination in the running direction of 1:1000 downward. The direction of running for competitors should be counterclockwise.

In races up to and including 400 m, competitors must stay in their own lanes, necessitating a staggered start to

Middle/long distance start
Positions just before the gun for a 1000-meter event.

equalize the distance for each runner, except in the case of races up to 110 m, which must be run on a straight course. Contests over 400 m and up to and including 800 m may be run in lanes as far as the end of the first bend, again with adjustments to the starting point in each lane. A single finish line should serve all lanes at the end of one straight.

Indoor tracks are shorter than outside ones because of limited space. Banking of bends is permitted. Races up to and including 60 m must be run on a straight course in lanes. In a race of 400 m on a track 200 m or less in length, the first two complete bends should be run in lanes, with a "break" line distinctly marked on the track.

Starting Places

Lanes for competitors should be drawn in all races. In straight course sprints, the competitor drawing No.1 should take the lane on the left facing the finishing line. The next lane is taken by the second-drawn runner and so on through the field. In events on the circular track, the first-drawn competitor should take the lane nearest the center, the second-drawn the next lane, and so on.

For reasons of safety and fairness, limits should be applied to the number of runners in races, with

The following rules are applicable for international competition at adult level. In some instances they may be at variance with rules applied for domestic and junior competition. If in doubt, the rulebook issued by the relevant national association (for example, the Athletic Congress of the United States) should also be consulted.

These rules should be followed wherever possible. Obviously, however, not all clubs, schools, or individuals may have access to facilities and apparatus meeting the recommended standards. That should not deter adaptation or improvisation —for example, laying out a 300-m (330-yd) outdoor running track if that is all that available space will allow.

competitors divided into heats at the discretion of the referee.

Starting blocks

Starting blocks, against which runners place their feet to gain traction, may be used for all races up to and including 400 m. This includes the first leg of a relay race, where that leg does not exceed 400 m.

Starting blocks consist of two adjustable foot plates, mounted on a rigid frame. Their construction and use comply with several rules:

• they must be made entirely of rigid materials;
• they must not give any unfair advantage to the runner;
• they should be fixed to the track by a number of pins or spikes (arranged to minimize damage to the running surface);
• they should be easily and quickly removable;
• they may be adjustable but should allow no movement during the actual start;
• where runners use their own starting blocks, these must be approved by the starter; and
• when in position on the track, the starting block must not overlap the starting line or extend into another lane.

The surface of the foot plates may have slots or recesses, or may be covered with suitable material to accommodate the use of spiked shoes.

For major international competitions starting blocks are linked to a false start apparatus. This provides an audible indication to the starter if an athlete's reaction time to the starting signal takes less than 100/1000ths of a second. The starter has to bring all runners back in such circumstances.

The start

A white line, 5 cm (2 in) wide at right angles to the inner edge of the running track, marks the starting point of a race. The distance is measured from the edge of the starting line farther from the finish, to the edge of the finish line nearer to the start. In races that are not run in lanes, the starting line is curved so that all the runners start the same distance from the finish.

All track events begin with a shot from the starter's gun, (or other approved starting apparatus), fired upward into the air. Prior to this, the starter checks that the competitors have been placed correctly in their respective stations by other race officials (3 m behind the starting line or, in races run wholly or partly in lanes, behind each starting line) and that the timekeepers are ready.

In races up to and including 400 m (including relay events), the starter calls "On your marks," then "Set" (when runners steady themselves motionless, and then fires the starting gun. In races longer than 400 m, competitors approach the starting line (without touching it or touching the ground with their hands) on the "On your marks" command. When all the competitors are steady, the starting gun is fired, without the "Set" command. The starter can order all runners to withdraw from their marks and take their places again if he is not satisfied that everything is ready for the start of the race.

False starts

Circumstances that could constitute a false start by a runner include:
• failure to comply with the commands "On your marks" or "Set" within a reasonable space of time;
• disturbing fellow runners in a race, through sound or otherwise, after the "On your marks" call; or
• moving after assuming a full and final set position and before the starting signal.

A competitor who is responsible for a false start is given a warning. Two false starts, or three in the case of a combined event (e.g., the pentathlon, heptathlon, or decathlon), warrant disqualification. If the starter (or start recaller) thinks that the start was not fair, the competitors are recalled with a second shot. When one or more competitors beat the gun, others are, in practice, inclined to follow—all of whom have made a false start according to the letter of the law. The starter should warn only such competitor or competitors who, in his opinion, were responsible for the false start. This may result in more than one competitor being warned. If an unfair start is not due to any competitor, no warnings are issued.

Off the blocks
England's Linford Christie just after starting a 100-meter sprint.

Right, crouch start and the use of starting blocks are compulsory under International Amateur Athletic Federation (IAAF) rules in all races up to and including 400 m. Competitors approach the starting line upon the "On your marks" command, assuming a crouching position within their allocated lanes behind the starting line (which they must not touch). Each runner should have both hands and at least one knee in contact with the ground, and both feet on the foot plates of the block. On the "Set" command, competitors raise their knees from the track and arch to their final starting positions, with hands on the ground and feet on the blocks.

Photo finish
*Fully automated timing uses
equipment that is started by the
starter's gun, or other
approved starting device. The
finish is recorded through a
camera, with a vertical
slit, positioned even to
the finish line. It uses a
continuous film
synchronized with a
uniformly marked
time-scale
graduated in
1/100ths of a second.*

Clothing and footwear

Top athletes wear tops and shorts (or equivalent), which are clean and non-transparent (even if wet). Competitors should not wear any attire that might impede the view of the judges. Distinctive number cards are generally provided to competitors.

Shoes should give traction and protection with minimum weight, although athletes may compete in bare feet, or with footwear on one foot, if they wish. Shoes may not be constructed so as to give a competitor any additional assistance (e.g., extra spring). Any number of spikes up to 11 may be used on the sole and heel of each shoe. In a competition taking place on a synthetic surface, the part of the spike projecting from the sole or heel must not exceed 9 mm (approx. 1/2 in) or 12 mm in the high jump and javelin events. The spikes should have a maximum diameter of 4 mm. For non-synthetic surfaces the maximum spike length should be 25 mm (1 in), again with a maximum diameter of 4 mm. For track and field events other than the high jump, a shoe's sole and/or heel may be any thickness. It may have grooves, ridges, or other design features, provided these are constructed of the same or similar material as the basic sole itself.

The race

In races run in lanes, competitors keep in their assigned lane from start to finish. IAAF rules make it a mandatory disqualification if a runner, unless forced to do so by another competitor, steps on or over the inner line of the lane when running around any part of a bend. Running over the outside lane line does not constitute an infringement unless the action impedes another runner. Competitors who jostle, run across, or impede others in a race risk disqualification. If a runner is so disqualified, the referee can order a race to be rerun (excluding that runner). The referee can also allow any competitor affected by such an incident to compete in a subsequent round of the event. Competitors on their marks may not be accompanied by an attendant, nor may they receive help in the course of a race. Runners are notified of the last lap usually by a bell. In races of 200 m or less, the wind speed should be recorded wherever possible, with a gauge set up 50 m from the finish line, not more than 2 m from the inner edge of the track, at a height of 1.22 m. The wind should be measured for a 13-second period in hurdle events and for 10 seconds in others (starting in the 200 m when the first runner enters the straight). An aiding wind of more than 2 m per second nullifies a record time.

The finish

The finishing line for a race should be 5 cm (2 in) wide and drawn across the track at right angles to the inner edge.

Except where their use may interfere with photo-finish equipment, two white posts may be placed along the finish line at least 1 foot from the edge of the track. The posts should be about 4 3/4 inches high, 3 inches wide, and 2 inches thick. Competitors are placed in the order in which any part of the body (meaning the torso rather than the head and neck or limbs) reaches the vertical plane of the edge of the finish line nearer to the start.

Should a tie occur in any heat affecting the qualification of runners to compete in the following round or in the final of the event, the tying competitors should all qualify. (IAAF rules stipulate that, in determining whether there has been a tie for a qualifying place, it is acceptable to review the times recorded by the competitors to a smaller margin than the official 1/100th of a second.) Should there be a tie for first place in any final, the referee has the power to decide whether it is practical to arrange for the tying competitors to run again. If the referee thinks otherwise, the results stand. Ties for places other than first always remain.

Timekeeping

A sufficient number of timekeepers for the number of competitors should be appointed, one of whom should be the chief timekeeper. Timekeepers must be in line with the finish, wherever possible on the outside of the track and at least 5 m from the outside lane. To ensure that they have an unimpeded view of the finish line and of the starter, an elevated position should be provided. A competitor's performance in a race should be timed from the flash of the starter's gun or other device to the instant when his or her body reaches the leading edge of the finish line (*see* The finish). In races of 800 m and over, lap times and the leader's number should be recorded, as should times at each 1,000 m in races of 3,000 m or more. In the case of a record claim, this information is essential. Only an official timekeeper or other designated person may indicate intermediate times to competitors or give times to be announced over the public address system.

Different track events require different running styles. Sprinters race to the finish line at top speed, involving high knee lift, free-swinging arm movements and a forward lean of about 25 degrees. Distance runners have to regulate their speed to avoid exhaustion. Knee action is less pronounced, the stride shorter, and the forward lean less extreme.

Fully automated timing

Fully automatic electrical timing is used at most important meets and is a specific requirement in international competition, such as the Olympic Games or the World Championships.

For races up to and including 10,000 m, the time read from the photo-finish picture should be recorded in 1/100ths of a second. Times for events longer than 10,000 m that are held entirely on the track should be read in 1/100ths of a second and converted to the next longer tenth of a second. For races held partly or wholly outside the stadium the time should be read in 1/100ths of a second and recorded to the next longer whole second.

Fully automatic times should be regarded as official, unless the chief photo-finish judge deems otherwise, in which case the chief timekeeper should provide manual times taken by back-up timekeepers. A timing device that operates automatically at either the start or the finish, but not at both, cannot be used to register official times. If possible, two photo-finish cameras should be deployed, one on each side of the finish. They should be technically independent of each other.

Times for all finishing competitors should be recorded, as should, where possible, lap times in races of 800 m and over and times at every 1,000 m in contests of 3,000 m or more.

Manual timing

Conventional watches (which have generally been superseded by manually operated electronic timers) may be used for timing races up to and including 3,000 m. Electronic timers may be used for hand timing in all races. For all hand-timed races on the track, timings recorded in 1/100ths of a second should be rounded up (unless ending in zero) to the next longer tenth of a second (e.g., a timing of 10.13 seconds should be read as 10.2). The times for races partly or wholly outside the stadium should be converted to the next longer full second. Each timekeeper should act independently and declare the recorded time to the chief timekeeper who may inspect the readings for verification (which must be done if a record claim is involved). The chief timekeeper should then decide the official time for each competitor, applying as necessary the following provisions:
• when two out of three timekeepers timing one placing agree and one does not, the time shown by the two should be the official time;
• if all three timekeepers disagree, the middle time should be the official one;
• should only two times be available for any reason and they disagree, the longer should be the official time.

Relay races

Relay races are for teams of four runners, each carrying a baton for a given distance or stage before passing it to the next team member. The handover needs to be accomplished with speed and dexterity within a defined take-over zone.

Lines should be drawn across the track to mark the distances of the relay stages and to denote the "scratch line." Lines drawn 10 m before and after the scratch line denote the take-over zone. These lines should be included in the zonal measurements.

In 4 x 100 m events (in which each of four teammates runs 100 meters) all teams should stay in their lanes throughout the race. Members of a team may not begin running more than 10 m outside the takeover zone. This limit should be marked distinctively in each lane.

In 4 x 400 m races (each of four teammates runs 400 meters) teams stay in lanes for the first lap and for part of the second, although IAAF rules recommend only the first bend to be run in lanes if only two or three teams are competing. The waiting runners must start their run within the take-over zone. The second runners in each team may break from their lanes immediately after passing the exit from the first bend (marked by a 2-inch white line across the track). The runners in the third and fourth stages should, under official direction, place themselves in their waiting position in the same order (from inside to out) as the order of their respective team members as they complete 200 m of their stages.

In other relay races, if lanes are not used, waiting runners can move to an inner position on the track as incoming teammates arrive, provided another competitor's progress is not impeded.

If a runner drops the baton, he or she can retrieve it, leaving the lane to do so if necessary. However, other athletes must not be impeded and the distance to be covered must not be lessened, otherwise disqualification may result.

Once a team has started in a competition, only two additional athletes may be used as team substitutes for subsequent rounds. A substitution may only be made from among those athletes already entered for the meets.

Outdoor track events generally include:
sprints: 100-, 200-, 400-meters;
middle distance: 800-, 1,500-meters;
long distance: 5,000- and 10,000-meter runs;
steeplechase: 3,000-meters;
hurdles: 110- and 400-meters (100 meters for women); and
relays: 4 x 100- and 4 x 400-meters

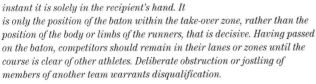

Passing the baton
A baton pass starts when it is first touched by the receiving runner and is completed the instant it is solely in the recipient's hand. It is only the position of the baton within the take-over zone, rather than the position of the body or limbs of the runners, that is decisive. Having passed on the baton, competitors should remain in their lanes or zones until the course is clear of other athletes. Deliberate obstruction or jostling of members of another team warrants disqualification.

The baton
A rigid hollow tube, 12–13 cm (approx. 5 in) in circumference. It should be no more than 30 cm or less than 28 cm (approx. 1 ft) in length, and no less than 50 gm (1 ¾ oz) in weight. It should be distinctly colored to be visible during a race. In all relay races the baton must be passed between runners within the take-over zone.

Hurdles

The standard outdoor hurdling distances for men are 110 m and 400 m, and 100 m and 400 m for women (50 m and 60 m indoors). All hurdle races are run in lanes, the hurdles in each lane being set out in accordance with the specifications in the chart on the following page.

A hurdle consists of two bases and two uprights supporting a rectangular frame reinforced by one or more crossbars. It is made of metal and wood. The uprights are fixed at the extreme end of each base, and the hurdle should be placed on the track so that the ends carrying the uprights face an approaching competitor.

The hurdle should be designed so that only a force at least equal to the weight of 3.6 kg (7 lb) applied to the center of the top of the crossbar can overturn it. It may be adjustable in height for each event. The counterweights should be adjustable so that at each height a force at least equal to the weight of 3.6 kg (7 lb) and not more than 4 kg (approx. 9 lb) is required to overturn the hurdle. Where hurdles comply with these specifications, knocking down any in a race will not warrant a competitor's disqualification, nor any entitlement to claim a record.

A competitor should be disqualified if he or she:
• trails a foot or leg below the horizontal plane of the top of any hurdle at the instant of clearance;
• jumps any hurdle not in his or her own lane; or
• deliberately (in the referee's opinion) knocks down any hurdle by hand or foot.

Obstacle course
Hurdling events combine sprinting with clearing a series of obstacles called hurdles. A good hurdling style involves leaning far forward and clearing each hurdle in a smooth action without breaking the rhythm of the running stride.

Hurdle dimensions
The maximum width of a hurdle should be 1.2 m (4 ft) and the maximum length of the base should be 70 cm (27 1/2 in). The top bar should be 7 cm (2 3/4 in) in width and between 1 cm (1/2 in) and 2.5 cm (1 in) thick. It should be striped in distinctive contrasting colors. The lighter stripes should appear at the end of the hurdle and should be at least 22.5 cm (9 in) wide.

Hurdle race specifications

Men

distance of race	height of of hurdle	distance from start line to first hurdle	distance between hurdles	distance from last hurdle to finish line
		outdoor		
110 m	1.067 m	13.72 m	9.14 m	14.02 m
400 m	0.914 m	45 m	35 m	40 m
		indoor		
50 m	1.067 m	13.72 m	9.14 m	8.86 m
60 m	1.067 m	13.72 m	9.14 m	9.72 m

Women

distance of race	height of of hurdle	distance from start line to first hurdle	distance between hurdles	distance from last hurdle to finish line
		outdoor		
100 m	0.840 m	13 m	8.5 m	10.5 m
400 m	0.762 m	45 m	35 m	40 m
		indoor		
50 m	0.840 m	13 m	8.5 m	11.5 m
60 m	0.840 m	13 m	8.5 m	13 m

The steeplechase

The steeplechase combines long-distance running with hurdling. The two standard distances for the steeplechase are 2,000 m and 3,000 m (although it is sometimes run over 1,500 m too). In a 3,000-m event there should be 28 hurdle jumps and seven water jumps, while for 2,000 m there should be 18 and five respectively. For a 3,000 m course, there should be five evenly spaced jumps per lap, the fourth being the water jump.

Water jumps have to be constructed on an arena either inside or outside the track. This has the effect of shortening or lengthening the normal distance of the lap. It is not possible therefore to lay down any rule specifying the exact length of a steeplechase lap or to state exactly the position of the water jump.

To prevent overcrowding among competitors, there needs to be sufficient distance from the starting line to the first hurdle. In the 3,000-m event, the distance from the start to the beginning of the first lap should not include any jumps (the hurdles being removed until the runners have entered the first lap). There should also be about 62.2 m from the last hurdle to the finish line. Competitors may go over each hurdle in any manner (for example, by jumping, vaulting, or placing one or both feet on them). However, disqualification results if a runner steps to either side of the water jump, or if he or she trails a foot or leg below the horizontal plane of the top of any hurdle at the instant of clearance.

Steeplechase hurdle
Should be made of heavy timber, or of metal with a timber bar, constructed so that they cannot be easily overturned. They should be 91.4 cm (3 ft) in height—76.2 cm (2½ ft) for women's events—and at least 3.96 m (13 ft) in total width. The section of the top bar of hurdles, and the hurdle at the water jump, should be 12.7 cm (5 in) square. Weighing 80–100 kg (176–220 lb), a hurdle should be placed on the track so that about 30 cm (12 in) of the top bar overlaps the track's inner edge into the field. The top bar should be striped in distinctive contrasting colors. The lighter stripes should appear at the end of the bar and should be at least 30 cm (12 in) wide.

Water jump
The water jump, including the hurdle, should be 3.66 m (12 ft) in length and width. The hurdle should be firmly fixed in front of the water at the same height as the others in the event. The water should be 70 cm (2 ft) in depth at the hurdle end, remaining at that depth for a distance of 30 cm (12 in), and then rising to the level of the track at the farther end of the water jump. The bottom of the water jump should be covered at the farther end with a suitable material that ensures the safe landing of the runners. This covering should be at least the same width as the water jump and 2.5 m (18¼ ft) in length, its thickness not exceeding 2.5 cm (1 in).

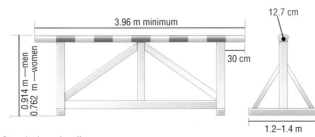

Steeplechase hurdle

Fields events at an outdoor meet include jumping and throwing disciplines—high jump, pole vault, long jump, triple jump, shot put, hammer throw, discus, and javelin. The hammer, discus, and javelin are not contested indoors.

General conditions

For field events, where the aim is to out-jump or out-throw other contestants, a draw first decides the order in which the participants compete. Each throw or jump by a competitor is called a trial, a number of trials being allowed in each round of the competition. Except for the high jump and pole vault, competitors cannot save any of their trials for a subsequent round. In circumstances where competitors are entered in more than one event taking place simultaneously, the judges can allow them to take their trials in an order different from that decided by the initial draw. No competitor may have more than one trial recorded in any one round, except for the high jump and pole vault.

Once a competition begins, athletes may not use runways, takeoff areas or throwing sites for warm-up purposes or practice trials. In any field event, the referee has the power to change the place of the competition if conditions justify it. This should not be done in the course of a round.

All measurements should be made with a calibrated steel tape or with a scientific apparatus. The accuracy of any measuring equipment should be certified by an appropriate authority.

Qualifying rounds

A qualifying round should be held in field events when the number of competitors is too large for a single round. The participants are divided into two or more groups, each group competing in turn unless facilities allow them to compete at the same time under the same conditions. Those competitors who reach the pre-set standard of performance in the qualifying round go on to the competition. If less than the prescribed number of athletes achieve that standard, the group of finalists should be increased to that number by adding competitors according to their performances in the qualifying round.

Competitors should be allowed up to three trials each in a qualifying round (apart from

High jump— details on next page

the high jump and pole vault). Performance at this stage should not be considered part of the competition. Once a competitor achieves the qualifying standard, he or she does not take any more trials.

Competitors who have qualified in preliminary rounds or heats for further participation in any event, but do not then

High jump construction

The diagram gives the specifications for the crossbar, uprights, and supporting pegs in the high jump event. The uprights, of any style, must be rigid. The bar, made of fiberglass, metal, or other suitable material, should be circular in cross-section except for end pieces, which rest on the pegs of the uprights. The front of the bar should be painted, and its weight should not exceed 2 kg (4½ lb).

The pegs supporting the bar should be firmly fixed to the uprights, each facing the opposite upright so that the ends of the bar can rest on them. The pegs may not have any kind of springs, nor may they (or those parts of the bar that rest on them) be covered in any kind of friction-increasing material.

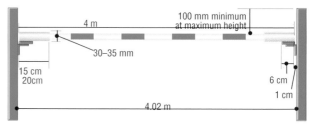

continue without giving the referee a valid reason, should be excluded from participating in any further events at the meet. In meets extending over more than one day, such an exclusion should apply to all subsequent events.

Vertical jumps

In the high jump and pole vault, competitors try to propel themselves over a crossbar, at successively greater heights without knocking it off its supporting uprights. The height at which the competition starts, and to what height the bar is raised at the end of each round,

is decided by the judge.

Competitors are always allowed to attempt a jump higher than the standard, both at the start and at any point throughout the meet. Exit from the event follows three consecutive failures at any height (except in the case of a tie). After failing once or twice, competitors may forgo their remaining trials at a height, but still attempt a subsequent height. However, if they forgo a trial, no subsequent attempts at that height may be made, except in the case of a tie.

A single remaining competitor can continue until three consecutive failures are recorded. In such a case, the height or heights to which the bar is raised rests with the official in charge after consultation with that competitor (not applicable for combined events competitions).

All height measurements should be made in whole centimeters perpendicularly from the ground to the lowest part of the upper side of the crossbar. Any measurement of a new height should be made before competitors attempt that height (and must be checked, in the case of a record claim, after it has been cleared). Unless only one competitor remains, the bar should not be raised by less than 2 cm (approx 1 in) in the high jump and 5 cm (2 in) in the pole vault after each round.

Ties

If there is a tie, the competitor with the lowest number of attempts at the height at which the tie occurs is awarded the higher place. If it is still a tie, the lowest number of failures up to and including the height last cleared prevails. If it is still a tie

---

Delay

A participant in a field event who unreasonably delays making a trial may have the delay disallowed and recorded as a fault. A second delay at any time during the competition may incur disqualification from taking any further trials (although performances up to that point still stand in the final result of the event). Although the referee decides what constitutes an unreasonable delay, the following times for each trial should not normally be exceeded:

* one and a half minutes for the high jump, long jump, triple jump, shot put, discus, hammer, and javelin.
* two minutes for the pole vault (beginning when the uprights have been adjusted to the

satisfaction of the competitor).
* where only two or three participants remain in the competition in the high jump and pole vault, the above times should be increased to three minutes for the former and four minutes for the latter (and to five and six minutes respectively under IAAF rules when there is only one competitor left). This is not applicable in a combined events competition.
* the period between consecutive trials by the same athlete should be at least four minutes for the pole vault and three minutes for other field events.

If the time allowed elapses after the competitor has started his or her trial, that trial should not be disallowed.

Pole-vault construction

The uprights for pole-vaulting may be of any style provided they are rigid. They should be not less than 4.3 m, or more than 4.37 m (approx. 14 ft) apart. The crossbar is made of fiberglass, metal, or other suitable material, and should be circular in cross-section with a diameter of 29–31 mm (approx. 1 in) except for end pieces (each 30–35 mm wide and 15–20 cm long), which rest on the supports of the uprights. The overall length of the bar is between 4.48 m and 4.52 m (approx. 15 ft), and its weight is 2.25 kg (5 lb).

The pegs supporting the bar extend horizontally not more than 7.5 cm (3 in) from the face of the uprights on the side farther from the runway. They should be not more than 13 mm in diameter. Alternatively the pegs may be positioned upon extension arms permanently attached to the uprights, thereby allowing the uprights to be placed wider apart without increasing the length of the crossbar. This lessens the chance of injury to competitors. The uprights should extend 35–40 mm above the supports. Neither the pegs nor the ends of the crossbar may be covered in any kind of friction-increasing material, and the pegs may not have any kind of springs.

and concerns first place, the competitors should have one more jump, starting at the lowest height at which any of them failed. If no decision is reached, the bar should be raised or lowered 2 cm for the high jump and 5 cm (approx. 1 in) for the pole vault, each competitor attempting one jump at each height until the tie is resolved. For other than first place, the tied competitors should be awarded the same place in the competition.

High jump

In this event the uprights should not be moved during a competition unless the referee thinks that the takeoff or landing area has become unsuitable. This should not be done during a round. Competitors may place markers (which must not leave any indelible residue) to help them in their approach and takeoff.

Competitors are judged to have failed if they:
• take off from both feet;
• dislodge the crossbar so that it falls from the supports (pegs) on the uprights; or
• touch the ground, including the landing area, beyond the plane of the uprights (either between or outside them) with any part of the body without first clearing the bar (unless the judge considers no advantage has been gained).

Competitors may not wear shoes with a sole thickness of more than 13 mm (½ in) or a heel thickness over 19 mm (¾ in).

The minimum length of the runway should be 15 m (or 20 m for more important competitions), and the landing area should measure not less than 5 m in length and 3 m in width. The takeoff area should be level although there may be a maximum overall inclination of 1:250 in the direction of the center of the crossbar.

Pole vault

Positioning the uprights

The following rules for the event apply in addition to the general conditions outlined on the previous page. Athletes may have the uprights moved in either direction, but not more than 40 cm (16 in) in the direction of the runway, and not more than 80 cm (31½ in) to the landing area from the continuation of the inside edge of the top of the takeoff box. (A white line 1 cm wide may be drawn at right angles to the axis of the runway, at the level of the inside edge of the top of the box. It should be drawn as far as the outside edge of the uprights.) Before the competition starts, competitors should inform the appropriate official where they want the uprights for their first

Pole vault

In pole-vaulting a competitor tries to clear a high crossbar with the aid of a long flexible pole. Holding the pole a little way from its top, the athlete sprints along a runway toward the uprights and digs the end of the pole into a box sunk below ground level. He or she then swings upward toward the bar, arching over it feet first and face down before dropping onto a thick, soft pad.

attempt, and that position should be recorded. If they subsequently want to make any changes, they should immediately inform the official before the uprights have been set in accordance with their initial request.

The jump

Athletes may place markers next to the runway to help them in their approach and takeoff. They may not use tape on their hands or fingers unless to cover an open wound, but can use an adhesive substance on their hands or on the pole to improve their grip. Competitors are judged to have failed in a vault if they:
• dislodge the crossbar so that it falls from the supports (pegs) on the uprights;
• touch the ground, including the landing area beyond the vertical plane of the upper part of the box, with any part of the body or with the pole, without first clearing the bar; or
• change grip after leaving the ground (moving the lower hand above the upper one or the upper hand higher on the pole).

No one should be allowed to touch the pole unless it is falling away from the bar or the

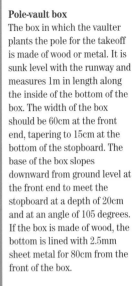

uprights. If it is touched, however, and the referee thinks that the bar would otherwise have been knocked off, the vault should be recorded as a failure. If a competitor's pole breaks during a vault, the attempt should not be recorded as a failure.

The runway should be level and not less than 40 m in length. As with a lane on a running track, the width should be not less than 1.22 m (4 ft) and not more than 1.25 m. For record purposes, the maximum allowance for lateral inclination of the runway should not exceed 1:100 and the overall inclination in the running direction 1:1000. The landing area should measure at least 5 m by 5 m.

The pole

The pole can be made of any material or combination of materials and have any length or diameter, provided that the basic surface is smooth. It may have a binding of not more than two layers of smooth adhesive tape of uniform thickness. The lower 30 cm of the pole may have additional protective layers of tape to protect it when it strikes the back of the takeoff box.

Pole-vault box

The box in which the vaulter plants the pole for the takeoff is made of wood or metal. It is sunk level with the runway and measures 1m in length along the inside of the bottom of the box. The width of the box should be 60cm at the front end, tapering to 15cm at the bottom of the stopboard. The base of the box slopes downward from ground level at the front end to meet the stopboard at a depth of 20cm and at an angle of 105 degrees. If the box is made of wood, the bottom is lined with 2.5mm sheet metal for 80cm from the front of the box.

Long jump/triple jump

General conditions

Where there are more than eight athletes in the competition, each is allowed three trials and the eight competitors with the best valid jumps are allowed three additional trials. If there is a tie for the eighth place, any competitor tied receives the three extra trials. If there are eight competitors or fewer, each is allowed six trials.

As they complete their approaches, competitors take off from a board, the "takeoff line" being the edge of the board that is nearer to the landing area. They may place markers alongside the runway to help them in their approach and takeoff, but may not mark the runway itself. Nor may they place any mark beyond the takeoff line. Competitors are judged to have failed a trial if they:
* touch the ground beyond the takeoff line with any part of the body, whether in the act of jumping or running without jumping;
* take off from outside either end of the takeoff board, whether beyond or before the extension of the takeoff line;
* in the course of landing, touch the

ground outside the landing area at a point nearer to the takeoff than the nearest break in the sand made by the jump;
* walk back through the landing area after a completed jump; or
* somersault in any fashion while in their approach or in the act of jumping.

If an athlete takes off before reaching the board, but within its width span, the jump should not be counted as a failure.

Measurement

The length of a long jump or triple jump is the distance between the takeoff line and the nearest break in the landing area's sand made by any part of a competitor's body. (The measurement is made at right angles from the nearest break.) Distances are recorded to the nearest 1 cm below the distance measured if that distance is not a whole centimeter.

In the case of a tie in the competition, the second best jump of the tied competitors determines the result. Then, if necessary, the third best and so on. If the tie is still not resolved and it concerns first place, the competitors involved compete again in the same order until the tie is decided. Each athlete is credited with the best of all his or her jumps in the competition, including those achieved in deciding a tie for first place.

Wind speed

As for track events, the wind speed should be measured and recorded for both the long jump and triple jump wherever

possible. A gauge should be set up 2 m from the takeoff line, not more than 2 m from the edge of the runway, at a height of 1.22 m (4 ft). The wind component should be measured for a 5-second period from the time the competitor passes a mark positioned 40 m from the takeoff board in the case of the long jump and 35 m for the triple jump. If the competitor's

approach is less than these distances, the reading should be taken from the time the competitor starts to run.

General specifications

The takeoff board is sunk level with the runway and rigidly fixed. Painted white, it is made of wood, measuring 1.21 m to 1.22 m long (approx. 4 ft), between 19.8 cm and 20.2 cm (approx. 8 in) wide, and 10 cm deep. The minimum length of the runway is 40 m, with a minimum width of 1.22 m. For record purposes, the maximum allowance for lateral inclination of the runway does not exceed 1:100 and the overall inclination in the running direction 1:1000. Before a competition the sand in the landing area should be dampened, as this aids accurate measurement. The sand should be level with the top of the takeoff board.

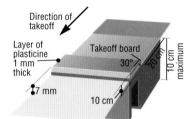

Tell-tale

A plasticine indicator board should, if possible, be positioned immediately beyond the takeoff line to record a competitor's footprint in the event of a foot fault. It consists of a rigid board, between 9.8 cm and 10.2 cm (approx. 4 in) wide and 1.21–1.22 m (approx. 38 in) long. Covered with plasticine, the surface rises from the level of the takeoff board at an angle of 30 degrees in the running direction to a maximum height of 7 mm (2⅓ in) above the takeoff board. If such an installation is not possible, soft earth or moist sand can be sprinkled to a height of 7 mm for 10 cm (4 in) beyond the takeoff board. The landing area should be between 2.75 m and 3 m wide and 9 m long (approx. 3 by 10 yds).

Triple jump in action—the hop stage.

Right: A gauge for measuring wind speed

Long jump

In addition to those rules already described, the takeoff board in the long jump should be placed between 1–3 m from the nearer end of the landing area. There should also be a distance of at least 10 m between the takeoff board and the far end of the landing area.

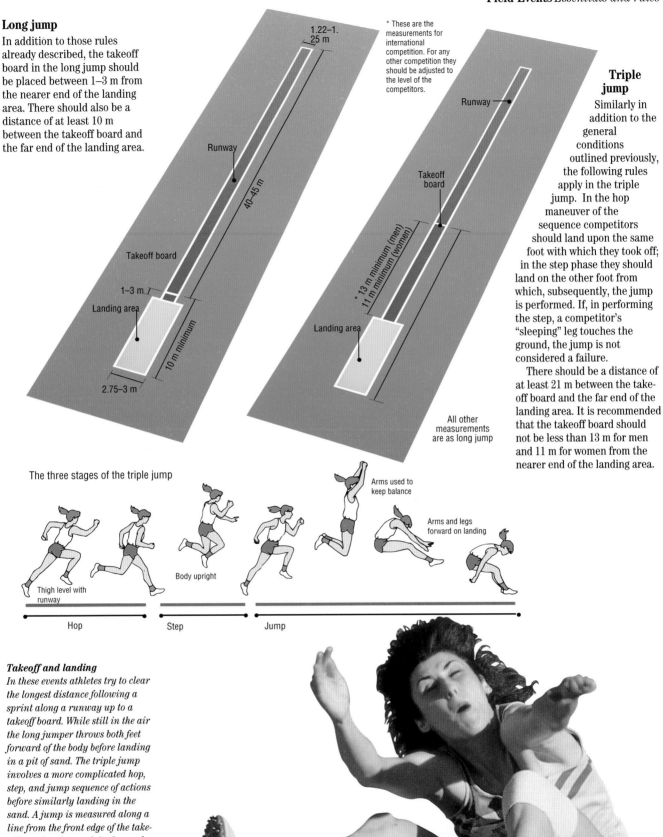

1.22–1.25 m

Runway

40–45 m

Takeoff board

1–3 m

Landing area

10 m minimum

2.75–3 m

* These are the measurements for international competition. For any other competition they should be adjusted to the level of the competitors.

Runway

Takeoff board

* 13 m minimum (men)
11 m minimum (women)

Landing area

All other measurements are as long jump

Triple jump

Similarly in addition to the general conditions outlined previously, the following rules apply in the triple jump. In the hop maneuver of the sequence competitors should land upon the same foot with which they took off; in the step phase they should land on the other foot from which, subsequently, the jump is performed. If, in performing the step, a competitor's "sleeping" leg touches the ground, the jump is not considered a failure.

There should be a distance of at least 21 m between the take-off board and the far end of the landing area. It is recommended that the takeoff board should not be less than 13 m for men and 11 m for women from the nearer end of the landing area.

The three stages of the triple jump

Arms used to keep balance

Arms and legs forward on landing

Thigh level with runway

Body upright

Hop   Step   Jump

Takeoff and landing

In these events athletes try to clear the longest distance following a sprint along a runway up to a takeoff board. While still in the air the long jumper throws both feet forward of the body before landing in a pit of sand. The triple jump involves a more complicated hop, step, and jump sequence of actions before similarly landing in the sand. A jump is measured along a line from the front edge of the take-off board to the mark in the sand made closest to the takeoff board by any part of the jumper's body on landing.

Long jumper

Landing sector

Stop board

Shot circle

*Shot put circle and
landing sector*

Throwing events

General conditions

The four standard throwing
events in field competition—
the shot put, hammer, discus,
and javelin—all involve
hurling items of
various weights and
shapes as far as
possible.

Where there are
more than eight
athletes in an event,
each is allowed
three trials, and
the eight
competitors
with the best
valid throws are
allowed three
additional trials. If
there is a tie for the
eighth place, those
competitors receive three extra
trials. If there are eight
competitors or fewer, each is
allowed six throws.

In the case of a tie (other
than that outlined above), the
second-best throw of the tied
competitors determines the
result. Then, if necessary, the
third best and so on. If the tie is
still not resolved and it
concerns first place, those
involved compete again in the
same order until the tie is
decided. Each athlete is
credited with the best of all his
or her throws in the
competition, including those
achieved in deciding a tie for
first place.

Athletes may not place any
marker within the throwing
sector. The taping of fingers
(except in the hammer event)
or anything else that may aid a
competitor when making a
throw is not allowed. However,
for a better grip, competitors
may use an adhesive substance
on their hands. They may also
wear a belt of suitable material
to help protect the spine.

Shot putting

Shot putting entails pushing,
rather than throwing, a solid
metal ball through the air.
Holding the shot in the
throwing hand, the athlete rests
that hand against the shoulder,
with the shot positioned under
the chin. The competitor then
moves across the throwing
circle in a twisting movement,
gathering momentum,
before rapidly
straightening
the arm and
pushing
the shot
into the
air
within the throwing sector.

Each competitor may have
two practice trials
(from the
throwing circle
only) before the
competition
begins. Athletes
may not wear gloves, nor
apply any substance
on their shoes or on
the surface of the
throwing circle.

The throw, or "put"
Competitors should
commence their
throws from a
stationary position
within the circle. Having
started to make the
throw, competitors may
not touch the ground
outside the circle, the
top of the circle rim, or
the top of the
stopboard (see
opposite page) with
any part of the body.
To do so constitutes a
foul throw, as does
improperly releasing the shot in
making any attempt. A foul
throw constitutes a trial. A
competitor should not leave the
circle until the shot has
touched the ground. When
leaving the circle, the first
contact with the top of the
circle rim or the ground outside
the circle has to be completely
behind the white line drawn
outside the circle that
theoretically runs through its
center. Provided the above rules
have not been infringed, a
competitor may interrupt a trial
once started, may lay the shot
down inside or outside the
circle, and may leave the circle
(in the manner described
above), before returning to a
stationary position and
beginning a fresh trial. Any
such moves are included in the
maximum time normally
allowed for a trial.

As a competitor takes his or
her stance in the circle to begin
a put, the shot should be near
or touching the chin, and the
hand must not drop below this
position during the throwing
action. The shot must not be
taken behind the line of the
shoulders.

Measurement

For a put to be valid, the shot
has to land completely within
the inner edges of lines marking
a sector of 40 degrees. The put
is measured from the nearest
indentation in the ground made
by the shot to the inside of the
circumference of the throwing
circle, along
a line drawn
to the
center of
the circle.

Measurements
should be made
immediately after
each put,
recorded to the
nearest 1cm
($\frac{1}{2}$ in) below the
distance measured
if that distance is not
a whole centimeter.

The shot

The shot is made of
any metal not softer
than brass, or a shell
of such metal filled
with lead or other
material. It has a smooth
finish. No unorthodox shot
surface is permissible.
The minimum weight of a
shot is 7.26 kg (16 lb) in
men's competition and
4 kg (9 lb) in women's. In
men's events, the shot
has a minimum diameter of 110
mm (4 $\frac{1}{4}$ in) and a maximum of
130 mm (5 in). For women's,
the equivalents are 95 mm
(3$\frac{3}{4}$ in) and 110 mm (4$\frac{1}{2}$ in)

Indoor competition

In indoor competition the 40
degree landing sector should
extend as far as the limitations
of space allow, and should be of
some suitable material on
which the shot will make an
imprint. There needs to be a
stopping device at the end of
the putting area. Specifications
are the same as for outdoors,
although special plastic or
rubber cased shots may be used.

Safety is paramount in the
throwing events. They
should be conducted only
in a strictly controlled
situation, with competition
areas being adequately
roped off. Whether in
practice or competition,
any item thrown should be
carried back to the starting
area by hand.

*Below, shot put release;
left and above left,
different buildup styles*

CZECH
TDK
1212
STUTTGART '93

Shot circle construction

The interior of the shot circle is constructed of concrete, asphalt, or similar firm and non-slippery material. The surface of the inside of the circle is level and 14 mm–26 mm (¹/₂ in) lower than the upper edge of the circle rim (which should be level with the ground outside). The circle rim is made of band iron, steel, or other suitable material. Measured from inside the rim, the diameter of the circle should be 2.135 m (7 ft), with a 5 mm (¹/₄ in) deviation either way. A white rim should be 6 mm (¹/₄ in) thick. A white line, 5 cm wide (2 in), should be drawn from the top of the metal rim, extending for at least 75 cm (30 in) on either side of the circle. The plane of the line should form an imaginary bisection of the circle dividing it into front and rear halves, the rear edge of the line passing through the center of the circle.

A stopboard, with a curved inner edge coinciding with the inner edge of the circle, is positioned in the middle of the circumference of the front half of the circle (midway between the sector lines). The board, painted white, should be fixed firmly to the ground. Its dimensions are as follows: 1.21–1.23 m (approx. 4 ft) long on the inside, 11.2–11.4 cm wide, and 9.8–10.2 cm high in relation to the level of the inside of the circle.

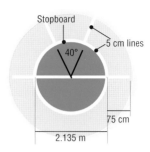

A forty degree sector emanating from the center of the throwing circle can be laid out accurately by making the distance between two points on the inside edge of the sector lines 20m from the center of the circle exactly 13.68m apart (and 27.36m apart at 40m from the center).

Throwing the hammer

In the hammer throw, the object used is not a conventional hammer but a metal ball attached to a wire with a handle at its other end. The competitor grips the handle with both hands and begins by whirling the ball around in a circle, passing above and behind the head and just below the knees. The thrower then spins around three or four times within the throwing circle, building up centrifugal force, before releasing the hammer upwards and outwards.

Hammer cage

The competition area should be roped off and throws should be made from an enclosure or cage to ensure the safety of spectators, officials, and competitors. The cage should be capable of stopping a hammer moving at a speed of up to 32 m (105 ft) per second, arranged to eliminate any danger of ricocheting or rebounding back towards the athlete or over the top of the cage. Provided it satisfies those requirements, any form of cage design and construction can be used.

Competition

Each competitor may have two practice trials before competition begins. Athletes may wear gloves, and may tape individual fingers, but may not apply any substance to their shoes or to the surface of the throwing circle. They should start their throws from a stationary position within the circle, at which

Landing sector

Hammer circle

40°

2.5 m

point the head of the hammer may be on the ground either inside or outside the circle. Having started to make the throw, a competitor may not touch the ground outside the circle or the top of the circle rim with any part of the body. Doing so constitutes a foul

throw (which counts as a trial). The head of the hammer may touch the ground during a competitor's preliminary swings and turns but, should the competitor then interrupt the throw so as to begin a trial again, it will be considered a foul throw. A competitor should not leave the circle until the hammer has touched the ground. When leaving the circle, the first contact with the top of the circle rim or the ground outside the circle has to be completely behind the white line drawn outside the circle theoretically running through its center.

Provided the above rules have not been infringed, a competitor may interrupt a trial once started, may lay the hammer

down, and may leave the circle (in the manner described), before returning to a stationary position and beginning a fresh trial. Any such moves should be included in the maximum time

normally allowed for a trial.

For a throw to be valid, the hammer head must land completely within the inner edges of lines marking a sector of 40 degrees set out on the ground. If the hammer first strikes the cage before landing within the sector, the throw is considered valid. If the hammer breaks during a throw or while in the air, the competitor may throw again. If such an incident results in the competitor losing balance and committing a foul, it should similarly not be counted.

Measurement

A throw is measured from the indentation in the ground made by the hammer head that is nearest to the inside of the circumference of the throwing circle, along a line drawn to the center of the circle.

Measurements are made immediately after each throw, recorded in even centimeters to the nearest unit below the distance measured if that distance is not a whole even centimeter.

Left, hammer world championship competitor

Below, stages in the hammer throw.

1 2 3 4

5 6 7 8

Hammer circle and equipment
The specifications for the hammer circle are the same as for the shot put circle (but without a stopboard). The hammer is made of any metal not softer than brass, or a shell of such metal filled with lead or other material. The steel wire, connected to the head by means of a swivel, is at least 3mm in diameter. The handle or grip on the other end of the wire may be of single or double loop construction, but rigid and without hinging joints. The minimum weight of a hammer is 7.26 kg (16 lb) in men's competition and 4kg (9 lb) in women's. In men's events, the hammer has a minimum diameter of 110 mm (4¼ in) and a maximum of 130 mm. In women's, the equivalents are 95 mm and 110 mm.*

Throwing a discus

In this event the athlete holds the discus—a platter-shaped object—against the palm of the hand and forearm of the throwing arm, with the finger ends around the edge. Facing away from the direction of the throw, he or she then rapidly makes one and half spins before propelling the discus into the air with a sidearm throw. For safety reasons, as in the hammer-throwing event, discus trials are made from an enclosure or cage. Most of the specifications for the discus circle are the same as those for the hammer circle, except that the inside diameter of the circle is 2.5 m.

Competitors may have two practice trials. They may not wear gloves, nor apply any substance on their shoes or in the throwing circle. Adopting any position they choose, athletes commence a throw from a stationary position within the circle. It is a foul if, having started to make the throw, a competitor touches the ground outside the circle or the top of the circle rim with any part of the body. A competitor must

Discus circle

2.5 m   40°

Landing sector

not leave the circle until the discus has touched the ground. The rules relating to leaving the circle, or beginning a fresh trial, are the same as for the hammer and shot events outlined previously.

For a throw to be valid the discus must land completely within the inner edges of lines marking a sector of 40 degrees. If the discus first strikes the cage before landing within the sector, the throw is considered valid. If it breaks during a fair throw, it does not count as a trial.

Measurement

Immediately after a fair throw, the distance is measured from the nearest mark in the ground made by the discus to the inside of the circumference of the circle, along a line drawn to the center of the circle.

Measurements are recorded in even centimeter units to the nearest unit below the distance measured if that distance is not a whole even centimeter.

Discus
Below, the body of the discus is made of wood or other suitable material, with a metal rim, the edge of which is circular. Each side is identical, without any indentations or projections. The minimum weights are 2 kg (4½ lb) for men and 1 kg (2½ lb) for women. The approved discus dimensions for men's and women's competition are shown in the diagram below.

Men 219–221 mm
Women 180–182 mm

1   2   3   4   5

6   7   8   9

Above, stages in the discus throw.

Throwing the javelin

A javelin is like a spear, thrown over the shoulder or upper part of the throwing arm by an athlete at the end of an approach run. It may not be slung or hurled, and no unorthodox styles are allowed.

No practice throws are permissible after the competition has begun, and gloves may not be worn. The javelin is held in one hand only, and at the grip, so that the smallest finger is nearest to the point. Two parallel lines mark the javelin runway, and during their run-up to throw, competitors may not cross either of these lines. In the course of a throw, until the javelin has been launched, a competitor may not turn completely around so that his or her back is toward the throwing arc of the scratch line (the arc represents part of a circle drawn with a radius of 8 m with its center in the middle of the runway).

If a competitor steps on or beyond the arc or extended scratch line in the course of a throw, it is a foul. A foul throw, or letting the javelin go in an attempt, counts as a trial, but not if a javelin breaks during a fair throw. For a throw to be valid, the tip of the metal head must strike the ground before any other part of the javelin. It must also be within the inner edges of the landing sector. When the javelin has touched the ground, the competitor may leave the runway from behind the white line

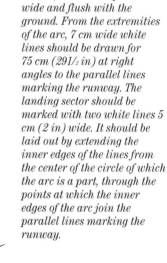
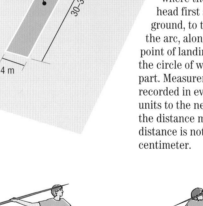

Landing sector

29°

Throwing arc

Runway

30–36.5 m

4 m

of the arc at right angles to the parallel lines.

Immediately after a fair throw, the distance should be measured from where the tip of the metal head first struck the ground, to the inside edge of the arc, along a line from the point of landing to the center of the circle of which the arc is a part. Measurements should be recorded in even centimeter units to the nearest unit below the distance measured if that distance is not a whole even centimeter.

The runway should be 30–36.5 m in length. The parallel lines should be 5 cm (2 in) wide and 4 m apart. The throw should be made from behind the arc, a white strip 7 cm wide and flush with the ground. From the extremities of the arc, 7 cm wide white lines should be drawn for 75 cm (29½ in) at right angles to the parallel lines marking the runway. The landing sector should be marked with two white lines 5 cm (2 in) wide. It should be laid out by extending the inner edges of the lines from the center of the circle of which the arc is a part, through the points at which the inner edges of the arc join the parallel lines marking the runway.

Javelin action.

Combined events
In combined events, athletes compete in several different disciplines over a period of up to two days. Athletes gain points for each event, and the one with the highest score at the end of the competition is the winner.

Combined events include the pentathlon, decathlon, and heptathlon. The first may be contested at outdoor level by men and indoors by both men and women. Only male athletes contest the decathlon. The heptathlon is contested by men at indoor level, but only by women outdoors. The breakdown (and competing order) of events in each case is as follows:
* *Outdoor pentathlon (men):*
one-day event—long jump, javelin, 200-m run, discus, and 1,500-m run.
* *Indoor pentathlon (men):*
one-day event—60-m hurdles, long jump, shot put, high jump, 1,000-m run.
* *Indoor pentathlon (women):*
one-day event—60-m hurdles, high jump, shot put, long jump, 800-m run.
* *Outdoor heptathlon (women):*
two-day event—100-m hurdles, high jump, shot put, 200-m run, long jump, javelin, 800-m run.
* *Indoor heptathlon (men):*
two-day event—60-m run, long jump, shot put, high jump, 60-m hurdles, pole vault, 1,000-m run.
* *Outdoor decathlon (men):*
two-day event—100-m run, long jump, shot put, high jump, 400-m run, 110-m hurdles, discus, pole vault, javelin, 1,500-m run.

In combined competition, athletes are allowed three trials in the long jump and in each throwing event. There should, at the discretion of the referee, be an interval of at least 30 minutes between the time one event ends and another starts for an individual athlete. In running and hurdle races, competitors are disqualified in any event in which they are responsible for three false starts. For the high jump and pole vault, heights should be increased uniformly throughout the competition by 3 cm (approx. 1 in) and 10 cm (4 in) respectively.

Any athlete who fails to participate in any of the required events may not participate further. In the event of a tie, the winner should be the competitor who, in the greater number of events, has received more points than the other tied competitor(s). If that does not resolve it, the winner should be the athlete scoring the highest number of points in any one of the events (this applies also for any other place in the competition).

The javelin
A javelin is a metal shaft, with a pointed metal head and a cord grip. The finish of the shaft should be smooth and uniform. The cord grip, covering the javelin's center of gravity, should not exceed the diameter of the shaft by more than 8 mm (⅓ in). The cross-section of the javelin should be circular throughout, the maximum diameter of the shaft being immediately in front of the grip. From the grip, the javelin tapers regularly to the tip at the front and the tail at the rear.

2.2–2.3 m

2.6–2.7 m

Women's

Men's

Javelin specifications in men's (and women's) competition:

minimum weight—
   800 (600) gm

overall length—
   2.6(2.2) m (min)
   2.7(2.3) m (max)

length of metal head—
   250(250) mm (min)
   330(330) mm (max)

distance from tip of metal head to center of gravity—
   0.9(0.8)m (min)
   1.06(0.95) m (max)

diameter of shaft at thickest point—
   25(20)mm (min)
   30(25)mm (max)

Golf
Essentials

The game of golf originated in Scotland during the late Middle Ages, probably on the grassy dunes of Scotland's eastern coast. In 1457, King James II of Scotland tried to ban his subjects from playing the game, because he felt that they were neglecting archery, a martial skill required to defend the kingdom. Today, players of varying ability can legally enjoy a fair competition thanks to the handicap system. The world's best players compete for large cash prizes on a roving "tour" of organized competitions.

The teams
Players compete against one competitor, in a field of competitors, or with a partner against another pair.

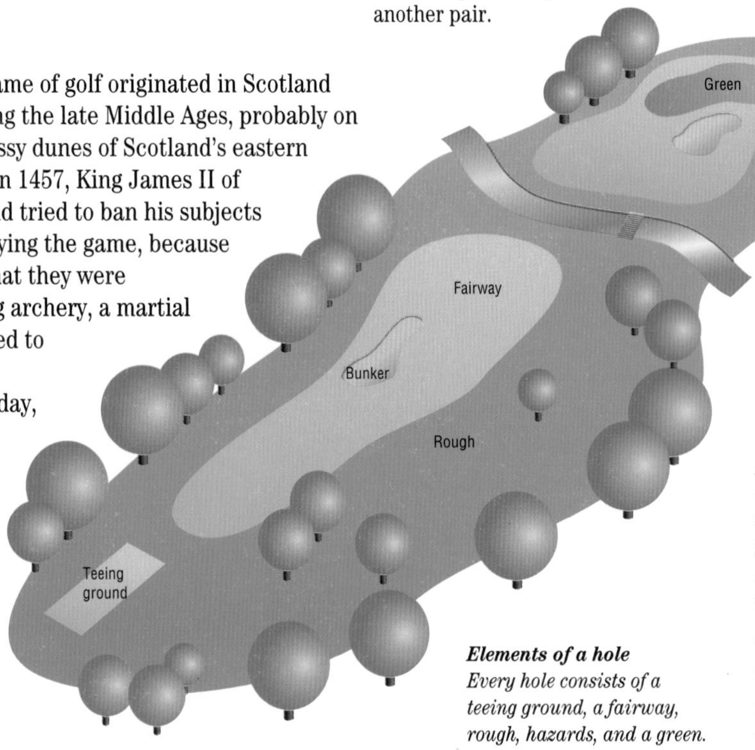

Officials
A marker records a player's score in strokes. A fellow competitor may act as a marker. In competitions, a referee decides on questions of fact and applies the rules, although in general, officials are far less involved in the competition than in most other sports.

Ryder cup—awarded for team golf matching Europe versus the USA.

Elements of a hole
Every hole consists of a teeing ground, a fairway, rough, hazards, and a green.

Labels on diagram: Green, Fairway, Bunker, Rough, Teeing ground

The hole
The hole must be 4.25 in in diameter and at least 4 in deep.

The tee
A peg made of plastic or wood on which the ball is placed for the first stroke of each hole.

The ball
The maximum ball weight is 1.62 oz and the minimum size is 1.68 in. Balls come in a variety of materials, ranging from the inexpensive one-piece Surlyn ball to the more costly balata-covered ball with a liquid center bound with yarn. For regulations concerning usage and condition of the ball see Rule 5, The Ball (page 196). See also Rule 21, Cleaning Ball (page 203).

The course
A golf course normally consists of 18 holes, although short, 9-hole courses also exist. Each hole starts with a teeing ground. The fairway is an area of short grass that connects the tee to the green, an area of fine, well-maintained grass where the player putts the ball into a hole. The surrounding landscape of trees, rough grass, water features, and sand bunkers provides challenging obstacles.

Courses vary in length, from around 5,500 to 7,000 yds (up to 4 miles). The length of each hole and the sequence of long and shorter holes also varies from one course to another, as golf course architects design holes, that are unique. Each hole is indicated by a flag.

Golfing mecca
Augusta National, home of the U.S. Masters tournament.

Golf bag
The bag carries clubs and accessories such as a ball cleaner, field mark repairer, and ball marker—as well as towel, water bottle, and snacks. Golf bags can be carried over the shoulder or attached to a trolley for easy transport across the course.

On the green
Renowned for his long drives, Greg Norman ("the Great White Shark") often gets the ball on the green with a single stroke. But like every player, he takes immense care both choosing his iron and preparing his putting stroke on the green.

Clubs

Players take a set of clubs with them around the course, each designed for a certain type of stroke. There are two types of clubs—irons and woods—although most of today's "woods" are actually made of metal. The basic design of the club has changed little, but manufacturers have been experimenting with construction techniques and materials for over a century—woods such as persimmon and hickory gave way to steel, and other materials such as graphite, boron, and titanium are also now used.

Generally, woods are designed for power, and irons for precision. Each club has a different "loft," or head angle, according to the required trajectory of the ball. Woods are normally numbered from 1 (the driver) to 9, and irons usually range from 1 to 10. In the range of clubs, the loft increases as the length of the trajectory decreases. The sand wedge has an extreme loft designed for getting the ball out of the bunker. Putters are designed for precision shots on the green. The maximum number of clubs that a player is permitted to take on a round of golf is 14.

Wood

Iron

Club class
Woods are designed for long drives; irons for accuracy over a short distance.

Dress

Nice dress is customary; jeans and T-shirts are banned by many clubs. A glove may be worn on the player's dominant hand to ensure a good grip on the club.

Buying equipment

Golf can be an expensive pastime, so it is best to buy a minimum amount of equipment before you commit yourself to the sport. You don't have to acquire a full set of clubs to start with—you may be able to buy suitable second-hand clubs. Basic Surlyn balls are fine for beginners. Even at an early stage, though, a pair of good quality shoes with leather uppers is well worth buying. Golf, clubs often insist on golf shoes (rather than sneakers or tennis shoes).

HOW TO PLAY

Each hole starts at the teeing ground. The player strikes the ball with an appropriate club, selected for power or precision, aiming to land it on the green. Other shots are taken as necessary to move the ball closer and closer to the hole. Finally, the player putts the ball into the hole. An "ace," or hole-in-one, is quite a rare feat.

Good driving
Big hitter John Daly demonstrates excellent stance and posture before his downswing for a power drive. See also The swing (pages 198–199).

How to win

There are two forms of golf: stroke play and match play. In stroke play, the final score is calculated according to the total number of strokes made over the 18 holes of the round. In match play, the players' score indicates the number of holes they have won; a player wins a hole by completing it using fewer strokes than his competitors. *See Rule 2 and Rule 3 (page 196).*

The score card indicates the distance for each hole in yards (or meters) as well as the par for that hole (the score that an expert would be expected to achieve on that hole). In a handicap competition, the score is adjusted according to each player's handicap and the player with the lowest score wins.

A player's handicap is calculated by the club where the player is a member, on the basis of a series of completed score cards. A good player will have a lower handicap than a less proficient one. The handicap is deducted from the player's final score. Professionals do not have a handicap.

KEY RULES

• Golf has its own code of behavior, based on safety, honesty, and consideration. The player should look around and behind before teeing off, to ensure that fellow competitors or spectators will not be struck.

• If the player is responsible for marking a score card, as is frequently the case in non-competition golf, he is honor-bound to mark the card honestly and accurately.

• Violations sometimes add a penalty stroke (or strokes) to a player's score in stroke play, or incur the loss of the hole in match play. For instance, in stroke play, if a player starts a hole from outside the teeing ground, he is penalized by two strokes. *See Rule 11-4b (page 197); there are many other examples of penalty strokes.*

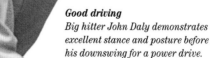

RULES OF GOLF
••••••••••

Rule 1. The Game

1-1. General
The game of golf consists in playing a ball from the teeing ground into the hole by stroke or successive strokes in accordance with the rules.

1-2. Exerting Influence on Ball
No player or caddie shall take any action to influence the position or the movement of a ball except in accordance with the rules.

1-3. Agreement to Waive Rules
Players shall not agree to exclude the operation of any rule or waive any penalty incurred.

1-4. Points Not Covered by Rules
If any point in dispute is not covered by the rules, the decision shall be made in accordance with equity.

Rule 2. Match Play

2-1. Winner of Hole; Reckoning of Holes
See How to win (page 195).

2-2. Halved Hole
A hole is halved if each side holes out in the same number of strokes.

2-3. Winner of Match
A match (which normally consists of a stipulated round) is won by the side that is leading by a number of holes greater than the number of holes remaining to be played. For the purpose of settling a tie, the stipulated round may be extended to as many holes as are required for a match to be won.

2-4. Concession of Next Stroke, Hole, or Match
When the opponent's ball is at rest or is deemed to be at rest under Rule 16-2, the player may concede the opponent to have holed out with his next stroke and the ball may be removed by either side with a club or otherwise.

A player may concede a hole or a match at any time prior to the conclusion of the hole or the match. Concession of a stroke, hole or match may not be declined or withdrawn.

2-5. Claims
In match play, if a doubt or dispute arises between the players and no duly authorized representative of the committee is available within a reasonable time, the players shall continue the match without delay. Any claim, if it is to be considered by the committee, must be made before any player in the match plays from the next teeing ground or, in the case of the last hole of the match, before all players in the match leave the putting green.

2-6. General Penalty
The penalty for a breach of a rule in match play is loss of the hole except when otherwise provided.

Rule 3. Stroke Play

3-1. Winner
The competitor who plays the stipulated round or rounds in the fewest strokes is the winner.

3-2. Failure to Hole Out
If a competitor fails to hole out at any hole and does not correct his mistake before he plays a stroke from the next teeing ground or, in the case of the last hole of the round, before he leaves the putting green, he shall be disqualified.

3-3. Doubt as to Procedure
a. Procedure
In stroke play only, when during play of a hole a competitor is doubtful of his rights or procedure, he may, without penalty, play a second ball. After the situation that caused the doubt has arisen, announce to his marker or his fellow competitor his decision to invoke this rule and the ball with which he will score if the rules permit.

b. Determination of Score for Hole
If the rules allow the procedure selected in advance by the competitor, the score with the ball selected shall be his score for the hole.

3-4. Refusal to Comply with a Rule
If a competitor refuses to comply with a rule affecting the rights of another competitor, he shall be disqualified.

3-5. General Penalty
The penalty for a breach of a rule in stroke play is two strokes except when otherwise provided.

Rule 4. Clubs
See also Clubs (page 195).

4-1.
The player's clubs shall conform with the provisions of this rule and with the specifications and interpretations set forth in Appendix II (Design of Clubs).

If a player's club ceases to conform with Rule 4-1 because of damage sustained in the normal course of play, the player may:
(i) use the club in its damaged state, but only for the remainder of the stipulated round during which such damage was sustained; or
(ii) without unduly delaying play, repair it.

4-2. Playing Characteristics Changed
During a stipulated round, the playing characteristics of a club shall not be purposely changed by adjustment or by any other means.

4-3. Foreign Material
Foreign material must not be applied to the club face for the purpose of influencing the movement of the ball.

4-4. Maximum of Fourteen Clubs
See Clubs (page 195).

Rule 5. The Ball
See also The ball (page 194).

5-1. General
The ball the player uses shall conform to requirements specified in Appendix III (The Ball).

5-2. Foreign Material
Foreign material must not be applied to the ball for the purpose of changing its playing characteristics.

5-3. Ball Unfit for Play
A ball is unfit for play if it is visibly cut, cracked, or out of shape.

Rule 6. Player's Responsibilities

6-1.
The player is responsible for knowing the conditions under which the competition is to be played

6-2 Handicap
a. Match Play
Before starting a match in a handicap competition, the players should determine from one another their respective handicaps. If a player begins the match having declared a higher handicap that would affect the number of strokes given or received, he shall be disqualified.

b. Stroke Play
In any round of a handicap competition, the competitor shall ensure that his handicap is recorded on his score card before it is returned to the committee.

6-3. Time of Starting and Groups
a. Time of Starting
The player shall start at the time laid down by the committee.

b. Groups
In stroke play, the competitor shall remain throughout the round in the group arranged by the committee.

6-4. Caddie
The player may have only one caddie at any one time.

6-5. Ball
The responsibility for playing the proper ball rests with the player. Each player should put an identification mark on his ball.

6-6. Scoring in Stroke Play
a. Recording Scores
After each hole the marker should check the score with the competitor and record it. On completion of the round the marker shall sign the card and hand it to the competitor.

b. Signing and Returning Card
After completion of the round, the competitor should check his score

for each hole and settle any doubtful points with the committee. He shall ensure that the marker has signed the card, countersigning the card himself and return it to the committee.

c. Alteration of Card
No alteration may be made on a card after the competitor has returned it to the committee.

d. Wrong Score for Hole
The competitor is responsible for the correctness of the score recorded for each hole on his card. If he returns a score for any hole lower than actually taken, he shall be disqualified.

6-7. Undue Delay; Slow Play
The player shall play without undue delay and in accordance with any pace of play guidelines that may be laid down by the committee.

6-8. Discontinuance of Play
a. When Permitted
The player shall not discontinue play unless:
(i) the committee has suspended play;
(ii) he believes there is danger from lightning;
(iii) he is seeking a decision from the committee on a doubtful or disputed point; or
(iv) there is some other good reason, such as illness.

Rule 7
Covers practice before or during rounds.

Rule 8. Advice; Indicating Line of Play

8-1. Advice
During a stipulated round, a player shall not give advice to anyone in the competition except his partner. A player may ask for advice during a stipulated round from only his partner or either of their caddies.

8-2. Indicating Line of Play
The "line of play" is the direction that the player wishes his ball to take after a stroke, plus a reasonable distance on either side of the intended direction.

a. Other Than on Putting Green
A player may have the line of play indicated to him by anyone, but no one shall be positioned by the player on or close to the line or an extension of the line beyond the hole while the stroke is being played.

b. On the Putting Green
When the player's ball is on the putting green, the player, his partner, or either of their caddies may, before but not during the stroke, point out a line for putting, but in doing so the putting green shall not be touched.

Rule 9. Information as to Strokes Taken

9-1. General

The number of strokes a player has taken shall include any penalty strokes incurred.

9-2. Match Play
A player who has incurred a penalty shall inform his opponent as soon as practicable.

An opponent is entitled to ascertain from the player, during the play of a hole, the number of strokes he has taken, and, after play of a hole, the number of strokes taken on the hole just completed.

If during the play of a hole the player gives or is deemed to give the wrong information as to the number of strokes taken, he shall incur no penalty if he corrects the mistake before his opponent has played his next stroke. If the player fails so to correct the wrong information, he shall lose the hole.

9-3.
A competitor who has incurred a penalty should inform his marker as soon as practicable.

Rule 10. Order of Play
10-1 Match Play
a. Teeing Ground
The side entitled to play first form the teeing ground is said to have the "honor."

The side that shall have the honor at the first teeing ground shall be determined by the order of the draw. In the absence of a draw, the honor should be decided by lot.

b. Other Than on Teeing Ground
When the balls are in play, the ball farther from the hole shall be played first. If the balls are equidistant from the hole, the ball to be played first should be decided by lot.

c. Playing Out of Turn
If a player plays when his opponent should have played, the opponent may immediately require the player to cancel the stroke so played and, in correct order, play a ball without penalty as nearly as possible at the spot from which the original ball was played.

10-2. Stroke Play
a. Teeing Ground
The competitor entitled to play first from the teeing ground is said to have the "honor."
See 10-1 (a) for the procedure for determining the honor.

b. Other Than on Teeing Ground
See 10-1 (b).

c. Playing Out of Turn
If a competitor plays out of turn, no penalty is incurred and the ball shall be played as it lies. If, however, the committee determines that competitors have agreed to play in an order other than that set forth in Clauses 2a and 2b of this rule to give one of

them an advantage, they shall be disqualified.

10-3. Provisional Ball or Second Ball from Teeing Ground
If a player plays a provisional ball or a second ball from a teeing ground, he should do so after his opponent or fellow competitor has played his first stroke. If a player plays a provisional ball or a second ball out of turn, Clauses 1c and 2c of this rule shall apply.

10-4. Ball Moved in Measuring
If a ball is moved in measuring to determine which ball is farther from the hole, no penalty is incurred and the ball shall be replaced.

Rule 11. Teeing Ground
11-1. Teeing
In teeing, the ball may be placed on the ground, on an irregularity of surface created by the player on the ground or on a tee, sand, or other substance in order to raise it off the ground. A player may stand outside the teeing ground to play a ball within it.

11-2. Tee-Markers
Before a player plays his first stroke with any ball from the teeing ground of the hole being played, the tee-markers are deemed to be fixed.

11-3 Ball Falling Off Tee
If a ball, when not in play, falls off a tee or is knocked off a tee by the player in addressing it, it may be re-teed without penalty, but if a stroke is made at the ball in these circumstances, whether the ball is moving or not, the stroke counts but no penalty is incurred.

11-4. Playing from Outside Teeing Ground
a. Match Play
If a player, when starting a hole, plays a ball from outside the teeing ground, the opponent may immediately require the player to cancel the stroke so played and play a ball from within the teeing ground, without penalty.

b. Stroke Play
If a competitor, when starting a hole, plays a ball from outside the teeing ground, he shall incur a penalty of two strokes and shall then play a ball from within the teeing ground.

If the competitor plays a stroke from the next teeing ground without first correcting his mistake or, in the case of the last hole of the round, leaves the putting green without first declaring his intention to correct his mistake, he shall be disqualified.

Strokes played by a competitor from outside the teeing ground do not count in his score.

11-5. Playing from Wrong Teeing Ground
The provisions of Rule 11-4 apply.

Rule 12. Searching for and Identifying Ball
12-1. Searching for Ball; Seeing Ball
In searching for his ball anywhere on the course, the player may touch or bend long grass or other vegetation, but only to the extent necessary to find and identify it, provided that this does not improve the lie of the ball, the area of his intended swing, or his line of play.

In a hazard, if a ball is covered by loose impediments or sand, the player may remove as much thereof as will enable him to see a part of the ball. If the ball is moved in such removal, no penalty is incurred; the ball shall be replaced and, if necessary, re-covered.

If a ball lying in casual water, ground under repair or a hole, cast, or runway made by an animal or bird is accidentally moved during search, no penalty is incurred; the ball shall be replaced, unless the player elects to proceed under Rule 25-1b.

If a ball is believed to be lying in water in a water hazard, the player may probe for it with a club or otherwise. If the ball is moved in so doing, no penalty is incurred; the ball shall be replaced, unless the player elects to proceed under Rule 26-1.

12-2. Identifying Ball
Except in a hazard, the player may, without penalty, lift a ball he believes to be his own for the purpose of identification. If the ball is the player's ball, he shall replace it. Before lifting the ball, the player must announce his intention to his opponent in match play or his marker or a fellow competitor in stroke play and mark the position of the ball. He must then give his opponent, marker or fellow competitor an opportunity to observe the lifting and replacement.

13-1. Ball Played as It Lies
The ball shall be played as it lies, except as otherwise provided in the rules.

13-2. Improving Lie, Area of Intended Swing, or Line of Play
Except as provided in the rules, a player shall not improve or allow to be improved the position or lie of his ball, the area of his intended swing, his line of play, or a reasonable extension of that line beyond the hole or the area in which he is to drop or place a ball by any of the following actions:
moving, bending or breaking anything growing or fixed, or removing or pressing down sand, loose soil, replaced divots, or other irregularities of surface, except as follows:

as may occur in fairly taking his stance, in making a stroke or the backward movement of his club for a stroke, on the teeing ground in creating or eliminating irregularities of surface as provided in Rule 16-1a or on the putting green in removing sand and loose soil or in repairing damage as provided in Rule 16-1c.

The club may be grounded only lightly and shall not be pressed on the ground.

13-3. Building Stance
A player is entitled to place his feet firmly in taking his stance, but he shall not build a stance.

13-4. Ball in Hazard
Except as provided in the rules, before making a stroke at a ball that is in a hazard or that, having been lifted from a hazard, may be dropped or placed in the hazard, the player shall not:
a. Test the condition of the hazard or any similar hazard;
b. Touch the ground in the hazard or water in the water hazard with a club or otherwise; or
c. Touch or move a loose impediment lying in or touching the hazard.
Exceptions:
1. Provided nothing is done that constitutes testing the condition of the hazard or improves the lie of the ball, there is no penalty if the player (a) touches the ground or water in any hazard as a result of or to prevent falling, in removing an obstruction, in measuring or retrieving or lifting a ball under any rule or (b) places his clubs in a hazard.
2. The player after playing the stroke, or his caddie at any time without the authority of the player, may smooth sand or soil in the hazard, provided that nothing is done that improves the lie of the ball or assists the player in his subsequent play of the hole.

Rule 14. Striking the Ball
Definition
A "stroke" is the forward movement of the club made with the intention of fairly striking at and moving the ball, but if a player checks his downswing voluntarily before the clubhead reaches the ball he is deemed not to have made a stroke.

14-1. Ball to Be Fairly Struck at
The ball shall be fairly struck at with the head of the club and must not be pushed, scraped, or spooned.

14-2. Assistance
In making a stroke, a player shall not accept physical assistance or protection from the elements.

➡ *page 200*

TACTICS

It is useful to arrive at the golf course in good time before the game, in order to limber up and practice driving and swinging on the practice range. The tactics involved in golf are known as course management—this entails being able to select the best club for a shot, based on the need for power, precision, or loft. In addition, it is a good idea to pack a bottle of water and a snack in the golf bag—a round of golf can last a long time.

Putters
Putters come in a variety of different shapes and weights to suit different greens. Heavier putters, for instance, help on slower greens.

A putting grip
The thumbs overlap facing directly down the putter handle.

Practice makes perfect
Players of all abilities seek regular practice and instruction. Below and right, golf coach David Leadbetter offers guidance.

Putting position
For a smooth putting action the golfer needs a completely stable stance with the knees relaxed and slightly flexed and the upper body weight firmly placed on the feet.

SKILLS

Developing a good *swing* (the arc made by the golf club before striking the ball) is the key factor in becoming a proficient golfer. The execution of the swing depends on the player's *address* (the posture adopted before the ball is struck), powers of concentration, and grip. As he swings, the player should keep his head still, looking down on the ball. Essentially, the swing comes from the arms, not the wrist.

Putting is the other essential skill; a player must control his hands and deliver a delicate, accurate stroke to get the ball in the hole.

Although brute strength is not essential, and can even be counterproductive, exercises that develop the strength of the wrists, legs, and stomach are beneficial. Exercises designed to strengthen and protect the back are essential.

The swing (A)
Getting the swing right is something that obsesses every golfer and golfers may spend hours practicing. One of the keys to success is the correct stance. The aim is to swing the arms, upper body, and club so that the club head addresses the ball at the maximum possible speed. The stroke begins with the golfer addressing the ball with the face of the club to align it properly (1). The golfer then takes a half swing back to prepare the stroke. The swing then begins with the golfer swinging the club back behind his head, then forward to strike the ball in one smooth action (2)—see opposite.

1

2

Gray Area

Rule 26-1 Ball in Water Hazard

This rule states that "In order to treat the ball as lost in the [water] hazard, there must be reasonable evidence that the ball lodged in it."

During play, there may be some difficulty in agreeing on what constitutes "reasonable evidence." Further insight was given in the 1997 Decisions on the Rules of Golf:

> The term "reasonable evidence" in Rule 26-1 is purposely and necessarily broad so as to permit sensible judgements to be reached on the basis of all the relevant circumstances of particular cases. As applied in this context, a player may not deem his ball lost in a water hazard simply because he thinks the ball may be in the hazard. The evidence must be preponderantly in favour of its being in the hazard. Otherwise, the ball must be considered lost outside the hazard and the player must proceed under Rule 27-1. Physical conditions in the area have a great deal to do with it. For example, if a water hazard is surrounded by a fairway on which a ball could hardly be lost, the existence of reasonable evidence that the ball is in the hazard would be more likely than if there was deep rough in the area. Observing a ball splash in a water hazard would not necessarily provide reasonable evidence as splashing balls sometimes skip out of hazards. It would depend on all the circumstances.

Pitching and chipping

There are a number of other ways of striking the ball apart from a full swing drive and a putt. When the golfer is within 55 yds of the green he needs a shot that will drop the ball on the green with the minimum of rolling after it lands. This is where the "pitch stroke" comes into play, which uses a pitching wedge to gently loft the ball into the air in an action a bit like an underarm throw. Once within about 10 ft of the green the golfer may use a "chip shot" with a wedge to lift the ball over rougher grass so that it lands on the green.

3

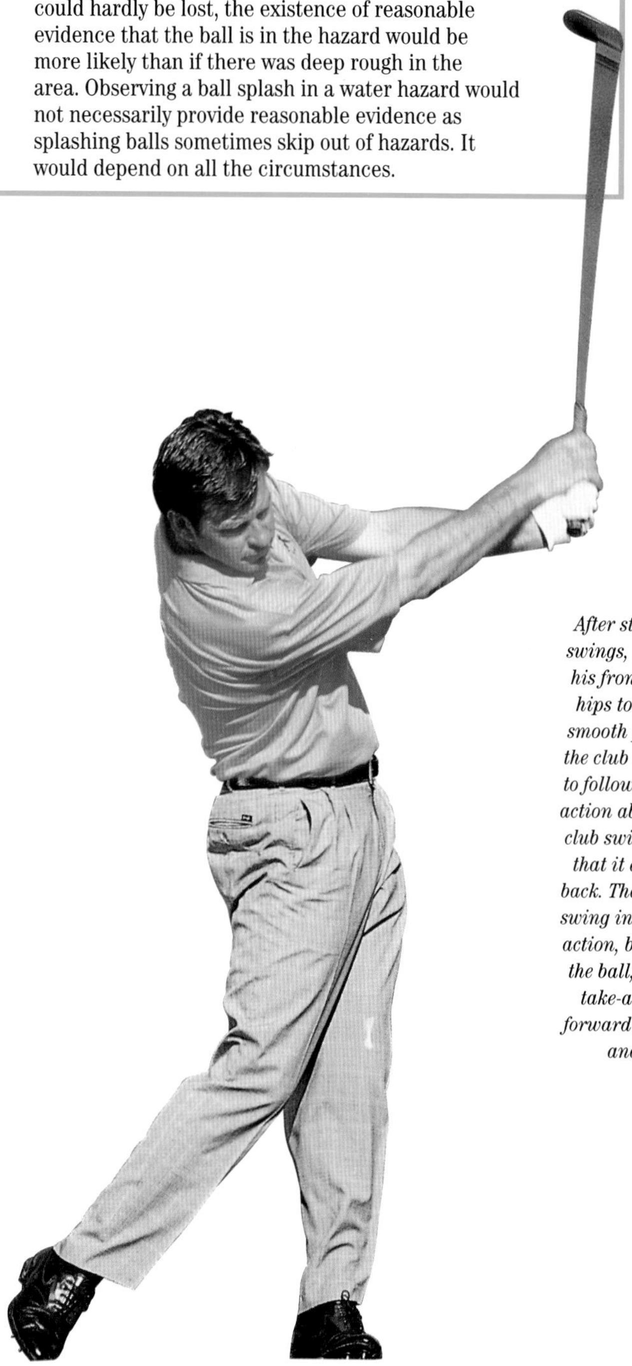

The Swing (B)

After striking the ball, the golfer swings, transferring his weight to his front foot and unwinding his hips to push the ball away with smooth power (3). He then allows the club and his entire upper body to follow through freely to keep the action absolutely balanced (4). The club swings all the way around so that it ends up down the golfer's back. The aim is to make the entire swing into one smooth, continuous action, beginning with addressing the ball, and continuing with the take-away, the backswing, the forward swing, the swing through and the follow-through.

4

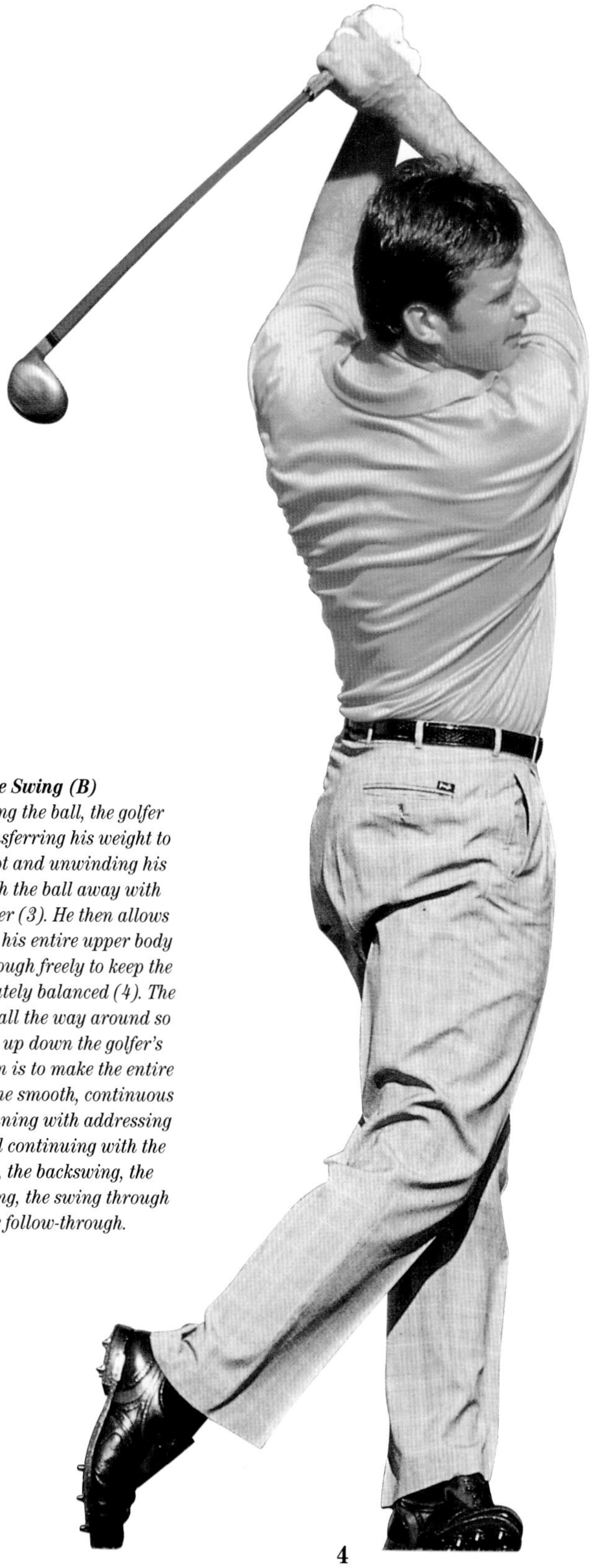

continued from page 197

14-3. Artificial Devices and Unusual Equipment
Except as provided in the rules, during a stipulated round the player shall not use any artificial device or unusual equipment:
a. That might assist him in making a stroke or in his play; or
b. For the purpose of gauging or measuring distance or conditions that might affect his play; or
c. That might assist him in gripping the club, except that:
  (i) plain gloves may be worn;
  (ii) resin, powder, and drying or moisturizing agents may be used;
  (iii) tape or gauze may be applied to the grip; and
  (iv) a towel or handkerchief may be wrapped around the grip.

14-4. Striking the Ball More than Once
If a player's club strikes the ball more than once in the course of a stroke, the player shall count the stroke and add a penalty stroke.

14.5 Playing Moving Ball
A player shall not play while his ball is moving.
Exceptions:
Ball falling off tee (11-3).
Striking the ball more than once (14-4).
Ball moving in water (14-6).
When the ball begins to move only after the player has begun the stroke or the backward movement of his club for the stroke, he shall incur no penalty under this rule for playing a moving ball, but he is not exempt from any penalty incurred under the following rules:
  Ball at rest moved by player (18-2a).
  Ball at rest moving after address (18-2b).
  Ball at rest moving after loose impediment touched (18-2c).
(Ball purposely deflected or stopped by player, partner, or caddie—see Rule 1-2).

14-6. Ball Moving in Water
When a ball is moving in water in a water hazard, the player may, without penalty, make a stroke, but he must not delay making his stroke in order to allow the wind or current to improve the position of the ball. A ball moving in water in a water hazard may be lifted if the player elects to invoke Rule 26.

Rule 15. Wrong Ball; Substituted Ball

Definition
A "wrong ball" is any ball other than the player's:
a. Ball in play,
b. Provisional ball, or
c. Second ball played under Rule 3-3 or Rule 20-7b in stroke play.
15-1. General

A player must hole out with the ball played from the teeing ground unless a rule permits him to substitute another ball. If a player substitutes another ball when not so permitted, that ball is not a wrong ball; it becomes the ball in play and, if the error is not corrected as provided in Rule 20-6, the player shall incur a penalty of loss of hole in match play or two strokes in stroke play.

15-2. Match Play
If a player plays a stroke with a wrong ball except in a hazard, he shall lose the hole.

15-3. Stroke Play
If a competitor plays a stroke or strokes with a wrong ball, he shall incur a penalty of two strokes, unless the stroke or strokes played with such a ball were played when it was in a hazard, in which case no penalty is incurred.

The competitor must correct his mistake by playing the correct ball. If he fails to correct his mistake before he plays a stroke from the next teeing ground or, in the case of the last hole of the round, fails to declare his intention to correct his mistake before leaving the putting green, he shall be disqualified.

Strokes played by a competitor with a wrong ball do not count in his score.

If the wrong ball belongs to another competitor, its owner shall place a ball on the spot from which the wrong ball was first played.

Rule 16. The Putting Green

The "line of putt" is the line that the player wishes his ball to take after a stroke on the putting green. Except with respect to Rule 16-1e, the line of putt includes a reasonable distance on either side of the intended line. The line of putt does not extend beyond the hole.

16-1. General
a. Touching Line of Putt
The line of putt must not be touched except:
  (i) the player may move sand and loose soil on the putting green and other loose impediments by picking them up or by brushing them aside with his hand or a club without pressing anything down;
  (ii) in addressing the ball, the player may place the club in front of the ball without pressing anything down;
  (iii) in measuring (10-4);
  (iv) in lifting the ball (16-1b);
  (v) in pressing down a ball marker;
  (vi) in repairing old hole plugs or ball marks on the putting green (16-1c); and
  (vii) in removing movable obstructions (24-1).

b. Lifting Ball
A ball on the putting green may be lifted and, if desired, cleaned. A ball so lifted shall be replaced on the spot from which it was lifted.

c. Repair of Hole Plugs Ball Marks and Other Damage
The player may repair an old hole plug or damage to the putting green caused by the impact of a ball, whether or not the player's ball lies on the putting green. If the ball is moved in the process of such repair, it shall be replaced, without penalty. Any other damage to the putting green shall not be repaired if it might assist the player in his subsequent play of the hole.

d. Testing Surface
During the play of a hole, a player shall not test the surface of the putting green by rolling a ball or roughening or scraping the surface.

e. Standing Astride or on Line of Putt
The player shall not make a stroke on the putting green from a stance astride, or with either foot touching, the line of putt or an extension of that line behind the ball.

f. Position of Caddie or Partner
While making a stroke on the putting green, the player shall not allow his caddie, his partner, or his partner's caddie to position himself on or close to an extension of the line of putt behind the ball.

g. Playing Stroke While Another Ball in Motion
The player shall not play a stroke while another ball is in motion after a stroke from the putting green, except that, if a player does so, he incurs no penalty if it was his turn to play.

16-2. Ball Overhanging Hole
When any part of the ball overhangs the lip of the hole, the player is allowed enough time to reach the hole without unreasonable delay and an additional 10 seconds to determine whether the ball is at rest. If by then the ball has not fallen into the hole, it is deemed to be at rest. If the ball subsequently falls into the hole, the player is deemed to have holed out with his last stroke, and he shall add a penalty stroke to his score for the hole; otherwise there is no penalty under this rule.

Rule 17. The Flagstick

17-1. Flagstick Attended, Removed, or Held Up
Before and during the stroke, the player may have the flagstick attended, removed, or held up to indicate the position of the hole.

This may be done only on the authority of the player before he plays his stroke.

17-2. Unauthorized Attendance
a. Match Play
In match play, an opponent or his caddie shall not, without the authority or prior knowledge of the player, attend, remove, or hold up the flagstick while the player is making a stroke or his ball is in motion.

b. Stroke Play
In stroke play, if a fellow competitor or his caddie attends, removes or holds up the flagstick without the competitor's authority or prior knowledge while the competitor is making a stroke or his ball is in motion, the fellow competitor shall incur the penalty for breach of this rule. In such circumstances, if the competitor's ball strikes the flagstick, the person attending it or anything carried by him, the competitor incurs no penalty and the ball shall be played as it lies, except that, if the stroke was played from the putting green, the stroke shall be cancelled, the ball replaced and the stroke replayed.

17-3. Ball Striking Flagstick or Attendant
The player's ball shall not strike:
a. The flagstick when attended, removed, or held up by the player, his partner, or either of their caddies, or by another person with the player's authority or prior knowledge; or
b. The player's caddie, his partner, or his partner's caddie when attending the flagstick, or another person attending the flagstick with the player's authority or prior knowledge or anything carried by any such person; or
c. The flagstick in the hole, unattended, when the ball has been played from the putting green.

17-4. Ball Resting Against Flagstick
If the ball rests against the flagstick when it is in the hole, the player or another person authorized by him may move or remove the flagstick and if the ball falls into the hole, the player shall be deemed to have holed out with his last stroke; otherwise the ball, if moved, shall be placed on the lip of the hole, without penalty.

Rule 18. Ball at Rest Moved

A ball is deemed to have "moved" if it leaves its position and comes to rest in any other place.

An "outside agency" is any agency not part of the match or, in stroke play, not part of the competitor's side, and includes a referee, a marker, an observer, and a forecaddie. Neither wind nor water is an outside agency.

18-1. By Outside Agency

If a ball at rest is moved by an outside agency, the player shall incur no penalty and the ball shall be replaced before the player plays another stroke.

18-2. By Player, Partner, Caddie, or Equipment

a. General

When a player's ball is *in play*, if:

(i) the player, his partner, or either of their caddies lifts or moves it, touches it purposely (except with a club in the act of addressing it), or causes it to move except as permitted by a rule, or

(ii) equipment of the player or his partner causes the ball to move, the player shall incur a penalty stroke. The ball shall be replaced unless the movement of the ball occurs after the player has begun his swing and he does not discontinue his swing.

b. Ball Moving after Address

If a player's ball in play moves after he has addressed it (other than as a result of a stroke), the player shall be deemed to have moved the ball and shall incur a penalty stroke.

c. Ball Moving After Loose Impediment Touched

Through the green, if the ball moves after any loose impediment, lying within a club-length of it has been touched by the player, his partner, or either of their caddies and before the player has addressed it, the player shall be deemed to have moved the ball and shall incur a penalty stroke.

On the putting green, if the ball or the ball marker moves in the process of removing any loose impediment, the ball or the ball marker shall be replaced. There is no penalty provided the movement of the ball or the ball marker is directly attributable to the removal of the loose impediment.

18-3. By Opponent, Caddie, or Equipment in Match Play

a. During Search

If, during search for a player's ball, the ball is moved by an opponent, his caddie, or his equipment, no penalty is incurred and the player shall replace the ball.

b. Other Than During Search

If the ball is touched or moved by an opponent, his caddie, or his equipment, except otherwise provided in the rules, the opponent shall incur a penalty stroke. The player shall replace the ball.

18-4. By Fellow Competitor, Caddie, or Equipment in Stroke Play

If a competitor's ball is moved by

a fellow competitor, his caddie, or his equipment, no penalty is incurred. The competitor shall replace his ball.

18-5. By Another Ball

If a ball in play and at rest is moved by another ball in motion after a stroke, the moved ball shall be replaced.

Rule 19. Ball in Motion Deflected or Stopped

19-1. By Outside Agency

If a ball in motion is accidentally deflected or stopped by any outside agency, it is a rub of the green, no penalty is incurred and the ball shall be played as it lies except:

a. If a ball in motion after a stroke other than on the putting green comes to rest in or on any moving or animate outside agency, the player shall, through the green or in a hazard, drop the ball, or on the putting green place the ball, as near as possible to the spot where the outside agency was when the ball came to rest in or on it, and

b. If a ball in motion after a stroke on the putting green is deflected or stopped by, or comes to rest in or on, any moving or animate outside agency except a worm or an insect, the stroke shall be cancelled, the ball replaced and the stroke replayed.

19-2. By Player, Partner, Caddie, or Equipment

a. Match Play

If a player's ball is accidentally deflected or stopped by himself, his partner, or either of their caddies or equipment he shall lose the hole.

b. Stroke Play

If a competitor's ball is accidentally deflected or stopped by himself, his partner, or either of their caddies or equipment, the competitor shall incur a penalty of two strokes.

19-3. By Opponent, Caddie, or Equipment in Match Play

If a player's ball is accidentally deflected or stopped by an opponent, his caddie, or his equipment, no penalty is incurred. The player may play the ball as it lies or, before another stroke is played by either side, cancel the stroke and play a ball without penalty as nearly as possible at the spot from which the original ball was last played.

19-4. By Fellow Competitor, Caddie, or Equipment in Stroke, Play

See Rule 19-1 regarding ball deflected by outside agency.

19-5. By Another Ball

a. At Rest

If a player's ball in motion after a stroke is deflected or stopped by a ball in play and at rest, the player shall play his ball as it lies.

In match play, no penalty is incurred. In stroke play, there is no penalty unless both balls lay on the putting green prior to the stroke, in which case the player incurs a penalty of two strokes.

b. In Motion

If a player's ball in motion after a stroke is deflected or stopped by another ball in motion after a stroke, the player shall play his ball as it lies. There is no penalty unless the player was in breach of Rule 16-1g, in which he shall incur the penalty for breach of that rule.

Rule 20. Lifting, Dropping, and Placing; Playing from Wrong Place

20-1. Lifting

A ball to be lifted under the rules may be lifted by the player, his partner, or another person authorized by the player. In any such case, the player shall be responsible for any breach of the rules.

The position of the ball shall be marked before it is lifted under a rule which requires it to be replaced.

If a ball or ball marker is accidentally moved in the process of lifting the ball under a rule or marking its position, the ball or the ball marker shall be replaced. There is no penalty provided the movement of the ball or the ball marker is directly attributable to the specific act of marking the position of or lifting the ball.

20-2. Dropping and Redropping

a. By Whom and How

A ball to be dropped under the rules shall be dropped by the player himself. He shall stand erect, hold the ball at shoulder height and arm's length, and drop it.

If the ball touches the player, his partner, either of their caddies or their equipment before or after it strikes a part of the course, the ball shall be redropped, without penalty.

b. Where to Drop

When a ball is to be dropped as near as possible to a specific spot, it shall be dropped not nearer the hole than the specific spot which, if it is not precisely known to the player, shall be estimated.

A ball when dropped must first strike a part of the course where the applicable rule requires it to be dropped. If it is not so dropped, rules 20-6 and 20-7 apply.

c. When to Redrop

A dropped ball shall be re-dropped without penalty if it:

(i) rolls into a hazard;

(ii) rolls out of a hazard;

(iii) rolls onto a putting green;

(iv) rolls out of bounds;

(v) rolls to a position where there is interference by the

condition from which relief was taken under 24-2 (immovable obstructions) or 25-1 (abnormal ground conditions), or rolls back into the pitch mark from which it was lifted under 25-2 (embedded ball);

(vi) rolls and comes to rest more than two club-lengths from where it first struck a part of the course; or

(vii) rolls and comes to rest nearer the hole than its original position or estimated position (see 20-2b) unless otherwise permitted by the rules.

(viii) rolls and comes to rest nearer the hole than the point where the original ball last crossed the margin of the area or hazard (25-11c(i) and (ii)) or the margin of the water hazard (Rule 26-1b) or lateral water hazard (26-1c).

If the ball when redropped or placed under this rule is not immediately recoverable, another ball may be substituted.

20-3. Placing and Replacing

a. By Whom and Where

A ball to be placed under the rules shall be placed by the player or his partner. If a ball is to be replaced the player, his partner, or the person who lifted or moved it shall place it on the spot from which it was lifted or moved. In any such case, the player shall be responsible for any breach of the rules.

If a ball or ball marker is accidentally moved in the process of placing or replacing the ball, the ball or the ball marker shall be replaced. There is no penalty provided the movement of the ball or the ball marker is directly attributable to the specific act of placing or replacing the ball or removing the ball marker.

b. Lie of Ball to Be Placed or Replaced Altered

If the original lie of a ball to be placed or replaced has been altered:

(i) except in a hazard, the ball shall be placed in the nearest lie most similar to the original lie which is not more than one club-length from the original lie, not nearer the hole and not in the hazard;

(ii) in a water hazard, the ball shall be placed in accordance with clause (i) above, except that the ball must be placed in the water hazard;

(iii) in a bunker, the original lie shall be recreated as nearly as possible and the ball shall be placed in that lie.

c. Spot Not Determinable

If it is impossible to determine the spot where the ball is to be placed or replaced:

➡ *page 202*

continued from page 201

(i) through the green, the ball shall be dropped in the hazard as near as possible to the place where it lay but not in a hazard or on a putting green;

(ii) in a hazard, the ball shall be dropped in the hazard as near as possible to the place where it lay;

(iii) on the putting green, the ball shall be placed as near as possible to the place where it lay but not in a hazard.

d. Ball Fails to Come to Rest on Spot

If a ball when placed fails to come to rest on the spot on which it was placed, it shall be replaced without penalty. If it still fails to come to rest on that spot:

(i) except in a hazard, it shall be placed at the nearest spot not nearer the hole or in a hazard where it can be placed at rest;

(ii) in a hazard, it shall be placed in the hazard at the nearest spot not nearer the hole where it can be placed at rest.

If a ball when placed comes to rest on the spot on which it is placed, and it subsequently moves, there is no penalty and the ball shall be played as it lies, unless the provisions of any other rule apply.

20-4. When Ball Dropped or Placed Is in Play

If the player's ball in play has been lifted, it is again in play when dropped or placed.

A substituted ball becomes the ball in play when it has been dropped or placed.

20-5. Playing Next Stroke from Where Previous Stroke Played

The player shall proceed as follows: if the stroke is to be played from the teeing ground, the ball to be played shall be played from anywhere within the teeing ground and may be teed; if the stroke is to be played from through the green or a hazard, it shall be dropped; if the stroke is to be played on the putting green, it shall be placed.

20-6. Lifting Ball Incorrectly Substituted, Dropped, or Placed

A ball incorrectly substituted, dropped, or placed in a wrong place may be lifted, without penalty, and the player shall then proceed correctly.

20-7. Playing from Wrong Place

For a ball played from outside the teeing ground or from a wrong teeing ground, see 11-4 and 11-5.

a. Match Play

If a player plays a stroke with a ball that has been dropped or placed in a wrong place, he shall lose the hole.

b. Stroke Play

If a competitor plays a stroke with his ball in play (i) that has been

dropped or placed in a wrong place or (ii) that has been moved and not replaced in a case where the rules require replacement, he shall, provided a serious breach has not occurred, incur the penalty prescribed by the applicable rule and play out the hole with the ball.

If, after playing from a wrong place, a competitor becomes aware of that fact and believes that a serious breach may be involved, he may, provided he has not played a stroke from the next teeing ground or, in the case of the last hole of the round, left the putting green, declare that he will play out the hole with a second ball dropped or placed in accordance with the rules. The competitor shall report the facts to the committee before returning his score card; if he fails to do so, he shall be disqualified. The committee shall determine whether a serious breach of the rule occurred. If so, the score with the second ball shall count and the competitor shall add two penalty strokes to his score with that ball.

If a serious breach has occurred and the competitor has failed to correct it as prescribed above, he shall be disqualified.

Rule 21. Cleaning Ball

A ball on the putting green may be cleaned when lifted under Rule 16-1b. Elsewhere, a ball may be cleaned when lifted except when it has been lifted:
a. To determine if it is unfit for play (5-3);
b. For identification (12-2), in which case it may be cleaned only to the extent necessary for identification; or
c. Because it is interfering with or assisting play (22).

If a player cleans his ball during play of a hole except as provided in this rule, he shall incur a penalty for breach of Rule 20-3a, but no additional penalty under Rule 21 shall be applied.

22. Ball Interfering with or Assisting Play

Any player may;
a. Lift his ball if he considers that the ball might assist any other player; or
b. Have any other ball lifted if he considers that the ball might interfere with his play or assist the play of any other player, but this may not be done while another ball is in motion. In stroke play, a player required to lift his ball may play first rather than lift. A ball lifted under this rule shall be replaced.

Rule 23 Loose Impediments

Definition

"Loose impediments" are natural objects such as stones, leaves, twigs, branches, and the like, dung, worms and insects, and casts or heaps made by them, provided they are not fixed or growing, are not solidly embedded and do not adhere to the ball.

Sand and loose soil are loose impediments on the putting green but not elsewhere.

Snow and natural ice, other than frost, are either casual water or loose impediments, at the option of the player. Dew and frost are not loose impediments.

23-1. Relief

Except when both the loose impediment and the ball lie in or touch the same hazard, any loose impediment may be removed without penalty. If the ball moves, see 18-2c.

When a ball is in motion, a loose impediment which might influence the movement of the ball shall not be removed.

Rule 24. Obstructions

Definition

An "obstruction" is anything artificial, including the artificial surfaces and sides of roads and paths and manufactured ice, except:
a. Objects defining out of bounds, such as walls, fences, stakes, and railings;
b. Any part of an immovable artificial object that is out of bounds; and
c. Any construction declared by the committee to be an integral part of the course.

24-1. Movable Obstruction

A player may obtain relief from a movable obstruction as follows:
a. If the ball does not lie in or on the obstruction, the obstruction may be removed. If the ball moves, it shall be replaced without penalty.
b. If the ball lies in or on the obstruction, the ball may be lifted, without penalty, and the obstruction removed. The ball shall through the green or in a hazard be dropped, or on the putting green be placed, as near as possible to the spot directly under the place where the ball lay in or on the obstruction, but not nearer the hole.

When a ball is in motion, an obstruction that might influence the movement of the ball, other than an attended flagstick or equipment of the players, shall not be removed.

24-2. Immovable Obstruction

a. Interference by an immovable obstruction occurs when a ball lies in or on the obstruction, or so close to the obstruction that the obstruction interferes with the player's stance or the area of his intended swing. If the player's

ball lies on the putting green, interference also occurs if an immovable obstruction on the putting green intervenes on his line of putt. Otherwise, intervention on the line of play is not, of itself, interference under this rule.

b. Relief

Except when the ball is in a water hazard or a lateral water hazard, a player may obtain relief from the interference by an immovable obstruction, without penalty, as follows:

(i) **Through the Green**: If the ball lies through the green, the point on the course nearest to where the ball lies shall be determined (without crossing over, through, or under the obstruction) which (a) is not nearer the hole, (b) avoids interference (as defined), and (c) is not in a hazard or on a putting green. The player shall lift the ball and drop it within one club-length of the point thus determined on a part of the course that fulfills (a), (b), and (c) above.

(ii) **In a Bunker**: If the ball is in a bunker, the player shall lift and drop the ball in accordance with Clause (i) above, except that the ball must be dropped in the bunker.

(iii) **On the Putting Green**: If the ball lies on the putting green, the player shall lift the ball and place it in the nearest position to where it lay that affords relief from interference, but not nearer the hole nor in a hazard.

c) Ball Lost

Except in a water hazard or a lateral water hazard, if there is reasonable evidence that a ball is lost in an immovable obstruction, the player may, without penalty, substitute another ball and follow the procedure prescribed in 24-2b.

Rule 25. Abnormal Ground Conditions and Wrong Putting Green

"Casual water" is any temporary accumulation of water on the course that is visible before or after the player takes his stance and is not in a water hazard. Dew and frost are not casual water.

25.1 Interference

a. Interference by casual water, ground under repair, or a hole, cast, or runway made by an animal or bird occurs when a ball lies in or touches any of these conditions or when such a condition on the course interferes with the player's stance or the area of his intended swing.

If the player's ball lies on the putting green, interference also occurs if such condition on the putting green intervenes with his line of putt.

If interference exists, the player may either play the ball as it lies or take relief as provided in Clause b.

b. Relief

If the player elects to take relief, he shall proceed as follows:

(i) **Through the Green:** If the ball lies through the green, the point on the course nearest to where the ball lies shall be determined that (a) is not nearer the hole, (b) avoids interference by the condition, and (c) is not in a hazard or on a putting green. The player shall lift the ball and drop it without penalty within one club-length of the point thus determined on a part of the course that fulfills (a), (b), and (c) above.

(ii) **In a Hazard:** If the ball is in a hazard, the player shall lift and drop the ball either:

(a) Without penalty, in the hazard, as near as possible to the spot where the ball lay, but not nearer the hole, on a part of the course that affords maximum available relief from the condition; or

(b) Under penalty of one stroke, outside the hazard, keeping the point where the ball lay directly between the hole and the spot on which the ball is dropped, with no limit to how far behind the hazard the ball may be dropped. Exception: If a ball is in a water hazard, the player shall play the ball as it lies or proceed under 26-1.

(iii) **On the Putting Green:** If the ball lies on the putting green, the player shall lift the ball and place it without penalty in the nearest position to where it lay that affords maximum available relief from the condition, but not nearer the hole nor in a hazard.

c. Ball Lost Under Condition Covered by Rule 25-1

It is a question of fact whether a ball lost after having been struck toward a condition covered by Rule 25-1 is lost under such condition. In order to treat the ball as lost under such condition, there must be reasonable evidence to that effect. In the absence of such evidence, the ball must be treated as a lost ball and Rule 27 applies.

(i) **Outside a Hazard:** If a ball is lost outside a hazard under a condition covered by Rule 25-1, the player may take relief as follows: the point on the course nearest to where the ball last crossed the margin of the area shall be determined which (a) is not nearer the hole than where the ball last crossed the margin, (b) avoids interference by the condition and (c) is not in a hazard or on a putting green. He

shall drop a ball without penalty within one club-length of the point thus determined on a part of the course that fulfills (a), (b), and (c) above.

(ii) **In a Hazard:** If a ball is lost in a hazard under a condition covered by Rule 25-1, the player may drop a ball either:

(a) Without penalty, in the hazard as near as possible to the point at which the original ball last crossed the margin of the area, but not nearer the hole, on a part of the course which affords maximum available relief from the condition; or

(b) Under penalty of one stroke, outside the hazard, keeping the point at which the original ball last crossed the margin of the hazard directly between the hole and the spot on which the ball is dropped, with no limit to how far behind the hazard the ball may be dropped.
Exception: If a ball is in a water hazard, the player shall play the ball as it lies or proceed under 26-1.

25-2. Embedded Ball

A ball embedded in its own pitch mark in the ground in any closely-mown area through the green may be lifted, cleaned, and dropped, without penalty, as near as possible to the spot where it lay but not nearer the hole. The ball when dropped must first strike a part of the course through the green.

25-3. Wrong Putting Green

A player must not play a ball that lies on a putting green other than that of the hole being played. The ball must be lifted and the player must proceed as follows: The point on the course nearest to where the ball lies shall be determined that (a) is not nearer the hole and (b) is not in a hazard or on a putting green. The player shall lift the ball and drop it without penalty within one club-length of the point thus determined on a part of the course that fulfills (a) and (b) above.

Rule 26. Water Hazards

Water hazards (other than lateral water hazards) should be defined by yellow stakes or lines.

A "lateral water hazard" is a water hazard or that part of a water hazard so situated that it is not possible or practicable to drop a ball behind the water hazard in accordance with Rule 26-1b. Lateral water hazards should be defined by red stakes or lines.

26-1. Ball in Water Hazard

It is a question of fact whether a ball lost after having been struck toward a water hazard is lost inside or outside the hazard. In order to treat the ball as lost in

the hazard, there must be reasonable evidence that the ball lodged in it. In the absence of such evidence, the ball must be treated as a lost ball and Rule 27 applies.

If a ball is in or is lost in a water hazard (whether the ball lies in water or not), the player may under penalty of one stroke:
a. Play a ball as nearly as possible at the spot from which the original ball was last played (see 20-5); or
b. Drop a ball behind the water hazard, keeping the point at which the original ball last crossed the margin of the water hazard directly between the hole and the spot on which the ball is dropped, with no limit to how far behind the water hazard the ball may be dropped; or
c. As additional options available only if the ball last crossed the margin of a lateral water hazard, drop a ball outside the water hazard within two club-lengths of and not nearer the hole than (i) the point where the original ball last crossed the margin of the water hazard or (ii) a point on the opposite margin of the water hazard equidistant from the hole.

26-2. Ball Played Within Water Hazard

a. Ball Comes to Rest in the Hazard

If a ball played from within a water hazard comes to rest in the same hazard after the stroke, the player may:

(i) proceed under Rule 26-1; or
(ii) under penalty of one stroke, play a ball as nearly as possible at the spot from which the last stroke from outside the hazard was played (see 20-5).

If the player proceeds under Rule 26-1a, he may elect not to play the dropped ball. If he so elects, he may:
(a) proceed under Rule 26-1b, adding the additional penalty of one stroke prescribed by that rule; or
(b) proceed under Rule 26-1c, if applicable, adding the additional penalty of one stroke prescribed by that rule; or
(c) add an additional penalty of one stroke and play a ball as nearly as possible at the spot from which the last stroke from outside the hazard was played (see 20-5).

b. Ball Lost or Unplayable Outside Hazard or Out of Bounds

If a ball played from within a water hazard is lost or declared unplayable outside the hazard or is out of bounds, the player, after taking a penalty of one stroke under Rule 27-1 or 28a, may:

(i) play a ball as nearly as possible at the spot in the hazard from which the original ball was

last played (see 20-5); or
(ii) proceed under Rule 26-1b, or if applicable Rule 26-1c, by the rule and using as the reference point the point where the original ball last crossed the margin of the hazard before it came to rest in the hazard; or
(iii) add an additional penalty of one stroke and play a ball as nearly as possible at the spot from which the last stroke from outside the hazard was played (20-5).

Rule 27. Ball Lost or Out of Bounds; Provisional Ball

If the original ball is lost in an immovable obstruction (24-2) or under a condition covered by Rule 25-1 (casual water, ground under repair, and certain damage to the course), the player may proceed under the applicable rule. If the original ball is lost in a water hazard, the player shall proceed under Rule 26.

Definitions

A ball is "lost" if:
a. It is not found or identified as his by the player within five minutes after the player's side or his or their caddies have begun to search for it; or
b. The player has put another ball into play under the rules, even though he may not have searched for the original ball; or
c. The player has played any stroke with a provisional ball from the place where the original ball is likely to be or from a point nearer the hole than that place, whereupon the provisional ball becomes ball in play.

27-1. Ball Lost or Out of Bounds

If a ball is lost outside a water hazard or is out of bounds, the player shall play a ball, under penalty of one stroke, as nearly as possible at the spot from which the original ball was last played (see 20-5).

27-2. Provisional Ball

a. Procedure

If a ball may be lost outside a water hazard or may be out of bounds, to save time the player may play another ball provisionally as nearly as possible at the spot from which the original ball was played (see 20-5). The player shall inform his opponent in match play or his marker or a fellow competitor in stroke play that he intends to play a provisional ball, and he shall play it before he or his partner goes forward to search for the original ball. If he fails to do so and plays another ball, such ball is not a provisional ball and becomes the ball in play under penalty of stroke and distance (Rule 27-1); the original ball is deemed to be lost.

➡ *page 204*

continued from page 203

b. When Provisional Ball Becomes Ball in Play

The player may play a provisional ball until he reaches the place where the original ball is likely to be. If he plays a stroke with the provisional ball from the place where the original ball is likely to be or from a point nearer the hole than that place, the original ball is deemed to be lost and the provisional ball becomes the ball in play under penalty of stroke and distance (Rule 27-1).

c. When Provisional Ball to Be Abandoned

If the original ball is neither lost outside a water hazard nor out of bounds, the player shall abandon the provisional ball and continue play with the original ball. If he fails to do so, any further strokes played with the provisional ball shall constitute playing a wrong ball and the provisions of Rule 15 shall apply.

Rule 28. Ball Unplayable

The player may declare his ball unplayable at any place on the course except when the ball is in a water hazard. The player is the sole judge as to whether his ball is unplayable.

If the player deems his ball to be unplayable, he shall, under penalty of one stroke:

a. Play a ball as nearly as possible at the spot from which the original ball was last played (see 20-5); or

b. Drop a ball within two club-lengths of the spot where the ball lay, but not nearer the hole; or

c. Drop a ball behind the point where the ball lay, keeping that point directly between the hole and the spot on which the ball is dropped, with no limit to how far behind that point the ball be dropped.

If the unplayable ball is in a bunker, the player may proceed under clause a, b, or c. If he elects to proceed under clause b or c, a ball must be dropped in the bunker.

Rule 29. Threesomes and Foursomes

Definitions

Threesome: A match in which one plays against two, and each side plays one ball.

Foursome: A match in which two play against two, and each side plays one ball.

29-1 General

In a threesome or a foursome, during any stipulated round , the partners shall play alternately from the teeing grounds and alternately during the play of each hole. Penalty strokes do not

affect the order of play.

29-2 Match Play

If a player plays when his partner should have played, his side shall lose the hole.

29-3 Stroke Play

If the partners play a stroke or strokes in incorrect order, such stroke or strokes shall be cancelled and the side shall incur a penalty of two strokes. The side shall correct the error by playing a ball in correct order as nearly as possible at the spot from which it first played in incorrect order (see Rule 20-5). If the side plays a stroke from the next teeing ground without first correcting the error or, in the case of the last hole of the round, leaves the putting green without declaring its intention to correct the error, the side shall be disqualified.

Rule 30, Three-Ball, Best-Ball, and Four-Ball Match Play

Definitions

Three-Ball: A match play competition in which three play against one another, each playing his own ball. Each player is playing two distinct matches.

Best-Ball: A match in which one plays against the better ball of two or the best ball of three players.

Four-Ball: A match in which two play their better ball against the better ball of two other players.

30-1 Rules of Golf Apply

The Rules of Golf, so far as they are not at variance with the following special Rules, shall apply to three-ball, best-ball, and four-ball matches.

30-2 Three-Ball Match Play

a. Ball at Rest Moved by an Opponent

Except as otherwise provided in the Rules, if the player's ball is touched or moved by an opponent, his caddie, or equipment other than during search, Rule 18-3b applies. That opponent shall incur a penalty stroke in his match with the player, but not in his match with the other opponent.

b. Ball Deflected or Stopped by an Opponent Accidentally

If a player's ball is accidentally deflected or stopped by an opponent, his caddie, or equipment, no penalty shall be incurred. In his match with that opponent the player may play the ball as it lies or, before another stroke is played by either side, he may cancel the stroke and play a ball without penalty as nearly as possible at the spot from which the original ball was last played (see Rule 20-5). In his match with the other opponent, the ball shall be played as it lies.

Exception: Ball stroking person attending flagstick—see Rule 17-3b.

(Ball purposely deflected or stopped by opponent—see Rule 1 2).

30-3 Best-Ball and Four-Ball Match Play

a. Representation of Side

A side may be represented by one partner for all or any part of a match; all partners need not be present. An absent partner may join a match between holes, but not during play of a hole.

b. Maximum of Fouteen Clubs

The side shall be penalized for a breach of Rule 4-4 by any partner.

c. Order of Play

Balls belonging to the same side may be played in the order the side considers best.

d. Wrong Ball

If a player plays a stroke with a wrong ball except in a hazard, he shall be disqualified for that hole, but his partner incurs no penalty even if the wrong ball belongs to him. If the wrong ball belongs to another player, its owner shall place a ball on the spot from which the wrong ball was first played.

e. Disqualification of Side

(i) A side shall be disqualified for a breach of any of the following by any partner: Rule 1-3; Rule 4-1, -2, -3; Rule 5-1 or -2; Rule 6-2a; Rule 6-4; Rule 6-7; Rule 14-3; Rule 6-3; Rule 6-8.

f. Effect of Other Penalties

If a player's breach of a Rule assists his partner's play or adversely affects his opponent, the partner incurs the applicable penalty in addition to any penalty incurred by the player.

In all other cases where a player incurs a penalty for breach of a Rule, the penalty shall not apply to his partner. Where the penalty is stated to be loss of hole, the effect shall be to disqualify the player for that hole.

g. Another Form of Match Played Concurrently

In a best-ball or four-ball match when another form of match is played concurrently, the above special Rules shall apply.

Rule 31. Four-Ball Stroke Play

In four-ball stroke play, two competitors play as partners, each playing his own ball. The lower score of the partners is the score for the hole. If one partner fails to complete the play of a hole, there is no penalty.

31-1. Rules of Golf Apply

The Rules of Golf, so far as they are not at variance with the following special Rules, shall apply to four-ball stroke play.

31-2. Representation of Side

A side may be represented by either partner for all or any part of a stipulated round; both partners need not be present. An absent competitor may join his partner between holes, but not during play of a hole.

31-3. Maximum of Fourteen Clubs

The side shall be penalized for a breach of Rule 4-4 by either partner.

31-4. Scoring

The marker is required to record for each hole only the gross score of whichever partner's score is to count. The gross scores to count must be individually identifiable; otherwise the side shall be disqualified. Only one of the partners need be responsible for complying with Rule 6-6b. (Wrong score—see Rule 31-7a.)

31-5. Order of Play

Balls belonging to the same side may be played in the order the side considers best.

31-6 Wrong Ball

If a competitor plays a stroke or strokes with a wrong ball except in a hazard, he shall add two penalty strokes to his score for the hole and shall then play the correct ball. His partner incurs no penalty even if the wrong ball belongs to him.

If the wrong ball belongs to another competitor, its owner shall place a ball on the spot from which the wrong ball was first played.

31-7. Disqualification Penalties

a. Breach by One Partner

A side shall be disqualified from the competition for a breach of any of the following by either partner: Rule 1-3; Rule 3-4; Rule 4-1, -2 or -3; Rule 5-1 or -2; Rule 6-2b; Rule 6-4; Rule 6-6b;Rule 6-6d; Rule 6-7; Rule 7-1; Rule 14-3; Rule 31-4.

(b) Breach by Both Partners

A side shall be disqualified:

(i) for a breach by both partners of Rule 6-3 (Time of Starting and Groups) or Rule 6-8 (Discontinuance of Play) or

(ii) if, at the same hole, each partner is in breach of a Rule the penalty for which is disqualification from the competition or for a hole.

c. For the Hole Only

In all other cases where a breach of a Rule would entail disqualification, the competitor shall be disqualified only for the hole at which the breach occurred.

31-8. Effect of Other Penalties

If a competitor's breach of a Rule assists his partner's play, the partner incurs the applicable penalty in addition to any penalty incurred by the competitor.

In all other cases where a competitor incurs a penalty for

breach of a Rule, the penalty shall not apply to his partner.

Rule 32. Bogey, Par, and Stableford Competitions

32-1. Conditions

Bogey, par, and Stableford competitions are forms of stroke competition in which play is against a fixed score at each hole. Generally the Rules for stroke play apply, but there are some special conditions. For details, see *The Rules of Golf.*

Rule 33. The Committee

33-1. Conditions; Waiving Rule

The Committee shall lay down the conditions under which a competition is to be played.

The Committee has no power to waive a Rule of Golf.

Certain special rules governing stroke play are so substantially different from those governing match play that combining the two forms of play is not practicable and is not permitted. The results of matches played and the scores returned in these circumstances shall not be accepted.

In stroke play the Committee may limit a referee's duties.

33-2. The Course

a. Defining Bounds and Margins

The Committee shall define accurately:

(i) the course and out of bounds.

(ii) the margins of water hazards and lateral water hazards.

(iii) ground under repair, and

(iv) obstructions and integral parts of the course.

b. New Holes

New holes should be made on the day on which a stroke competition begins and at such other times as the Committee considers necessary, provided all competitors in a single round play with each hole cut in the same position.

Exception: When it is impossible for a damaged hole to be repaired so that it conforms with the Definition, the Committee may make a new hole in a nearby similar position.

Note: Where a single round is to be played on more than one day, the Committee may provide in the conditions of a competition that the holes and teeing grounds may be differently situated on each day of the competition, provided that, on any one day, all competitors play with each hole and each teeing ground in the same position.

c. Practice Ground

Where there is no practice ground available outside the area of a competition course, the Committee should lay down the area on which players may practice on any day of a competition, if it is practicable to do so. On any day a stroke competition, the Committee should not normally permit practice on or to a putting green or from a hazard of the competition course.

(d) Course Unplayable

If the Committee or its authorized representative considers that for any reason the course is not in a playable condition or that there are circumstances that render the proper playing of the game impossible, it may, in match play or stroke play, order a temporary suspension of play or, in stroke play, declare play null and void and cancel all scores for the round in question. When play has been temporarily suspended, it shall be resumed from where it was discontinued, even though resumption occurs on a subsequent day. When a round is cancelled, all penalties incurred in that round are cancelled. (Procedure in discontinuing play—see Rule 6-8.)

33-3. Times of Starting and Groups

The Committee shall lay down the times of starting and, in stroke play, arrange the groups in which competitors shall play.

When a match play competition is played over an extended period, the Committee shall lay down the limit of time within which each round shall be completed. When players are allowed to arrange the date of their match within these limits, the Committee should announce that the match must be played at a stated time on the last day of the period unless the players agree to a prior date.

33-4. Handicap Stroke Table

The Committee shall publish a table indicating the order of holes at which handicap strokes are to be given or received.

33-5 Score Card

In stroke play, the Committee shall issue for each competitor a score card containing the date and the competitor's name or, in foursome or four-ball stroke play, the competitors' names.

In stroke play, the Committee is responsible for the addition of scores and application of the handicap recorded on the card.

In four-ball stroke play, the Committee is responsible for recording the better-ball score for each hole and in the process applying the handicaps recorded on the card, and adding the better-ball scores.

In bogey, par, and Stableford competitions, the Committee is responsible for applying the handicap recorded on the card and determining the result of each hole and the overall result or points total.

33-6. Decision of Ties

The Committee shall announce the manner, day, and time for the decision of a halved match or of a tie, whether played on level terms or under handicap.

A halved match shall not be decided by stroke play. A tie in stroke play shall not be decided by a match.

33-7. Disqualification Penalty: Committee Discretion

A penalty of disqualification may in exceptional individual cases be waived, modified, or imposed if the Committee considers such action warranted.

Any penalty less than disqualification shall not be waived or modified.

33-8. Local Rules

a. Policy

The Committee may make and publish Local Rules for abnormal conditions if they are consistent with the policy of the Governing Authority for the country concerned as set forth in Appendix I to these Rules.

b. Waiving Penalty

A penalty imposed by a Rule of Golf shall not be waived by a Local Rule.

Rule 34. Disputes and Decisions

34-1. Claims and Penalties

a. Match Play

In match play, if a claim is lodged with the Committee under Rule 2-5, a decision should be given as soon as possible so that the state of the match may, if necessary, be adjusted.

If a claim is not made within the time limit provided by Rule 2-5, it shall not be considered unless it is based on facts previously unknown to the player making the claim and the player making the claim had been given wrong information (Rules 6-2a and 9) by an opponent. In any case, no later claim shall be considered after the result of the match has been officially announced, unless the Committee is satisfied that the opponent knew he was giving wrong information.

There is no time limit on applying the disqualification penalty for a breach of Rule 1-3.

b. Stroke Play

Except as provided below, in stroke play, no penalty shall be rescinded, modified, or imposed after the competition has closed. A competition is deemed to have closed when the result has been officially announced, or in stroke play qualifying followed by match play, when the player has teed off in his first match.

Exceptions: A penalty of disqualification shall be imposed after the competition has closed if a competitor:

(i) was in breach of Rule 1-3 (Agreement to Waive Rules); or

(ii) returned a score card on which he had recorded a handicap that, before the competition closed, he knew was higher than that to which he was entitled, and this affected the number of strokes received (Rule 6-2b); or

(iii) returned a score for any hole lower than actually taken (Rule 6-6d) for any reason other than failure to include a penalty that, before the competition closed, he did not know he had incurred; or

(iv) knew, before the competition closed, that he had been in breach of any other Rule for which the prescribed penalty is disqualification.

32-2. Referee's Decision

If a referee has been appointed by the Committee, his decision shall be final.

34-3. Committee's Decision

In the absence of a referee, any dispute or doubtful point on the Rules shall be referred to the Committee, whose decision shall be final.

If the Committee cannot come to a decision, it shall refer the dispute or doubtful point to the Rules of Golf Committee of the Royal and Ancient Golf Club of St. Andrews, whose decision shall be final.

If the dispute or doubtful point has not been referred to the Rules of Golf Committee, the player or players have the right to refer an agreed statement through the Secretary of the Club to the Rules of Golf Committee for an opinion as to the correctness of the decision given. The reply will be sent to the Secretary of the Club or Clubs concerned.

If play is conducted other than in accordance with the Rules of Golf, the Rules of Golf Committee will not give a decision on any question.

The rest of the rule book consists of: **Appendix I** Local Rules; **Appendix II** Design of Clubs; **Appendix III** The Ball; **Rules of Amateur Status** (defines amateur status); and **Royal & Ancient Policy On Gambling.**

These rules are reprinted by permission of the copyright holders, the Royal and Ancient Gold Club of St Andrews. Copies of the rules are also available from the Professional Golfers Association of America.

Boxing
Essentials

The rules first published in 1867 by the Marquess of Queensberry (for whom they are still named) form the basis of a modern sport—both professional and amateur. The latter, presented here, are a stricter, more safety-conscious code. Players wear headguards, and bouts are limited to five rounds—as opposed to as many as 15 in professional contests.

4.90m (16 ft)–6.10 m (20 ft)

4.90m (16 ft)–6.10 m (20 ft)

The ring

Minimum 4.90 m (16 ft) square, maximum 6.10 m (20 ft) square. Fitted with four corner posts and a floor covered with felt, rubber, or other approved material. Three or four ropes of thickness 3–5 cm (approx 1.5 in) are tightly drawn from the corner posts at 40 cm (1.3 ft), 80 cm (2.6 ft), and 1.30 m (4.3 ft) high.

Square ring
Boxers are kept in close proximity during the fight in a square enclosure called, oddly, a ring.

Officials

A referee (in the ring), five judges, and a timekeeper.

Dress

Gloves weighing 284 g (10 oz), light boots or shoes, socks, shorts, and T-shirts. (For top-level amateur competitions, boxes wear either a red or blue shirt, depending on the color of their corner.) Only soft surgical bandaging may be worn beneath gloves for protection. Harmful or objectionable products may not be worn. Beards are forbidden and long hair must be covered by the headgear. Professionals do not wear either headgear or shirts.

Boxing gloves

Exposed
Although boxing involves a great deal of violent physical contact, boxers wear surprisingly little protection. The only body armor apart from the gloves is a headguard and gumshield. Professionals don't even wear the headguard.

Players

Two players. Each boxer is also allowed two "seconds," who are generally coaches or trainers. (Only one second may enter the ring.) The seconds service the boxer and clear the ring of towels, buckets, and so on prior to a round. They may retire their boxer by throwing the towel into the ring if they think he is in danger.

The international weight classifications are as follows:

Light Fly:
Up to 48 kg (106 lb).
Fly:
Over 48 kg and up to 51 kg
(106 lb–112 lb).
Bantam:
Over 51 kg and up to 54 kg
(112 lb–119 lb).
Feather:
Over 54 kg and up to 57 kg
(119 lb–126 lb).
Light:
Over 57 kg and up to 60 kg
(126 lb–132 lb).
Light Welter:
Over 60 kg and up to 63.5 kg
(132 lb–140 lb).

Welter:
Over 63.5 kg and up to 67 kg
(140 lb–148 lb).
Light Middle:
Over 67 kg and up to 71 kg
(148 lb–157 lb).
Middle:
Over 71 kg and up to 75 kg
(157 lb–165 lb).
Light Heavy:
Over 75 kg and up to 81 kg
(165 lb–179 lb).
Heavy:
Over 81 kg and up to 91 kg
(179 lb–201 lb).
Super Heavy:
Over 91 kg (201 lb).

Contestants must weigh in, without clothes, on the day of a bout.

HOW TO PLAY

Two opponents score points with blows to one another, using the knuckle part of their gloves. Hits must land on the front or sides of the head, or anywhere on the body above the belt.

Starting

At the start of the bout, everyone, apart from the referee and the two boxers, leaves the ring. The opponents shake hands and then wait in their separate corners until the timekeeper announces the round and strikes the bell or gong to start it.

How to win

A boxer can win in a number of different ways. The most dramatic is by knockout, although this occurs less frequently in amateur boxing than in professional contests.

Generally, a bout is won on points. An electric scoring system is now used at all AIBA competitions. (AIBA is the French acronym for the International Amateur Boxing Association.) Judges feed correct hits into a computer by pressing keys and a final result is calculated automatically. The winner is the boxer who has scored the most correct hits, the final result based only on blows that have been fed in simultaneously by at least three of the five judges. In the case of a boxer who is disqualified or outclassed (unable to continue in the opinion of the referee), his opponent wins the bout. *See Rule XVI, Decisions (page 208).*

The referee raises the hand of the winning boxer at the end of the bout.

KEY RULES

Amateur bouts generally consist of five rounds of two minutes each, with a one-minute interval between rounds. (Some international contests consist of three or four rounds of three minutes each, or six rounds of two minutes each.)

• When a boxer knocks his opponent to the floor he is sent to a neutral corner by the referee, where he remains while the referee counts out 10 seconds aloud, indicating each second with his hand to the boxer on the floor. If this boxer is unready to resume boxing after 10 seconds have passed, a knockout is declared. *See Rule XIX, Down (page 209).*

• Boxers must not hit below the belt, on the back of the neck or in the kidneys. They must not hit with an open glove nor hit an opponent who is down or in the act of rising. When a referee commands two boxers holding each other to "Break," they must take one step back before continuing. Failure to obey any rule is a foul and will result in a caution or warning. A third warning brings automatic disqualification. *See Rule XVIII, Fouls (page 209).*

SKILLS AND TACTICS

Sharp reflexes, speed, and power. Boxers train to be able to score maximum points with well-placed hits to target areas, while also dodging and blocking the blows of an opponent.

The *jab* is a short, sharp punch, the *uppercut* is delivered from below and aimed at the body or the lower part of the face, and the *hook* is a heavy blow, usually to the head. Combination punching makes use of all these in varying order, usually in rapid succession.

Jab on the jaw
The most common blow in boxing is the jab—a short, sharp punch, often aimed at the jaw, one of a boxer's weak points. Here the boxer leads with his right foot and also his right arm. This unorthodox combination can be tricky for opponents to deal with.

The "champ"
Because no single world body governs professional boxing, there may be as many as four "world champions" at any given time for a particular weight class. Above are professional boxers—hence no headgear or T-shirts.

THE RULES

RULE I: The Ring
See The Ring (page 206)
RULE II: Gloves
Rule III: Bandages
Rule IV: Dress
See Dress (page 206)
Rule V: Ring Equipment
Rule VI: Medical Examination and Weigh-in for International Competitions

RULE VII: Draws and Byes
A. The Draw. The draw shall take place after the medical examination and weigh-in. The draw must take place in the presence of official representatives of the teams concerned, and must ensure, where practicable, that no competitor shall box twice in the competition before all other competitors have boxed at least once. In special situations, the Executive Committee of A.I.B.A. has the right to depart from this rule. The draw shall proceed first for the boxers to box in the first series and then for the byes. However, no boxer may be awarded a World or Continental Championship or Olympic Games Medal without having boxed.

B. Byes. In competitions where there are more than four competitors, a sufficient number of byes shall be drawn in the first series to reduce the number of competitors in the second series to four, eight, 16, or 32. Competitors drawing a bye in the first series shall be the first to box in the second series. If there is an odd number of byes, the boxer who draws the last bye will compete in the second series against the winner of the first bout in the first series. Where the number of byes is even, the boxers drawing byes shall box the first bouts in the second series in the order in which they are drawn. No medal shall be awarded to a boxer who has not boxed at least once.

C. Order of the Program. In World Championships, the Olympic Games, and Continental Championships, the order of the program should be arranged as far as practicable in the order of weights so that in each series the lightest weights will be run off first and thence in order of weights up to the heaviest weights in that series followed by the lightest weights in the next series, and so on.

RULE VIII: ROUNDS
See Key Rules (page 207).

RULES IX–XV
Deal with the appointment and duties of the seconds, referee, judges, jury, and timekeeper.

Winning
Most contests are decided on points—that is, on points awarded by the judges for blows landed on an opponent. Only rarely is a bout decided by a knockout.

RULE XVI: Decisions
A. Types. Decisions shall be as follows:

1. Win on Points. At the end of a contest, the boxer who has been awarded the decision by a majority of the judges shall be declared the winner. If both boxers are injured, or are knocked-out simultaneously, and cannot continue the contest, the judges shall record the points gained by each boxer up to its termination, and the boxer who was leading on points up to termination, or the actual end of the contest, shall be declared the winner.

2. Win by Retirement. If a boxer retires voluntarily owing to injury or other cause, or if he fails to resume boxing immediately after the rest between rounds, his opponent shall be declared the winner.

3. Win by Referee Stopping Contest:
a. Outclassed. RSC is a term used to stop a bout when a boxer is outclassed or is unfit to continue. If a boxer, in the opinion of the referee is being outclassed or is receiving excessive punishment, the bout shall be stopped and his opponent declared the winner.

b. Injury. If a boxer, in the opinion of the referee, is unfit to continue because of injury sustained from correct blows or other action or is incapacitated for any other physical reasons, the bout shall be stopped and his opponent declared the winner. The right to make this decision rests with the referee, who may consult the doctor. Having consulted the doctor, the referee must follow his advice. It is recommended that the referee checks the other boxer for injury also before he makes this decision. The Ringside Medical Officer has the right to request that the bout be suspended if he thinks, for medical reasons, the bout should not be allowed to continue. He must first inform the Jury President and the latter shall inform the referee that the bout shall be suspended. The suspension shall last a maximum of one minute by the referee for examining the fitness of a boxer by the Medical Officer.

4. Win by Disqualification. If a boxer is disqualified, his opponent shall be declared the winner. If both boxers are disqualified, the decision shall be announced accordingly.

5. Win by Knockout. If a boxer is "down" and fails to resume boxing within 10 seconds, his opponent shall be declared the winner by a knockout.

6. No Contest. A bout may be terminated by the referee inside the scheduled distance owing to a material happening outside the responsibility of the boxers, or the control of the referee, such as the ring becoming damaged, the failure of the lighting supply, exceptional weather conditions, etc. In such circumstances, the bout shall be declared "no contest" and in the case of Championships, the jury shall decide the necessary further action.

7. Win by Walkover. Where a boxer presents himself in the

ring fully attired for boxing and his opponent fails to appear after his name has been called out by the public address system, the bell sounded and a maximum period of three minutes has elapsed, the referee shall declare the first boxer to be the winner by a "Walkover." He shall first inform the judges to mark their papers accordingly, collect them and then he summons the boxer to the center of the ring and after the decision is announced, raises his hand as winner.

8. A Draw (Dual Matches Only). Two clubs or two nations in a friendly dual match may agree to a draw decision, when the majority of judges scored the competition equally. Likewise, an injury in the first round may result in a draw in dual matches.

9. Incidents in the Ring Outside the Control of the Referee.

a) If something happens that does not allow the bout to continue within one minute after the bell has rung for the beginning of the first or second round (e.g., power failure), the bout shall be stopped and the boxers will box again in the last bout of the same session.

b) If the incident occurs in the third round of a bout, the contest shall be terminated and the judges are asked to give a decision as to the winner of the bout.

c) If the incident occurs in the last three bouts of a session on the program, the boxers shall be asked to box the first bout on the program of the next session. The boxers shall be weighed and medically examined again for that bout.

RULE XVII: Awarding of Points
See How to Win (page 207).

RULE XVIII: Fouls
A. Cautions, Warnings, Disqualifications. The competitor who does not obey the instructions of the referee, acts against the boxing rules, boxes in any unsportsmanlike manner, or commits fouls, can, at the discretion of the referee, be cautioned, warned, or disqualified without warning. A referee may, without stopping a contest, caution a boxer at some safe opportunity. If he intends to warn a boxer, he shall stop the contest, and will demonstrate the infringement. He will then point to the boxer and to each of the five judges. A referee having once administered a warning for a particular foul, e.g., holding, cannot issue a caution for the same type of offense. A third

Out for the count
When the boxer is on the canvas or outside the ropes the referee counts the seconds. If the boxer is not back on his feet by the count of 10, the bout ends as a knockout.

caution for the same type of foul will mandatorily require a warning to be issued. Only three warnings may be given to the same boxer in one contest. The third warning brings automatic disqualification.

B. Types of Fouls. The following are fouls:

1. Hitting below the belt, holding, tripping, kicking, and butting with foot or knee.

2. Hits or blows with head, shoulder, forearm, elbow, throttling of the opponent, pressing with arm or elbow in opponent's face, pressing the head of the opponent back over the ropes.

3. Hitting with open glove, the inside of the glove, wrist, or side of the hand.

4. Hits landing on the back of the opponent and especially any blow on the back of the neck or head and kidney punch.

5. Pivot blows.

6. Attack while holding the ropes or making any unfair use of the ropes.

7. Lying on, wrestling, and throwing in the clinch.

8. An attack on an opponent who is down or who is in the act of rising.

9. Holding.

10. Holding and hitting or pulling and hitting.

11. Holding, or locking, of the opponent's arm or head, or pushing an arm underneath the arm of the opponent.

12. Ducking below the belt of the opponent in a manner dangerous to his opponent.

13. Completely passive defense by means of double cover and intentionally falling to avoid a blow.

14. Useless, aggressive or offensive utterances during the round.

15. Not stepping back when ordered to break.

16. Attempting to strike the opponent immediately after the referee has ordered "Break" and before taking a step back.

17. Assaulting or behaving in an aggressive manner toward a referee at any time.

18. Spitting out gumshield (teeth protector).

19. Keeping the advanced hand straight in order to obstruct the opponent's vision.

C. Seconds. Each boxer is responsible in the same way for his second.

D. Referee Consults judges. If a referee has any reason to believe that a foul has been committed that he himself has not seen, he may consult the judges.

RULE XIX: Down
A. Definition. A boxer is considered "down":

1. if he touches the floor with any part of his body other than his feet as the result of a blow or series of blows, or

2. if he hangs helplessly on the ropes as a result of a blow or series of blows, or

3. if he is outside or partly outside the ropes as the result of a blow or series of blows, or

4. if following a hard punch he has not fallen and is not lying on the ropes, but is in a semi-conscious state and cannot, in the opinion of the referee, continue the bout.

B. The Count. In the case of a knock-down, the referee shall immediately begin to count the seconds. When a boxer is "down" the referee shall count aloud from one to 10 with intervals of a second between the numbers, and shall indicate each second with his hand in such a manner that the boxer who has been knocked down may be aware of the count. Before the number "one" is counted, an interval of one second must have elapsed from the time when the boxer has fallen to the floor, and the time of announcing "one." If the opponent should not go to the neutral corner on the command of the referee, the referee shall stop counting until the opponent has done so. The counting shall be then continued where it has been interrupted.

C. Opponent's Responsibilities. If a boxer is down, his opponent must at once go to the neutral corner as designated by the referee. He may only continue against the opponent who is knocked down after the latter has got up and on the command "Box" of the referee.

D. Mandatory Eight Count. When a boxer is "down" as the result of a blow, the bout shall not be continued until the referee has reached the count of eight, even if the boxer is ready to continue before then.

E. The Knockout. After the referee has said "ten" and the word "out," the bout ends and shall be decided as a "knock-out." (Points F–J of RULE XIX give further details of the Down Rule.)

These rules are abridged and reprinted here by permission of the International Amateur Boxing Association (AIBA). A complete copy of the Rules of Boxing, including Rules XX to XXVIII and Appendices I–VII, can be obtained from the Association.

GRAY AREA

Q. Can a medical officer stop a fight for medical reasons?

A. No. A new rule, XVI, A 3b, adopted in 1994, states that the medical officer has the right to request that the bout be suspended for medical reasons. Some people interpret this to mean that the medical officer has the right to stop the bout. In fact a medical officer must first inform the Jury President who in turn instructs the referee to stop the bout; he cannot stop it himself or stop it immediately.

Karate
Essentials

Karate (Japanese for "empty hand") is a form of unarmed self-defense dating back to 16th-century Okinawa. Denied the right to carry weapons by their overlords, the Okinawans secretly developed a system of combat that relied on the power of their hands and feet. *Kumite* is the sparring form of karate involving two opponents in combat, delivering (or blocking) kicks and punches. Another form, using a set of movements as if in combat with an imaginary opponent, is called Kata. Of Korean origin, Tae Kwon Do is a related form of martial art with greater emphasis on offensive techniques.

The competition area

A flat, area with a mat, 8 m (26 ft) square, which may be elevated to a height of up to 1 m (3 ft). A referee's line, 0.5m (1½ ft) long, is drawn 2 m (3¼ ft) from the center of the area and two lines, each 1 m long, are drawn at right angles to this and 1.5 m (5 ft) from the center. These lines are used to position the competitors. Another line is drawn 1 m (3 ft) on the inside of the competition area. The area enclosed by it may be a different color.

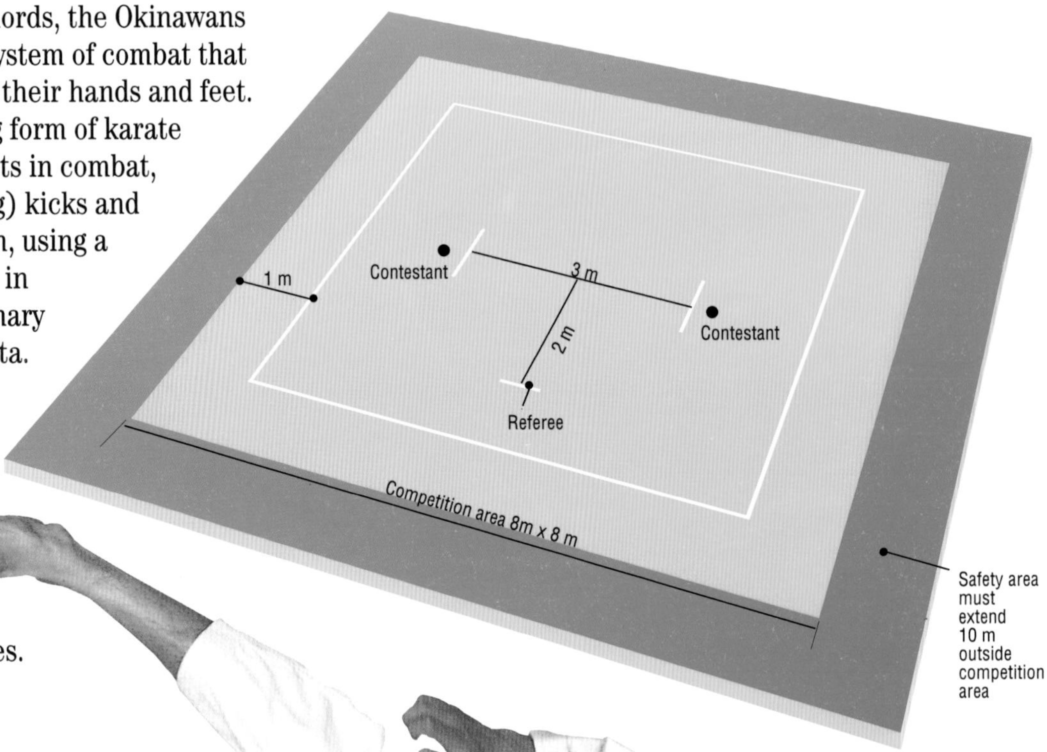

1 m

Contestant

3 m

2 m

Contestant

Referee

Competition area 8m x 8 m

Safety area must extend 10 m outside competition area

Players

Two contestants for Kumite competitions, in which individual results may contribute to a larger team score. Individual matches are divided into weight divisions and an open category. Kata competitions do not involve direct competition. Contestants compete for scores from a panel of judges (as in figure skating or gymnastics).

Karate kids

Inspired by movies such as The Karate Kid, *the martial arts are very popular with young people. Today, Tae Kwon Do is the most widely practiced martial art.*

Dress

A white, unmarked *gi*, consisting of jacket (at least hip length) and trousers (must cover at least two-thirds of the shin). One contestant wears a red belt, the other a white one. Mitts and gumshields are required, and soft shin pads may also be worn. Shin/instep protectors are forbidden.

To avoid injury, fingernails must be kept short and contestants must not wear glasses or any other potentially dangerous objects.

Degrees of achievement are recognized by the color of a contestant's belt—the highest being the black belt (or *Dan*), which, itself, is divided into 10 grades of expertise.

Side kick

One of the most powerful kicks in karate is the "yoko-geri," here used as an attacking move. The yoko-geri can be either a thrust kick in which the foot travels in essentially a straight line, or a snap kick where the foot travels upwards in an arc.

Officials

One referee (shushin), two judges (fukushin), and one arbitrator (kansa). Timekeepers, caller-announcers, and record-keepers facilitate the operation of matches.

HOW TO PLAY

In Kata competitions, contestants compete individually for points from the judges. In Kumite competitions (discussed here), two contestants meet on the mat. Each tries to score points (or half points) by attacking particular areas of their opponent's body. Contact is never excessive and parts of the body are out of bounds.

Starting

The two opponents take their place on the mat and bow to each other, with their feet touching their starting lines. The referee announces "Shobu sanbon hajime!" to start the bout.

How to win

Contestants score either full points (ippon) or half points (waza-ari). A half point is awarded for a technique that is not quite worthy of an ippon; for example, it may have lacked precision or conviction in its delivery. A contestant who gains sanbon (three points) wins automatically, otherwise the win is awarded to the contestant with the most points when time expires. *See Article 7 (page 212).* Contestants may also win the bout if their opponent is given a hansoku

---

GRAY AREA

Scoring in karate depends on the judges' subjective view of a bout. Each judge makes a skilled assessment of a competitor's technique, considering the following criteria:
• Would the technique have worked in real combat?
• If so, was it delivered on time?
• If two opponents seem to have delivered a technique almost simultaneously, who was the first to do so?
   In this way, scoring depends very much on the personal interpretation of events by a judge.

(for a serious foul), a shikkaku (disqualification), or a kiken (if he is absent, withdraws or is withdrawn).

KEY RULES

• A karate bout is three minutes long for senior male contestants and two minutes long for women and juniors. A warning buzzer sounds 30 seconds before the end of a bout.

If one opponent achieves sanbon (3 points) the match ends at that point.

• Each time a contestant scores, the referee calls "yame!" and the clock is stopped. The referee and judges award points and the fighting then resumes with the call "tsukete hajime!" *See Article 13, Starting, Suspending, and Ending of Matches (page 213).*

• For reasons of safety, contestants may only attack certain areas on the body, including the head, face, neck, abdomen, chest, back (excluding shoulders), and side. They must not attack the throat, groin, joints, or instep. Nor must excessive force be used, especially in attacks to the head and neck. All techniques must be controled. *See Article 8, Prohibited Behavior (page 212).*

• Scoring is based on the quality of a technique. A blow must have good form. It must be made with a good attitude, a good sense of timing, and from the correct distance. Judges take all these things, and more, into account when awarding points. *See Article 6 , Scoring (page 212).*

• Penalty points

may be awarded to an opponent for misconduct. The scale of penalties is given in *Article 9, Penalties (page 212).*

SKILLS AND TACTICS

Years of hard work and self-discipline are required to acquire a black belt. Speed, technique, strength, and flexibility are the key components of karate expertise. The beginner must first acquire the basic chops, punches, kicks, and blocking techniques. The next step is to learn a series of combinations of these made up techniques.

Overall fitness is crucial. Warming up and stretching are essential in order to avoid injury. Deep-breathing techniques are also an important part of karate.

The key to success in competition is a finely-tuned control over the delivery of kicks and punches as well as a keen sense of timing, alertness, and the ability to surprise.

In focus
Karate is a very elaborate sport. Whether Kata or Kumite, it involves repeating set drills over and over again with an emphasis on perfection. In any kind of karate a number of different elements are essential: "kime," which is a frame of mind; "kokyu," which is breath control; and "zanshin," which is an almost meditative state of total awareness.

KUMITE KARATE THE RULES
• • • • • • •

This is an abridged version of the official Rules of Karate Competition.

Article 1: Competition Area
See The competition area (page 210).

Article 2: Official Dress
See Dress (page 210).

Article 3: Organization of Kumite Competitions

Article 4: The Referee Panel

Article 5: Duration of Bout
See Key rules (page 211).

Article 6: Scoring

6.1 The result of a bout is determined by either contestant scoring three ippons, six waza-ari, or a combination of the two totaling sanbon, or obtaining a decision, or by a hansoku, shikkaku, or kiken imposed against a contestant.

6.2 It must be noted that an ippon is worth two waza-ari.

6.3 An ippon is awarded on the basis of the following:

   6.3.1 A scoring technique counts as an ippon when it is performed according to the following criteria to a scoring area.

      6.3.1.1 Good form.

      6.3.1.2 Correct attitude.

      6.3.1.3 Vigorous application.

      6.3.1.4 Zanshin (perfect finish).

      6.3.1.5 Proper timing.

      6.3.1.6 Correct distance.

6.4 An ippon may also be awarded for techniques deficient in one of the above criteria but which conform to the following schedule:

   6.4.1 Jodan kicks or other technically difficult techniques.

   6.4.2 Deflecting an attack and scoring to the unguarded back of the opponent.

   6.4.3 Sweeping or throwing followed by a scoring technique.

   6.4.4 Delivering a combination technique, the individual components of which each score in their own right.

   6.4.5 Successfully scoring at the precise moment the opponent attacks.

6.5 A waza-ari is awarded for a technique almost comparable to that needed to score ippon. The refereeing panel must look for ippons in the first instance and only award a waza-ari in the

second instance.

6.6 A victory over an opponent who has been given a hansoku or shikkaku will be worth sanbon (3 full points or ippons). If a contestant is absent, withdraws, or is withdrawn, the opponent will be credited with a win by kiken (sanbon, or three ippons).

6.7 Attacks are limited to the following areas:

   6.7.1 Head.

   6.7.2 Face.

   6.7.3 Neck.

   6.7.4 Abdomen.

   6.7.5 Chest.

   6.7.6 Back (but excluding shoulders).

   6.7.7 Side.

6.8 An effective technique delivered at the same time that the end of the bout is signaled, is considered valid. An attack, even if effective, delivered after an order to suspend or stop the bout shall not be scored and may result in a penalty being imposed on the offender.

6.9 No technique, even if technically correct, will be scored if it is delivered when the two contestants are outside the competition area. However, if one of the opponents delivers an effective technique while still inside the competition area and before the referee calls "yame," the technique will be scored.

6.10 Simultaneous effective scoring techniques delivered by both contestants the one on the other, shall not score.

Article 7: Criteria for Decision

7.1 In the absence of a sanbon score, or of a defeat caused by kiken, hansoku, or a shikkaku during the bout, a decision is taken on the basis of the following considerations:

   7.1.1 Whether there have been any ippons or waza-ari awarded.

   7.1.2 The attitude, fighting spirit, or strength demonstrated by the contestants.

   7.1.3 The superiority of tactics and techniques.

7.2 In individual category where there is no score superiority, then the following procedure will be followed:

   7.2.1 If, at the end of a bout, the two contestants have no score, the winning decision shall be given by hantei (judgment).

   7.2.2 If, at the end of a bout, the two contestants have scored equally, the decision for victory shall be given by hantei.

   7.2.3 If, at the end of a bout, neither contestant has established a superiority, then

the decision for the bout shall be a draw ("hikiwake") and encho-sen (an extension) should be announced.

   7.2.4 A penalty or warning incurred in the bout will be carried forward to the encho-sen.

7.3 In team competition the winning team is the one with the most bout victories.

7.4 If two teams have the same number of victories, the winner is the one whose contestants have scored the most points, taking both winning and losing fights into account.

7.5 If two teams have the same number of victories and scores, a deciding bout must be held between representatives of the two teams. In the event of a continuing tie, there is an extension ("encho-sen"). The first contestant to score ippon or waza-ari is declared the winner.

7.6 If there is no decision after a bout of an individual match, an extension ("encho-sen") will be fought. In the event of a tied encho-sen, the majority decision of the panel will be announced by the referee.

Article 8: Prohibited Behavior

8.1 The following are forbidden:

   8.1.1 Techniques that make contact with the throat.

   8.1.2 Techniques that make excessive contact, having regard to the scoring area attacked. All techniques must be controlled. Any techniques that impact the head, face, or neck and result, in visible injury must be penalized, unless caused by the recipient.

   8.1.3 Attacks to the groin, joints, or instep.

   8.1.4 Attacks to the face with open hand techniques ("teisho" or "nukite").

   8.1.5 Dangerous throws that by their nature preclude or prejudice the opponent's ability to land with safety.

   8.1.6 Techniques that by their nature, cannot be controlled for the safety of the opponent.

   8.1.7 Direct attacks to arms or legs.

   8.1.8 Repeated exits from the competition area (jogai), or movements that waste too much time. Jogai relates to a situation where a contestant's body, or part thereof touches the floor outside of the area. An exception is when the contestant is actually pushed or thrown from the area by his opponent.

   8.1.9 Wrestling, pushing, or seizing without an immediate technique.

8.1.10 Mubobi is the term used to describe a situation where one or both contestants display a lack of regard for his, or their own safety.

   8.1.11 Feigning of injury to gain advantage.

   8.1.12 Any discourteous behavior from a member of an official delegation can earn the disqualification of the offender or the entire team delegation from the tournament.

Article 9: Penalties

9.1 The following scale of penalties shall operate.

9.1 Atenai Yoni: may be imposed for intended minor infractions or for the first (Warning) instance of a minor infraction.

9.2 Keikoku: this is a penalty in which waza-ari is added to the opponent's score. Keikoku is imposed for minor infractions for which a warning has previously been given in that bout, or for infractions not sufficiently serious to merit hansoku-chui.

9.3 Hansoku-chui: this is a penalty in which ippon is added to the opponent's score. Hansoku-chui is usually imposed for infractions for which a Keikoku has previously been given in that bout.

9.4 Hansoku: this is imposed following a very serious infraction. It results in the opponent's score being raised to sanbon. Hansoku is also invoked when the number of hansoku-chuis and keikokus imposed raise the opponent's score to sanbon.

9.5 Shikkaku: this is a disqualification from the actual tournament, competition, or match. The opponent's score is raised to sanbon. In order to define the limit of shikkaku, the referee council must be consulted. Shikkaku may be invoked when a contestant commits an act which harms the prestige and honor of karate-do and when other actions are considered to violate the rules of the tournament.

Article 10: Injuries and Accidents in Competition

10.1 Kiken or forfeiture is the decision given when a contestant or contestants are unable to continue, abandon the bout, or are withdrawn on the order of the referee. The grounds for abandonment may include injury not ascribable to the opponent's actions.

10.2 If two contestants injure each other at the same time or are suffering from the effects of previously incurred injury and are declared by the tournament doctor to be unable to continue, the bout is awarded to the contestant who has amassed the most points at that time. If the points score is equal, than a decision (hantei) will decide the outcome of the bout.

10.3 An injured contestant who has been declared unfit to fight by the tournament doctor cannot fight again in that competition.

10.4 An injured contestant who wins a bout through disqualification due to injury is not allowed to fight again in the competition without permission from the doctor. If he is injured, he may win a second bout by disqualification but is immediately withdrawn from further kumite competition in that tournament.

10.5 When a contestant is injured, the referee shall at once halt the bout and call the doctor. The doctor is authorized to diagnose and treat injury only.

10.6 Any competitor who falls, is thrown, or knocked down, and does not fully regain his feet within 10 seconds, is considered unfit to continue fighting and will be automatically withdrawn from the tournament.

Article 11: Protest

11.1 No one may protest about a judgment to the members of the refereeing panel.

11.2 If a refereeing procedure appears to contravene these rules, the official representative is the only one allowed to make a protest.

11.3 The protest will take the form of a written report submitted immediately after the bout in which the protest was generated. The sole exception to this is when the protest concerns an administrative malfunction. The area controller should be notified immediately the administrative malfunction is detected.

11.4 The protest must be submitted to a representative of the referee council. In due course the council will review the circumstances leading to the protested decision. Having considered all the facts available, it will produce a report and shall be empowered to take such action as may be called for.

11.5 Any protests concerning application of the rules must be made in accordance with the complaints procedure defined by the World Karate Federation Directing Committee (WKF-DC)

and submitted in writing on an approved form and signed by the official representative of the team or contestant(s).

11.6 The complainant must deposit a sum of money as may be agreed by the WKF-DC, with the treasury and a duplicate receipt will be issued. The protest, plus a copy of the receipt, must be lodged with the chairman of the referee council.

Article 12: Power and Duties of the Referee Council, Match Area Controllers, Referees, Judges, and Arbitrators.

Refers to officials.

Article 13: Starting, Suspending, and Ending of Matches.

13.1 The terms and gestures to be used by the referee and judges in the operation of a match shall be specified in Appendices 1 and 2.

13.2 The referee and judges shall take up their prescribed positions and, following an exchange of bows between the contestants, the referee will announce "Shobu sanbon hajime!" and the bout will commence.

13.3 The referee will stop the bout by announcing "Yame!" when a scoring technique is seen.

13.4 The referee will order the contestants to take up their original positions.

13.4.1 The referee returns to his position and the judges indicate their opinion by means of a signal.

13.4.2 The referee identifies the relevant score, awards waza-ari or ippon, and supplements the announcement with the prescribed gesture.

13.4.3 The referee then restarts the bout by calling "Tsuzukete hajime!"

13.5 When a contestant has scored sanbon during a bout, the referee shall call "Yame!" and order the contestants back to their standing lines as he returns to his. The winner is then declared and indicated by the referee raising a hand on the side of the winner and declaring "Shiro (aka) no kachi." The bout is ended at this point.

13.6 When time is up and the scoring situation tied:

13.6.1 The referee shall call "Yame!" and return to his position.

13.6.2 The referee will call "Hantei" and following his signal (by whistle) the judges will indicate their opinions.

13.6.3 The majority decision will be taken. The judges and referee have one vote each at hantei.

13.7 The referee will award the decision and announce the winner, or give a draw ("Hikiwake").

13.8 In the event of a tied individual bout, the referee will announce "Encho-sen"and start the extension with the command "Shobu hajime!"

13.9 When faced with the following situations, the referee shall announce "Yame!" and halt the bout temporarily. The bout will subsequently be restarted.

13.9.1 When both or either of the contestants are out of the area (or when a judge signals a jogai). The referee will order the two contestants to their initial positions.

13.9.2 When the referee orders the contestant to adjust his gi.

13.9.3 When the referee notices that a contestant appears about to contravene the rules, or when a signal concerning same from a judge is perceived.

13.9.4 When the referee notices that a contest has contravened the rules, or when the referee perceives a signal from a judge regarding same.

13.9.5 When the referee considers that one or both of the contestants cannot continue with the bout owing to injuries, illness, or other causes. Heeding the tournament doctor's opinion, the referee will decide whether the bout should be continued.

13.9.6 When a contestant seizes his opponent and does not perform an immediate effective technique, the referee will separate them.

13.9.7 When one or both contestants fall or are thrown and no effective techniques are immediately forthcoming.

These rules are reprinted here by permission of the English Karate Governing Body. A complete copy of the rules, including notes, explanations and guidelines, as well as the rules governing Kata competition are available from the Karate Governing Body.

Untouchable
The aim in karate is to break through your opponent's defense with a punch or a kick that stops just short of touching him. Note that an actual kick to the throat is illegal.

Judo
Essentials

Judo developed from an ancient Japanese method of unarmed combat known as *jujutsu* or *jujitsu*. Here, a contestant uses balance, leverage, and timing to pin or throw an opponent.

Combat team
In judo, contest bouts are fought by each of the six team members

Competition area

A minimum of 14 m (15 yds) square and a maximum of 16 m (17 ½ yds) square. Covered by tatami or a similarly acceptable material, generally green in color. The area is divided into two zones by a smaller square. The area in between (called the "danger zone") is indicated by a red area, approximately 1 m (3 ft) wide, parallel to the four sides of the competition area. The area within and including the danger zone is called the "contest area." It is a minimum of 8 m (26 ft) square or a maximum of 10 m (33 ft) square. The area outside the danger zone (called the "safety area") must be 3 m (10 ft) wide. A red line and a white line must be fixed on the center of the contest area 4 m (13 ft) apart, to indicate the positions where the contestants start and end the contest. The red tape is to the referee's right and the white to the referee's left. A free zone, a minimum of 50 cm (19 ½ in), must be maintained around the competition area.

The contestants

Two contestants participate in a contest.

Competition area 14–16 m (about 45–50 ft)

Starting positions

Danger zone 1 m

4 m

Contest area 8-10 m

Officials

Generally, the contest is conducted by one referee (who stays within the contest area) and two judges (who sit opposite each other at two corners outside the contest area), assisted by recorders and timekeepers.

Close contest
Combatants engage when the referee announces "hajime."

Dress

The contestants must wear *judogi* (judo uniform) made of cotton or similar material. The *judogi* must be in good condition and white, off-white or blue in color. The jacket must be long enough to cover the thighs and reach at least down to the fists when the arms are fully extended downwards. The trousers must be long enough to cover the legs to the ankle joint at their maximum reach and to 5 cm (2 in) above the ankle joint. Otherwise a strong belt of 4 to 5 cm wide must be worn over the jacket at waist level and tied with a square knot, tight enough to prevent the jacket from being too loose and yet long enough to go twice around the waist.

Equipment

Two chairs for the judges, each chair with a red and a white flag; two scoreboards; one timing clock for contest duration and two for *osaekomi* (indicating a pin to the mat); timekeepers' flags—one yellow, for contest stop, one blue for *osaekomi.*

On the mat
The aim in judo is to achieve a decisive throw or to hold an opponent on the mat for a particular length of time.

Thrown
Combatants are judged on their throwing technique (nagewaza) and holding technique (katamewaza).

HOW TO PLAY

Starting

The contestants stand facing each other on the contest area at the red or white tape, according to the sash they are wearing. They bow and take one step forward. The referee announces "hajime" to start the contest.

Duration of contest

The duration of the contest for World Championships and Olympic games is five minutes for men and four minutes for women. A bell or similar audible device indicates to the referee the end of the time allotted for the contest. Contestants are entitled to rest for a period of 10 minutes between contests.

How to win

A contestant wins the contest if he or she scores an *ippon*. If no one scores an *ippon*, the contestant with the highest score wins.

Scoring

Points are not cumulative (except for a *waza-ari*). An *ippon* scores 10 points, and wins the contest. A *waza-ari* scores seven points, and two *waza-ari* achieve an *ippon*. A *yuko* scores five points, and a *koka* scores three points. *Yuko* and *koka* can not contribute to *ippon*, and are used only to determine a winner in which *ippon* has not been achieved.

KEY RULES
• • • • • • • •

- *Ippon* (10 pts) is achieved:

  a) When a contestant, with control, throws the other contestant largely on his back with considerable force and speed.

  b) When a contestant holds with *osaekomi* (i.e., pins to the mat) the other contestant, who is unable to get away for 30 seconds.

  c) When a contestant gives up by tapping twice or more with his hand or foot or says *maitta* ("I give up"), generally as a result of grappling technique, *shime-waza* (strangle) or *kansetsu-waza* (armlock).

  d) When the effect of a strangle technique or armlock is sufficiently apparent.

  e) If one contestant gains two *waza-ari* in one contest, the contestant is awarded an *ippon*.

- *Waza-ari* (7 points) is awarded:

  a) When a contestant, with control, throws the other contestant, but the technique is partially lacking in one of the elements necessary for an *ippon*.

  b) When a contestant holds with *osaekomi* the other contestant who is unable to get away for 25 seconds or more, but less than 30 seconds.

- *Yuko* (5 points) is awarded:

  a) When a contestant, with control, throws the other contestant, but the technique is partially lacking in two of the other three elements necessary for an *ippon*.

  b) When a contestant holds with *osaekomi* the other contestant who is unable to get away for 20 seconds or more but less than 25 seconds.

- *Koka* (3 pts) is awarded:

  a) When a contestant, with control, throws the other contestant onto his thigh(s) or buttocks with speed and force.

  b) When a contestant holds with *osaekomi* the other contestant who is unable to get away for ten seconds or more but less than 20 seconds.

Penalties

Like points, penalties are not cumulative; however, the awarding of a second or

subsequent penalty automatically cancels an earlier penalty. When a contestant has already been penalized, any succeeding penalties must be awarded in higher value than the existing penalty. When a contestant is given a penalty, the opponent gains points.

Shido is given to any contestant who has committed a slight infringement. Slight infringements include:

- To make an action designed to give the impression of an attack but which clearly shows that there was no intent to throw the opponent (false attack).
- To put a hand, arm, foot, or leg, directly in the opponent's face. If one contestant is penalized shido, the other contestant is awarded *koka*.

Chui is awarded to any contestant who has committed a serious infringement (or having been awarded a *shido* commits a second slight infringement). Serious infringements include:

- To kick with the knee or foot, the hand or arm of the opponent, in order to make the opponent release their grip.
- To bend back the opponent's finger(s) in order to break the opponent's grip.

When one contestant is penalized *chui*, the other contestant is awarded *yuko*.

Keikoku is awarded to any contestant who has committed a grave infringement (or who having been penalized *chui*, commits a further slight or serious infringement). Grave infringements include:

- Making any action that might injure or endanger the opponent, or may be against the spirit of judo.
- Disregarding the referee's instructions.

When one contestant is penalized *keikoku*, the opponent is awarded *waza-ari*.

Hansoku Make is awarded to any contestant who has committed a very grave infringement (or having been penalized *keikoku*, commits a further infringement of any degree). Very grave infringements include:

- Intentionally falling backwards when the opponent is clinging to the contestant's back and when either contestant has control of the other's movement.
- Wearing a hard or metallic object (covered or not). If a contestant is penalized *hansoku-make*, their opponent is awarded *ippon*.

The ultimate aim in judo is to score an ippon, *hurling an opponent flat on his back.*

SKILLS
• • • • •

There are four key combat techniques used in judo contests:

Nage-komi-waza—throwing an opponent.

Osaekomi-waza—pinning an opponent to the ground.

Kansetsu-waza—armlocking an opponent.

Shime-waza—choking an opponent.

These are not the full rules of judo, only an overview. Full rules are available from judo associations.

Fencing *Essentials*

Fencing originated in the techniques of swordsmanship used in dueling. During the Renaissance, the vigorous Italian style of fencing, based on the use of the rapier, predominated in Europe. The épée (ay-PAY), or small sword, was invented in France during the eighteenth century, giving rise to a more formal, restrained style of fencing. The rules of modern fencing are for the most part derived from the French style, and many of the sport's technical terms are French words.

There are three forms of fencing, defined by the type of weapon used: foil, épée, or saber.

Officials

Bouts are judged by a referee who applies the right-of-way rules and awards touches.

The referee is assisted by two ground judges; when nonelectric weapons are used, there are four ground judges.

The referee has the authority to halt a bout if the play of the competitors is dangerous or contrary to the rules, or if one of the competitors is disarmed or leaves the piste.

Left, foil.

20 cm max

18 cm max

110 cm max

15 cm blade insulation for electric foil

Making a point
The épée is an old dueling weapon that is not bound by the conventions that govern the foil and the saber. Double hits are valid.

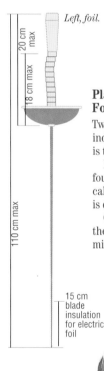

Point to point
Fencers combat each other on a narrow strip called the "piste."

14 m

Center line

On gaurd line

Start of 2-m signal area

Last 2 m of piste

Rear limit

Extensions of piste

2 m

3 m

2 m

Players
Forms of Competition

Two opponents involved in a "bout." In individual competitions, the result of a competition is the aggregate of the bouts.

In team competitions, the aggregate of the bouts fought between the fencers of two different teams is called a "match." The winner of a team competition is decided on an aggregate of the matches.

Competitions are distinguished by weapons; by the competitors' sex, age, or occupation (e.g., military, students); and by whether they are for individuals or for teams.

Competitions are said to be by "direct elimination" when the competitors are eliminated as soon as they have received their first defeat, or after their second, if the rules specify a system "with repêchage [reh-peh-SHAHJ]." A pool is the meeting of several competitors (or of all the competitors), each of whom fences all the others in order to establish a rank.

The piste ("peest")

The field of play is known as the piste. It measures 14 m (46 ft) in length and 1.5 to 2 m (5 to 6½ ft) in width. It may be made of various materials, such as cork, rubber, or plastic. In competitions where electrical apparatus is used to detect hits, a metallic mesh covers the piste.

Equipment

The three types of weapons are called the foil, épée, and saber. The blades of all three are made of tempered steel, the blunted end forming the "button." A variety of handles exist, including the Italian grip, which has a crossbar and is used with a wrist strap, and the French grip, which is slightly curved and has a pommel (or knob) at the end.

As it is light and flexible, the foil is used by most beginners. The épée is similar to the foil, but it has a larger hand guard and is heavier and more rigid. The design of the saber is based on that of the cavalryman's weapon, and it requires a cut-and-thrust technique based on military swordplay.

A fencer wears a protective face mask made of fine wire mesh, and a jacket, over which the plastron, a metallic chest protector, is worn. Women wear breast protectors made of metal or other rigid material. The sword hand is protected by a glove. The jacket, which must be white or a pale color, overlaps breeches or trousers. These are buttoned or fastened below the knee or at the ankle, respectively.

Electrical weapons are used in formal competitions to increase the accuracy of scoring. The weapons are wired. When the weapon blade's button makes contact with the opponent's metallic plastron, electricity is conducted to a body wire. The hit registers on

an electrical scoring apparatus: when a touch is scored, a light flashes on a screen on the sidelines. The referee awards touches accordingly.

Because fencing is a potentially hazardous sport, participants have to accept responsibility for safety, both for themselves and for others. Weapons and protective clothing must meet prescribed safety standards. Before competitions, clothing and weapons are checked. As well as checking for safety, officers ensure that electrical components such as the body wire will register touches accurately.

En garde
This fencer is warming up, indicated by the absence of his face mask.

HOW TO PLAY

Fencing tactics depend on fundamental stances and movements; defensive and attacking motions stem from the basic "on-guard" position, in which the knees are flexed, the rear arm crooked upwards, and the sword arm partly extended towards the opponent. The "lunge," the basic attacking action, is executed by stabbing at the target with the sword arm and thrusting forward on the front leg.

A defensive movement of the blade intended to block an attack is called a "parry." There are eight main parries in foil and épée fencing, each one designed to protect a different part of the body against attack. In saber fencing, there are just five parries. (The parries bear the names of the Old French words meaning "first" to "eighth"—*prime, seconde,*

tierce, quarte, quinte, sixte, septime, and *octave*). The return thrust made immediately after a parry is known as a "riposte." The "counter-riposte" is an offensive action made by the fencer who has parried the riposte.

How to win

Points are scored by touching valid parts of the opponent's body with the blade. In foil fencing, only the touches to the torso count, whereas in épée fencing the entire body is valid. In saber fencing, only touches above the hips count— but the edge of the sword may be used as well.

When nonelectric weapons are used, thrusts with the point must reach their target clearly and distinctly in order to be counted.

The effective duration of a bout is: at épée for one hit (in pentathlon): 3 minutes; at all weapons, for five hits: 4 minutes; for 15 hits: 9 minutes—consisting of up to three sets, each lasting 3 minutes.

KEY RULES

• The competitors fence in their own ways and at their own risk with the one condition that they must observe the fundamental rules of fencing.
• All bouts or matches must preserve the character of a courteous and frank encounter. All irregular actions (such as collisions, disorderly fencing, falls, irregular movements on the piste, hits achieved with undue violence, hits made while falling) are strictly forbidden.
• Before the beginning of the bout the two fencers perform a fencing salute to their opponent, to the spectators, and to the referee. The fencing salute is performed by lifting the weapon guard up to the chin. (If one of the two fencers does not comply with this rule, he receives a red card). When the final hit has been scored, the bout is not ended until the two fencers have saluted each other, the audience, and the referee.

• At foil it is forbidden, during the course of fencing, to advance the shoulder of the non-sword arm in front of the shoulder of the sword arm.
• The fencer, whether on or off the piste, must keep his mask on until the referee calls halt.
• Bodily contact between the competitors (known as *corps à corps*) is forbidden, even without brutality or violence.
• It is forbidden to turn one's back to one's opponent during the bout.

SKILLS

Concentration, alertness, precision, and anticipation are essential.

The technique of finger-play, or *doigté* (dwa-TAY), is important: one manipulates the weapon using the thumb and first finger in such a way that the blade moves via the shortest possible route in the quickest possible time.

An associated skill is blade-sense, or *sentiment du fer* ("feeling for the iron"). For an experienced fencer, the weapon feels like an extension of his own body. With this heightened sense of feeling, he can perceive his opponent's dexterity, strength, speed, and temperament.

TACTICS

A competitor on the offensive chooses from a number of attacking techniques to overcome his opponent's parries. A rapid single cut or thrust of the blade may hit the target before the defender can parry. A more complex tactic involves making a compound attack requiring several blade movements. The initial movements, which deceptively suggest an area of attack, may mislead the opponent into parrying in a different direction from the one in which the attack is finally made. An opponent may also be caught unaware by a running attack, or *flèche* ("flesh"). However, a competitor on the defensive may surprise an opponent by making a "stop-thrust," a counterattack made by thrusting without lunging. Another offensive technique is to beat or press the opponent's blade aside before attacking.

Winning hit
In top-level matches the winner is the fencer who scores the most hits in three rounds of five hits in six minutes. In foil and épée, hits are scored with the point; in saber, with the edge too.

Croquet

Essentials

Generally thought of as a recreational game played in backyards on warm summer days, croquet is actually a rapidly developing international sport, with the average age of competition players now around 25. It is a subtle game in which tactics and strategy are more important than strength.

Equipment and accessories

Six hoops, metal, painted white, fixed firmly to the ground, and measuring 12 in in height above the ground. The first hoop has a blue crown and the final hoop (the rover) has a red crown. A center peg is wooden, 18 in high, with a diameter of 1½ in. Four balls, colored blue, black, red, and yellow, each with a diameter of 3⅝ in and a weight of 1 lb. (Alternative colors green, brown, pink, and white are permitted.) Clips, the same color as the balls, are placed on the hoop or peg that the ball must be hit through next. A mallet has a head usually made of wood and two identical end faces.

Players

Two for singles—the striker and the outplayer—or four for doubles. The striker is the player whose turn it is to strike the ball. Each player has two balls for singles, or one ball for doubles.

Officials

A referee.

Dress

Generally white. Men wear a shirt and trousers or shorts and women may substitute a skirt. Suitable flat sports shoes.

Follow-through
Follow-through is important for achieving accuracy and distance.

The court

A rectangular lawn, 35 yds by 28 yds or smaller for non-competition games. The boundary is marked with a white line. Imaginary yard lines (not marked) lie one yard in from the boundary. The area contained within these is the yard-line area. Corners may be marked with flags. There is a *baulk line* at each end, consisting of 13 yds of the yard line, measured out from the corners.

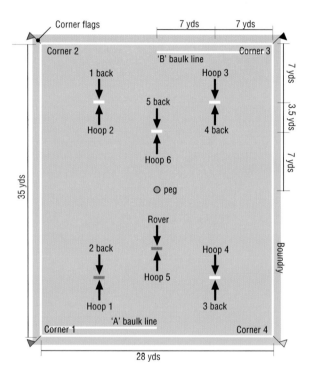

Diagram labels: Corner flags · 7 yds · 7 yds · Corner 2 · Corner 3 · 'B' baulk line · 1 back · Hoop 3 · 7 yds · 5 back · 3.5 yds · Hoop 2 · 4 back · 7 yds · Hoop 6 · 35 yds · peg · Rover · 2 back · Hoop 4 · Boundary · Hoop 5 · 3 back · Hoop 1 · 'A' baulk line · Corner 1 · Corner 4 · 28 yds

GRAY AREA
One issue that sometimes requires a referee's judgment is whether a ball has passed completely through a hoop. No part of the ball may show on the playing side of the hoop, so that a straight edge lowered on the playing side of the hoop would not touch the ball. The playing side is the side where the ball was before it was struck.

HOW TO PLAY

Both players or teams try to hit their balls with the head of their mallets through each of the six hoops on the court twice, and then against the center peg, before the opposition does. The six hoops form a circuit that must be completed in a set order in one direction and then in a reverse sequence.

Starting

The winner of the toss decides whether to opt for a choice of colors (to play the blue and black or the red and yellow) or to start the game. The player starting then places a ball anywhere on the baulk line and strikes it to begin the game. The opposing player does the same. Then two more alternating turns are taken so that all four balls are in play.

How to win

Each time a ball passes through a hoop in the correct order a point is scored. A point is also scored when the ball hits the center peg at the completion of the circuit. The points scored therefore total 13 for each ball. The winner is the player (or team) whose balls score these 12 *hoop points* and one *peg point* (26 in total) before the opposition.

KEY RULES

• Players take turns. In singles, either of a player's two balls may be played; at the beginning of each turn he chooses a *striker's ball* and this ball is played exclusively throughout that turn.

• Each turn consists of at least one initial stroke. However, if with this stroke the ball scores a hoop point., the player is allowed another (a *continuation stroke*).

• A player earns two extra strokes if he makes a *roquet* (hits another ball with his ball). For the first of these (the *croquet stroke*) he places his ball in any position, providing it is in contact with the roqueted ball, and then strikes his own ball, ensuring that both balls move. After this he takes a continuation stroke and, if this does not result in a roquet or a hoop point, his turn ends.

A croquet shot
Having roqueted the red ball, this striker now plays his croquet stroke. You may roquet and croquet not only your own partner ball but also those of your opponent.

against the center peg (directly or by another rover ball) for a peg point, after which it is removed from the court.

SKILLS AND TACTICS

A high degree of accuracy is needed when taking a shot. Because croquet is played over a relatively large area and the balls are only $\frac{1}{8}$ in narrower than the hoops, a player needs

• Within one turn, each of the other balls may be roqueted and croqueted only once. But, if the player is able to score by hitting his ball through the next hoop, he is entitled to roquet and croquet each ball anew.

• If during play a ball goes off the court or comes to rest in the yard-line area, it is retrieved and placed on the yard line at a point nearest to where it left the court.

• A turn ends when a player has no strokes left. It also ends if, *in a croquet stroke,* a ball goes over the boundary or if the player commits a fault. This occurs, for example, if he pushes his ball, hits his ball more than once (a *double tap*), squeezes his ball against a hoop or the peg (a *crush*), touches a ball other than his own with his mallet, or fails to move or shake the croqueted ball in a croquet stroke. In addition to the turn ending, a fault also means that a point cannot be scored off that particular stroke, and the balls are returned to their previous positions.

• A ball must pass completely through a hoop (and stay there) to score a point. If a ball other than the striker's ball passes through its next hoop (*peeled* through the hoop), it also scores a point. When a ball has completed both circuits of six hoops and has scored 12 points, it becomes a *rover ball*. It must then be *pegged-out* by being hit

to be accurate to within 6 in over 35 yds.

As well as trying to get his own ball through the hoops, a player must do everything he can to prevent his opponent from completing the circuit before him. Play therefore needs to be tactically defensive. Skilled players use spin, angle shots, and just the right amount of strength to place not only their own ball but also their opponent's ball, using roquet and croquet strokes. They try to retain the initiative while keeping the opponent on the defensive by thinking as much about what a particular shot might give away as what gain it could achieve. Advanced players use such finely tuned and elaborate tactics that they plan up to 20 strokes ahead, ideally seeking to build and maintain a four-ball break.

These are not the complete rules of croquet, but an overview. The complete rules are available from any croquet association.

Easy roquet
This player strikes his yellow ball towards the red in order to make a roquet. Once that's achieved, he plays the croquet shot (see above) in order to position his yellow in a good hoop-scoring position.

Index

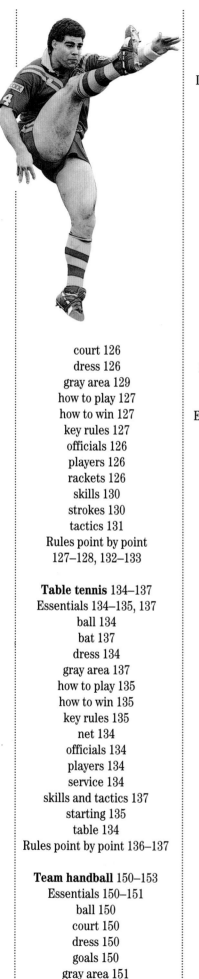

Australian Rules Football
United States Australian
Football Association
http://www.usfooty.com or
Australian Football Association
of North America, Inc.
P.O. Box 5423
Vienna WV 26105-5423
(888)4-AFANA-1
http://www.afana.com

Badminton
United States Badminton
Association
501 West 6th Street
Papillion NE 68046

Baseball
Major League Baseball
350 Park Avenue
18th Floor
New York NY 10022
(212) 339-7600 (American
League)
(212) 339-7700 (National
League)
http://www.major-
leaguebaseball.com

Basketball
National Basketball Association
Olympic Tower
645 Fifth Avenue
New York NY 10027
(212) 407-8000
http://www.nba.com

Boxing
USA Boxing
One Olympic Plaza
Colorado Springs CO 80909

Cricket
United States Cricket
Federation
P.O. Box 135
Haverford PA 19041
(610) 525-6975
http://www.uscf.org

Fencing
United States Fencing Coaches
Association
118 Fayette Street
Ithaca NY 14850

Field Hockey
USA Field Hockey
One Olympic Plaza
Colorado Springs, CO 80909
http://www.ifhockey.it

Football
National Football League
350 Park Avenue
New York NY 10022
(212) 450-2000
http://www.nfl.com

Golf
Professional Golfers Association
of America
Box 109601
Palm Beach Gardens FL

Ice Hockey
National Hockey League
650 Fifth Avenue
33rd Floor
New York NY 10019
(212) 789-2000
http://www.nhl.com

Judo
United States Judo Association
21 North Union Blvd.
Colorado Springs CO 80909
(719) 633-7750

Karate
National Karate-do Federation
P.O. Box 77083
Seattle WA 98177
http://www.usankf.org

Korfball
United States Korfball
Federation
11017 Bell Air Place
Oklahoma City OK 74132

Lacrosse (Men's)
United States Intercollegiate
Lacrosse Association
P.O. Box 928
Washington & Lee University
Lexington VA 24450

Lacrosse (Women's)
United States Women's
Lacrosse Association Inc.
20 East Sunset Avenue
Philadelphia PA 19118

Lawn Bowling
http://www.sportuk.com/
bowling/world/
full-memb.html

Netball
USA Netball Association
119 Glendwood Avenue #2C
Yonkers NY 10701
http://www.netball.org

Pétanque
Federation of Pétanque USA
138 Southern Heights Blvd.
San Rafael CA 94601
http://www.beachmedia.
com/www/epetclub.html

Rounders
National Rounders Association
3 Denehurst Avenue
Nottingham NG8 5DA
England

Rugby League
Rugby Football League
Red Hall
Red Hall Lane
Leeds LS17 8NB
England

Rugby Union
USA Rugby Football Union
3595 E. Fountain Blvd.
Colorado Springs CO 80910
e-mail: usarugby@rmii.com

Soccer
United States Soccer
Federation
United States Olympic Complex
1750 East Boulder Street
Colorado Springs CO 80909

Softball
International Softball
Federation
4141 NW Expressway
Suite 340
Oklahoma City OK 73116

Squash
United States Squash Racquets
Association
P.O. Box 1216
Bala-Cynwyd PA 19004
(610) 667-4006

Table Tennis
U.S. Table Tennis Association
Olympic Complex
1750 East Boulder Street
Colorado Springs CO 80909

Team Handball
United States Team Handball
Federation Olympic Complex
1750 East Boulder Street
Colorado Springs CO 80909

Tennis
United States Tennis
Association
51 East 42nd Street
New York, NY 10017

Track and Field
USA Track and Field
One RCA Dome
Suite 140
Indianapolis IN 46225

Volleyball
United States of America
Volleyball
3595 East Foundation Blvd.
Colorado Springs CO 80910-
1740

Editorial Director Andrew Duncan
Art Director Mel Petersen
Chief compiler Angela Koo
Assistant compilers Sarah Barlow, Richard German, and Huw Jones
Captions by John Farndon
Assistant Editors Nicola Davies and Sarah Barlow
Designers Chris Foley and Beverley Stewart
Illustrations Julian Baker
Photography Allsport Picture Library